D0452839

THE POLITICAL ECONOMY
OF LATIN AMERICA
IN THE POSTWAR PERIOD

iLAS Critical Reflections on Latin America Series

The Political Economy of Latin America in the Postwar Period

**Edited by
Laura Randall**

 **University of Texas Press, Austin
Institute of Latin American Studies**

Copyright © 1997 by the University of Texas Press
All rights reserved
Printed in the United States of America

First Edition, 1997

Requests for permission to reproduce material from this work should be sent to
Permissions, University of Texas Press, P.O. Box 7819, Austin, Texas 78713-
7819

♾ The paper used in this publication meets the minimum requirements of
American National Standard for Information Sciences—Permanence of Paper
for Printed Library Materials, ANSI Z39.48–1984.

Library of Congress Cataloging-in-Publication Data

The political economy of Latin America in the postwar period / edited by
  Laura Randall.
      p.   cm. — (ILAS critical reflections on Latin America series)
    Includes bibliographical references and index.
    ISBN 0-292-77086-3 (hardcover : alk. paper). — ISBN 0-292-77083-9
  (paperback : alk. paper)
    1. Latin America—Economic policy.   2. Latin America—Economic
  conditions—1945- . I. Randall, Laura. II. Series: Critical reflections on
  Latin America series.
  HC125.P644 1997
  338.98'009'045—dc21   97-34275

Contents

Tables and Charts

Introduction
Charts

Chile
Tables

Brazil
Tables

THE POLITICAL ECONOMY
OF LATIN AMERICA
IN THE POSTWAR PERIOD

1.
Introduction

Laura Randall
Hunter College, CUNY

Why edit a textbook on Latin American economies when there are texts describing Latin America as a whole? Because such generalizations do not adequately account for the importance of policies, people, and differences among Latin American nations in determining their economic development. Although Argentina, Brazil, Chile, Cuba, Ecuador, Mexico, and Peru—chosen to represent all major regions of Latin America—are linked by language and culture, they differ in size, resource endowments, and political and historical traditions; hence each nation is best studied in the context of its own history and world events. For those interested in an overview, this introduction provides a summary of some issues and trends common to the seven nations, against which the economic history, institutions, and policies of each nation can be evaluated. These are growth rates (see charts 1.1 and 1.2); development policies; the role of government; spending patterns, capital, and growth; foreign financing of Latin American development; exports, land reform, and growth; who benefits from Latin American growth (income distribution); and common development patterns.

Growth Rates

Latin American economies during many periods of their history compared favorably with the economy of the United States at similar stages of development. The Inter-American Development Bank suggests that because almost one-half of the Latin American labor force was in agriculture in 1965 it should be compared to the United States in 1870, when 48% of the labor force was in agriculture (Urrutia 1991b, pp. 46 and 55). For example, Latin America grew 3.5% per year in 1913–50 and 4.7% per year in 1950–73, compared to 1.1% for advanced countries in 1820–70, 1.4% in 1870–1913, and 1.2% in 1913–50 (Maddison 1983, p. 28; Maddison 1991, p. 17). The same pattern is observed in the growth of per capita gross domestic product, indicating a strong performance, because

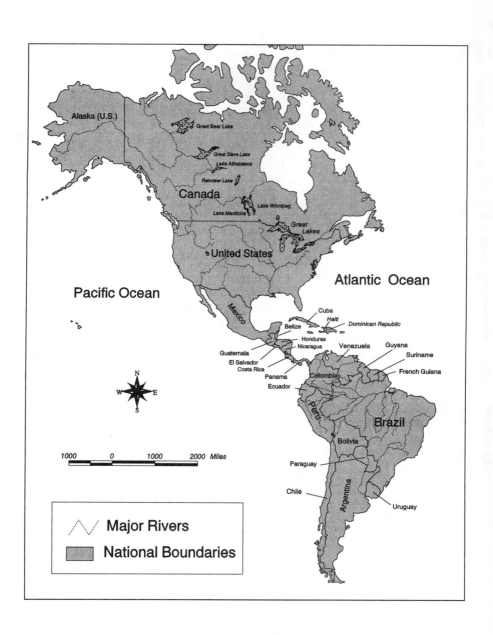

the first effect of economic growth is the increased life expectancy rates and consequent increase in population of a developing nation.

Inadequate worldwide adjustments to oil price increases contributed to a fall in the growth rate of Latin American nations to 3.8% in 1973–80; continuing gyrations in commodity prices and sharp changes in interest rates led to transfers of real resources to service their foreign debt in the 1980s—4% of Latin American gross domestic product was transferred abroad, compared to a prior inflow of 2%, for a shift of 6% of gross domestic product—with a consequent fall in real per capita income. Despite the problems from 1973 to the early 1990s, their long-run overall economic performance was still strong; the 1950–90 economic growth of Mexico and Brazil was more rapid than that of the United States. Latin American economic growth, however, was not uniform among the nations studied in this book: Argentina, Chile, and the United States grew more slowly than Brazil, Ecuador, Mexico, and Peru from 1950 to 1980 (Morley 1994, p. 1).

Development Policies

Development style shifted from export-led growth and government provision of infrastructure before World War I to increasing attention to development of the domestic market. The closing of world markets during World War I, preferential trading agreements during the Great Depression, and disruptions to trade during World War II made export-led growth appear to be unduly risky. Governments therefore protected local industries using raw materials in which the nation had a comparative advantage and took measures to develop financial and physical infrastructure. Direct investment by foreigners had led to conflicts about pricing, availability of products, and remittance of profits. In cases where domestic private investment did not enter fields believed essential for national economic development, the government took on the role of entrepreneur.

After World War II, the United Nations Economic Commission for Latin America often emphasized external rather than internal bottlenecks that inhibited growth. Emphasis was placed on the falling terms of trade, defined as the ratio between prices for Latin American exports and those for their imports. A conclusion was that producing goods formerly imported was a better growth strategy than emphasizing export growth. Resources were taken from agriculture and other sectors and used to protect industry. Manufactured products were protected from import competition, and industries were created, frequently by government entities acting alone or in combination with domestic or foreign investors. At the same time, concern with employment was greater than

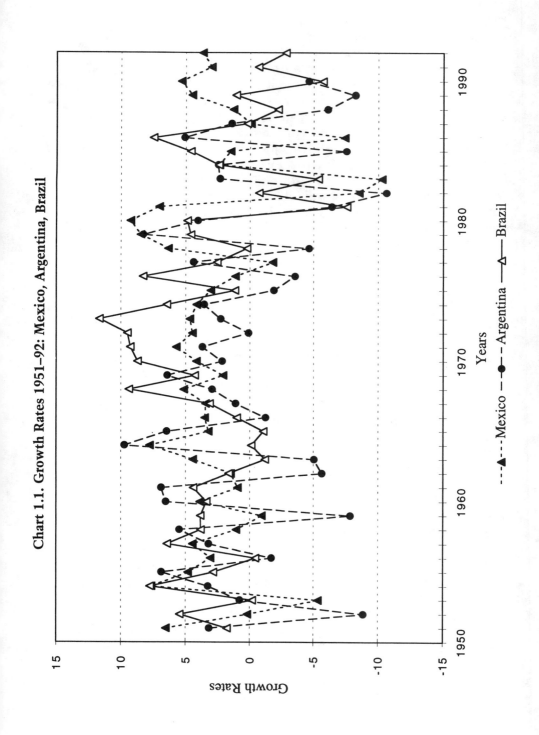

Chart 1.1. Growth Rates 1951–92: Mexico, Argentina, Brazil

Growth Rates

Years

- - ▲ - - Mexico — ● — Argentina — △ — Brazil

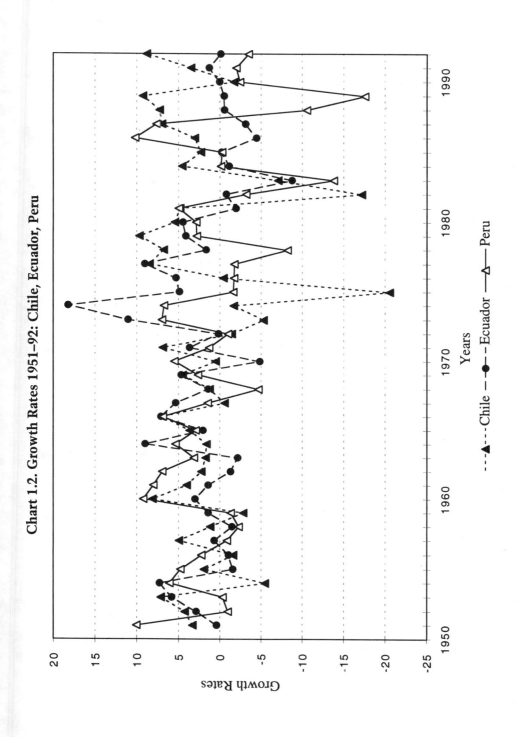

Chart 1.2. Growth Rates 1951–92: Chile, Ecuador, Peru

Growth Rates

Years

- - ▲ - - Chile — ● — Ecuador — △ — Peru

worries about inflation: both job creation—through government firms and other parts of the public sector more than through increases in central government employment—and inflation typified post–World War II Latin American economic development. Although there were many complaints about Latin American economic performance at the time, economic growth was stronger in 1950–73 than in later periods because of the disruption caused by skyrocketing oil prices in the 1970s and debt-related problems in the 1980s.

This led to changes in economic policy in the eighties and nineties, consistent with an analysis indicating that from 1950 to 1989 the restriction of individual liberties by the state reduced the rate of investment in Latin American economies; that anticipated inflation and current public spending reduced economic growth; that there was no proof that a fall in the terms of trade reduced long-term economic growth; and that the expansion of the export sector increased economic growth (Feliz 1992, p. 17). These findings confirm the policy prescriptions suggested and implemented from the mid-eighties: increase democratic political procedures, reduce government spending and inflation, and increase exports.

The Role of Government

Summarizing results for Argentina, Brazil, Chile, Mexico, and Peru, public sector spending—which except for Chile was largely financed by foreign borrowing—rose from 30% of gross domestic product in 1970 to almost 50% in 1985. In Chile, it rose from 41% in 1970 to 56% in 1972, under President Salvador Allende, falling after his death to 40% in 1985. The increase in public sector spending in rich nations occurred over the course of half a century. In Latin America, it took place in one decade (Larraín and Selowsky 1991, pp. 2–3 and 310).

This growth reflects not only the growth of central government expenditures, but also that of state and local governments, firms owned in whole or in part by the government, and other government entities whose budgets are not included in that of the central government. The share of public enterprises in total government spending rose from 34 to 50% during this period (Larraín and Selowsky 1991, pp. 308–9). The expansion was triggered by the oil crisis, with governments expanding their activities to earn money to pay for oil imports by increasing the production of tradable goods in oil-importing nations and expanding production of oil and its substitutes in all countries, as well as in industries that supply the expanded sectors. However, public sector growth was not the unique cause of external indebtedness. "Chile's indebtedness was due almost totally to . . . private sector overspending. . . . Part of [Argentina and Mexico's] increase in foreign debt was the result of a public sector deficit and part of an increase in the Central Bank's foreign debt. The funds received were used to support the currency and ended up as capital flight. Only in Brazil and Peru are public deficits accountable for the bulk of the build-up in foreign debt" (Larraín and Selowsky 1991, p. 10; also pp. 6, 308–9, 319).

Consequently, Larraín and Selowsky recommend that public sector finances be strengthened by improving the tax system; by eliminating transfers from the central government to public enterprises, ensuring that this is a result of increased efficiency rather than only of increases in the prices they charge; and by reducing deficits of state and provincial governments, usually from provincial banks and central monetary authorities. This requires adequate supervision of banking and a fully independent Central Bank. Chile and Mexico have recently implemented the latter reform (Larraín and Selowsky 1991, p. 316).

The tax system traditionally has been plagued by tax evasion, which increased with increased burdens of inflation, with falls in income, and with increased ratios of future to current income (Fishlow and Friedman 1994, p. 121). During the 1970s and 1980s, the tax system increased its coverage, but also tended to increase the burden on the poor: value added taxes and contributions to social security provided increasing shares of government revenue during the seventies, and value added taxes continued to do so in the eighties in Brazil, Chile, and Mexico. Taxes on income, profits, and capital gains fell substantially in Brazil, Mexico, and Peru (Werneck 1991, p. 59; International Monetary Fund, *Government Finance Statistics Yearbook*).

From the 1970s to the 1990s the share of spending on defense fell. Concern shifted in Argentina and Brazil to general government services and public order. During the 1980s, except for Chile and Argentina, the share of spending on education, health, social security, and welfare fell. The transfer of funds abroad to service or reduce the foreign debt clearly came at the expense of the welfare of the present generation of the poor and middle classes. The rationale was that renewed lending and structural reform, which were said to depend on repayment of at least some of the foreign debt, were necessary for the economic welfare of future generations. The pattern of government revenue collection and expenditure, designed to increase economic growth, worsened the distribution of income and welfare in the short run.

Spending Patterns, Capital, and Growth

Moreover, spending patterns became similar to those of rich nations, resulting in a lowering of growth rates. For example, Mexican private consumption patterns rapidly approached those of the United States, leaving less room for personal savings than other nations had obtained at similar stages of development. In consequence, if the level of consumption were to be maintained, increases in investment would have to be made by the government or obtained from foreign sources, which explains the opening to foreign investment in recent years. The composition as well as the level of investment is significant (Randall 1993a). Investment in people, homes, and infrastructure was necessary for the population's well-being, even though investment in machinery and equipment was directly related to economic growth (De Long and Summers 1991, p. 445).

The composition of investment varied among Latin American nations and indicated preferences for present comfort or future growth. Mexico emphasized investment in machinery, equipment, and housing. In Argentina, Brazil, and Chile, the share of investment in housing fell. Argentina and Chile concentrated investment in machinery and equipment, Brazil, in nonresidential structures. The Mexican distribution of investment was thought to balance needs of current housing and future growth more adequately than other nations and may explain why Mexico had relatively little violence until the 1994 economic and political crisis.

Foreign Financing of Latin American Development

Development can be financed by public or private savings and investment, from domestic or foreign sources. Developing nations traditionally use both domestic and foreign funds. Although foreign direct investment in Latin America rarely accounted for more than 10% of gross domestic capital formation, it was important both for its contribution to growth and for its provision of foreign exchange, which was used to import goods and services essential for growth that were not available within the nation that imported them. The massive reduction of direct investment and transfer of funds abroad to service the foreign debt in the early and mid-eighties severely reduced Latin America's economic capacity for growth. To reverse this trend, Latin American nations restructured their debt and opened their financial markets. Increasingly deep discounts in the secondary market for debt issues from 1987 to 1989 led, in some cases, to swapping government debt for equity (attractive because the debt was accepted at close to par for conversion purposes), while commercial debt was reduced under the 1989 Brady Plan, which facilitated forgiveness of private debt in exchange for International Monetary Fund and World Bank debt guarantees and greater Latin American reforms in fiscal, monetary, and international commercial policy. The private sector consequently increased its share in total investment from 57% in 1983 to 62% in 1990, although this was below the 1970s level of 64% (Pfeffermann and Madarassy 1992).

Exports, Land Reform, and Growth

Worldwide, the nations that had the most successful export-led growth stressed education and implemented land reform before the export expansion. In Latin America, education as a share of total central government expenditures was stagnant or falling from the mid-1970s to the mid-1990. Moreover, Mexico's land reform slowed significantly; Chilean land reform was partially reversed after Allende; limited land reforms were undertaken by Ecuador and Peru (Peru, however, ended restrictions on private land ownership in 1995). Only Cuba initiated a major land reform in the postwar era. Thus, the preconditions allowing the poor to benefit directly from export expansion—through owning land on which exports are produced (Morley 1994, p. 20) or obtaining skills to produce manufactured goods and other exports—are missing.

Export expansion, however, is a central Latin American economic policy in the 1990s, free trade agreements having been established among many Latin American nations and between Canada, Mexico, and the United States. (The most recent is the Association of Caribbean States: it was created in August 1995 to offer some protection for the small economies in the region that are endangered by rapid changes in global trade.) It is anticipated that a Western Hemisphere Free Trade Area will gradually be established during the next twenty years.

Who Benefits from Latin American Growth? Income Distribution

Latin American income is more unequally distributed than that of rich nations at a similar stage of development. In rich nations the top 10% of the population had 34–42% of the income from 1911 to 1938. In Latin America in the 1950s and 1960s they had roughly 50 to 60%. In 1970 the upper 10% had 22% of income in Argentina and 52% in Mexico. In 1980 the range was from 30% in Argentina to 50% in Peru. A comparison of Latin American nations to others found that in 1965 only Costa Rica, Panama, Uruguay, and Venezuela were more egalitarian than other nations with similar characteristics. Brazil, Honduras, Jamaica, and Mexico were much more unequal (Urrutia 1991b, p. 47). Poverty was nearly always reduced by economic growth, but it increased with the disruption of growth during the 1980s, when inequality increased: 31% of Latin America lived on less than $2 per day in 1989, compared to 26.5% in 1980 (Morley 1994, p. 14). Rural urban migrations reduced rural poverty, while urban poverty increased. More than half of Latin America's poverty is now urban, and Brazil has a 36% larger share of poor people than other Latin American nations. Mexico's stabilization policy after 1984 increased inequality of income distribution, while in Argentina urban poverty decreased (Altimir 1993).

For Latin America as a whole, the partial economic recovery did not restore income distribution to its earlier levels of somewhat greater equality, although inequality tends to decrease with economic growth through most of the developing world. Nations with more democratic political processes have more equal income distributions. A special feature of income distribution is that in Mexico and Peru 80% of the Indian population has an income of less than $2 per day, compared to 18% of Mexico's and 50% of Peru's nonindigenous population. Much of this difference in income reflects differing levels of education and, consequently, of employment (Psacharopoulos and Patrinos 1993, 1994, pp. 41–43).

To gain access to education and other services, women, national minorities, and "nonwhite" citizens are increasingly mobilized. In 1994 Colombia reserved seats in its legislature for minorities. This should ameliorate their poverty: there is an emerging consensus that income distribution does not vary automatically with stages of growth, but depends on national economic policy—which the minorities can now help to create—as well as world economic conditions (Altimir forthcoming). Moreover, both land reform and increased investment in education are recommended as policy measures that will increase the equality of income distribution.

One reason why the poor accept unequal distribution of income is the existence of safety net social programs. Brazil, with a highly unequal income distribution, had a rapid decline in infant mortality during the 1980s, in part due to availability of oral rehydration therapy and improved water supply and sanitation. Increased coverage of unemployment insurance, beginning in 1990, and the existence of food programs for children and workers moderated the plight of some of the Brazilian poor, although the poorest are not adequately helped. The improvements were strongest after 1985, and the opening toward democracy. Mexico similarly has increased its safety nets for the poor, although its adjustment policies have led to unemployment and poverty. On the other hand, when the poor have not initiated a revolution, they have increased robberies to stay alive, when they otherwise have no chance of getting a job. The striking worsening of income inequality has been matched by increasing robberies and kidnappings.

Not all of these developments result from market forces. Latin American governments often established marketing boards, requiring producers to sell their products to them. The marketing boards paid producers prices below those that they received for their products that they sold on world markets. This was done in part because it was easier to use marketing boards than to collect taxes. The government kept the funds arising from the difference between export receipts and payments to the producers. The funds were at least in part used to finance economic development. The low prices paid to producers, however, discouraged investment in agriculture. Investment in other sectors was more profitable.

As a result, the productivity of agriculture lagged behind that of other sectors, and incomes from agricultural activities were below average. Agricultural real income and wages fell 20% during the 1980s, compared to 5% in manufacturing and 7% in construction (Morley 1994, p. 20). Labor productivity in agriculture rose from 30% to 42% of average economy-wide GDP per worker in Chile and 36% to 45% in Brazil—which encouraged commercial, export promotion, and import substitution agriculture. It fell from 100% to 68% in Argentina, from 29% to 23% in Mexico, and from 34% to 21% in Peru. Labor migration from rural areas to the cities increased; reallocation of labor accounted for 28% of Latin America's productivity growth (Syrquin 1991, pp. 110–14). In the case of Mexico, the low productivity of traditional agriculture led the government to reform the Mexican agrarian reform, anticipating that long-run overall economic growth would absorb the estimated 16 million people who would be forced out of agriculture (Randall 1996a, 1996b). This assumed that the new economic policies would adequately attract investment and that the Mexican experience would therefore differ from that of Latin America during the 1980s, when urban indigence and poverty increased more rapidly than that of the rural areas (Altimir 1994, p. 11).

During the 1980s, falling individual incomes led to increased participation of women in the paid labor force. Women's wages were higher relative to men's wages in the government than in the private sector. The difference reflected the greater variation in educational level of Latin Americans, as well as the greater variation in levels of technology used in different industries. The size of the firm, union strength, government policy, and nationality of owner all influenced wages (Abuhada and Romaguero 1993, p. 203; Randall 1987, 1989, 1993). Workers in large and medium-sized enterprises lost 7% of their average real wages and incomes during the 1980s, compared to 30% in small enterprises and the public sector and 42% in the informal sector. During this period, urban minimum wages fell 24%.

The difference in wages received reflected the greater variation in educational level of Latin Americans, as well as the greater variation in levels of technology used in various industries (Infante and Klein 1991, p. 132). It seems reasonable to assume that when education, especially at the primary school level, is more widely available, dispersion in wages and in overall income will fall. In this respect, Latin America will increasingly resemble richer areas, with better-functioning markets.

Common Latin American Development Patterns

The history of Latin American economic development in the postwar period is detailed in the following chapters, which describe who owns the economy, how the economy grows, concepts of economic growth, who contributes to growth, and who is the first to benefit from growth.

At first, all seven nations had largely private ownership in a mixed capitalist system, in which the state provided infrastructure and regulated the economy, but had little direct ownership of wealth. Influenced by dependency and import substitution industrialization theories, governments increased their provision of infrastructure, their protection of industry, and their creation or takeover of firms. Only Cuba expanded this to almost complete state ownership of the economy.

These shifts in ownership changed the conditions of economic interdependence, but did not eliminate it. Oil imports and exports accounted for a large share of the balance of payments and influenced the selection of economic policies. These often were to borrow abroad and increase the supply of money at home, leading to an unacceptable debt burden and inflation. The government deficit led to foreign borrowing; escape from the debt required an increase in government tax revenue and a reduction in government spending, often by selling its enterprises, reducing the bureaucracy, or restricting the salaries of its employees. Many Latin American nations feared that they could not compete effectively with newly industrializing Asian economies in world markets. They could nonetheless obtain the benefits of expanded and competitive markets through the establishment of free trade agreements, most notably the North American Free Trade Agreement (NAFTA) and the Common Market of the South (MERCOSUR). This would make it easier to obtain funds for development. Moreover, foreign investment began to be welcomed as a supplement to domestic savings.

However, much of foreign investment was in short-term, highly liquid instruments. Investors could invest and withdraw funds instantaneously, with serious impacts on the money supply and stock market. The relatively small to medium size of Latin American economies limited the ability of national monetary authorities to compensate for such capital movements. Thus, limited controls on capital movements were introduced.

In the medium term, moreover, domestic savings would become available. It was expected that lower population growth rates would decrease the number of dependents per worker and enable families to save and invest more of their income and make it possible to increase investment in education and other infrastructure, in order to obtain a better distribution of the benefits of economic growth.

The country studies begin with Chile, whose sharp shifts between reform, revolution, and free market delineate the choices among policies and the means of obtaining them that are available to Latin American policymakers. Next comes Brazil, whose economic development provides an example of the results of emphasizing the domestic market and of the use of techniques such as indexing—tying prices to an indicator of inflation—on economic development. The study of Mexico incorporates analysis of policy shifts, the role of oil, and increased integration into the world economy. Argentine economic history highlights the impact of stop-go policies and reliance on macroeconomic policy tools in a politically divided nation. Peruvian economic policies incorporated land reform and state ownership, without continuing economic growth or stable redistribution of income. Ecuador has transformed its economy from predominantly rural, agricultural, and commercial activities to an urban economy dominated by oil. Economic recession has forced increased reliance on the state, as private savings have dried up. Cuba for many years led Latin America in increasing benefits available to its poor. Cuba's policy shifts among several models of a state-dominated economy precluded steady economic growth. The breakup of the Union of Soviet Socialist Republics removed significant economic support. Cubans' level of living, including government-provided services, declined.

Country Studies

The following sections outline central points in the country studies.

Chile

William Maloney notes that Chilean economic history is as much a story of reconstituting a social contract as of restructuring an economy. In the immediate postwar period, the largely foreign-owned copper industry was the motor of economic growth. Domestic industry was developed by protection and was financed in large part by the Chilean Development Corporation (CORFO), while agriculture was controlled by traditional groups. High inflation and stop-go policies hindered exports during the fifties. Orthodox stabilization attempts failed. In 1959–61 monetary and commercial reforms brought a larger role for market mechanisms. The government adopted a ten-year program that included land reform and shifted toward structuralist analysis of industrial stagnation, inflation, balance of payments crises, and dependency. The small domestic market limited the possibility of successful import substituting industrialization. Small scale of production led to high costs and an inability to expand exports. In the sixties the government turned to land reform with compensation, in part paid for by increased revenues from copper.

The fragmentation of Chilean politics allowed Allende to win the presidency with one-third of the vote. He completed the nationalization of the copper industry—begun in the sixties—intervened in firms that had labor disputes, and expropriated 60% of Chile's agricultural land. Increased wages led to an increase in demand for food; this, combined with the fall in agricultural output, led to food shortages, a rise in wheat imports, and a trade deficit. Deteriorating economic conditions contributed to the military coup of 1973.

Twenty years later, Chile had obtained a market-based economy and democratic politics. Since 1987 output, savings, and real wages have grown impressively, with low rates of unemployment and inflation. Greater integration in the world economy has increased exports tenfold since 1975, eliminating import bottlenecks for industry. These developments ended stop-go policy cycles and helped to insulate Chile from the effects of short-term outflow of foreign capital. Spending on social programs began to increase and was directed to the very poor.

In the transition from an interventionist to a market economy, economic power was concentrated when government enterprises were sold to private owners at 50 to 70% of their net worth. Some 35% of redistributed agricultural land was returned to its owners. Labor market reform included the replacement of the government pension fund system with mandatory workers' savings in a personal account.

Maloney concludes that the Chilean achievements indicate that the ability to establish credible and permanent rules of the game may be as important as the relative importance of the market and of the state in the economy.

Brazil

Werner Baer and Claudio Paiva characterize Brazil's government as both a policymaker and a direct participant in economic activities. International trade provides a smaller share of gross domestic product than in many other Latin American nations. Brazil's economy grew rapidly, gradually shifting from primary exports to industry. Starting in the early fifties, this transformation was intensified by policies designed to produce goods in Brazil that had previously been imported (import substituting industrialization) and to increase public and private investment, especially in infrastructure and modern industry. Development was concentrated in the Center-South, and income distribution became more concentrated.

Brazil's reaction to the oil price increase in 1973 was not to reduce economic activity in response to the oil shock, but instead to increase exploration for oil and to produce alcohol as a substitute for gasoline. By the early 1980s the increase in world interest rates made it difficult for Brazil to meet its debt service obligations, while budget deficits and inflation led to stagnation of the economy in the 1980s and early 1990s.

Attempts were made to gradually open the economy to foreign competition, to privatize some government enterprises, to control federal, state, and public enterprise expenditures, to improve tax collection, and to introduce a new currency, in order to restore confidence in the credibility of Brazilian economic policy. New inflows of foreign funds were primarily invested in government securities and in the stock market. The Brazilian economy consequently was vulnerable to rapid responses to changing interest rates, which could lead to a sudden outflow of funds.

Brazilian economic policy has included indexing prices and contracts to the rate of inflation; agricultural policies favoring the landowning elite and commercial farmers, while neglecting technical change and agricultural support policies; and a shift in import substituting industrialization policy from favoring consumer goods to benefiting basic inputs and capital goods and to expanding manufactured goods exports. The favored sectors have grown, as has the informal economy, largely in services.

Mexico

Miguel Ramírez points out that active participation of the government in Mexico's economy began with an alliance between the state, landed elites, and foreign capital under Porfirio Díaz (1876–1911). The Mexican Revolution (1910–17) tried to shift state actions to benefit peasants, workers, and small businessmen, especially under President Lázaro Cárdenas (1934–40), who implemented land reform and nationalized the oil industry.

In 1940 emphasis shifted to private capital formation, which was aided by protection of Mexican markets, first through shortages of imports during World War II and then through government provision of infrastructure, including credit through a development bank.

In the postwar period, Mexico implemented import substituting industrialization policies, while also promoting the development of exports by the commercial agricultural sector. A sharp devaluation in 1954 led to a shift in policies, which emphasized "Stabilizing Development" (1955–70). It combined price stability with investment in social infrastructure and basic industry. Increasing social and political problems led the Echeverría administration (1970–76) to abandon Stabilizing

Development and instead to increase government spending, creating state enterprises. Attempts at tax reform failed, and the government turned to foreign investors and the Central Bank for financing. Inflation and devaluation followed. Inflation, increasing interest rates, and the collapse of the price of oil led to capital flight and devaluation, a temporary moratorium on debt payments, and nationalization of banks in 1982.

In 1983 Mexico turned to neoliberal economic policies, emphasizing expenditure cuts, instead of shifting expenditure to investment in infrastructure. The new administration tried to reassure the business community. It first imposed a stabilization plan and then established solidarity pacts, starting in 1987, that were signed with representatives of business and labor. A continuation of these policies, and the establishment of NAFTA during the Salinas administration (1988–94), contributed to the massive inflow of foreign capital. Economic policy mistakes and political assassinations led to capital flight, collapse of the peso, and a massive fall in income. There was a displacement of peasants as a result of the reform of traditional collective agricultural landholdings (the ejido).

Funds from privatization eased government finances, but the economy suffered from a banking crisis, as well as failures of small and medium-sized businesses as a result of debt burdens. The continuing political and economic crisis suggests that until Mexico renews its emphasis on social development in a sound economy there will be only limited possibilities for further growth.

Argentina

Robert McComb and Carlos Zarazaga's study indicates that Argentina developed with scarce labor and scarce mineral resources. The economy was primarily agricultural. Its products were the basis of light industry, which began to be protected in the early twentieth century. Economic regulation of the economy by relying on a Central Bank began in 1935; Juan Domingo Perón substantially increased government ownership and control of the economy in the forties and early fifties.

The small size of the highly protected Argentine market made it difficult to export goods. This gave rise to "stop-go" policy cycles that began with a devaluation to promote exports and reduction in real income designed to reduce imports. The increased price of imports led to inflation, which made Argentine goods uncompetitive in world markets.

The continuing alternation of economic policies, as well as shifts between civilian and military governments, led to recurring economic crises and, in 1973, to Perón's return to the presidency. The policy cycles of renewed intervention in the economy and inflation contributed to the 1976 military coup. The new government followed disastrous economic policies, culminating in the economic sphere in banking scandals and financial crises, and in the political sphere in the Malvinas/Falkland war with Great Britain. The discredited military government was replaced by the elected president Raúl Alfonsín in 1983. His flawed economic policies led to a run on dollars and the election of Carlos Menem, who was faced with hyperinflation. He abandoned his populist platform and implemented wide-ranging free market economic reforms, opening the economy to foreign trade, reducing public sector employment, and privatizing state enterprises.

Inflation fell and growth spurted from 1993 to 1995, but was interrupted by the "tequila effect," a panic in 1995 spreading from Mexico, which had devalued sharply, to other Latin American nations. Growth was resumed in 1996, in part as a result of the creation of MERCOSUR. Income distribution was inequitable, and there was resistance to Menem's reforms, leading to fears of increased political and economic conflict, as Menem sought to modify the constitution so that he could succeed himself in office—a strategy followed by President Alberto Fujimori in Peru and considered by President Fernando Henrique Cardoso in Brazil.

Peru

Efraín Gonzales de Olarte emphasizes that since the 1950s the Peruvian economy has been transformed, but has not developed. Income distribution was unequal throughout the postwar period and worsened during recessions. The nation relied on the export of raw materials, whose export was financed by foreign investment. Domestic production was insufficient to supply consumer goods for the rapidly increasing population. In the mid-fifties import substituting industrialization policies were adopted. From the sixties to the eighties Peru followed a semi-industrial primary export growth–led economic policy, based on mining and fishing exports.

The military regime of 1968–75 increased foreign borrowing, but also nationalized the International Petroleum Company as well as the principal mining and fishing enterprises, creating labor communities to own them. Land reform did not increase the share of agriculture in output. The role of government in the economy increased. The state became the principal investor and employer. The increasing burden left insufficient funds for domestic needs. In the early 1980s Sendero Luminoso attacks disrupted the nation. In reaction, the newly elected president, Alberto Fujimori, tried to reverse the economic conditions that had contributed to their rise by undertaking a drastic stabilization policy.

The "Fujishock" policies included, successfully, privatization and reform of fiscal administration and, less successfully, liberalization of foreign trade and deregulation of markets.

Peru's savings did not provide as much economic growth as expected because of maldistribution of investment. Peru educated its population, but did not create enough jobs, which led to emigration of large numbers of professionals and students. Five percent of the Peruvian population now lives abroad. Some 81% of the economically active are unemployed, underemployed, or engaged in unreported activities. During the post–World War II period, the government maintained questionable relative prices, overvalued the exchange rate, allowed real salaries to decline, and permitted interest rate instability. This, combined with political instability, led to declining willingness to invest in the Peruvian economy. Nonetheless, average levels of education increased, economic expectations changed from dependence on the state to self-reliance, and it is increasingly understood that the government needs to promote development without direct intervention in the economy.

Ecuador

Joan B. Anderson points out that physically Ecuador is one of the smallest countries in South America. Its regional split, with agribusiness and commerce on the coast and the traditional oligarchy and capital in the sierra, both prevented the development of a highly concentrated population in the capital and contributed to political instability. Economic instability was heightened by reliance on a single export, most recently, oil.

Primarily agricultural in 1950, by 1990 the nation was more than half urban, living in coastal areas because rural well-being was below that in urban areas. Ecuador's population tripled and real annual per capita growth was 2.3%, although there was negative growth and inflation during the 1980s.

Industrialization was encouraged by import substituting industrialization policies that began in 1957 and tax, education, and agrarian reform in the early sixties. Oil exports beginning in the early 1970s led to increased receipts and a faster increase in imports financed by increases in the foreign debt. General improvements in the level of economic welfare through the early 1980s did not result in major changes in Ecuador's highly unequal income distribution or adequately develop a domestic market.

In the mid-eighties Ecuador adopted a free market approach to economic policy, which was modified by more government intervention in the economy at the end of the decade. In the 1990s the economy again grew; economic "adjustment" measures were adopted. Their cost was borne by the poor. The inequality in Ecuador's income distribution was largely the result of protection, rather than of differences in productivity.

Agriculture has had both large landholdings and farms too small to support the rural population. Rural-urban migration resulted; attempts at land reform have been frustrated, while policies favoring industry also have hindered the development of agriculture.

The public sector now pays more than half of the nation's wage bill, but has decreased its investment in infrastructure and has begun to privatize government firms. It opened the oil industry to foreign participation in the early 1990s. Foreign participation in the economy must supply savings no longer available from Ecuadoreans, whose savings decreased when the nation's gross domestic product fell. Increased attention to agriculture, infrastructure, and human capital is needed to increase Ecuador's economic development.

Cuba

Carmelo Mesa-Lago indicates that in the 1950s Cuba was ranked as one of the most advanced Latin American economies. Unlike similar Latin American nations, it had small state ownership of production and services, other than in education, banking, and public health. There was great dependence on sugar exports and therefore on shifting sugar prices and on U.S. policies governing overall sugar quotas and preferences granted according to sugar imports' country of origin.

Fidel Castro seized power in 1959. His government replaced a capitalist system with a series of socialist economic systems and shifting emphases on sugar and other economic sectors. Despite these shifts, until 1990, when 94.1% of the civilian sector worked for the state, Cuba steadily moved toward collectivization of production and more equal distribution of income. The collapse of socialist nations has led to an opening to foreign investment and some private ownership in the 1990s: this has provided only a small fraction of the funds previously obtained from the Soviet bloc. Remittances of funds from Cubans living abroad and the expansion of self-employment and free agricultural markets have contributed to an increase in inequality of income distribution.

Plans for industrialization were replaced in 1966 by emphasis on sugar. Shifting reforms characterized planning until 1986, when Cuba moved away from a market economy, until Russia's economic collapse and the end of its subsidies to the Cuban economy. This forced a more radical shift toward a market economy, while the decline in value of socialist countries' currencies has significantly reduced the burden of repaying Cuba's debt to them. Cuba has been unable to make debt service payments to countries with stronger currencies, because of insufficient exports and lack of access to hard currency credit. The nation's growth was intermittent and declined by about one-half in 1990–94, when it began to lose its earlier gains in provision of employment, free social services, and increased equality of income distribution.

Conclusion

The studies in this book indicate that, despite long-run success, the depression of the eighties and early nineties makes it essential to redistribute income and invest in the population for political stability and economic growth with development to prevail in Latin America.

Note

The author expresses appreciation to the University Seminars of Columbia University for assistance in the preparation of the manuscript for publication. The ideas presented reflect discussions in the University Seminar on Latin America and in the University Seminar on Brazil.

Works Cited

Abuhada, Mario, and Pilar Romaguero. 1993. Inter-Industrial Wage Differentials: Evidence from Latin American Countries. *Journal of Development Studies* 30(1).

Altimir, Oscar. 1993. Income Distribution and Poverty through Crisis and Adjustment. In Economic Commission for Latin America and the Caribbean—ECLAC *Working Paper No. 15* (September).

———. 1994. Distribución del ingreso e incidencia de la pobreza a lo largo del ajuste. *Revista de la Cepal* 52 (April).

———. Forthcoming. Changes in Inequality and Poverty in Latin America. *Journal of Development Economics*.

De Long, J. Bradford, and Lawrence H. Summers. 1991. Equipment Investment and Economic Growth. *Quarterly Journal of Economics* (May).

Feliz, Raúl Aníbal. 1992. *Determinantes del crecimiento económico en América Latina: La evidencia empírica, 1950–1989*. Documento de Trabajo 7, Economía. Mexico City: Centro de Investigación y Docencia Económicas.

Fishlow, A., and J. Friedman. 1994. Tax Evasion, Inflation, and Stabilization. *Journal of Development Economics* 43.

Infante, Ricardo, and Emilio Klein. 1991. The Latin American Labour Market, 1950–1990. *CEPAL Review* 145.

International Monetary Fund. *Government Finance Statistics Yearbook* (several issues).

Larraín, Felipe, and Marcelo Selowsky, eds. 1991. *The Public Sector and the Latin American Crisis*. San Francisco: International Center for Economic Growth.

Maddison, Angus. 1983. A Comparison of Levels of GDP Per Capita in Developed and Developing Countries, 1700–1980. *Journal of Economic History* 43.

——. 1991. Economic and Social Conditions in Latin America, 1913–1950. In M. Urrutia, ed., *Long-term Trends in Latin American Economic Development*. Washington, D.C.: Inter-American Development Bank/Johns Hopkins University Press.

Morley, Samuel A. 1994. Changes in Poverty and the Distribution of Income in Latin America during the 1980's. Paper presented at First Annual Meeting of Latin American Economics Association, Boston.

Pfeffermann, Guy P., and Andrea Madarassy. 1992. *Trends in Private Investment in Developing Countries, 1992 Edition*. Discussion Paper 14. Washington, D.C.: International Finance Corporation.

Psacharopoulos, George, and Harry A. Patrinos, eds. 1993. *Indigenous People and Poverty in Latin America*. LAT Regional Studies Report No. 30. Washington, D.C.: World Bank (August).

——. 1994. Indigenous People and Poverty in Latin America. *Finance and Development* (March).

Randall, Laura. 1987. *The Political Economy of Venezuelan Oil*. New York: Praeger.

——. 1989. *The Political Economy of Mexican Oil*. New York: Praeger.

——. 1993a. *Economic Structure and the North American Free Trade Area*. New York: Bildner Center for Western Hemisphere Studies.

——. 1993b. *The Political Economy of Brazilian Oil*. New York: Praeger.

——, ed. 1996a. *Changing Structure of Mexico: Political, Social and Economic Prospects*. New York: M. E. Sharpe.

——, ed. 1996b. *Reforming Mexico's Agrarian Reform*. New York: M. E. Sharpe.

Syrquin, Moshe. 1991. A Comparative Analysis of Structural Transformation in Latin America. In M. Urrutia, ed., *Long-term Trends in Latin American Economic Development*. Washington, D.C.: Inter-American Development Bank.

Urrutia, Miguel, ed. 1991a. *Long-term Trends in Latin American Economic Development*. Washington, D.C.: Inter-American Development Bank.

——. 1991b. Twenty-five Years of Economic Growth and Social Progress. In M. Urrutia, ed., *Long-term Trends in Latin American Economic Development*. Washington, D.C.: Inter-American Development Bank.

Werneck, Rogério F. 1991. Public Sector Adjustment to External Shocks and Domestic Pressures in Brazil. In F. Larraín and M. Selowsky, eds., *The Public Sector and the Latin American Crisis*. San Francisco: International Center for Economic Growth.

2.
Chile

William F. Maloney
University of Illinois, Urbana-Champaign

Postwar History

Chilean economic history in the postwar period holds a special fascination for students of development. Though the challenges facing Chilean policymakers—dependency, stagnation, macroeconomic instability, and extreme income inequality—were those facing governments throughout Latin America, policy responses have careened between extremes that bracket the range of development paradigms. The socialist era under Salvador Allende offered an answer through the dramatic expansion of Latin America's only democratically elected socialist workers' state. The equally radical "neoliberal" experiment that followed under the military embraced an unprecedented faith in markets and minimization of discretionary state power. The lessons taken from the much studied successes and catastrophic failures of this period continue to transform development thinking and policymaking around the globe.

Yet any attempt to understand Chilean economic history must also acknowledge that the problems to which these disparate economic experiments would be solutions had deep sociopolitical roots of which their designers were acutely aware. The history from World War II is one of a progressive erosion of the traditional structures of governance that set electoral politics on a path to hypermobilization then brutal repression and only recently to a return to Chile's democratic tradition. Chilean economic history is as much a story of reconstituting a social contract as of restructuring an economy.

The Immediate Postwar Period

For much of the twentieth century the fortunes of copper would constitute the leitmotif around which other socioeconomic themes would be woven. As with nitrates before, foreign development of copper was accepted as the driving force in economic growth. Chilean investors, largely unaware of technological advances in the processing and extraction of low-grade ores, and unable or unwilling to make the mammoth

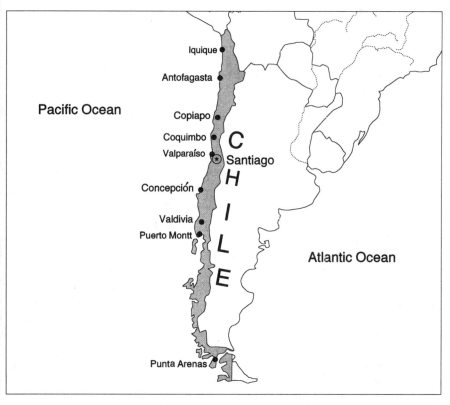

Iquique

Antofagasta

Pacific Ocean

Copiapo

Coquimbo

Valparaíso

Concepción

Valdivia

Puerto Montt

Punta Arenas

Santiago

C
H
I
L
E

Atlantic Ocean

1000   0   1000   2000   Miles

⊛ Capital
Major Rivers
• Major Cities
National Boundary
Countries

N

W   E

S

investments required, had deferred to two U.S. firms, Kennecott and Anaconda (Baklanoff 1975; Moran 1974). What became known as the Gran Minería grew to dominate the Chilean economy, accounting for 85–90% of the up to 80% of exports and 20% of gross domestic product that copper represented. Productivity was ten times that of other industries and twenty times that of agriculture, making miners' wages among the highest in the country. Again, as with nitrates before, copper revenues would be essential to the stability and development of central-ized state power (Monteón 1982). Taxation of the Gran Minería rose from 3% in 1930–34 to 70% by 1952 and would finance up to 40% of government expenditure.

Despite virtually exclusive government focus on the promotion of traditional extractive and agricultural exports, from the 1860s to the 1890s Chile experienced a period of rapid industrial development under a traditional liberal regime with tariff rates of 15–25% (Marshall 1988). The Manufacturing Development Society (SOFOFA), founded in 1883, was the first to urge the protection of nascent industry as a means of accelerating growth, as it argued had been done in the United States and the United Kingdom (Muñoz 1968). Though the response to SOFOFA's lobbying was modest, a low-capital, highly labor-absorptive industry prospered. By 1930 Santiago, Valparaíso, and Concepción were leading national suppliers of cotton and woolen textiles, ceramics, refined sugar, glass, fish- and whale-based products, and processed agricultural goods (Mamalakis 1976).

The Great Depression hit Chile with special fierceness, driving exports down 90% and national income by half. The next forty years would see a dramatic growth in protection and state intervention as the development strategy turned decidedly inward, both to reduce the global dependence on final products and to insulate the economy from sharp fluctuations in primary good exports. From 1931 to 1938 successive governments would double tariffs and embrace quotas, import licenses, exchange rate controls, and multiple exchange rates (Stallings 1974). The period of the leftist-centrist Popular Front alliance from 1938 to 1952 saw a sharp rise in de facto protection arising from the cessation of industrial imports during World War II as well as a marked shift toward direct impetus to industry through subsidies, tax exemptions, low-cost credits, technical assistance, and state entrepreneurship. A 15% addi-tional tax on copper in 1939 partially financed the Promethean efforts of the Chilean Development Corporation (CORFO), which grew by the 1950s to control 30% of investment in plant and equipment and to play the dominant role in fomenting Chilean industrialization.

On its twentieth birthday, CORFO published an overview of its achievements: the founding in 1941 of the linen, rayon, and silk indus-tries and a joint venture to produce rubber products, tires, and batteries;

the electrification of the country, beginning in 1944 with the creation of the National Electric Company; and the establishment from 1946 to 1950 of the National Petroleum Company to develop newly discovered petroleum reserves in Magallanes. Chilean history, CORFO boasted, consisted of two eras: before and after its construction of the massive steel works in Huachipato, near Concepción, beginning in 1947. This catalyst transformed the region into one of the most dynamic centers of manufacturing in Latin America, hosting peripheral industries in steel wires, ferrous alloys, zinc and tin recovery plants, electrical equipment, and tools and machinery (Mamalakis 1965). CORFO also promoted the mechanization of agriculture, engaged in vast irrigation projects, introduced the sugar beet in Bío Bío, and in 1952 created the National Sugar Industry to process it. Its vast and eclectic agenda extended to financing the Chilean Radio Corporation, the Bacteriological Institute of Chile, and the Chilean Film Company.

The corporation's efforts would lay the foundations for the dynamic export industries of the next half-century. It financed and promoted prospecting for gold, silver, manganese, and iron. To develop the fishing industry, CORFO contracted technical assistance missions, established a marine biology station near Valparaíso in 1945, granted sizable tax exemptions in 1952, and joined the army and the University of Chile in surveying the coastal waters in 1954. It took the first inventories of forest stocks, contracted the 1944 Haig technical assistance mission, which revealed "the indisputable truth that an adequate management of our forests could become the basis for a . . . great industry of forest products" (CORFO 1962, p. 80), and in 1953 financed processing plants for cellulose and newsprint. In the fruit industry as well, CORFO financed technical assistance missions, extended credit for cultivation and experimental plots, and invested in supporting infrastructure. In 1941 it cofinanced efforts to promote exports of wood products and wine.

The government thus became principal promoter of Chile's import substitution–based industrialization (ISI). From 1937 to 1950 industrial output and employment increased almost 7% per year, output by roughly 3.7%, and per capita income roughly 2% (Mamalakis 1976). From 1925 to 1950 import substitution reduced the share of consumer goods in imports from 44% to 25% (Moran 1974). However, the rapid growth of the interventionist and distributive state resulted as much from the need to incorporate new actors into the extant democratic order as from the need to address the vulnerability highlighted by the Great Depression (Valdés 1995). In the period of the Popular Front, Marxist parties and organized labor, with its nerve center in the copper fields, were successfully incorporated as "junior partners" in mainstream politics and their demands moderated and intermediated by the party system. This cooptation was made possible by the left's identification with the state's industrialization project as a necessary precondition for a revolutionary society and concern with fascist advances in Europe, modest government concessions on social and labor reform, and brutal repression (Valdés 1995; Velasco 1994; Scully 1992; Drake 1978).

In exchange for the popular initiatives and increasing government intervention in the economy, the traditional agricultural interests received a tacit agreement by the left parties to moderate worker demands and to desist from mobilizing the rural peasantry. Thus, largely excluded from the largesse of the distributive state were the rural workers, who lived in an isolated world of extreme inequalities, dependent on their patron and reliable in their support at the polls. The lock on the peasant vote gave the right a veto in the Congress and thus the ability to temper the statist agenda and demands for social reform (Scully 1992). The implicit taxation of agriculture implied by the overvalued exchange rate common to ISI generated relatively muted conflict. This was partly due to repressed rural wages, heavily subsidized credit, fertilizer, and transport, and a commitment not to levy taxes (Velasco 1994; Scully 1992; Moran 1974). As Maurice Zeitlin and Richard Ratcliff (1988) demonstrate, it was also due in part to the fact that the agricultural and industrial elites were essentially the same groups. Andrés Velasco (1994) argues that the growing middle class consisted primarily of government bureaucrats and remained dependent on the growth of the state.

Yet the foundations of this order that had generated relatively high growth and social stability were intrinsically fragile and showed increasing strains as the second half of the century approached. First, the vulnerability revealed in the depression and its perceived remedy in the national industrial project contributed to reframing the dependent relationship with the industrialized world. Copper became the central metaphor. As the dominant provider of export earnings, copper served as the umbilical cord to an industrialization strategy that had replaced dependence on finished goods with a greater dependence on imported raw materials and capital equipment. There was widespread concern that the 30% fall in copper production from 1944 to 1950 and disadvantageous pricing by foreign interests foreshadowed industry's progressive starvation. During the U.S. recession of 1949, copper prices fell to 7¢ per pound from their customary range of 13¢ to 22¢ at time when a 1¢ fall decreased exports by 2% and government revenues by 3% (Moran 1974). But while Chile bore the magnified burdens of downturns, it appeared not to reap the benefits of booms. Where World War I had led to almost a tripling of copper prices, the price caps imposed by the U.S government during World War II and the Korean War left the country's import capacity 40% below that of 1925. The free play of the markets appeared to be permitted only when it benefited the industrialized country. Further, Kennecott and Anaconda's position as controllers of half the world's copper production suggested monopolistic control that made possible an alliance between northern consumers and producers to keep prices artificially low at Chile's expense (Moran 1974).

Much of the conspiratorial alarm was misplaced. Theodore H. Moran (1974) argues that as more producers came on line and as aluminum emerged as a substitute, a weakened copper cartel moderated price increases to preserve market share. Further, as Eric N. Baklanoff (1975) argues, the decline in Chilean output was due largely to the pressures of increased taxes and mandatory foreign exchange conversions at prejudicial rates that raised labor costs and pushed implicit taxation far above that in competitor countries (see table 2.1). But Chileans lacked the technical capacity to monitor and confidently critique the actions of the Gran Minería: in 1952 the controller general admitted that he had no idea of what went on in the companies (Moran 1974). Many found resonance instead in the re-articulation of their dependent relationship in the works of Raúl Prebisch and the Economic Commission for Latin America (ECLA). Dependency theorists dismissed comparative advantage and liberal economics in general as inappropriate analytical frameworks. They argued that a continuing decline in the terms of trade meant that Chile would get progressively fewer imports in exchange for its copper. More profoundly, they called into question the possibility of developing as a primary exporter in a dependent context (Love 1996). Political leaders across the spectrum, allied with economists from ECLA and the University of Chile, proposed interventionist measures, and even conservative critics of state intervention saw a need to establish a "just price for copper." In 1952 the government established an ill-fated state sales monopoly that priced Chilean copper 13% above the global rate (Baklanoff 1975; Moran 1974).

There would also be a progressively deeper search for "structural" determinants of increased dependency, inflation, and industrial stagnation with a special focus on the heretofore off-limits agricultural sector. After World War II, output of what foreign observers had called "probably the best piece of farm real estate in the world" (Theodore Schultz cited in Crosson 1970, p. xiii) outside of California had not kept pace with population growth, and food imports became a steady drain on foreign exchange. In 1940 agriculture's share in GDP was a slight 15% and would continue to decline to half the Latin American average. Production of some industrial agricultural products such as oils and fibers and to a lesser extent fruits and vegetables increased, but output of cereals and meat products fell below the growth of internal demand, and they had to be imported. Gains in industrial independence seemed offset by growing dependence on food (Mamalakis 1976).

Analysts fell into two camps. The first saw extensive opportunities for investment at current prices going unexploited due to the fact that

Table 2.1. Gross Domestic Product by Sector of Origin, 1950–95 (1977 pesos, millions)

Year	Total	Agriculture	Mining	Manufacturing	Electricity and Gas	Construction	Commerce	Transport	Other*
1950	135,802	17,019	13,224	27,385	1,546	10,865	22,999	5,573	35,242
1955	157,996	20,172	11,393	35,569	2,064	13,175	32,480	6,454	36,745
1960	187,100	19,875	14,431	41,648	2,752	14,285	34,056	7,880	49,093
1965	224,990	20,257	16,799	55,839	3,882	17,539	35,838	10,499	57,748
1970	283,096	24,070	18,595	69,911	4,792	20,034	47,494	13,765	70,700
1975	253,043	25,992	20,094	54,404	5,786	19,127	42,296	13,262	84,700
1980	363,446	30,031	26,077	78,332	7,754	15,669	59,767	20,176	109,385
1985	448,029	30,612	31,074	72,692	9,150	20,593	59,639	19,961	120,924
1990	509,153	40,194	37,060	104,451	12,847	29,581	94,196	37,419	149,110
1995	635,532	43,629	50,494	106,905	17,163	34,674	109,860	51,026	160,852
(Share of GDP)									
1950	100.0	12.5	9.7	20.2	1.1	8.0	16.9	4.1	26.0
1955	100.0	12.8	7.2	22.5	1.3	8.3	20.6	4.1	23.3
1960	100.0	10.6	7.7	22.3	1.5	7.6	18.2	4.2	26.2
1965	100.0	9.0	7.5	24.8	1.7	7.8	15.9	4.7	25.7
1970	100.0	8.5	6.6	24.7	1.7	7.1	16.8	4.9	25.0
1975	100.0	10.3	7.9	21.5	2.3	7.6	16.7	5.2	33.5
1980	100.0	8.3	7.2	21.6	2.1	4.3	16.4	5.6	30.1
1985	100.0	6.8	6.9	16.2	2.0	4.6	13.3	4.5	27.0
1990	100.0	7.9	7.3	20.5	2.5	5.8	18.5	7.3	29.3
1995	100.0	6.9	7.9	16.8	2.7	5.5	17.3	8.0	25.3

Source: Banco Central de Chile, *Indicadores económicos*, 1960–80, and *Boletín mensual*, various issues.
* Other: Banking, Housing, Defense and Public Administration, Services.

4.4% of owners controlled 80% of arable land, one of the most concentrated patterns of land ownership in the world. Large landowners felt no pressure to farm intensively, while smaller farmers lacked the collateral to secure credit for productivity-enhancing inputs (Jarvis 1985; Crosson 1970). This concentration was also seen as a barrier to expanding the domestic market for industrial production. The second camp blamed the adverse terms of trade between agriculture and the urban areas implicit in the ISI strategy for making agricultural investment unprofitable.

Though support could be found for both views, there was increasing evidence throughout the economy of strong disincentives to produce and export posed by regulatory distortions, the poor quality of state intervention, and persistent macro-instability. These had their roots, to large measure, in the very dynamics of bargain and compromise that maintained political stability. In particular, the arrangement where the centrist Radical party served as the intermediary processing diverse societal demands on the distributive state, alternating alliances with right- and left-wing groups, had deleterious effects on policy coherence and rationality. This showed up dramatically in the external sector. The partnership between industry and the dirigiste state, and labor's desire for employment stability in the absence of unemployment insurance or other measures to facilitate job mobility, lent an inherent bias toward protection (De la Cuadra and Hachette 1986). High tariff walls, combined with the byzantine complexity of the protectionist structure, made industry increasingly capital intensive, unable to compete abroad, and more dependent on copper revenues for intermediate inputs (Mamalakis 1976; Muñoz 1968). Many perceived the exhaustion of the easy phase of ISI by 1950 and were calling for liberalization of the trade regime and a rationalization of trade policy. A compilation of seminars given in the business community in 1954 entitled *Negative Aspects of Economic Intervention: Failures of an Experiment* praised CORFO's irreplaceable role in creating the electricity and fishing industries, but derided the gross inefficiency of Huachipato and the National Petroleum company and saw the capriciousness of exchange controls as the overriding disincentive to needed foreign investment. The halving of export volume over the previous decade, the stagnation of agriculture, and the frustration of Chile's tremendous potential in vegetable and fruit exports were laid at the feet of irrational intervention in the price mechanism and the persistently overvalued exchange rate (Correa Prieto 1954; see table 2.2).

What drove the instability of the real exchange rate and posed an insuperable barrier to liberalization were inflationary pressures arising from the inability to maintain consistent and coherent macroeconomic policy (Hirschman 1963). Excessive subsidies, tax breaks, and transfers

Table 2.2. Composition of Exports, 1950–95 (millions of U.S. dollars)

	1950	1955	1960	1965	1970	1975	1980	1985	1990	1995
TOTAL	307	486	469	684	1,111	1,552	4,818	3,706	8,375	16,039
Mining	257	415	406	557	950	1,075	2,771	2,124	4,640	7,850
Copper	151	327	321	428	839	890	2,152	1,685	3,810	6,847
Agriculture	36	36	24	22	32	86	339	375	995	1,449
Fruit	1	3	4	9	12	38	169	299	757	1,055
Industry	13	35	39	103	128	390	1,558	1,168	2,739	6,739
Fishmeal	0.2	1	2	8	16	29	233	279	380	628
Lumber, furniture	0.2	0.4	1	3	9	25	286	112	370	735
Paper, cellulose	0.9	1.5	5	20	40	89	511	210	423	1,629
Chemicals	0.4	0.9	3	4	11	46	163	96	308	621
Metal products									153	496
(As a Share of Exports)										
TOTAL	100.0	100.0	100.0	100.0	100.0	100.0	100.0	100.0	100.0	100.0
Mining	83.7	85.4	86.6	81.4	85.5	69.3	57.5	57.3	55.4	48.9
Copper	49.2	67.3	68.4	62.6	75.5	57.3	44.7	45.5	45.5	42.7
Agriculture	11.7	7.4	5.1	3.2	2.9	5.5	7.0	10.1	11.9	9.0
Fruit	0.3	0.6	0.9	1.3	1.1	2.4	3.5	8.1	9.0	6.6
Industry	4.2	7.2	8.3	15.1	11.5	25.1	32.3	31.5	32.7	42.0
Fishmeal	0.1	0.2	0.4	1.2	1.4	1.9	4.8	7.5	4.5	3.9
Lumber, furniture	0.1	0.1	0.2	0.4	0.8	1.6	5.9	3.0	4.4	4.6
Paper, cellulose	0.3	0.3	1.1	2.9	3.6	5.7	10.6	5.7	5.1	10.2
Chemicals	0.1	0.2	0.6	0.6	1.0	3.0	3.4	2.6	3.7	3.9
Metal products									1.8	3.1

Source: Banco Central de Chile, *Indicadores económicos,* 1960–80, and *Boletín mensual,* various issues. Data from 1950 to 1965 tabulated and adjusted from *Indicadores de comercio exterior.*
Note: Shares may not sum to 100 due to rounding.

led to creeping budget deficits that were monetized. These, combined with the ability of CORFO and other development banks to expand the money stock through their lending activities, led to chronically high rates of inflation, which rose from 3% in the 1920s to 40% in the early 1950s (Velasco 1994). Sporadic attempts to control aggregate demand led to stop-go cycles that inhibited investment and contributed to lackluster growth. As Velasco (1990) summarizes:

> These cycles were of the type well known to students of Latin American macroeconomics: aggregate demand expansion under fixed exchange rates leads to growing real exchange rate overvaluation and a deteriorating trade performance; eventually the near exhaustion of reserves leads to a devaluation of the currency and the corresponding sharp acceleration of inflation; once inflation becomes excessively high, alarmed authorities enact emergency stabilization measures, which often tend to be merely temporary, thus serving as the preface to the next phase of unsustainable expansion.

The evolution of anti-inflation strategy across the century was conditioned to a degree by gains in understanding on a technical level (Hirschman 1963). But, as important, it reflected the perceived tradeoff between development and equity on the one hand and inflation reduction on the other, and a growing suspicion that money creation was a symptom of deeper diseases, both structural and political. As early as 1932–38 monetary stability and balanced budgets were seen as fetishes of the privileged classes that locked in an unequal distribution of income that the Popular Front would see as part of its mandate to alter through large wage and salary increases, credit expansion, and development bank activity (Hirschman 1963). The degree of adjustment of wages to past inflation, in particular, became a symbolic measure of how much of the stabilization burden labor would bear. Unhappily, these cost of living adjustments were also a critical determinant of the budget deficit through their impact on the public sector wage bill. Increasingly, inflation would be framed as resulting from competition between groups for a share in national income, which Hirschman argued proxied for repressed civil war. To varying degrees, governments sought anti-inflation programs that would share the necessary sacrifice: money caused inflation, but could not be controlled without political consensus.

Such agreement would become progressively more elusive after 1950. The left would grow disenchanted with the limited fruits of its cooptation and would look for influence outside the traditional alliances in a workers' front strategy. After aggressive mobilization both in the rural areas and among government bureaucrats, the Communist party garnered an unexpectedly high 16.5% of the vote in the 1947 congressional elections. Rightist alarm and U.S. pressure led the Radical-dominated government of rightist Gabriel González Videla to repress the Communist party, its coalitional partner, and shift right in its alliances. More fundamentally, the perception of opportunistic alliance forming and corruption of the Radical party led to its exhaustion as a centrist honest broker and arbiter of increasingly disparate societal demands (Scully 1992).

Ibáñez, Alessandri, and the First Return to Liberal Economics

Chile thus entered the 1950s with the traditional political system in profound crisis and the economy in disarray. General Carlos Ibáñez's withering antiparty campaign of 1952 attacked the inefficiency and corruption of traditional politics and in particular the inability to stop inflation (Scully 1992; Hirschman 1963). Elected on a loose coalition of left-wing and nationalist parties with no organized movement, he was widely expected to assume dictatorial powers to override previous parliamentary gridlock. In the absence of organized and committed allies, his refusal to do so left him largely ineffectual.

On the economic front, proponents of the state sales monopoly in copper had vastly overestimated Chile's market power. Chile's share of the world market fell from 22% to 14%, leading to a large fall in copper revenues with attendant effects on industry. Falling government revenues caused deep cuts in public investment and large and monetized deficits that pushed inflation from the 23% inherited to 40% in 1953 and 64% in 1954. Large devaluations led to speculative behavior in the external sector, a tarnished foreign image, and withdrawal of foreign credit. Labor unrest heightened.

In what Hirschman cites as "a truly heroic attempt at equitable sharing of the burden of anti-inflationary austerity" (Hirschman 1963, p. 198), Ibáñez submitted a stabilization program in November 1954 that limited salary readjustments and forbade strikes. In exchange he offered low-cost housing and a minimum wage for workers and, insisting that "the powerful also pay" (Hirschman 1963, p. 195), proposed a progressive tax system to increase public revenues. However, relations with labor and with Congress had decayed after Ibáñez's declaration of a state of siege in September, and the program was stillborn in an ambiance of heightened class conflict. By 1955 inflation had risen above 80%, the highest in Chilean history, and income per capita was falling. Amid strikes, and rumors of immanent military takeover, Ibáñez turned to the right and initiated a series of reforms of a more liberal cast that would foreshadow many of the policies implemented by the military twenty years later.

The Klein Saks advisory mission from the United States arrived in September 1955 and stayed for three years and was integral to facilitating the policy shift. The mission communicated little in new northern wisdom, and many of the recommended policies could be found in Central Bank recommendations of a year earlier. However, it did serve as a mechanism through which polarized political actors could coordinate the policies on which there was general consensus (Hirschman 1963). The prescription was orthodox, stressing a general reorganization and reduction in the role of the state, increased taxes to put fiscal policy on sound footing, consolidation and tightening of monetary policy, and reduced backward indexing of wages. Ibáñez also unified and stabilized the exchange rate and initiated the first serious attempt at trade liberalization, moving from a discretionary quota system to a more impersonal one offering a greater role for market forces. Shifting back from confrontation to a posture of pragmatic accommodation with the copper companies, the Nuevo Tratado, or New Deal, of 1955 decreased taxation as an incentive to further foreign investment (Baklanoff 1975). The program succeeded in reducing inflation to 24% by 1957. However, the tax bill failed in the Congress, and the monetary contraction, combined with another fall in copper prices in 1956, would cause a deep recession through 1955–58 that led to bloody riots and general strikes.

The experience spurred and legitimized analyses that saw little hope in orthodox stabilization attempts and found additional resonance in the structuralist diagnoses articulated at ECLA. Monetary growth, rather than being viewed as the cause of inflation, was increasingly seen as accommodating inflationary pressures arising from unresolved structural problems, among them the low supply response of agriculture. Monetary contractions would serve only to drive up unemployment (Hirschman 1963). The structuralist line generated its antithesis in 1955. Under the aegis of a U.S. government concerned with the leftist orientation of Chilean economics, the University of Chicago and the Catholic University in Santiago signed a cooperative agreement that would convert a moribund department into a dynamic group of economists trained abroad. Strongly at odds with the new structuralist analysis, and confident in the efficacy of market mechanisms, this group would become increasingly active in public policy over the next four decades (Valdés 1995).

The Ibáñez years also hastened the transformation of party politics and class conflict. In 1953 a revitalized labor confederation, the Unified Workers' Central (CUT), was formed, which rejected traditional alliances with bourgeois parties, especially the centrist Radicals. In response to government repression of a CUT national strike protesting a wage freeze, working-class and Marxist parties formed a single Popular Action Front (FRAP) in 1957. The same year, two hitherto electorally insignificant Christian reform parties fused to become the party that would replace the Radicals at the center of the political spectrum, the Christian Democrats. Ibáñez's compliance with a prior campaign pledge to legalize the Communist party made it eligible again to participate openly in the 1958 presidential campaign. In addition, his promulgation of a series of reform laws that proscribed vote buying, introduced the secret ballot, and reduced vote fraud would prove to be the catalytic event in loosening the traditional control of the hacienda *patrón* over the rural vote. Both measures weakened the right and put it firmly on the defensive as the left scrambled for new votes in the countryside. And in the 1958 elections this was precisely where the FRAP and its candidate, Salvador Allende, experienced its fastest electoral growth (Scully 1992).

Rightist candidate Jorge Alessandri's narrow victory over Allende was seen as the last chance for the traditional elites to deal with the country's problems, among them inflation and an economy at a standstill (Stallings 1974; Hirschman 1963). Alessandri held the state-led model of development, and CORFO in particular, responsible for the stagnation and inefficiency of the economy and sought a larger role for market mechanisms and for both domestic and foreign investment. Working broadly along the lines of the Klein Saks mission, his government freed most prices, revised the system of credit control, and undertook a currency reform. From 1959 to 1961 the commercial reforms were deepened as quantitative restrictions were eliminated and tariffs lowered, making the economy the most open since the Great Depression and almost as open as under the first three years of the military (De la Cuadra and Hachette 1986; Behrman 1976). In another foreshadowing of future policies, Alessandri unified and then devalued the exchange rate to an export-promoting level and pegged it in January 1959 as a means of reducing expectations of inflation and restoring confidence in trade and credit management. Full convertibility was guaranteed, and the Central Bank assumed sole responsibility for foreign exchange policy (De la Cuadra and Hachette 1986; Ffrench-Davis 1973).

Again, the program initially succeeded in bringing inflation down to a postwar low of 5.4%. However, the balance of payments crisis that erupted in 1961 cut short the longer-term experiment of stimulating a larger role for the private sector. The plan to severely limit cost of living adjustments, seen as essential to stopping both inflationary inertia and fiscal hemorrhaging, was stymied by labor's violent resistance to bearing the costs of stabilization (see table 2.3). The fiscal gap rose beyond 4.6% of GDP and was monetized. Though inflation would be repressed by abundant imports and the fixed exchange rate, the fiscal imbalance

Table 2.3. Main Economic and Social Indicators, 1960–92
(percent unless otherwise indicated)

Indicator	Alessandri Government 1959–64	Frei Government 1965–70	Allende Government 1971–73	Pinochet Regime 1974–89	Aylwin Government 1990–93
GDP growth[a]	3.9	4.1	0.7	3.4	5.9
Rate of inflation[b]	26.6	26.3	285.7	79.9	19.6
Public sector deficit[c]	4.7[d]	2.1	16.1	0.5	-0.3
Unemployment rate[e]	5.2[d]	5.9	4.8	17.1	6.5
Average real wage[f]	62.2[d]	84.2	90.0	81.4	94.7
Minimum real wage[f]	116.8[d]	101.8	134.0	83.0	83.0
Public sector real wage[f]	–	81.4	87.9	75.3	78.3[g]
Social expenditure[c]	–	–	–	4.5	3.6
Price of copper[h]	32.4[d]	61.0	59.6	78.7	110.2
Gini[i]	.48	.50	.49	.50	.51
5th/1st quintile	18.1	19.5	17.9	23.0	18.1
Population (1,000s)	7,993		9,851	12,748	
Infant mortality rate[j] (per 1,000 live births)	109		73	19	

Sources: Marcel and Solimano 1994; Raczinski 1994.
[a] Annual average.
[b] December–December.
[c] Percent of GDP.
[d] 1960–64.
[e] Percent of labor force.
[f] 1970 = 100.
[g] 1990–91.
[h] US$ per pound.
[i] Calculated by author.
[j] Numbers correspond to 1962, 1972, and 1988.

manifested itself in a ballooning trade deficit financed with short-term external capital (Stallings 1974; Ffrench-Davis 1973; see table 2.4). By the end of 1961 the government had devalued and resorted again to piece-meal policies to restrict imports (Behrman 1976). The consequent surge in inflation set off yet another round of bloody strikes and riots as workers positioned themselves to preserve their purchasing power, dealing the coup de grâce to the stabilization program. Pondering the long-term implications of this exacerbation of class conflict, Eduardo Frei of the Christian Democrats would ask: "Are we building something positive in this country, or are we accumulating a foundation of hate in the people which tomorrow no one will be able to contain, neither one man nor any political party?" (Stallings 1974, p. 90).

A historically unprecedented flattening of industrial growth and a dismal decadal per capita growth rate of 0.5%, far below the 2.6% of the region as a whole, revived with renewed force the charge that development was being sacrificed for price stability. Further, weak investment

Table 2.4. Macroeconomic Indicators, 1952–92

Year	Growth of GDP	Inflation[a]	Budget Surplus[b]	Trade Balance Surplus[c]	Real Exchange Rate[d]	Real Wage[e]
1952	4.5	21.2	-4.0			
1953	3.8	49.8	-4.6			
1954	-2.3	58.7	-3.8			
1955	0.2	88.7	-4.0			
1956	-1.4	44.6	-2.5			
1957	-1.7	23.7	-3.1			
1958	-0.1	24.6	-3.1			
1959	0.9	33.1	-3.6			
1960	3.7	5.4	-4.7	-8.2	40.5	0.0
1961	6.1	9.4	-4.4	-9.6	37.4	6.8
1962	5.7	28.6	-5.5	-7.2	36.0	4.0
1963	4.0	45.9	-4.8	-6.6	40.9	-6.7
1964	4.8	40.4	-4.0	-7.4	36.7	-2.7
1965	6.5	27.3	-4.3	-7.0	38.6	13.3
1966	10.1	17.9	-3.1	-12.2	40.4	12.2
1967	1.2	22.8	-1.7	-9.3	42.5	15.5
1968	3.5	29.1	-1.8	-10.6	45.8	0.8
1969	5.5	30.6	-0.8	-12.8	48.2	9.1
1970	3.6	36.2	-3.5	-12.5	48.5	10.2
1971	8.0	22.1	-9.8	-13.3	45.2	17.0
1972	-0.1	260.5	-14.2	-15.9	41.9	-10.1
1973	-4.3	605.1	-10.5	-15.1	62.7	-32.1
1974	1.0	369.2	-6.6	-11.3	95.0	-5.4
1975	-12.9	343.3	0.0	-1.2	123.8	-2.7
1976	3.5	197.9	3.0	2.1	111.4	10.8
1977	9.9	84.2	0.9	-1.8	100.0	21.5
1978	8.2	37.2	2.2	-3.2	119.3	14.3
1979	8.3	38.9	5.1	-5.2	122.9	10.9
1980	7.8	31.2	5.5	-6.7	106.5	8.6
1981	5.7	9.5	2.9	-12.9	92.6	9.0
1982	-14.3	20.7	-2.3	0.2	103.3	0.3
1983	-0.7	23.1	-3.0	4.1	124.0	-10.9
1984	6.3	23.0	-3.5	2.2	129.6	0.2
1985	2.4	26.4	-3.7	6.4	159.2	-4.5
1986	5.5	17.4	-1.0	6.5	175.1	2.0
1987	5.7	21.5	2.4	5.2	182.7	-0.2
1988	7.4	12.7	4.2	3.9	194.7	6.5
1989	10.0	21.4	4.9	2.0	190.2	1.9
1990	2.1	27.3	3.4	3.9	197.4	1.8
1991	6.0	18.7	2.2	5.3	186.3	4.9
1992	10.4	12.7	2.0	2.3	171.8	4.5
1993	6.1	12.2	1.5	-1.5	168.4	3.1
1994	3.8	8.9	1.5	1.7	165.2	5.3
1995	7.4	8.2	1.3	3.5	156.3	7.0

Sources: Velasco 1994. Updates from 1992–95 using Banco Central de Chile, Boletín mensual, several issues.
[a] December–December CPI change.
[b] Definition of government corresponds to the general government, excluding state enterprises and local and regional governments.
[c] % GDP.
[d] 1977 = 100.
[e] Wage and salary index deflated by CPI, annual averages.

and a decline in average copper production by the multinationals of roughly 20%, despite the incentives offered under the Nuevo Tratado, offered new evidence of bad faith. This, with the U.S recessions in 1957–58 and 1960–61, brought out traditional anxieties about maintaining import capacity (Moran 1974). Copper policy again turned confrontational. In 1960–61 the Congress overwhelmingly rejected a request by the Gran Minería to lock in a tax level for twenty years in exchange for additional investments and instead levied additional taxes (Baklanoff 1975). Orthodox measures and market mechanisms had become widely discredited and the government radically shifted tack. It adopted a ten-year development plan drawn up by CORFO that explicitly contemplated agrarian reform and brought an economist of confirmed structuralist bent into the cabinet (Hirschman 1963).

The Rise of Christian Democracy

The election of Eduardo Frei in 1964 marked the rise of a new, more ideological center party. The Christian Democrats shared the growing awareness of the vulnerabilities of the ISI strategy, but also embraced a structuralist diagnosis of industrial stagnation, inflation, balance of payments crises, and dependency. Although Frei would come to power with the support of the right, who saw the close-running Allende as a greater threat and ran no candidate, the "Revolution with Liberty" conceived an integrated approach to altering the fundamental political economy of the country within the legal framework. This explicitly included redistributing income and integrating popular elements in the political and industrial decision-making processes (Behrman 1976; Stallings 1974; and Ffrench-Davis 1973).

The Christian Democrats sought to implement the project without the traditional political maneuvering and compromise that they held in contempt. To this end, the party followed a double and initially successful strategy of seeking to retain an apolitical stance above the increasingly polarized right and left, while poaching on their constituencies to build its own. Frei could also count on strong support from the United States, which, alarmed by leftist advances and Castro's revolution in Cuba, would seek to make Chile the showcase for reform under the Alliance for Progress (Scully 1992; Stallings 1974).

The government inherited an economy with an inflation rate of 46% and a large accumulated external debt. The Christian Democrats conceived of stabilization as a necessarily gradual process since they identified the source of the macro-disequilibria in the structural deficiencies of the economy: excess capacity, low savings, unstable government revenues, and poor agricultural production. The reduction of inflation could not occur without, and was not accorded a higher priority than, the resolution of these obstacles, or renewed growth. Frei created the National Planning Office (ODEPLAN) to coordinate the stabilization effort, renegotiated the external debt run up under Alessandri, and implemented a partial reform of the banking system and Central Bank. Of critical importance, he also passed a progressive wealth tax with provisions to maintain real collection in the face of future inflation. In another foreshadowing of future military policies, the program announced progressively decreasing inflation targets to control expectations. Starting in 1966, the program fully indexed wages to inflation to prevent disproportionate sacrifice by labor, counting on productivity gains to permit eventual price stability (Ffrench-Davis 1973).

The first three years would see moderate success as inflation rates halved to 18%. But resuscitating growth posed the challenges faced by governments across the continent at this time. After the "easy" phase of import substitution, output could increase along three dimensions: production of heavier producer and industrial goods, export promotion, or expansion of the domestic market through redistribution. Growth along the first dimension was brisk but fundamentally unsound. From 1960 to 1967 annual production of refrigerators grew 26%, washing machines, 21.4%, electric and gas stoves, 13.7%, automobiles, 28%; and from 1963 to 1978 TV, radio, and stereo production grew 64%, 12.9%, and 21.4%, respectively (Muñoz 1968). But Chile had fewer than 10 million people and a distribution of income that implied a very small market for these products. As an extreme example, the number of auto producers or assemblers in 1967 exceeded that of the entire United States. The narrowness of the market and the excess diversification precluded reaping economies of scale and pushed costs far above world prices. Further, all of these industries were highly capital intensive and hence absorbed little labor. They were also built on imported technology, which implied large royalty and licensing fees and were heavily dependent on imports and foreign technical expertise (Mamalakis 1976).

Industry had also become extremely concentrated in *grupos*, large collections of vertically integrated groups of diverse industries with interlocking directorates, typically with a large bank at the center. Among the largest, the Grupo Banco Sud-Americano controlled or influenced 40% of total corporate capital, Grupo Banco de Chile, 35%, and Banco A. Edwards, 21%. Together, the eleven groups represented what Lagos (1962) called a "super grupo" that controlled 22.4% of all corporations and 70.6% of national capital. In the absence of discipline from exposure to the world market these groups wielded extraordinary power over the functioning of the economy. They also exercised substantial control over the media and politics, and their concentration was thought to perpetuate the persistent income inequalities (Lagos 1962).

Compounding the concentration question was the issue of sovereignty. Foreign firms in 1960 constituted 60 of the 1,300 corporations, but controlled over half of the capital of the country (Zeitlin and Ratcliff 1988). Profit remittances abroad accounted for roughly 20% of export revenues. But it was also the case that historically very low rates of domestic savings made foreigners a critical source of investment.

The cultivation of the heavy consumer durable industries, the gross inefficiency, and the extremes of concentration were the logical culmination of a system of protection and incentives that had mutated to literally incomprehensible degrees of distortion. Teresa Jeanneret (1972, p. 50) argued that "in 1965, the multiplicity of instruments used, and the frequency with which they were modified, had arrived at such extremes that it was humanly impossible to have a clear vision of their final impact by sector or for the economy as a whole." She found effective rates of protection extreme by global standards, ranging from -100 to 650, compared to -50 to 500 for Brazil, -25 to 200 for Malaysia, and -17 to 106 for Norway.

In addition to implying costly products for home consumers, these distortions precluded growth along the second dimension, export expansion. Many industries that were widely recognized to be areas of Chilean comparative advantage stagnated. Jeanneret (1972, p. 95) noted that heavy negative effective rates of protection implied that ten of twenty-one manufacturing industries studied could export only at a loss and that "some of these sectors, principally, wood, paper, paper products, fish and other minerals, would have become, perhaps, significant exporters." Markos Mamalakis (1976, p. 151) also wondered at the inability of the agro-export industry to grow, given that "export demand for raw or processed Chilean fruit, seafood, oils, wine and so forth [was] almost unlimited."

This situation was at least partially appreciated by the Christian Democrat intelligentsia and CORFO, who viewed promotion of nontraditional and traditional exports, combined with greater control over mineral exports, as essential to stimulating growth, reducing the country's dependency, and mitigating recurrent balance of payments pressures (Foxley 1971). Frei loosened exchange controls, readjusted many controlled agricultural prices to world parity, and matched depreciation to inflation through a crawling peg to prevent further exchange rate appreciation (Ffrench-Davis 1973). In 1966 he implemented an export promotion scheme consisting of duty drawbacks and special export credits. Both industrial food exports, 80% of which were fishmeal, and forestry-based products of wood, paper, and cellulose quadrupled between 1960 and 1969 (Mamalakis 1976). Together with metallic and chemical products, these were the four industries that CORFO intensively nurtured and targeted for export. Through the 1950s and early 1960s CORFO had established an experimental fishing station in Arauco, financed construction of modern boats and dock facilities in Tarapacá and Valdivia, and founded fish canneries and fishmeal mills (CORFO 1962). The World Bank–financed Paper and Carton Manufacturing Company in Bío Bío stimulated paper and cellulose-related forestry activities after 1957 (Weaver 1968). But for most industries the incentives did not outweigh the disincentives implied by the still overvalued exchange rate and distorting tariff structure (Behrman 1976).

Frei would not pursue substantial liberalization or opening and even less a reduction in state influence. It is not surprising that a party skeptical of the benefits of free trade, with a mandate to increase employment and wages, and competing for the support of an increasingly radicalized working class, would not choose to weather the dislocations that the 1970s reform would show liberalization implied. But more profound, the Christian Democratic agenda of taking control of Chile's destiny, both from foreign and from domestic agents, and addressing fundamental issues of equity required the expansion of a meta-economic actor, the state. Managing an economy where the government was already responsible for 70% of investment, the Christian Democrats would search for a third way, neither Communist nor capitalist (Foxley 1971, 1972). They were confident in the state's ability to rectify dependency, inefficiency, and inequality through extensive planning and structural reform. This was especially clear in the willingness to tackle copper nationalization and agrarian reform.

As a central plank in Frei's platform, progressive "Chileanization" of copper was essential both to assert greater national control over the mineral resources that generated the bulk of the foreign exchange and to finance the Christian Democratic modernizing agenda (Behrman 1976). Even before Frei took office, Kennecott offered to bring Chile in as a majority partner in production and marketing and proposed a plan to expand production by 50% in return for restitution as well as the twenty-year tax stability denied in 1960–61. The resulting agreement in the Convenios de Cobre led to almost a doubling of output by 1970 and the expansion of markets as the new smelting capability made possible direct shipments to Japan and the European Economic Community (EEC). Anaconda, while agreeing to measures to expand output, refused equity participation. However, rising nationalism would lead to such virulent attacks that by 1969 the firm requested nationalization with compensation of its principal properties. In January 1970 Chile purchased 51% at book value and planned a full buyout by 1981 (Moran 1974).

Several factors coalesced to grant the government increasing leverage over the companies and make nationalization feasible. First, Frei could rely on an expanding group of well-trained *técnicos* who could monitor and bargain with the copper companies and provide technical depth for the Chileanization program. The staff at the mines was now largely Chilean and the companies were no longer perceived as having a monopoly on technology, marketing, or entrepreneurship. The success of the government's 1966 pricing policy, this time coinciding fortuitously with the Vietnam War boom and a strike in U.S. mines, encouraged a more aggressive stance toward nationalization and made plausible the severing of this most symbolic of dependency links. Second, the failure to lock in taxation guarantees and increasing criticism from across the political spectrum had led Kennecott to doubt the credibility of any long-run guarantees. It had dropped major investment projects and was looking to divest. Finally, by defecting from its traditional noninterventionist probusiness stance, the right effectively held the copper companies hostage as a means of mitigating pressures from the Alliance for Progress for tax and, more fundamentally, agrarian reforms (Baklanoff 1975; Moran 1974).

The Frei administration's embrace of the structuralist view of agricultural stagnation and its emphasis on redistribution, both as an issue of social justice and as a means of expanding markets, made land reform central to the Christian Democratic agenda. Enhancement of the little-used Alessandri 1962 land reform law in 1968 with a more expansive expropriation law (Jarvis 1985) was to have profound ramifications for the political economy of the country. First, its success as one of the most far-reaching efforts within Latin America to alter the initial distribution of assets required tampering with the core tenets of Chilean society. Although Frei was elected with 56% of the vote and the reform laws were approved by Congress, the traditional parties, and business organizations like SOFOFA, saw land reform not simply as the death of the latifundium, but also as a fundamental challenge to the sacrosanctity of private property that carried unforeseeable consequences (Scully 1992; Stallings 1974). Their concerns were not without merit. In a country renowned for respect for due process and order, the reforms would offer legal cover for the more aggressive and controversial redistributions that would occur under Allende.

Second, the land reforms were part of a deliberate strategy on the part of the Christian Democratic party to accelerate the erosion of the agricultural oligarchy's clientelistic control over the rural electorate and build its own rural-urban coalition. Freed by Ibáñez's electoral reforms, having suffered a real wage decline of roughly 40% across the 1950s, and finding a new ally in the Catholic Church, which had renounced its traditional alliance with the oligarchy for a more radical agenda, rural workers were ripe for a political realignment. The aggressive recruitment of these and previously unmobilized marginal urban groups propelled the explosive growth of the Christian Democratic party. It also drove the alienated right to form a new coalition in 1966, the National party, which would form a second, noncooperative bloc going into the elections of 1970 (Scully 1992).

As numerous authors have documented (Velasco 1994; Scully 1992; Larraín and Meller 1991; Valenzuela 1978) the period became one of high political mobilization. From 1958 to 1970 the number of voters increased by a factor of 2 to 30% of the population and the number of workers affiliated with unions doubled: blue-collar workers to 38%, white-collar workers to 90%. In 1969, 12% of the workforce was involved in strikes (Velasco 1994, p. 394). The legalization of rural unionization in 1967 led to a rise from 0.7% in 1964 to 20.7% in 1970 (Scully 1992).

While this was a situation that the Christian Democrats hoped to use to consolidate their position, it also carried the potential to escape the control of the elites and to destabilize the economy. Macro-economic policy across the period was competent: growth rates averaged 4.1% and unemployment 5.9%, real wages increased 9.7%, the fiscal deficit averaged 2.1%, and inflation hovered at the standard postwar level of 26%. But the numbers conceal the rising demands on the government's resources, which reflected a larger dissatisfaction and undermined fiscal control. Real current expenditure grew 19% in 1965 and swelled 21.2% in pre-election 1970. Only the dramatic increase in copper revenues allowed a reasonable fiscal position to be maintained (Velasco 1994). The high costs of reimbursing landowners for expropriated land put a heavy burden on the urban middle and working sectors, who in effect paid for them, and eroded the core of urban support for the Christian Democracy (Scully 1992). Even so, the land reform affected only the 15–20% of the rural population who were relatively well off permanent workers on haciendas, leading to socialist demands for more extensive reform.

Trouble managing their labor base also undermined the Christian Democrat stabilization program, particularly the inability to control wage rises. The government's commitment to full wage indexation was taken as the first negotiation position by the unions, and it found itself attacked not only by irate business, but also from the left for resisting even higher readjustments (Ffrench-Davis 1973). Amid massive strikes, the resulting rise in wages above those programmed led to further deterioration of the fiscal position. Despite advances in the coordination of macropolicy and a good technical staff, these factors would drive up inflation to over 30% again in 1967 and force a reversion to orthodox monetary restraint. In retrospect, Ffrench-Davis would conclude with dismal prescience:

The failure of the program showed that in a society where the workers have a high degree of organization and power, a comprehensive and efficient program from the technical point of view is not sufficient by itself. The truth is that a law that remuneration should move a certain way is not enough. It also requires the utilization of force or of persuasion. The "Revolution with Liberty" program was directed to advance the working class and transform the social structure of the country within the margins of the present political system. For this reason, the only road was that of persuasion. . . . The results were completely the opposite. (Ffrench-Davis 1973, p. 62)

As Felipe Larraín and Patricio Meller (1991) argue, a somewhat paradoxical situation emerged in which, contrary to other populist episodes, Chile's socialists would successfully run against an economy with moderate growth and stability where genuine attention had been paid to issues of equity and structural reform. "Rather than stagnation or outright depression, Chile's case at the time was better characterized by one of pent-up expectations that went unfulfilled" (Larraín and Meller 1991, pp. 211–12). Combined with these expectations in a highly combustible mixture was the erosion of the legitimacy of traditional politics encouraged by the open disdain in which the Christian Democratic party held the compromise and bargaining of the past. Velasco asserts that this led to the belief that "it was possible and acceptable to seek redistribution by means other than political bargaining in a highly institutional environment. In some senses, the populist experience that followed under Allende was the logical culmination of this process" (Velasco 1994, p. 395).

The Popular Unity Government

The Christian Democratic party's competition for the left's traditional urban constituency to complement its gains among the rural electorate, and Fidel Castro's example in Cuba, had driven the Socialist party to stake out increasingly extreme positions (Scully 1992). Benefiting from the unbreachable gap between the right and center parties, Allende would win with only a third of the vote on a platform committed to remedying what was seen as the monopolistic, externally dependent, oligarchic, and capitalist,ic nature of the Chilean economy by establishing a socialist workers' state.

External dependence and excessive foreign influence in the mineral sector were clearly not new issues on the political agenda, nor was the Popular Unity government's concern with the concentration of ownership unprecedented or without basis. The Frei reforms had already gone some way toward redistributing agricultural land and had nationalized much of copper production. But, as Larraín and Meller (1991) summarize, the Popular Unity diagnosis implied a prescription for truly radical reform beyond anything envisioned by previous governments:

> Chile was characterized by a vicious circle where the unequal original income distribution pattern generated a highly monopolistic productive structure, which reinforced the existing skewed income pattern. The structure of the economy got more and more oriented toward the satisfaction of consumption patterns of the high income groups while there existed stagnation of productive sectors producing (essential or basic) wage goods for the majority. The income and wealth inequalities led to a high degree of concentration of power, that is, only a few had control upon the main decisions. Thus, the interrelationships between political and economic power reinforce the prevailing structure of the country. In order to change the economic conditions it was required to alter substantially the property structure. (Larraín and Meller 1991, p. 181)

By definition this position required a further challenge to property rights, yet the mandate supporting the Popular Unity government was far narrower than Frei enjoyed for even his relatively limited reforms. Allende was able to finish the nationalization of the copper industry early in his term with the support of both houses of Congress. But to advance in other spheres established legal precedent was pushed to the point of distortion, and frequently extralegal means came into play. To justify taking over firms the government resorted to an obscure law passed in the 1930s during the short period of the Socialist Republic that offered numerous conditions for legitimate expropriation yet required full compensation and thus became too expensive. Another little-known law of the 1940s was found that allowed firms to be "intervened" by the state in the event of severe labor disputes, which in the charged environment were common and, not uncommonly, provoked. The Popular Unity government also pushed the existing land reform to the limit so that all parcels over 80 basic hectares had been redistributed by 1972. It then sought to extend land reform to farms below the legal limit of 80 basic hectares, but lacked the legislative majority to do it. Increasingly, takeovers by campesinos occurred that would be validated, again, with the aid of a law that permitted intervention in the case of labor disputes (Thiesenhusen 1995). By 1973, 10 million hectares from almost 6,000 farms, 60% of Chile's agricultural land, had been expropriated, two-thirds of which had been accomplished in Allende's three-year tenure (see tables 2.5 and 2.6). The purchase of the remaining copper

Table 2.5. Distribution of Agricultural Properties by Size, 1965–76

	1965	1972	1976
< 5 BIH*	9.7	9.7	9.7
5–20 BIH	12.7	13.0	37.2
20–80 BIH	22.5	38.9	22.3
> 80	55.3	2.9	24.7

Source: Jarvis 1985; 1976 numbers represent estimated values of the Department of Agricultural Economy at Catholic University.
*BIH = Basic irrigated hectare.

Table 2.6. Share of the Public Sector in Economic Activities, 1965–88

Sector	1965	1973	1981	1988
Mining	13	85	83	–
Industry	3	40	12	–
Utilities	25	100	75	–
Transport	24.3	70	21	–
Communications	11.1	70	96.3	–
Financial	–	85	28.3	–
Output to all sectors	14.2	39.0	24.1	15.9

Source: Hachette and Lüders 1993.

mines owned by the U.S. firms Kennecott and Anaconda occurred in effect without any restitution to the foreign investors after the value of "excess profits" was deducted from the book value and generated substantial external opposition (Larraín and Meller 1991; Baklanoff 1975).

The politically charged climate precluded the maintenance of a coherent macroeconomic policy, and extreme disequilibria emerged that would contribute to undermining the Popular Unity program. In an attempt to build support among urban workers, wages were raised dramatically and the fiscal burden of government wages and social security payments rose 7 percentage points of GDP in the first two years. Public subsidies needed for continued operation of nationalized firms would claim almost 9% of GDP in 1973. A sharp fall in tax revenues of over 15% of GDP (Larraín and Meller 1991) and the fall in international copper prices in 1971 pushed the fiscal deficit from 3.5% to 14%. In the absence of an astronomical increase in private savings, government dissavings of this order of magnitude implied an overwhelming excess demand for goods that was manifested through both a sharp increase in inflation and current account deficits. Despite batteries of price controls that generated an extensive black market, inflation rose to 605% in 1973, which, with imperfect wage indexation measures, led to a 40% fall in real wages by the third quarter of 1973 (Larraín and Meller 1991). The fall in agricultural production led to severe internal food shortages and a rise in wheat imports by a factor of five, exacerbating a deteriorating trade balance. International reserves fell from the five months of imports inherited from the Frei administration to roughly twenty-two days.

By 1973 Chile would be thrown into a chaos so indelibly etched in the memories of a broad cross section of Chileans that predicting its return under civilian rule would be a central theme in the campaign to extend President Augusto Pinochet's term fifteen years later. In part, the Chilean road to socialism was undermined, as in many other populist experiments, by a misalignment of the key prices in the economy and a fatal inattention to internal and external constraints. But the crisis reached another level altogether. Uncertainty paralyzed the private sector, and, at the same time that the state assumed control of vast sectors of the economy, it became largely dysfunctional. The Popular Unity government proved unable to discipline members of its own coalition and drove important domestic and external actors to obstructionism, most notably in the monthlong national strike in October 1972 that brought the economy to a standstill. Whatever may have been the alternative to the military government that took over in 1973, with traditional mechanisms for resolving social tensions eviscerated, return to the previous social equilibrium was no longer possible.

Twenty Years Later

The contrast twenty years later could not be greater. Chile's current prosperity and refound democratic politics have made it the reference case to be emulated, both within the multilateral institutions and by governments around the world contemplating reform. Across the last decade, Chile has successfully consolidated a rocky transition to a substantially market based economy, with impressive results.

Since 1987 output growth has averaged almost 7%, supported by a stunning rise in national savings rates to above 26%, up from the single digits of the 1970s. Real wages have grown at 3% and unemployment is below 5%. The budget often shows large surpluses and inflation now hovers around 8%, low by global standards and truly enviable within Latin America. The goal of growth with price stability, elusive for most of the century, has been attained.

The solution to the problems of external dependence and exhausted markets has been sought in relentless pursuit of greater integration with the global economy. Exports have increased by almost a factor of ten since 1975, essentially eliminating the traditional import bottlenecks

Table 2.7. Income and Spending of Central Government, 1974–90 (percentage of GDP)

	1974	1975	1976	1977	1978	1979	1980	1981	1982	1983	1984	1985	1986	1987	1988	1989	1990
Income	28.4	33.3	37.2	38.6	32.4	34.1	33.9	35.5	36.2	30.7	31.8	31.6	32.9	33.6	34.7	33.2	28.3
Taxes	20.4	24.2	23.6	22.9	21.8	18.9	19.2	19.5	18.9	19.4	20.4	20.0	20.2	20.8	19.8	19.3	17.8
Social Security	3.1	3.4	3.4	3.7	3.7	5.3	5.5	4.2	2.6	2.4	2.2	2.1	2.2	2.0	1.6	1.4	2.0
Other current income	6.8	7.3	10.3	12.1	7.7	7.7	7.4	9.5	9.8	6.9	6.7	7.6	7.8	7.4	9.5	9.4	6.8
Net capital income	-1.9	-1.6	-0.1	-0.1	-0.8	2.2	1.7	2.3	5.0	2.0	2.4	1.8	2.8	3.4	3.8	3.2	1.7
Spending	35.0	33.3	34.2	37.2	30.2	28.9	28.0	32.3	38.8	34.3	34.8	33.5	33.4	31.1	30.7	27.6	26.8
Personnel & goods & services	14.3	13.6	12.6	15.9	14.7	11.1	10.3	11.0	12.8	11.8	11.3	10.3	9.7	98.1	8.2	7.7	7.4
Social Security	4.5	7.2	6.9	7.0	6.9	7.0	6.9	7.9	10.3	9.4	9.7	9.0	8.8	8.0	7.0	6.4	6.9
Other current spending	7.6	6.8	11.5	10.1	5.2	5.8	5.8	7.9	9.6	9.0	8.9	8.9	8.8	7.8	7.6	8.6	6.6
Capital formation	8.7	5.7	3.1	4.2	3.5	5.1	5.0	5.4	6.2	4.1	4.9	5.3	6.1	6.2	8.0	4.8	5.9
Global deficit/surplus	-6.6	0.0	3.1	1.4	2.2	5.1	5.8	3.2	-2.6	-3.6	-2.9	-1.9	-0.5	2.5	3.9	5.6	1.6
Social Security deficit/surplus	-1.4	-3.8	-3.6	-3.4	-3.2	-1.7	-1.4	-3.8	-7.7	-7.1	-7.4	-6.9	-6.6	-6.0	-5.4	-5.1	-4.8

Source: Contraloría General de la República.

for industry. Foreign investment in copper and other minerals is again a key player. But the long-recognized potential in other exports has also been realized as part of a diversification of the economy that has seen copper's export share fall to 45%. From their levels in 1975, export shares of fruit, fishmeal, and lumber and wood furniture have risen from 2% to peaks of 9%, 8%, and 6%, respectively, paper and cellulose from 4% to 11%, chemicals from 1% to 4%. The combination of abundant exports, high savings, and fiscal balance has largely eliminated the current account-driven stop and go cycles of the past and left the country less dependent on capital inflows and susceptible to tequila-type shocks than its neighbors (Morandé 1996).

The credibility of its commitment to the current economic structure and to paying its debt led Chile to be the first Latin American country to receive voluntary new private lending from foreign banks. Japan has energetically cultivated investment, trade, and political links with Chile as its bridge of choice to Latin America, and in some areas Japan's presence overshadows that of the United States. The evident dynamism and solidity of the economy led the *Wall Street Journal* to laud Chile as "Latin America's Tiger," thereby likening it to the similarly named growth miracles of East Asia.

Although a third of the population still lives below the U.N.-defined poverty line, the last half decade has seen a decrease in the level of poverty and improvements in some social indicators such as infant mortality and life expectancy to among the best in Latin America. Spending on social programs has rebounded from the depressed levels of the mid-1980s and has been targeted effectively toward the very poor (Hojman 1993; World Bank 1990).

At a more profound level, some observers detect changes in the character of the Chileans themselves. Surveys suggest "the emergence of a generation characterized by an 'entrepreneurial spirit' which the Chilean lacked in the past, an independent and cosmopolitan social identity, [and] a more pragmatic, less ideological or paternalistic conception of the firm" (Montero 1990, p. 91). Others find that the average citizen has become more independent and savvy in choosing between private health care facilities or weighing which private pension fund will yield retirement funds a greater return (Constable and Valenzuela 1991). Such evidence, however impressionistic, suggests that the transformation wrought over the last two decades has reached deeper than economic indicators alone would suggest.

This recent record is even more remarkable because it occurred during a delicate period of political transition clouded by uncertainty about how gracefully the military would relinquish power and what changes in the economic model the new democratic government might have in mind. In fact, credible assurances from the government of Patricio Aylwin to the business community, both domestic and foreign, that policy moves would be moderate forestalled any substantial economic dislocation. By rapidly shepherding through the 1990 tax bill, which raised substantial resources to attack the "social debt," the government managed to create an environment of stability and consultation while making an important gesture to the popular sectors. The economic team under finance minister Alejandro Foxley enjoyed wide respect in the global economic community and received only minimal criticism from the opposition. By historical standards, social conflict has been virtually absent and a peaceful and relatively uneventful transition in 1994 installed Eduardo Frei, son of the previous Christian Democratic leader, as president.

The Economic Model

At the foundation of Chile's present success rest the economic policies implemented over the last twenty years. That said, there is a tendency to a kind of vulgar reductionism in drawing inferences from the period: enthusiasts credit a "free market model" as the demiurge of the positive results enumerated earlier; detractors see the repression, declining social indicators, and other negatives as necessary concomitants of an equally poorly articulated "neoliberal" model. Such polarization is unfortunate for two reasons. First, the useful lessons for countries contemplating following Chile are in the details as much as the broad generalities—which characteristics or mechanisms of the model generated or required each outcome; what can be appropriately imitated.

Second, the Chilean model stimulates controversy not only because of the repression that accompanied its installation, but because of the extreme position it holds in the spectrum of development strategies with respect to the role of government. Yet it is exactly this extremeness that gives it value. Competent state intervention does appear to have facilitated the spectacular growth rates of the East Asian newly industrializing countries (Haggard 1990; Wade 1990). But it also seems that in the hands of administratively "weaker" or "distributive" states such policies may be counterproductive and that for these countries a hard adherence to minimal economic intervention might be seen as a "second best" strategy. Chile is therefore perhaps most fruitfully viewed as an evolving case study on the minimum level and type of government intervention necessary for a small open economy with a very skewed initial wealth distribution to grow at a moderate pace.

Military Government Policies

The military government came to power without a firm commitment to the free market positions with which it would later become associated and in the past had shown leanings toward an activist role for government. Over time, Pinochet would increasingly be influenced by the Chicago-inspired economists at the Catholic University who articulated a compelling global vision of an economy with a dominant role played by a freely functioning market and a far reduced role for the state. This was outlined in a voluminous critique and game plan nicknamed, and still published under the title, *The Brick*.

The government first undertook an accelerated program to reprivatize banks and other state firms that had been nationalized under the Allende administration: in the first year after the coup 350 expropriated or intervened firms were privatized, and from 1974 to 1982 another 92 firms and 11 banks were sold. The pace was rapid, the manner of transfer often cavalier, and the program was sharply criticized. Most of these firms were sold in the depths of economic depression at discounts of 30–50% of net worth with few safeguards against or, some have argued, with the explicit intention of concentrating economic power in a few hands. Despite laws prohibiting private citizens or holding companies from purchasing more than 5% of any bank, Edwards (see Edwards and Cox Edwards 1987) suggests that it was well known that these regulations were being routinely evaded while nonfinancial corporations had no safeguards against excessive concentration and were frequently sold off to a single buyer.

A new generation of *grupos* emerged that, while as dominant as their forerunners, were less family organized, more aggressive and prone to risk, and more modern and technocratic, their leaders having been trained at foreign business schools (Edwards and Cox Edwards 1987). By 1979 the ten largest groups had grown to control 135 of the 250 largest corporations and almost 70% of all corporate stock traded on the stock exchange. *The Brick* was not averse to this concentration, imagining, as with the Japanese *zaibatsu* or Korean *chaebols*, that it would permit the exploitation of economies of scale and penetration of export markets (El Ladrillo 1992). In an important difference from the situation faced by previous governments, the discipline of external competition reduced their monopoly power.

In the agricultural sector as well, the government moved to return roughly 35% of the redistributed land (see table 2.5). As Lovell Jarvis (1985) argues, the military saw most of the takeovers under the Popular Unity as illegal. But it also needed to reduce the fiscal costs of compensation of previous owners and saw larger farmers as the key to resuscitating agriculture from its depressed state. In both the industrial and agricultural spheres, it saw the security of property as essential for future investment.

Across the next eight years, the government would let fly a barrage of liberalization measures, all of which would lead to transformation of the country to a textbook model neoclassical small economy. Soon after the coup, it freed prices on 3,000 goods on which they were controlled and would eventually free those few remaining. In 1974–75 the financial system was privatized, and allocative quotas and interest rate ceilings were abolished. The budget deficit was reduced to zero by 1976, by cutting expenditures and installing a value added tax that would provide public finances some insulation from the instability of copper revenues. By 1979 tariffs had been reduced to a uniform level of 10% and controls on external capital flows were largely eliminated.

Labor market reform was an especially high priority. Among the greatest successes was the replacement of an arbitrary, underfunded, and costly pension fund system with a mandatory fully paid up program where workers accumulated savings in a personal account in a Pension Fund Administrator (AFP) that earned interest and became available upon retirement. This system has been widely imitated elsewhere and is credited with deepening capital markets and, less convincingly, with boosting savings rates. Many institutions and elements of the labor protection system that were thought to induce rigidities and raise costs in labor markets were reformed or eliminated (Wisecarver 1985).

More traumatically, union and worker bargaining institutions were dismantled, arguably also to increase labor market flexibility (Drake 1996). But the demobilization of labor also short-circuited the tensions driving a half-century of Chilean macroeconomic and industrial policy. Burden sharing and full employment could be dropped as considerations in stabilization policy and the amelioration of long-standing income and power disparities could be demoted as a developmental objective.

In fact, the military was embarked on a much broader agenda that extended well beyond the confines of economics to a redefinition of the relation between the citizen, the state, and the economy. As Tomás Moulián and Pilar Vergara argue in their study of ideology and economic policy in the Chilean junta:

> The revolutionary idea was expressed less in the clear outlines of a defined project than in the assigning to the military government the role of re-founders. The revolutionary innovation that the regime espoused was not "economistic," and was not limited to . . . reinstalling or reconditioning the previous forms of capitalist development. It was presented as a global project of the construction of a new type of society and even a new culture. . . . The economic policy was presented as the only one that would assure the unrepeatability of the dangers of the past. The virtue of the model and of the economic program was related to its capacity to overcome endemic economic stagnation but also to create a new social conscience. (Moulián and Vergara 1980, pp. 67–68)

To cast the state in a much diminished, less paternalistic role, privatization would not only encompass steel and electric companies, but also the education, health, and pension systems that are frequently considered appropriately in the public domain. Diffusing shares in state corporations through popular capitalism was thought to develop support for privatization and more profoundly to "create a national consensus around the idea of unrestricted respect owed to private property" and lay the foundations for "true democracy" (minister of the economy Modesto Collados, 1985; cited in Maloney 1993).

The goal of the military, which traditionally saw itself as the guardian of law and order, was not merely to reconstruct the economy, but also to restrict the universe of potential state-led change and ensure that the events leading up to the coup could not reoccur. Private capital markets would replace a politicized CORFO as the allocator of investment. An independent Central Bank would be the sole emitter of currency and ensure that political conflict would not translate into inflationary pressures. A uniform external tariff ensured transparency in the protective structure and discouraged favoritism in industrial policy (Velasco 1994). "In truth," reflects Juan Valdés (1995, p. xi), "the essential political discourse of state, so much a part of Chilean democratic culture, had been replaced by an analytical matrix that propounded economic and market solutions for practically all problems in society." These innovations, of course, embodied normative views on the nature of a good society that were imposed on a reluctant polity. Making the vision stick after the return to democracy was a challenge that received as much attention as any economic issue.

The First Miracle

Confronting triple-digit inflation, the government would first rely on an orthodox closed economy monetarist strategy based on closing the fiscal gap and maintaining a tight monetary stance. Inflation came down again to double digits, 84% in 1977, but the resultant contraction in aggregate demand was compounded by a further fall in copper prices and the oil shocks leading to a 13% decline of GDP in 1975 and the first of two large bouts of severe unemployment. As the reforms to liberalize trade took hold, the government embraced the more open economy "global monetarist" approach to the balance of payments and sought to use the exchange rate to reduce inflationary expectations. It first preannounced the rate of devaluation of the peso and then in mid-1979 pegged it to the dollar for three years. It was announced that through the automatic adjustment mechanism implicit in the monetary approach to the balance of payments the money stock would be determined passively by foreign reserve movements and the economy would self-regulate. The year 1980 ushered in the first Chilean miracle as inflation fell slowly to zero, the economy boomed with a vast expansion in consumption and imports, and capital flows rose to unprecedented levels. However, in one of the enduring economic puzzles of the period, the peso in real terms became increasingly overvalued and interest rates rose to 40% in real terms over the three years to 1982. Domestic industry and agriculture contracted sharply. Faced with an unsustainable current account deficit and uncertain flows of external capital, the government devalued the peso, initiating a dramatic collapse. Output fell on the order of 18% amid the complete disintegration of the financial sector brought on by a variety of factors, among them poor supervision and unsound financial practices among the *grupos* and affiliate banks.

To the state fell the task of normalizing the financial sector as a first step in revitalizing the economy. Fourteen financial institutions were declared in liquidation. Two very large and visible institutions—the Banco de Santiago and the Banco de Chile—and three smaller institutions were put under provisional state administration. Their portfolios of bad debts, in some cases reaching six times the institution's capital and reserves, were purchased completely by the Central Bank at the stupefying cost of 15% of 1982 GNP. By the end of 1983 the state again controlled 60% of the deposits in the financial system and 68% of the resources of the privatized pension funds that had been invested in the Banco de Santiago and the Banco de Chile. With much of the previous decade's reprivatization reversed, talk was heard of the "Chicago road to socialism."

After contracting a program with the IMF in 1982, macroeconomic policy took a more "pragmatic" turn. Most visibly, this meant a lessened faith in the automatic adjustment mechanism, a targeting of interest rates to be compatible with a reasonable return to physical investment, and maintenance of a high real exchange rate as part of a shift to a deliberate export promotion stance (Corbo and Fischer 1994). After several years of lackluster economic performance, Chile would recover from the second major recession in ten years, and this recovery would evolve into the second miracle.

But at the time of the 1988 plebiscite ending the Pinochet regime, Chile's record was not one that a country contemplating reform would necessarily desire to replicate. Per capita income stood only 8% above the 1971 level and per capita consumption slightly *below*. The average GDP growth rates of 3.4% fell below those during the Alessandri (3.9%) and Frei (4.2%) presidencies (Meller 1990). Unemployment was savage by any standard, averaging 17% and during the recessions exceeding 30% while the real wage averaged just above its 1965 level. The extremely low rates of investment (16.6%), below those of any presidential term since 1959, including Allende's (Alessandri, 21%; Frei, 19%; and Allende,

16.9%), implied that competitiveness had to be achieved as much by repressing the real wage as by increasing productivity. The unemployment and low wages led to a deterioration of Chile's already very unequal distribution of income and left 45% of the population below the poverty level, 20% of whom were classified as extremely poor or indigent (Marcel and Solimano 1993; Larraín 1991; Meller 1991).

The large private debts accumulated in the late 1970s and early 1980s were nationalized and, combined with the crisis of 1982, generated persistent adverse ripple effects throughout the economy. Servicing what was in 1984 the largest per capita foreign debt in Latin America required yearly transfers abroad on the order of 3% of GDP (Ffrench-Davis 1989; Larraín 1988). These debt payments, a vast national employment program, and the recession-induced decline in tax revenues contributed to a severe deterioration of the fiscal accounts, squeezing spending across the board, most particularly on social programs (Larraín 1988). Rescuing the financial sector gave rise to a "quasi-fiscal" deficit of about 2% of GDP yearly, roughly equal to the entire additional revenues from the 1990 tax bill dedicated to social spending (Larraín 1988, p. 20). The need for seigniorage to cover this debt was cited as a likely impediment to reducing inflation below double-digit levels (Morandé 1992; Larrañaga 1991; TASC 1990). The complications induced by having several large financial institutions that, because of vast debts incurred during the boom, were unlikely to make profits in the foreseeable future made the banking system far from transparent and required careful monitoring and management of competition by the superintendency of banks (Baeza 1985).

This litany is not meant to belittle the country's substantial achievements or as a critique of the current economic model: Chile's neighbors would love to have its problems. Nonetheless, the present situation came at a very high price in both economic and human terms, the weight of which is not fully allayed by the argument that "reform takes time." Nor is it enough to argue that relative to the other heavily indebted countries of the region Chile did rather well unless we believe that amassing the debt was somehow an unavoidable consequence of the reforms or, more generally, of being Latin.

Many of the disappointing outcomes can be laid at the door of the crisis of 1982. Although the potential for such a major detour is present in all reforms, it cannot be seen as a necessary element of transition to a more market based economy. This observation is essential since many inferences from the Chilean reforms (e.g., Chile's income distribution worsened during its experiment with neoliberal reforms) carry great rhetorical weight, but are of unclear import for policymakers. If, instead of the 1979–82 boom and collapse, the economy had grown steadily at even a languid pace, the Chilean reform package would be more palatable. The massive unemployment and decline in real wage of the 1980s, held by Mario Marcel and Andrés Solimano (1994) to explain much of the degradation in income distribution and absolute poverty, would have been far less. The public debt would have remained insignificant, public finances would not have been squeezed, and social spending would have been maintained at a higher level. The banking sector would be less murky, the Central Bank would be less dependent on seigniorage, and inflation might have fallen more quickly. The bankruptcies and accompanying uncertainty that were in part responsible for the collapse of investment in the 1980s would have been largely absent. Lower social unrest in the 1983–85 period might have led to less repression. The counterfactual evolution of the economy without the crisis is far more compelling than the rather bleak record to 1987. Other economic transitions can produce results more quickly and at a far lower social cost if they can avoid a debacle on the scale of 1982.

What Caused the Crash?

Though both Argentina and Chile were adversely affected by the world recession and the latter by the fall in the price of copper, analysis of the failed reform experiments in those countries has focused almost entirely on deficient government policy. In particular, the 1980s saw the emergence of a vast literature on the optimal sequencing of reform measures, the key themes of which have been well summarized elsewhere (Edwards 1989; Edwards and Cox Edwards 1987; Choski and Papageorgiou 1986). Heavy emphasis has been placed on the absolute necessity of the government's implementing a consistent, hence credible, plan, almost to the exclusion of all other issues. In an early and influential contribution to this literature, Edwards and Cox Edwards argued that "it is . . . in the credibility sphere where the most important lesson on the sequencing of liberalization lies. In a sense, the implementation of a consistent and credible policy package is more important than determining 'the correct' order of liberalization" (Edwards and Cox Edwards 1987, p. 193).

The policy inconsistency most commonly cited in the Chilean case was indexing wages to the inflation rate of the previous period at a time when the nominal exchange rate was fixed and when inflation, although low, was still substantial. The result was a dramatic overvaluation of the peso, which in turn led to expectations of depreciation that led investors to demand very high interest to hold Chilean versus foreign assets. This combination of the strong peso and the prohibitive cost of capital dealt a fatal double blow to the productive sector. Consumers, seeing this, sensed that the current trade regime would not last and borrowed heavily to purchase cheap imported goods before they became more expensive again, leaving the country massively in debt. The policy inconsistency, the backward indexing of wages, led to a loss in credibility in the reforms and their ultimate failure.

At first glance, the policy implications of this view are reassuring: theory is adequately describing the transition and governments should simply ensure that their actions are consistent with theory. We presumably know what Chile did wrong and therefore how other countries can avoid these mistakes. But it is also, in fact, a somewhat disheartening view. Few countries will have so politically able an autocrat as Pinochet, giving economists with such a coherent economic worldview such free reign to implement their vision. What may we expect from less pristine reform environments? More fundamentally, why did they make these mistakes?

The Perils of Policymaking during Reform

A partial answer is that the errors reflect the difficulty of making policy amidst the uncertainty inherent in the process of reform. While economics can tell convincing before-and-after stories about the economy's response to freeing markets, we are virtually in the dark about the dynamics of getting from here to there. In general policymakers cannot know the outcome of their policy measures since in very act of taking that policy measure they change the underlying structure of economy from the one on which they based their actions. In the case of liberalizations, we see this idea writ large.

As an example, there is general support for the idea that the backward indexing of wages was at least a partial cause of the critical appreciation of the peso. But when one prominent observer argues that this policy was "a mistake enhanced by the arrogant stupidity of policymakers who watched growing overvaluation without recognizing early on the fatal flaw or later, the inevitable collapse" and that they should have looked to past values as reference, he may understate the difficulty of distinguishing between the consequences of errant policy and the necessary pain of any extensive restructuring program (Dornbusch 1985, p. 8). The three rationales offered at the time for why the exchange rate was "correct" all enjoyed a respectable supporting body of theoretical literature and could be heard until recently in Mexico City, justifying Mexico's overvalued exchange rate; there was little history of similar reforms to refer to for guidance; and the international community was pouring money into Chile as a tangible acknowledgment of the wisdom of its policies. When we consider in addition the need to maintain the exchange rate as an anchor for expectations of inflation, a more charitable appraisal might be that these were educated and informed men who, faced with limited information and multiple goals, made a bad call. Though many would agree that the policy team showed excessive confidence in its paradigm, it also seems likely that critical errors in judgment by even very reasonable and modest policymakers are endemic to the reform process.

Would We Do Better Now?

In fact, the problem runs deeper. Whatever the judgment of the policy team, there is the presumption that in the backward indexing of wages we have identified the critical deviation from theoretically sound policy and that if we were able to rerun Chilean history we would know how to avoid the collapse. This view is probably excessively sanguine. Though the crash must rank with the Great Depression as one of the most heavily studied and debated economic events of the twentieth century, even with the benefit of ten years of hindsight there is still considerable confusion about what happened. Arriving in Santiago in 1988, a visitor would have found prominent economists spanning the political spectrum puzzling over the same resistant anomalies not fully explained by the backward indexing story.

An alternative explanation of the boom and collapse can be constructed from this thinking that approximates the data better and that has radically different implications for policy (Conley and Maloney 1995). Numerous Chilean authors find the source of the massive indebtedness in the reigning ambience of "triumphalism" or the conviction that Chile had overcome a decade of stagnation and "in ten years would be a developed nation . . . where 70% of the population would have color television" (labor minister José Piñera, cited in Eyzáguirre 1988; Velasco 1991; Barandiarán 1987; Schmidt-Hebbel 1987; Zahler 1985). This sudden upward revision in perceived future income prompted the volcanic surge in borrowing for consumption, on both foreign and domestic durable goods, that, in fact, took off very early in 1980, long before the trade regime appeared in peril. The same optimism was reflected in the quintessential nontradables sector, real estate, where prices in some areas of Santiago were rising at 400% per year and construction of housing and shopping malls was growing at rates 2.5 times the historical high. The behavior of both consumption and real estate suggests that the boom was not purely speculative, that people believed Chile would be far more prosperous than in the end it turned out to be, and that the dramatic fall in savings and increase in borrowing resulted from an *overconfidence* in the reforms rather than the reverse.

This "triumphalist" view, diametrically opposed to the lack of credibility scenario posited above, can also explain the movements in interest and exchange rates that proved so deleterious to the economy. The increase in borrowing contributed to a persistent excess demand for loans that, in conjunction with a sharp contraction in domestic credit by the Central Bank, forced up interest rates. Short-term capital inflows were prohibited, so the differential with the world rate was never fully arbitraged away, despite substantial quantities of long-term flows that arrived intermittently (Maloney 1997). These, rather than the backward indexing, caused the exchange rate to appreciate (Morandé 1988).

This alternate explanation is not intended as the last word on a very complex period, but it is plausible and it has important policy implications. First, designing "consistent" policy is no longer a question of simply eliminating backward indexing. We must now understand why people were demanding credit in the quantities they were, to what degree this may be attributable to the transition process itself, and what policy measures should have been taken to prevent such a demand from undermining the reforms. More profoundly, if after ten years substantially different interpretations of what happened can coexist, how could we expect contemporaneous policymakers to have known which world they were in and what corrective measures they should have taken? It is not just that they made a bad call, but that it is far from obvious that today's scholars, given the opportunity to replay Chilean history, would get it right either.

The lesson is perhaps not that the reform program was inconsistent as usually understood, or not credible, but rather that we understand the dynamics of economic transitions fairly poorly and that reform packages must be designed with this uncertainty in mind. Almost by definition, structural reform puts the policymaker in a world where what is consistent and prudent policy is difficult to evaluate and where the impact of the policies depends on the process through which people learn about the new structure: the way they stumble about guessing new prices for land, what their future income will be, which firms will be profitable and which not, how banking techniques must change. That policymakers must act with limited information on the final state of the economy and, in addition, must know how agents are learning about this new structure may argue that we should add a concern with the program's robustness to reform-related misjudgments and shocks to the conventional emphasis on credibility and consistency in the sequencing and reform literature.

In sum, the collapse was a tragic misstep that probably cost the reform program five years and is responsible for many of the negative outcomes of the neoliberal experiment. But there is no inexorable logic or theory that states that such a setback is an essential element of reform. The extreme unemployment, indebtedness, and collapse of investment during the 1980s were all avoidable. Nonetheless, as the coexistence of at least two plausible explanations for the crash shows, transitions are never likely to be reform-by-number affairs and policymakers must be prepared for the unexpected, both in the design of a program and in its implementation.

Taking Lessons from Chile: The Evolving Model

The fact that the economic strategy is evolving over time cannot be overemphasized. The conceptual canon laid down by the military in the early seventies continues to define the broad contours of the model—the belief in the sacrosanctity of private property, the benefits of openness and competition, the efficacy of the market as an allocative mechanism, the primacy of the private sector as the provider of goods and services, and the pursuit of market solutions to social problems that might previously have defaulted to the public sector. However, the period of extremely unfettered markets ended with the collapse of the boom in 1982, when economic policy took its more "pragmatic" turn.

At the microlevel there has been ongoing and bold experimentation with the scope and nature of state activities, expanding in some areas, withdrawing in others. Experience has taught some very costly lessons on the indispensability of the government as regulator that were not well appreciated before the crash. The rampant self-lending practices of large conglomerates that undermined the 1979–82 boom demonstrated the need for extensive oversight and regulation of the financial sector, both to guarantee its own stability and to make possible downstream programs such as the private pension fund system. Similarly, a transparent, credible, and permanent regulatory structure has come to be seen as equal in importance to the transfer of the enterprises themselves if the benefits of privatization are to be reaped (Bitrán and Sáez 1994; Spiller 1993). Competent and politically insulated regulatory systems are costly and slow to build and thus constrain the pace of reforms, but they are essential. It may also be the development of technical capacity to monitor and regulate that critically prevents the renewed foreign presence in mining, industry, and infrastructure from reviving atavistic patterns of dependency and permits both the reality and the perception of a more even playing field.

The successful export drive has revealed the importance of some pre-1973 public policies and there has been a reintroduction of the state in selected areas. In addition to maintaining a competitive and stable exchange rate, the government extends subsidies and offers duty drawback schemes to emerging industries, underwrites market research through the government agency Pro-Chile (thought to be relatively ineffectual), manages tariff-free zones, and establishes price stabilization bands for certain tradable agricultural commodities (Chacra and Jorquera 1991; Ossa 1988). The story of the fruit sector is one of rapid technological adaptation in an open economy, driven largely by the private sector, that has had a demonstration effect for potential exporters in the rest of the country. Yet the acceleration of fruit exports after 1974 owes much to public initiatives fostering scientific expertise established in the 1950s and 1960s, as well as the establishment of a dynamic land market made possible by the agrarian reforms (Jarvis 1992). The forestry sector was given its initial impulse in the 1930s with tax exemptions, direct state planting of forests, and protection from competition. From 1974 to the present the government has absorbed 75% of the cost of new plantings and offered a subsidized line of credit (Wisecarver 1988). The fisheries industry also benefited early on from CORFO's surveying, studies, and explicit promotion of fleets, facilities, and processing plants. It is fair to wonder if these, three of the most dynamic export sectors, could have responded to the play of market forces in the manner they have without the earlier and concurrent government support. More generally, business can count on a very high level of human capital generated by decades of state educational policies.

There are also acknowledged areas of weakness in the economy where the state's remedial role is still in the process of being defined. Numerous environmental laws are being discussed that concern the management of native forests and fisheries and reduction of the extreme pollution in Santiago. As an example, in 1991 the Fishing Development Institute (IFOP) announced that the majority of important commercial species in Chile showed signs of overexploitation, thus putting a limit to the expansion of future fishmeal exports. The fishing law passed in the same year implemented a system of transferable quotas to prevent collapse (Gómez Lobo and Jiles 1993).

Other factors seem likely to require fundamental alterations in the patterns of growth. The 20% appreciation of the peso since 1990 has sharply eroded the profitability of much of the agro-export industry and will become a drag on the fruit and vegetable export juggernaut (Álvarez and Soto 1995). Although copper, silver, and gold production is expected to almost double by 2000, government projections allow only another twenty years of production at the current pace with the largest mines, like Chuquicamata, lasting sixty years at the outside. These three products still jointly account for roughly half of the country's export earnings. The government talks of a "second phase" of exports shifting away from primary resources to finished products by providing technology transfer incentives and access to credit, but some observers see the need for a more substantial role for the state in guiding the transition (Porter 1996).

The debate over the government's proposed extension of the 1990 tax bill was in part over whether explicit government programs are necessary to address poverty and extreme income inequality or whether growth alone will suffice. The hard fact is that Chile's distribution is still among the worst in the world, and while it has not deteriorated significantly under the neoliberal regime, it has not improved (see table 2.3).

What distinguishes these debates is the close attention paid to weighing possible adverse effects of the intervention against the severity of the market failure being addressed and to designing mechanisms that minimize distortions and potential abuse. As an example, emerging export industries do receive subsidies, but in many cases they cease automatically when the industry "graduates" out of its infant class. The possibility of institutionalizing distortions or creating continued dependency on state largesse, as occurred under import substitution, is far reduced.

The privatization program that gained momentum after 1985 represents a categorical rejection of a role for the state as a provider of goods and services. It also serves as an object lesson on how complex the process of drawing inferences from the Chilean case can be. The dramatic improvements in some highly visible sectors, such as telecommunications, appear to confirm the beneficial effects of privatization, yet most studies find that the bulk of the efficiency gains in the public sector had been realized *before* the firms were sold (Hachette and Lüders 1993). This would seem to suggest that a country with a government that is politically insulated, resistant to capture by interest groups, and philosophically disinclined to use parastatals for social policy may have little efficiency to gain by their transfer to the private sector (Bitrán and Sáez 1994; Galal et al. 1992). But privatization did serve several non-efficiency-related purposes in Chile. Receipts from the sales of enterprises were important in closing the budget deficits of the 1980s, and private owners provided much-needed investment that the state's weak fiscal position prohibited. The pace and scope of the program served as a signal to international investors of the government's respect for private property, guaranteed the irreversibility of the reform program, and prevented any potential abuses of the state sector that might occur under future democratic regimes. Given the historical context and the long-term agenda of the military, it is not surprising that privatization was pushed so far. But it is not clear for which of these reasons we would advise Spain to privatize the state telecommunication company that, in 1990, purchased its Chilean counterpart.

Finally, keeping the more dirigiste NICs in mind, the ability to establish credible and permanent rules of the game may be as important, within moderate tolerances, as how great a role the market plays in the economy (Spiller 1993). The shelving of investment plans by the Gran

Minería when unable to lock in stable tax rates, and the disappointing investment response more generally under Alessandri, is perhaps the most obvious example. Chile began its social transformation with a long tradition of respect for legal process, by both government and governed, perhaps unusual for the region (Rosenberg 1991). But as mentioned above, the military was very deliberate in both its political and economic policies to cultivate long-term stability, seeking to isolate state institutions from political pressures and to ensure that the reforms would not be reversed at a later date. Assuming the international debt signaled a willingness to play by international rules and a long-term concern for the future health of the export sector that would generate the foreign exchange to make payments. The privatization program demonstrated a long-run favoring of private enterprise and a systematic removal of some levers of power from the state's grasp. The uncertainty-reducing and -signaling properties of various policy measures may thus be as important as their merit on efficiency grounds.

Re-establishing Consensus

The fabric of Chilean society was not suddenly and unexpectedly rent by Allende's election or the military coup. It was slowly pulled apart by forces fifty years in gestation, each conceiving the challenges to development in ways that would grow mutually incompatible. Economic policies reflected these conflicts both in their design and in their failure. The eventual success of the Chilean reforms and the stability and growth witnessed under the new democratic regime testify to a political evolution as profound as the economic.

Pinochet's ruthlessness and effectiveness in consolidating the military behind the market agenda must be granted. But it is also the case that he came to power at a time when the business community and much of the political spectrum, including some of what now constitutes the democratic government, were traumatized by the chaos of the Popular Unity period and feared a resurgence of the left. They were thus willing to offer at least skeptical forbearance toward the radical economic policies being implemented, policies with a limited constituency even within the military, to prevent this (Silva 1991, 1993). Other dissonant sectors of the population that enjoyed less leverage with the regime were simply repressed.

What is remarkable about the lifting of the dictatorship in Chile is that economic policy could remain subtle, rational, and reassuring to investors when these groups were suddenly given voice for the first time in fifteen years. The challenge presented is reflected in a comment by one of Alejandro Foxley's advisors that one of the primary goals of the Aylwin presidency was to show that a democratic government in Latin America can be fiscally responsible. The modesty of that goal suggests the difficulty of attaining it. As the Allende period showed, democratic institutions do not have the capacity to mediate all degrees of social conflict and ideological diversity. Until some consensus emerges on the broad outlines of the organization of the economy, what features are fair game to change, and what constraints sound macroeconomic policy dictates, neither democracy nor economic reform can be consolidated.

Returning to democracy from their arduous authoritarian odyssey, Chileans appear to have reached such a consensus, both on the need for political moderation and on the legitimacy of the economic model. In the political sphere, both Scylla and Charybdis stand in clear view. Pinochet's strong showing in the plebiscite (43%) suggests a persistent, deep reservoir of fear about a return of the radical left and of the chaos of 1973. In more recent memory remain the brutality of the dictatorship, the tortuous navigation of the return to civilian rule, and the general's recurring saber rattling from the barracks. What this tension has forged, argue Pamela Constable and Arturo Valenzuela in *A Nation of Enemies*, is "a new appreciation for the values of moderation and compromise that had once been bitterly discarded—and a firm rejection of the utopian visions that had inspired and scarred a generation" (Constable and Valenzuela 1991, p. 319).

Any modification of the present economic vision is clearly circumscribed by legal restrictions and by the desire to maintain a favorable business climate as understood by foreign investors. But here too there appears to exist broad agreement across much of the political spectrum that, while purchased at a high cost and spread inequitably across the population, the current model has the potential to bring prosperity. This has emerged partly from a careful observation and assimilation of the successes and failures of the last half century, both in Chile and abroad. It is not at all unusual to hear socialists reflect critically on the Allende period or the failed promise of the former Eastern bloc and talk approvingly of market solutions to social problems (Constable and Valenzuela 1991). Eduardo Silva (1991) and Barbara Stallings (1990) have described the slow conversion of the regime's more centrist opposition to accepting the more pragmatic, export-oriented model as functional and therefore broadly legitimate: those defending import substitution's losing force with the success of the export drive, those supporting substantial state intervention fading with the success of the privatization program. Critical to this process was the willingness of some very high profile opposition economists, such as Alejandro Foxley, to appraise dispassionately the merits and shortcomings of the new economic structure and accept the implications of their thinking. This is not to imply by any means complete convergence of vision. But by 1988 the opposition was advocating only relatively minor modifications to the model, which it explicitly negotiated with the business community in the final bid for a smooth transition to democracy (Silva 1993).

This consensus is supported intellectually by a corps of well-trained and relatively like-minded economists who have been integral to framing discourse about development policy not only in Chile, but also in the principal multilateral institutions. Undergraduates of diverse political bents study together at economics departments that are rigorous by any standards and then attend graduate programs with broadly similar curricula in the United States. Though they hold substantially different opinions on key issues, they also share an understanding of the basic constraints under which an economy must work and of the properties and limitations of markets. The point is not that Chileans (or the discipline of economics more generally) have reached the economic analogy to the "End of History" and everybody knows *the model* and it works, only that it becomes less likely that a populist like Argentina's Perón can argue that "there is nothing more elastic than the economy" and find much support (Hirschman 1981, p. 102). This is a process evolving to different degrees throughout Latin America. While it is frequently said that there is a Washington consensus being imposed most particularly by the IMF and the World Bank, the charge of coercion, at this point, is exaggerated.

It is at the popular level where the present social concord is perhaps more vulnerable. "The model is able to generate national consensus as a shared project only if it is able to benefit everyone. If only a few benefit, and the majority remain in poverty, the model will not be viable in the medium and longer term" warns one columnist in *Mensaje*, a Catholic Church–affiliated monthly. A critical difference with the past that makes the present consensus possible is that the center-left now agrees that altering the distribution of power and income through intervention in the market or challenges to property rights is off the policy agenda. But the situation may be well described by Hirschman's tunnel allegory, where stalled motorists sit patiently watching the next lane of traffic advance, expecting that sooner or later they will move too (Hirschman 1981). The concern is whether those who remain relatively "parked" after ten years will rest content within the current consensus as the restraining memories of Allende and Pinochet fade.

However, at present, Chile provides a hopeful example to a continent emerging from a lost decade of economic stagnation. Though the conflicts of mid-century have been largely resolved or at least reduced in volume, the challenges, both in maintaining social consensus and in maintaining growth over the longer term, remain great. But Chile has shown that efficient growth with macrostability in a context of reduced dependency is possible in Latin America and will continue to offer lessons to other nations following its lead.

Note

An earlier version of the post-1973 section of this chapter was prepared for the 1993 University of Southern California Workshop on Economic and Political Transition and benefited from comments by Patricio Aroca, Lovell Jarvis, Michael Kevane, Joseph Love, Gay McDonald, Suzanne Meehan, Patricio Meller, Gerardo Munck, Moisés Naim, Timothy Scully, and Andrés Velasco. Thanks also to Michael Jacobson and Taimur Baig for able research assistance. The usual disclaimers apply.

Works Cited

Álvarez, Roberto, and Claudio Soto. 1995. Apreciación cambiaria y el sector exportador. In *Comentarios sobre la situación económica*. Departamento de Economía, Universidad de Chile. December 1995.

Baeza, V. Sergio. 1985. Capitalismo popular: Decisiones de inversión. In *Economía y sociedad*. Santiago, Chile: n.p.

Baklanoff, Eric N. 1975. *Expropriation of U.S. Investment in Cuba, Mexico, and Chile*. New York: Praeger.

Banco Central de Chile. *Boletín mensual*. Santiago, several issues.

——. *Indicadores económicos*. Santiago, several issues.

Barandiarán, Edgardo. 1987. La Gran Recesión de 1982. In *Del auge a la crisis de 1982*. Santiago, Chile: Instituto Interamericano de Mercados de Capital/ILADES/Georgetown.

Behrman, Jere R. 1976. *Foreign Trade Regimes and Economic Development: Chile*. New York: NBER and Columbia University Press.

Bitrán, Eduardo, and Raúl E. Sáez. 1994. Privatization and Regulation in Chile. In Barry Bosworth, Rudiger Dornbusch, and Raúl Labán, eds., *The Chilean Economy: Policy Lessons and Challenges*. Washington, D.C.: Brookings.

Bosworth, Barry, Rudiger Dornbusch, and Raúl Labán, eds. 1994. *The Chilean Economy: Policy Lessons and Challlenges*. Washington, D.C.: Brookings.

Chacra, Verónica, and Guillermo Jorquera. 1991. Bandas de precios de productos agrícolas básicos: La experiencia de Chile durante el período 1983–91. In Serie de Estudios Económicos, no. 36. Santiago: Banco Central de Chile.

Choski, A., and D. Papageorgiou, eds. 1986. *Economic Liberalization in Developing Countries*. Oxford: Basil Blackwell.

Collados Núñez, Modesto. 1985. Fundamentos sociales y económicos del capitalismo popular. Exposición del Sr. Modesto Collados N., Ministro de Economía. In *Capitalismo popular: Análisis y debate, Versión completa de las jornadas bursátiles realizadas en abril de 1985*. Santiago, Chile: Bolsa de Comercio.

Conley, John P., and William F. Maloney. 1995. Optimal Sequencing of Credible

Reforms with Uncertain Outcomes. *Journal of Development Economics* 48.

Constable, Pamela, and Arturo Valenzuela. 1991. *A Nation of Enemies: Chile under Pinochet*. New York: W. W. Norton.

Corbo, Vittorio, and Stanley Fischer. 1994. Lessons from the Chilean Stabilization and Recovery. In Barry Bosworth, Rudiger Dornbusch, and Raúl Labán, eds., *The Chilean Economy: Policy Lessons and Challenges*. Washington, D.C.: Brookings.

Corporación de Fomento de la Producción (CORFO). 1962. *Veinte años de labor, 1939–1959*. Santiago: Zig Zag.

Correa Prieto, Luis. 1954. *Aspectos negativos de la intervención económica: Fracasos de una experiencia*. Santiago: Zig Zag.

Crosson, Pierre R. 1970. *Agricultural Development and Productivity: Lessons from the Chilean Experience*. Baltimore: Johns Hopkins University Press.

De la Cuadra, Sergio, and Dominique Hachette. 1986. The Timing and Sequencing of Trade Liberalization Policy. Documento de Trabajo, Pontificia Universidad Católica de Chile.

Dornbusch, Rudiger. 1985. Inflation, Exchange Rates and Stabilization. Manuscript. MIT.

Drake, Paul W. 1978. *Socialism and Populism in Chile, 1932–52*. Urbana: University of Illinois Press.

——. 1996. *Labor Movements and Dictatorships: The Southern Cone in Comparative Perspective*. Baltimore: Johns Hopkins University Press.

Edwards, Sebastian. 1989. On the Sequencing of Structural Reforms. NBER Working Paper no. 3138.

Edwards, Sebastian, and Alejandra Cox Edwards. 1987. *Monetarism and Liberalization: The Chilean Experiment*. N.p.: Ballinger.

Eyzáguirre, Nicolás. 1988. La deuda interna chilena: 1975–1985. In Carlos Massad and Roberto Zahler, eds., *Deuda interna y estabilidad financiera, II*. Buenos Aires: CEPAL, Grupo Editor Latinoamericano.

Ffrench-Davis, Ricardo. 1973. *Políticas económicas en Chile, 1952–1970*. Santiago, Chile: Centro de Estudios de Planificación Nacional, Universidad Católica de Chile.

——. 1989. El conflicto entre la deuda y el crecimiento en Chile: Tendencias y perspectivas. Estudios CIEPLAN, 26. Santiago, Chile: Alfabeto Impresores.

Foxley, Alejandro R. 1971. Alternativas de decentralización en el proceso de transformación de la economía nacional. Documento no. 4. Santiago, Chile: Centro de Estudios de Planificación Nacional.

——. 1972. Opciones de desarrollo bajo condiciones de reducción en la dependencia externa. In *Proceso a la industrialización chilena*. Centro de Estudios de Planificación Nacional: Ediciones Nueva Universidad.

Galal, Ahmed, Leroy Jones, Pankaj Tandon, and Ingo Vogelsang. 1992. Synthesis of Case Studies and Policy Summary. World Bank Conference on Welfare Consequences of Selling Public Enterprises, Country Economics Department, World Bank, Washington, D.C.

Gómez-Lobo, Andrés, and Juan Jiles. 1993. La experiencia chilena en regulación pesquera. In Óscar Muñoz, ed., *Después de las privatizaciones, hacia el estado regulador*. CIEPLAN. Santiago, Chile: Alfabeto Impresores.

Hachette, Dominique, and Rolf Lüders. 1993. *Privatization in Chile: An Eco-*

nomic Appraisal. San Francisco: International Center for Economic Growth.

Haggard, Stephan. 1990. *Pathways from the Periphery: The Politics of Growth in the Newly Industrializing Countries.* Ithaca: Cornell University Press.

Hirschman, Albert O. 1963. Inflation in Chile. In *Journeys toward Progress.* New York: W. W. Norton.

———. 1981. The Changing Tolerance for Income Inequality in the Course of Economic Development. In *Essays in Trespassing, Economics to Politics and Beyond.* New York: Cambridge University Press.

Hojman, David E. 1993. *Chile: The Political Economy of Development and Democracy in the 1990s.* Pittsburgh: University of Pittsburgh Press.

Jarvis, Lovell. 1985. *Chilean Agriculture under Military Rule: From Reform to Reaction, 1973–1980.* Berkeley: Institute of International Studies, University of California.

———. 1992. Changing Private and Public Sector Roles in Technological Development: Lessons from the Chilean Fruit Sector. Mimeo. Davis: University of California.

Jeanneret, Teresa. 1972. El sistema de protección a la industria chilena. In *Proceso a la industrialización chilena.* Centro de Estudios de Planificación Nacional. Santiago, Chile: Ediciones Nueva Universidad.

El Ladrillo. 1992. *Bases de la política económica del gobierno militar chileno.* Santiago, Chile: Centro de Estudios Públicos.

Lagos Escobar, Ricardo. 1962. *La concentración de poder económico: Su teoría, realidad chilena.* Santiago, Chile: Editorial del Pacífico, Santiago.

Larraín, Felipe. 1988. Debt Reduction Schemes and the Management of Chilean Debt. Mimeo. Cambridge, Mass.: Harvard University.

———. 1991. The Economic Challenges of Democratic Development. In Paul Drake and Ivan Jaksic, eds., *The Struggle for Democracy in Chile, 1982–1990.* Lincoln: University of Nebraska Press.

Larraín, Felipe, and Patricio Meller. 1991. The Socialist-Populist Chilean Experience, 1970–1973. In Rudiger Dornbusch and Sebastian Edwards, eds., *The Macroeconomics of Populism in Latin America.* Chicago: University of Chicago Press.

Larrañaga, Osvaldo J. 1991. Autonomía y déficit del Banco Central. *Colección Estudios CIEPLAN,* 32. Santiago, Chile: Alfabeto Impresores.

Love, Joseph. 1996. *Crafting the Third World.* Stanford: Stanford University Press.

Maloney, William F. 1993. Privatization with Share Diffusion: Popular Capitalism in Chile: 1985–88. In W. Baer and M. Birch, eds., *Privatization in Latin America.* Westport, Conn.: Praeger.

———. 1997. Testing Capital Account Liberalization without Forward Rates: Another Look at Chile, 1979–1982. *Journal of Development Economics* 52.

Mamalakis, Markos. 1965. Public Policy and Sectoral Development, Case Study of Chile, 1940–1958. In Markos Mamalakis and Clark Reynolds, *Essays on the Chilean Economy.* Homewood, Ill.: Richard D. Irwin.

———. 1976. *The Growth and Structure of the Chilean Economy: From Independence to Allende.* New Haven: Economic Growth Center, Yale University Press.

Marcel, Mario. 1989. La privatización de empresas públicas en Chile 1985–88.

Notas Técnicas CIEPLAN, 125. Santiago, Chile: Alfabeto Impresores.

Marcel, Mario, and Andrés Solimano. 1994. Developmentalism, Socialism and Free Market Reform: Three Decades of Income Distribution in Chile. In Barry Bosworth, Rudiger Dornbusch, and Raúl Labán, eds., *The Chilean Economy: Policy Lessons and Challenges*. Washington, D.C.: Brookings.

Marshall, Jorge. 1988. La nueva interpretación de los orígenes de la industrialización en Chile. *Serie Investigación*, Programa Post-Grado de Economía, ILADES/Georgetown.

Meller, Patricio. 1990. Resultados económicos de cuatro gobiernos chilenos, 1958–1989. *Apuntes CIEPLAN* (October).

———. 1991. Adjustment and Social Costs in Chile during the 1980s. *World Development* 19(11).

Monteón, Michael. 1982. *Chile in the Nitrate Era: The Evolution of Economic Dependence, 1880–1930*. Madison: University of Wisconsin Press.

Montero, Cecilia. 1990. La evolución del empresariado chileno: ¿Surge un nuevo actor? *Colección Estudios CIEPLAN* 30 (Santiago, Chile).

Moran, Theodore H. 1974. *Multinational Corporations and the Politics of Dependence, Copper in Chile*. Princeton: Princeton University Press.

Morandé, Felipe G. 1988. Domestic Currency Appreciation and Foreign Capital Inflows: What Comes First? (Chile 1977–82). *Journal of International Money and Finance* 7.

———. 1992. The Dynamics of Real Asset Prices, the Real Exchange Rate, Trade Reforms and Foreign Capital Inflows, Chile, 1976–89. *Journal of Development Economics* 39 (North Holland).

———. 1996. Savings in Chile, What Went Right. Mimeo.

Moulián, Tomás, and Pilar Vergara. 1980. Estado, ideología y políticas económicas en Chile: 1973–78. *Colección Estudios CIEPLAN*. Santiago, Chile: Alfabeto Impresores.

Muñoz, Óscar G. 1968. *Crecimiento industrial de Chile, 1914–1965*. Instituto de Economía y Planificación, Universidad de Chile.

Ossa S., Fernando. 1988. Políticas de fomento al sector exportador chileno. Documento de Trabajo no. 114. Santiago, Chile: Pontificia Universidad Católica de Chile.

Piñera, José, and William Glade. 1991. Privatization in Chile. In William Glade, ed., *Privatization of Public Enterprises in Latin America*. San Francisco: International Center for Economic Growth.

Porter, Michael. 1996. Reported by Alejandro Kirk in "Problems Ahead for Chilean Economy?" Inter Press Service, January 24.

Raczinski, Dagmar. 1994. Social Policies in Chile: Origin, Transformations, and Perspectives. Democracy and Social Policy Series, Working Paper 4, Fall 1994. Kellogg Institute, University of Notre Dame.

Rosenberg, Tina. 1991. Beyond Elections. *Foreign Policy* 84.

Schmidt-Hebbel, Klaus. 1987. Consumo e inversión in Chile (1974–83): Una interpretación 'real' del boom. In *Del auge a la crisis de 1982*. Santiago, Chile: Instituto Interamericano de Mercados de Capital/ILADES/Georgetown.

Scully, Timothy. 1992. *Rethinking the Center: Party Politics in Nineteenth and Twentieth Century Chile*. Stanford: Stanford University Press.

Silva, Eduardo. 1991. The Political Economy of Chile's Regime Transition: From Radical to "Pragmatic" Neo-Liberal Policies. In Paul Drake and Ivan Jaksic, eds., *The Struggle for Democracy in Chile, 1982–1990*. Lincoln: University of Nebraska Press.

——. 1993. Capitalist Regime Loyalties and Redemocratization in Chile. *Journal of Interamerican Studies and World Affairs* 24(4).

Spiller, Pablo T. 1993. Institutions and Regulatory Commitment in Utilities Privatization. Unpublished. University of Illinois.

Stallings, Barbara. 1974. *Class Conflict and Economic Development in Chile, 1958–1973*. Stanford: Stanford University Press.

——. 1990. Politics and Economic Crisis: A Comparative Study of Chile, Peru and Colombia. In Joan M. Nelson, ed., *Economic Crisis and Policy Choice: The Politics of Adjustment in the Third World*. Princeton: Princeton University Press.

TASC (Trabajo de Asesoría Económica al Congreso Nacional). 1990. El déficit cuasi-fiscal. Santiago, Chile: ILADES/Georgetown (November).

Thiesenhusen, William. 1995. *Broken Promises: Agrarian Reform and the Latin American Campesino*. Boulder: Westview.

Valdés, Juan. 1995. *Pinochet's Economists: The Chicago School in Chile*. Cambridge: Cambridge University Press.

Valenzuela, Arturo. 1978. *The Breakdown of Democratic Regimes: Chile*. Baltimore: Johns Hopkins University Press.

Velasco, Andrés. 1991. Liberalization, Crisis, Intervention: The Chilean Financial System, 1975–85. In V. Sundararajan and Tomás J. T. Baliño, eds., *Banking Crises: Cases and Issues*. Washington, D.C.: International Monetary Fund.

——. 1994. The State and Economic Policy: Chile 1952–92. In Barry Bosworth, Rudiger Dornbusch, and Raúl Labán, eds., *The Chilean Economy: Policy Lessons and Challenges*. Washington, D.C.: Brookings.

Wade, Robert. 1990. *Governing the Market: Economic Theory and the Role of Government in East Asian Industrialization*. Princeton: Princeton University Press.

Weaver, Frederick Stirton, Jr. 1968. Regional Patterns of Economic Change in Chile, 1950–1964. Dissertation. Ithaca: Cornell University.

Wisecarver, Daniel. 1985. Economic Regulation and Deregulation in Chile, 1973–1983. In Gary M. Walton, ed., *The National Economic Policies of Chile*. London: JAI Press.

——. 1988. El sector forestal chileno: Políticas, desarrollo del recurso y exportaciones. Documento de Trabajo no. 112. Santiago, Chile: Pontificia Universidad Católica de Chile.

World Bank. 1990. *World Development Report 1990*. Oxford: Oxford University Press.

Zahler, Roberto. 1985. Las tasas de interés en Chile: 1975–82. In *El desarrollo financiero de América Latina*. Santiago, Chile: Instituto Interamericano de Mercados de Capital.

Zeitlin, Maurice, and Richard Ratcliff. 1988. *Landlords and Capitalists: The Dominant Class of Chile*. Princeton: Princeton University Press.

3.
Brazil

Werner Baer
University of Illinois, Urbana-Champaign

Claudio Paiva
International Monetary Fund

Introduction

In the mid-1990s Brazil had a population of 156 million and a gross domestic product (GDP) estimated at US$676 billion in 1995, placing its economy among the nine largest economies in the world. The per capita GDP was estimated at a little over US$3,000. Within the Third World Brazil is among the most industrialized countries, with industry's share having fluctuated between the low and high thirties, as against only about 10% for agriculture. Although it is a market economy, the state has played an unusually large role, as both a policymaker and a direct participant in economic activities. In 1985 a survey of the 8,094 largest firms revealed that the share of net assets of state enterprises was 48%, while the share of private Brazilian firms stood at 43% and of multinationals at 9%. And in 1990, just prior to the introduction of the privatization process, another survey examined the 20 largest firms by sectors and found that state firms had the following percentage of total sales: public utilities, 100%; steel, 67%; chemicals and petrochemicals, 67%; mining, 60%; transport services, 35%; gasoline distribution, 32% (Melhores e Maiores, *Exame*, August 1991).

Despite the rapid growth of nontraditional exports and recent efforts toward internationalization, Brazil's economy remains relatively closed, with external trade (exports plus imports) amounting to less than 14% of GDP in the early 1990s.

Growth Record

Brazil has experienced one of the highest growth rates among capitalist economies in the twentieth century. This observation is particularly true for the period ranging from the early 1950s to the mid-1990s, despite the crisis that lasted throughout most of the 1980s (the so-called lost decade) and into the early 1990s. A first assessment of the country's economic performance in the period can be made by noting that the

Atlantic Ocean

Belém
Manaus
São Luis
Fortaleza

Recife

Brazil

Salvador

⊛ Brasília

Belo Horizonte

Pacific Ocean

Rio de Janeiro

São Paulo
Curitiba

Porto Alegre

1000   0   1000   2000 **Miles**

⊛ **Capital**
Major Rivers
• **Major Cities**
National Boundary
Countries

N

W   E

S

Table 3.1. Average Yearly Real Growth Rates, 1950–95

Years	GDP	Industry	Agriculture	Services
1950–59	7.15	9.14	4.13	7.50
1960–69	6.12	6.90	5.00	6.61
1970–79	8.84	9.49	3.96	9.49
1980–89	2.93	2.00	4.04	3.73
1990–95	1.60	0.30	2.90	2.30

Sources: IGBE 1990 and 1992; *Conjuntura econômica,* August 1996.

Table 3.2. Some Yearly Average Macroeconomic Ratios, 1950–95
(as % of GDP)

Years	Gross Fixed Investment	Gross Fixed Investment (1980 prices)	Exports of Goods and Services	Imports of Goods and Services
1950–59	15.2		7.1	7.3
1960–69	16.1		6.6	6.5
1970–79	21.6	23.3	7.2	9.2
1980–89	21.0	18.2	10.2	7.7
1990–92	19.8	16.1	7.8	6.0
1993–94	20.4	14.5	9.2	7.5

Source: Calculated from data in *Conjuntura econômica.*

yearly GDP growth rates averaged 7.15% in the fifties, 6.12% in the sixties, 8.84% in the seventies, 2.93% in the eighties, and 1.60% in the years 1990–95 (see table 3.1). For a comparative vision, one should note that the United States economy grew at a yearly average rate of 3% in the period 1960–92.

Table 3.2 reveals some interesting aspects of Brazil's growth. It will be noted that the high yearly growth rates of the 1950s and 1960s took place with relatively low investment/GDP ratios, when compared with the 1970s and 1980s. This may have been due to the lower capital intensity of the prevailing technology and also due to the great emphasis on the promotion of industrial sectors with low capital/output ratios. In the 1970s and 1980s the higher investment/GDP ratios reflect an emphasis on industries with greater capital-intensive technologies (such as capital goods production) and a large amount of investment in infrastructure projects (such as the world's largest hydroelectric dam at Itaipu), which use up a huge amount of capital relative to short-term output. Also to be noted in table 3.2 is the decline of investments in the 1980s and early

Table 3.3. Sectoral Distribution of GDP, 1950–94 (percentages)

Year	Agriculture	Industry	Services	Total
1950	24.28	24.14	51.58	100.00
1960	17.76	32.24	50.00	100.00
1970	11.55	35.84	52.61	100.00
1980	10.20	40.58	49.22	100.00
1990	9.26	34.20	56.54	100.00
1992	9.89	31.56	58.55	100.00
1994	14.30	37.30	48.70	100.00

Sources: IGBE 1990 and 1992; *Conjuntura econômica*, August 1996.

1990s, which is even clearer when measured in constant 1980 prices. This reflects the crisis of the 1980s and early 1990s.

Table 3.2 also shows the low ratio of exports and imports of goods and services to GDP in the 1950s and 1960s. This reflects the emphasis on import substitution industrialization in those decades and the neglect of foreign trade. In the 1970s the export/GDP ratio rose slightly as a result of early efforts at export diversification. The much higher import/GDP ratio in the 1970s is the result of the dramatic increase of oil prices due to the OPEC oil shocks. The continued growth of the export/GDP ratio in the 1980s stems from a combination of a slower GDP growth rate and the attempts by many sectors to switch to exports as the domestic economy stagnated.

Besides the rapid increase in the national product, one should also note the structural changes that occurred in the economy during the growth process. Industry was the motor of growth and the centerpiece of all development strategies implemented throughout the period. Industrial production grew at a yearly average rate of 6.89% during the four decades but 8.5% if the lost decade is excluded. For the period as a whole, the yearly average growth rates of agriculture and services were 4.27% and 6.83%, respectively. As a result, the share of industry in GDP rose from about 24.14% in 1950 to 34.2% in 1990, after having reached 40.58% in 1980. Agriculture's share dropped from 24.28% to 9.26% in forty years, while the service sector's share rose from 51.58% to 56.54% (see table 3.3). It should be emphasized that besides showing the fastest growth rates, the industrial sector became the main determinant of the economy's dynamism, triggering both the upturns and the downturns of the growth cycles.

Structural changes also took place within Brazil's industry. The ISI (import substitution industrialization) process led to a greater diversification of the sector, both horizontally (industries in different sectors) and vertically (industries related to each other as suppliers or customers), producing not only various types of consumption goods, but capital goods and basic industrial inputs as well. For instance, machinery production increased 205% in the seventies, electrical equipment, 223%, and chemicals, 163%. The share of the machinery subsector in industrial production rose from 2.2% in 1949 to 12.5% in 1992; the share of electrical equipment went from 1.7% to 6.8% in the same period. Some of the early dominant industries of the first half of the twentieth century had their relative importance decreased. For example, the textile industry's share of industrial output declined from 20.1% in 1949 to 4.6% in 1992, and the food and beverage products' share declined from 24% to 15.7% in the same period.

Another characteristic of Brazil's industry that has emerged over the decades is its high degree of concentration. In the 1980s the share of the eight largest firms in total sales was 62% in transport equipment, 64% in pharmaceuticals, 100% in tobacco, 60% in printing and publishing, 72% in chemicals, 54% in beverages, and 81% in rubber. The average for industry as a whole was 52%.

There were also notable changes in Brazil's employment structure. The share of agriculture in total employment declined from 62% in 1950 to a little less than 23% in 1990, and that of services increased from 25% to 54% in the same period. Industry's share in total employment rose to a much smaller extent than its share in GDP; in 1950 it amounted to 13%, rising to 23% in 1990 (Baer 1995, table 15.4; and IGBE 1992).

Accompanying the changes in the production structure of the country was the diversification of the commodity composition of exports. This was especially the case after the first intensive import substitution industrialization, from the late sixties on. The basic idea of ISI was to produce domestically goods that were being imported, thus stimulating the economy. In 1950 the share of traditional export products (coffee, sugar, cotton, cocoa) was about 80%, while the share of manufactured products was about 13%; by 1992 the share of industrial products had risen to 66.7%, while the traditional exports' share had fallen to 5.2%. In addition, it should be noted that Brazil also diversified its agricultural exports. For instance, soybean and orange juice, which were almost nonexistent in Brazil's exports in the early 1970s, accounted for 7.3% of total exports each (totaling 14.6%) in the 1990s.

Background

Prior to the 1930s Brazil was a primary exporting economy. Its major export products were coffee, sugar, cocoa, cotton, and, for a short period, rubber. Although some manufacturing industries made their appearance from the 1890s on, industry was not a leading sector (Baer 1995, ch. 3; Villela and Suzigan 1973; Fishlow 1972b; Baklanoff 1969, pp. 19–35). Coffee exports were the engine of growth throughout most of the nineteenth century. Also, as in the latter part of the nineteenth century the coffee economy had shifted from the state of Rio de Janeiro to the state of São Paulo, so the economic center of the country gradually shifted to that region, where it has remained until the present day. The secondary effects of the São Paulo coffee economy—employment of free immigrant labor, foreign investment in infrastructure, capital accumulation of coffee growers, and some derived growth of industry—were to deepen regional dualism between the dynamic Center-South and the rest of Brazil (especially taking into account the Northeast).

The Great Depression of the 1930s had a severely negative effect on Brazil's exports, whose value fell from US$445.9 million in 1929 to US$180.6 million in 1932. The price of coffee in 1931 was at one-third of the average price in the years 1925–29. In addition to the decline of export receipts, the entrance of foreign capital had come to almost a complete halt by 1932. The decline of export earnings and the large amounts of foreign exchange needed to finance the country's external debt, not counting the remittances of the profits of private entities, forced the government to take some drastic actions. In August 1931 it suspended part of the foreign debt payments and introduced foreign exchange and other direct controls of imports. Combined with a devaluation of the currency, which increased the price of imports, these controls caused a decline of imports from US$416.6 million in 1929 to US$108.1 million in 1932.

Since at the beginning of the depression coffee accounted for 71% of total exports, and exports, in turn, stood at about 10% of GDP, the government's main concern was to support the coffee sector. The steep decline of world demand for coffee brought along by the depression also coincided with a huge coffee output, which was the result of plantings that had taken place in the 1920s. In order to protect the coffee sector, and thus the economy, from the full impact of the decline of world coffee markets and prices, the federal government, through the National Coffee Council, bought all coffee, destroying large quantities that could not be stored. Government protection of the coffee sector also included measures to help debt-plagued agricultural producers by having the government pay off the debt, thus creating new money and enabling the debtor to postpone payments.

The curtailment of imports and the continued domestic demand resulting from the income generated by the coffee support program caused shortages of manufactured goods and a consequent rise in their relative prices. This acted as a catalyst for a spurt of industrial production. In fact the growth was so pronounced that industry for the first time became the economy's leading sector, responsible for an early general recovery from the impact of the World Depression (Baer 1995, ch. 3; Abreu 1990, ch. 3; Furtado 1972, pp. 188–94). By 1931 industrial production had fully recovered from a decline that started in 1928, and in the following years it more than doubled. Especially noteworthy by 1939 was the rapid growth of production of such sectors as textiles (147% larger than in 1929), metal products (almost three times larger than in 1929), and paper products (almost seven times larger than in 1929).

World War II caused shortages of imported manufactured goods, which acted again as a stimulant to more intensive domestic production. But the war prevented a concerted development effort, as there was little investment in new productive capacity (Baer 1969). Output increased mainly through a more intensive utilization of existing capacity. Thus, at the end of the war Brazil's industrial capacity was obsolete, and transportation infrastructure was inadequate and badly deteriorated.

Since the wartime years made it possible for Brazil to earn a substantial amount of foreign exchange, the country found itself with a substantial amount of reserves at the end of the war. This made it possible in the early years after World War II for policymakers to decrease barriers to imports. However, trade liberalization was short-lived. The overvalued exchange rate established in 1945 and maintained fixed until 1953, a persistent inflation, and a repressed demand meant sharp increases in imports and a sluggish performance of exports, which soon led again to a balance of payments crisis.

Fearing a negative impact on inflation and having a pessimistic outlook on the future of Brazil's exports, the government, instead of devaluing the cruzeiro, decided to deal with the crisis with exchange controls. In 1950 a system of licensing was established, giving priority to the importation of essential goods and inputs, fuels, and machinery and discouraging that of consumer goods. These policies had the effect— initially unanticipated—of providing protection to the existing consumer goods industry.

Starting in the early 1950s, Brazil's policymakers adopted import substitution industrialization as the country's main development strategy. In the initial stages of ISI, exports were almost totally neglected, while from the mid-1960s on it was accompanied by simultaneous efforts to diversify exports.

Industrialization Policies

Two distinctive phases can be observed when analyzing Brazil's economic policies between 1950 and 1994. Economic growth, in general, and industrialization, in particular, were the main goals of policymakers until the 1980s. Thereafter, all efforts were concentrated on attacking the balance of payments crisis (early 1980s) and the inflationary process. In this section we focus on the growth strategies implemented in the period, leaving the stabilization policies to be discussed separately.

As already mentioned, from the early 1950s on Brazil's policymakers adopted import substitution industrialization (ISI) as the country's main development strategy. They had come to the conclusion that the only hope for rapid growth was to change the structure of the economy through ISI. This was achieved through (1) protection of the domestic market through tariffs, exchange controls, and import licensing; (2) the attraction of foreign direct investment through various incentives; (3) the creation of state enterprises in basic industries and public utilities; (4) the creation of a development bank (Banco Nacional de Desenvolvimento Econômico, BNDE) that, in the absence of an adequate capital market, provided long-term investment capital to both state and domestic private enterprises, often at subsidized interest rates; (5) the direct promotion of specific sectors (Baer 1995, ch. 4; Abreu 1990, ch. 7).

The 1950s began with a more relaxed fiscal and monetary policy, compared to the austerity years of the late 1940s. The exchange rate appreciated in real terms (i.e., the exchange rate remained fixed, while the domestic price level increased, thus making imported goods increasingly cheaper in cruzeiros), while import controls on consumption goods (especially consumer durables) were instituted. The combination of these measures with easy credit policies reduced investment costs and improved the prospective returns, stimulating investment and the importation of capital goods. The latter was further facilitated by increased revenues from coffee exports at the time. As a result of these policies, the rate of investment increased substantially, rising from 12% of GDP in 1950 to an average of 15.2% in the following four years, and the economy expanded by 47% in the first half of the 1950s.

In the second half of the 1950s a number of specific programs were introduced in order to better control the direction of the industrialization process, to remove bottlenecks, and to promote the vertical integration of a number of industries (Baer 1995, ch. 4). Special attention was given to industries considered basic for growth, such as the automotive, cement, steel, aluminum, cellulose, heavy machinery, and chemicals industries. The administration of the exchange rate, tariffs, and other import controls was used to stimulate these industries. For instance, foreign companies in such sectors as those mentioned above were given the privilege of importing machinery without foreign exchange cover. Without this privilege, foreign investors would have had to send dollars to Brazil at the free market rate and with the cruzeiros bought they would have had to repurchase dollars in the auction market at a higher price.

Also, the special Tariff Law of 1957 expanded protection of favored industries with tariffs as high as 60, 80, and 150%.

The government announced a very ambitious program of public investments in infrastructure, especially electricity generation and transportation. Illustrating the increasing participation of the public sector of the economy, the share of government expenditures in the national product went up from 19% in 1952 to 23.7% in 1956. Private investments were favored by facilitated access to internal and external credit, and expansionary monetary and fiscal policies completed the stimulation of the economy. Among the most impressive results of this phase were industry's growth rate of 16.8% in 1958 and the 10.8% GDP growth for the same year. Investment went up for four consecutive years, from 15.2% of GDP in the first half of the decade to 18% in 1959.

The ISI strategy also left and even created a number of problems (Donald Huddle in Baklanoff 1969, pp. 86–108). The type of growth that occurred resulted in a substantial increase of imports, notably of industrial inputs and capital goods, and the foreign exchange policies of the period resulted in an inadequate growth of exports (no efforts were made to diversify them). The balance of trade deficits in the second half of the 1950s were financed by a substantial influx of foreign capital, both in the form of direct investments and in the form of loans. By the beginning of the 1960s Brazil's foreign debt amounted to more than 2 billion dollars. A large proportion of the latter was short term, and both the interest and amortization payments, combined with profit remittances of foreign firms, produced increasing balance of payments difficulties.

Stagnation and Rapid Growth, 1960–74

The first half of this period was characterized by economic stagnation, while in the second half Brazil experienced the highest yearly growth rates ever achieved. The stagnation has been attributed to the end of the initial ISI cycle, to the imbalances it had created, to inflationary distortions, and to political instability. The subsequent boom was the result of structural changes brought about by military governments within a favorable international setting.

The above-mentioned period of stagnation occurred after a decade of prosperity. The GDP growth rate in 1963 was below 1%, and the inflationary impact of the policies adopted in the previous years started to be felt. The main explanations for the crisis were the completion of another stage of the ISI process and the resultant higher level of capital intensity of the domestic industry, which would inhibit new investments; low incentives to invest as a consequence of existing excess capacity and political instability; and insufficient domestic demand resulting from a highly concentrated income distribution.

In 1964 military forces took over Brazil's administration. Its first economic team believed that the main elements impeding growth were high inflation and an unfavorable balance of payments. Inflation, in turn, was considered to be caused by the public deficit, which was around 4% of GDP, the expansionary credit policies implemented in the late fifties, and the wage increases above productivity gains. In accordance with this diagnosis, economic policy until 1967 concentrated on reducing the deficit (which declined to 1.1% in 1966); controlling monetary expansion; and implementing a new formula to determine wage adjustments. The balance of payments problems were tackled by a reform and simplification of the foreign exchange system, with the introduction of a mechanism of periodic devaluations of the cruzeiro, taking into account inflation, and by stimulating a greater internationalizing of the economy by increasing exports and attracting foreign capital. Public investments were also expanded to improve the country's basic infrastructure and modernize and expand state-owned basic industries.

These policies succeeded in reducing inflation and attracting foreign capital, predominantly in the form of foreign loans. The adjustment was considered completed for the most part, and the economic team that took over in 1967 initiated a new development strategy. The remaining inflation was considered to be of a cost-push type, and the austerity policies were replaced by price controls. Interest rates were reduced, various forms of subsidies and tax incentives to encourage diverse types of investments (in backward regions, in sectors whose development was considered essential) were implemented, and measures to modernize capital markets were introduced. The resulting recovery of private investment was accompanied by an increase in public investments, especially in infrastructure (road building, power generation, telecommunications, etc.). Quite notable during this period was the expansion of such state enterprises as Petrobrás and Companhia Vale do Rio Doce. The former, founded in 1952, began with a monopoly in oil exploration. It expanded its activities into refining and various types of petrochemicals through the foundation of a number of subsidiaries (Randall 1993). Vale do Rio Doce, which was founded in the 1940s to export iron ore, expanded into other types of mining activities, steel mills, and various types of forest products. Foreign investment also increased significantly, responding to a more favorable legislation on dividend repatriation, the existence of a well-defined growth strategy, and the country's political stability.

These measures, together with the rapid expansion of the world economy, helped to bring about a time of very rapid growth between 1968 and 1974, during which the yearly growth rate of GDP was 11.1%, with industry expanding at over 13% a year. Its leading sectors consisted of consumer durables, transportation equipment, steel, cement, and electricity generation. The period also witnessed a rapid increase in demand for automobiles, luxury goods, and upscale housing, which was brought about by a rapid growth of upper-strata income and by credit schemes created by the capital market reform.

As a result of the post-1964 policies, external trade expanded substantially faster than the economy as a whole. There was a significant growth of exports, especially of manufactured products, but imports grew considerably faster, rapidly increasing the trade deficit. This did not present a problem, however, since there were massive inflows of capital, and the balance of payments showed surpluses.

In the 1968–74 period the concentration of personal income worsened and the regional disparities became larger. Industrial expansion took place more vigorously in Brazil's Center-South, the region that had benefited most from the ISI strategy. Its per capita income considerably exceeded the national average, its infrastructure was more developed, and it had an adequate supply of skilled workers and professionals. This enabled the region to take advantage of the opportunities and incentives offered by the military regime. Although there was a special regional development strategy for the poor Northeast of the country, it promoted a distorted industrialization that benefited only a few of that region's large cities; its linkages with the Center-South were stronger than those within the region.

Debt-Led Growth, 1974–80

The late-1973 oil shock (which quadrupled the price of oil) hit Brazil very hard as the country was importing more than 80% of its oil needs at the time. Contrary to most countries, Brazil did not accept the conventional thought that it would have to face a slowdown of economic activity as a response to the oil shock. In fact, Brazil's response to the international crisis was to implement an ambitious program of investments and to reinforce the economic policy instruments used to stimulate ISI.

Import substitution was promoted in basic industrial sectors like steel, aluminum, fertilizers, and petrochemicals. More intensive efforts were made in oil exploration both by Petrobrás and through risk contracts with foreign oil multinationals. In addition, Brazil engaged in a vast program to substitute alcohol for gasoline (Randall 1993, pp. 178–82; Barzelay 1986). Large public investments were also made to expand the country's economic infrastructure and to promote and further diversify exports. Besides the usual fiscal incentives and market protection through import controls, private investments were stimulated by subsidized credit and faster capital depreciation rates. Due to these policies, Brazil was able to maintain a high growth rate, the annual real GDP and industrial growth rates in the 1974–80 period being 6.9% and 7.2%, respectively.

Although the goal of these investments was to reduce imports, their immediate growth impact resulted in a higher quantum of imports (especially of capital goods). In addition, the rising value of imports was also attributable to the higher prices of imported oil. The resulting large deficit in the current account balance, which rose from US$1.7 billion in 1973 to US$12.8 billion in 1980, forced the country to borrow heavily in the international financial market. This borrowing was facilitated by the glut of petrodollars, which international banks were eager to lend. Policymakers expected that the combined effect of import substitution and export expansion would eventually bring about trade surpluses needed to service and repay the debt. By the end of the decade, however, interest rates rose dramatically (most of Brazil's external debt was on a flexible interest rate basis), forcing the country to borrow more just to meet its debt service obligations. As a consequence, the foreign debt rose from US$6.4 billion in 1973 to US$54 billion in 1980. The situation was worsened by the Mexican foreign debt moratorium of August 1982, which resulted in the closure of the international credit market to most Latin American countries, including Brazil, and the debt crisis became the major concern of Brazil's government.

In the same period Brazil experienced an acceleration of inflation and a steady worsening of its public finances. Not only were revenues decreasing because of the many tax incentives, but government expenditures were also rising rapidly due to many subsidies (especially to public service state firms whose prices were not allowed to rise with increased costs and whose resulting deficits had to be covered by government subsidies), the high level of public investments, and the rising domestic and foreign debt servicing obligations. While between 1968 and 1973 the rate of inflation had steadily declined, the trend was reversed from 1974 on. Yearly price increases rose from 16.2% in 1973 to 110.2% in 1980.

Stagnation, Inflation, and Crisis, 1981–92

Throughout the 1980s and early 1990s Brazil suffered from both inflation and economic stagnation. This contrasts with most advanced industrial economies, where long periods of stagnation have usually been accompanied by either no or very low rates of price increases. Brazil's stagflation comes as no surprise to the observer since both inflation and stagnation can be interpreted as different manifestations of the same imbalance.

The Fiscal and Monetary Crisis

Over many years Brazil's public sector experienced chronic budget deficits that were financed by increases in the indexed domestic debt. The problem in the 1980s was the gradual decline of the government's credibility with the public: there was increasing doubt about the government's capacity to service the debt and eventually to repay the principal. This gradual loss of credibility required the shortening of the terms of financing, reaching a point at which most of the debt had to be refinanced daily through the overnight market. Extremely high real interest rates were also required to roll over the debt, which substantially increased the government's financial expenditures. This created a vicious cycle of rising debt leading to rising deficit leading to further increases in the debt.

Besides the negative impact on the budget, the debt had an additional perverse effect on monetary control due to the characteristics of its financing. On top of the short terms and high rates, the government was forced to offer an extra attraction to financial institutions that acted as intermediaries in the sale of public bonds. The Central Bank was committed to repurchase from these institutions those bonds that did not find buyers in the market. This hindered the control over monetary policy, as net withdrawals of funds from the overnight market implied automatic increases in the money supply (Paiva 1993).

The large fiscal deficit, debt, and high interest rates also had a profound impact on resource allocation and economic growth. There was an increasing allocation of credit to the government, as the financial system became less and less an intermediator of resources to the private sector and increasingly a facilitator of the transfer of savings to the public sector. For instance, in 1980 the private sector received 74% of total credit, the rest going to the public sector. In 1990 this composition had changed significantly, as the private sector received only 47% and the public sector, 53%. The rising amount of funds placed in the financial rather than in the productive sector implied a decline in economic activity. In the years 1981–90 the average growth rate of the financial sector was 5% per year, which was double the growth rate of the GDP. As a result, the share of the financial sector in the GDP rose from 8.56% in 1980 to more than 19% in 1989 (von Doellinger 1991, pp. 281–82).

Adjustment Policies, 1981–82

The external debt crisis, the emerging fiscal and monetary problems discussed above, and the acceleration of inflation (see table 3.4) forced Brazil to abandon the former priority given to growth in favor of adjustment programs. The first of these programs was carried out in

Table 3.4. Yearly Inflation Rates, 1980–96

1980	110.0
1981	95.0
1982	100.0
1983	211.0
1984	224.0
1985	235.0
1986	65.0
1987	416.0
1988	1,038.0
1989	1,783.0
1990	1,477.0
1991	480.0
1992	1,158.0
1993	2,709.0
1994	1,094.0
1995	14.8
1996*	9.9

Source: *Conjuntura econômica.*
*Yearly rate in July.

1981–83 and served two purposes: by reducing domestic demand, it was supposed to simultaneously slow price increases and decrease imports, generating trade surpluses. The standard austerity measures used included reduction of subsidies and fiscal incentives to diminish the budget deficit; control of the expansion of the monetary aggregates; increase of interest rates; and reduction of real wages.

Most of the intermediate targets of the program were achieved, but the same cannot be said about the final objectives. The impact on economic activity became clear as GDP decreased by 7.4% from 1981 to 1983 and industrial production fell by more than 14% in the same years; the government deficit was reduced and the money supply grew at negative real rates. Inflation, however, increased from 100% in 1982 to 211% in 1983. The balance of trade improved due to the decline of imports. The latter resulted both from the lower growth of the economy and from the impact of the import substitution investments of the 1970s. Exports, however, did not rise until 1984, when international conditions became more favorable.

With the end of the military regime in 1985, stabilization programs were given a different orientation. Economists and policymakers involved in the new administration considered traditional austerity policies inappropriate for controlling Brazil's inflation. They believed that price increases were being determined by formal and informal index-ation mechanisms. Economic agents (i.e., groups that participate in the economy, such as business leaders, workers, firms, banks, the govern-ment) would increase their prices in response to the inflation that occurred in the previous period, which would thus tend to repeat itself. Given its inertial characteristic, inflation would not be significantly affected by contractionary orthodox policies. Following this diagnosis, five stabilization plans involving price freezes were attempted between 1986 and 1991. The idea was that if prices, wages, and the exchange rate were simultaneously frozen and stabilized, economic agents would have no further reason to increase their prices and inflation would disappear.

None of these plans had more than a temporary impact on the rate of inflation, which would continue to accelerate in the months succeeding the price and wage freeze. Explanations for each individual failure were given based on implementation and administration problems. It seems, however, that the plans failed mainly by not implementing a long-run fiscal adjustment. The latter, in turn, was sometimes overlooked by the policymakers in charge and sometimes aborted for political reasons (Baer 1995, ch. 9; Baer and Paiva 1994).

One program that deserves special note is the Collor Plan. When Fernando Collor de Mello assumed the presidency in March 1990, inflation had reached a monthly rate of 81%. Facing a runaway hyperin-flation, Collor immediately introduced a dramatic new anti-inflation program that consisted of the following measures: a price freeze; an 18-month freeze of 80% of all of the economy's financial assets, including checking and savings accounts; new temporary taxes; suspension of internal debt servicing; elimination of various types of tax incentives; indexation of taxes; an increase in the price of public goods; liberaliza-tion of the exchange rate and the adoption of various measures to promote the gradual opening of the Brazilian economy to external competition; measures to institute a process of privatization; and the introduction of a new currency.

The immediate impact of the plan was to dramatically reduce the country's liquidity, as the broader money supply (M_4) as a percentage of GDP fell from about 30% to 9%. Within a month, inflation declined to a single-digit monthly rate. The sharp decrease in liquidity led to a pronounced fall in economic activities. The fear of a long recession and the pressure from various socioeconomic groups led the government to release many blocked financial assets ahead of schedule. The many concessions that were made, the impact of the surplus on the balance of payments, and the budgetary process of the public sector (which could pay taxes in old blocked currency, but which made expenditures in the new currency) led to a rapid remonetization process. After forty-five days there had been a 62.5% expansion of the money supply, raising it to 14% of GDP.

One of the main targets of the Collor Plan was to reduce the primary budget deficit from 8% of GDP to a surplus of 2%, and the actual surplus achieved in 1990 was 1.2%. This result, however, was mostly due to artificial or temporary measures, such as the once-and-for-all tax on financial assets and the reduced debt servicing accomplished by the assets freeze.

The temporary decline in the financial component of the deficit created a situation in which government expenditures on personnel and related social charges amounted to 37% of total expenditures, while the transfers to states and municipalities, instituted by the 1988 constitution, represented 23%. The government's attempts to lay off workers was also constrained by the constitution, which stated that all government employees who were employed for more than five years could not be laid off. Thus further reforms aimed at permanently improving the government's fiscal situation were dependent on modifications in the constitution. These, in turn, required approval of two-thirds of Congress, which Collor was unable to obtain.

The Collor Plan had a strong recessive impact on the economy due to the dramatic decline in the stock of liquid assets. Real GDP declined by 7.8% in the second quarter of 1990. With the unblocking of a number of frozen assets within the following months, economic activity rebounded slightly, but for 1990 as a whole the GDP declined by 4.4%.

Collor's privatization program, which began in April 1994, was viewed as an integral part of his policies to modernize the Brazilian economy through a general liberalization process. Most sales occurred at public auctions, and acceptable currencies included various types of government debt certificates, foreign debt papers, and hard foreign currencies. The first sales of state enterprises occurred in the steel and petrochemical sectors. Although the government of Collor's successor, Itamar Franco, stalled privatization for a few months in 1993, it was soon resumed, and by the middle of 1994 twenty-nine companies had been privatized for US$9.57 billion. Foreign participation in privatization was quite small, occurring in only thirteen companies for the relatively small sum of US$263 million. In late 1984 the government also privatized an airplane manufacturing concern (EMBRAER) and in 1995 was planning to privatize public utilities.

On the external side, the Collor government began a process of liberalization, which continued throughout the first half of the 1990s. A gradual reduction of tariffs was initiated, and the exchange rate was allowed to fluctuate.

After an initial drop, following the introduction of the Collor Plan, inflation started to rise again. As price increases began to accelerate, various measures were tried to cope with it, such as financial reform, new wage and price freezes, and attempts at controlling expenditures of state enterprises. The ultimate failure of the Collor Plan to control inflation can be attributed to the lack of a permanent fiscal adjustment (since the surplus achieved was mostly due to temporary effects) and a monetary regime that had little credibility.

The Itamar Franco Presidency

By the time Itamar Franco took over as interim president in October 1992, it was clear that the economy's performance was not improving significantly. Inflation continued around a monthly rate of 25% in the last three months of 1992, and by the second half of 1993 it rose to a monthly rate of over 30%. Although the GDP recovered slightly in the last quarter of 1992, it declined again in the first quarter of 1993. Workers continued to be laid off; as mentioned above, there was opposition for a while in certain quarters to privatization, and there was no consensus about how to implement a fiscal adjustment.

Itamar Franco's initial ineffectiveness in providing political and economic leadership did not improve once he graduated from interim to full-time president. It took him over four months to resume the privatization program, and it also took a considerable amount of time to switch from a nationalist stance vis-à-vis foreign capital to a more welcoming attitude. Also unhelpful was the instability of his economic team, as he changed finance ministers three times within a period of six months.

Until the middle of 1993 the successive economic policy teams of Itamar Franco refrained from price freezes, seizing of savings, new indexation, or the breaking of existing contractual agreements. As it became increasingly clear to the Franco government that one of Brazil's major problems in coming to grips with inflation was a fiscal adjustment, a special temporary tax on financial movements (IPMF) was proposed and gradually passed by Congress. The constitutionality of this tax came into question, but it was allowed to linger on under special provisions until the end of 1994. The government also made efforts to organize tax collection more effectively and counteract tax evasions, which had grown substantially over the previous years. By the middle of 1993 the privatization program was fully instituted again and plans were broadened to include a number of infrastructure sectors in it (such as electric utilities and railroads).

In May 1993 President Franco appointed his fourth finance minister, Fernando Henrique Cardoso, who presented an austerity plan in June, called the Immediate Action Plan. Its centerpiece was a US$6 billion cut in government spending (amounting to 9% of federal spending and 2.5% of the spending of all levels of government). The plan also called for the tightening of tax collection and for resolving the financial relationships with state governments. The latter owed the federal government US$36 billion in 1993 and were about US$2 billion in arrears. Cardoso stated that the federal loan guarantees would be withheld from states until these arrears were cleared and that state governments would be required to allocate 9% of their revenues to clear their debts with the federal government. A campaign was also begun in mid-1993 to fight tax evasion, which had grown dramatically over the previous decade. It was claimed that the government was losing between US$40 and 60 billion a year due to evasion.

The Immediate Action Plan came out as economic activity was rising again. GDP increased by 4% in the first quarter of 1993 in relation to the first quarter of 1992. This was due partly to higher real wages and increased agricultural income. Rising economic activity also manifested itself in increased imports, especially raw materials and machinery. For 1993 as a whole GDP growth was 5%, with manufacturing industry growing at 10%.

Inflation, however, continued unabated, reaching monthly rates of over 30% in the middle of 1993. This led labor leaders and politicians to introduce a wage law requiring monthly wage adjustments for all low-income workers. Although this law was first passed, it was vetoed by President Franco. The government then succeeded in having Congress pass a wage law that limited monthly wage adjustments to 10 percentage points below the monthly inflation rate.

The Plano Real

In December 1993 Fernando Henrique Cardoso, Brazil's finance minister, proposed a new stabilization program that was supposed to avoid some of the weaknesses of the previous plans. Unlike the previous plans, the new program was at first presented as a "proposal," which was to be amply discussed in Congress and implemented gradually. The program had two basic thrusts: first, a fiscal adjustment, and, second, a new indexing system that would gradually lead to a new currency.

The principal fiscal adjustment measures consisted of (1) an across-the-board tax increase of 5%; (2) giving 15% of all tax receipts to a newly created Social Emergency Fund (Fundo Social de Emergência); and (3) spending cuts on government investments, personnel, and state companies of about US$7 billion. As the fund was only a temporary measure, the government announced long-term plans for constitutional amendments that would transfer to state governments and municipalities responsibilities in the areas of health, education, social services, housing, basic sanitation, and irrigation and would decrease the automatic transfer of federal tax receipts to state and local governments as contained in the 1988 constitution.

The new indexing system was introduced at the end of February 1994. It consisted of an indexer called the Unit of Real Value (URV, Unidade Real de Valor) that was tied to the dollar on a one-to-one basis. The URV's quotation in cruzeiros reais rose daily, accompanying the exchange rate, according to the prevailing inflation. Official prices, contracts, and taxes were denominated in URV, and the government encouraged its use on a voluntary basis by private economic agents. Gradually, an increasing number of prices were stated in URVs, although transactions occurred in cruzeiros reais.

By the middle of 1994, as an increasing proportion of prices were quoted in URVs, the government decided to introduce a new currency whose unit was equal to the URV. This was done on July 1 with the introduction of the "real," equal to one URV, or one US$, equal to 2,750 of the former currency units, the cruzeiros reais. At the time of the price conversion from the old currency into the real there occurred a wave of price increases in many supermarkets and stores, as many businesses took advantage of the initial confusion of the public about relative prices in the new currency. In addition, many business leaders also expected the introduction of a price freeze, which had been customary in previous stabilization attempts. However, the government refrained from any freezes, using its public relations network to suggest that the public minimize purchases of necessities in order to force a price retrenchment. As the public now was in possession of a currency that it believed would retain its purchasing power, consumers were in a position to "bargain" (i.e., to wait and not pay for goods at the recently increased prices). In fact, very soon some prices began to decline, and the first results were felt by a decline in the weekly inflation rates.

Along with the introduction of the new currency the government adopted a restrictive monetary policy. It consisted of a short-term limit on loans to finance exports, a 100% reserve requirement on new deposits, and a limit on the expansion of the monetary base of R$9.5 billion until the end of March 1995. For the quarter July–September 1994 the expansion had been limited to R$7.5 billion. By August, however, the government was forced to revise that number, admitting an increase of R$9 billion by September. This had some impact on inflationary expectations, although most of the overshooting of the planned expansion could be attributed to an increase in the demand for money.

The monetary authorities also kept interest rates high in order to control a possible increase of consumption and to discourage speculative stockpiling. As a complementary measure to discourage large capital inflows that high interest rates might attract, the authorities fixed the sales prices of the real to be equal to US$1, while they allowed the buying price of the real to appreciate according to market forces. With the substantial capital inflows and continued trade surpluses, the real indeed appreciated, reaching 84 centavos to the dollar in November.

The initial results of the plan were positive. Inflation was brought down from a monthly rate of about 47% in June to 1.5% in September and 0.57% in December; in 1995 its highest increase was 2.6% in June and its lowest level was an actual price decline of 1% in September. As can be seen in table 3.5, the monthly price stability continued to prevail in 1996. Also, the initial impact of the Plano Real on economic activity was quite pronounced, as the growth rate rose from 0.8% in the second quarter of 1994 to 3.1% in the third quarter and 3.6% in the fourth quarter. This was in large part due to rising sales, reflecting especially the purchases of the lower income groups, whose real incomes were boosted by the fact that their monthly losses from quasi-hyperinflation disappeared (*Conjuntura econômica*).

Although price stability continued throughout 1995 and 1996, it was maintained at the cost of a decline of growth and a worsening situation in the trade balance and public finances.

The appreciation of the exchange rate, resulting from a policy of high interest rates (which were deemed necessary to avoid capital outflows when the Real Plan was introduced and were later necessary to finance the government deficit), convinced some policymakers that an appreciated exchange rate would also be a useful additional instrument to control inflation (this was called an exchange rate anchor).

Since, however, there was still a considerable inflationary residual in the economy, the real appreciation of the exchange rate continued throughout 1995 and 1996. The degree of appreciation varied, depending on what price indexes were used to compare Brazil's inflation with that of the principal trade partners. For instance, comparing the cost of living indexes, the real appreciation was estimated to have been about 47% in the first two years of the Real Plan. Since these indexes contain a large proportion of nontradable goods, especially services, whose prices increased more than tradables, some analysts have claimed that the correct comparison would be wholesale prices, which more faithfully represent tradable goods. Estimates of real exchange rate appreciation based on the latter show an appreciation of about 29% (see *Conjuntura econômica*, August 1996, p. 5). Whether the appreciation represented an overvaluation of the real was a matter of considerable controversy. Some have argued that at the time of the introduction of the Real Plan the currency was undervalued and that an appreciation of 30% would expose the

Table 3.5. Monthly Inflation Rates, 1986–96

	1986	1987	1988	1989	1990	1991	1992	1993	1994	1995	1996
January	18.0	12	19	36	72	20	27	29	42	1.4	1.8
February	15.0	14	18	12	72	21	25	26	42	1.1	0.8
March	-.1	15	18	4	81	7	21	28	45	1.8	0.2
April	-.6	20	20	5	11	9	18	28	43	2.3	0.7
May	.3	28	19	13	9	6	22	32	41	0.4	1.7
June	.5	26	21	27	9	10	21	31	47	2.6	1.2
July	.6	9	21	38	13	13	22	32	25	2.2	1.1
August	1.3	4	23	36	13	15	25	34	3.3	1.3	
September	1.1	8	26	39	12	16	27	37	1.5	-1.1	
October	1.4	11	28	40	14	26	25	35	2.5	0.2	
November	2.5	14	28	44	17	26	24	37	2.5	1.3	
December	7.6	16	29	49	16	22	24	36	0.6	0.3	

Source: Conjuntura econômica.

formerly protected and high-cost Brazilian economy to healthy competition and thus force many sectors to increase their efficiency. Others maintained that such an appreciation was too severe and could result in permanent damage to many sectors.

The exchange appreciation, combined with the country's trade liberalization, caused a substantial increase of imports (from US$33 billion in 1994 to US$50 billion in 1995). Exports grew more modestly (from US$43 billion to US$46 billion), and thus Brazil experienced a trade deficit for the first time in thirteen years. This continued in 1996. Although this deficit helped to stabilize the economy, as the huge increase of imports resulted in a price-stabilizing foreign competition, some sectors (especially the automobile industry) found this situation so threatening that they convinced the government to reimpose higher tariff and direct import controls in 1995 and 1996. The government stated that this return to protectionism was only of a temporary nature, and its purpose was to give more time to the affected sectors to readjust.

The trade deficit, however, more than compensated by large capital inflows, which rose on a net basis from US$14 billion in 1994 to US$30.7 billion in 1995. This influx continued in the first half of 1996. Although substantial amounts of this influx consisted of direct investment (about US$4.8 billion in 1995 and close to US$7 billion in 1996), most of the inflow consisted of investments in government securities and funds for the stock market. A combination of lower interest rates in Brazil and rising rates abroad could easily reverse this flow.

The most worrisome aspect of the implementation of the Real Plan in 1995–96 was the delay in attaining a basic fiscal adjustment. As the temporary measures to attain such an adjustment ran out in the course of 1995, the government was finding it difficult to get constitutional amendments through Congress that would make it possible to balance the budget (this involved such measures as abolishing tenure of public servants, readjusting retirement age and changing the amount and method of fiscal transfers). Also, in the first two years of the Real Plan the rate of privatization proceeded at a very slow pace, thus keeping government revenues from that source relatively low. Government expenditures, however, kept rising—as a result of the rise of both government employment and wages, the rise of interest payments, and the need to rescue failing private and state banks that could not cope with operating in a noninflationary environment. In 1995 government receipts grew by 7.6%, while expenditures grew at 18.5% (*Gazeta mercantil*, August 14, 1996, p. A-5). The operational deficit of the government amounted to about 3% of GDP in 1995, and the estimates for 1996 were not more promising.

The government deficit was financed by borrowing from the public at high interest rates. Although this was not inflationary as the Central Bank was not involved, it resulted in a rapidly rising government debt. It rose from R$63.4 billion in January 1995 to R$151.3 in May 1996, and it was estimated that by the end of 1996 this debt would grow to about 40% of GDP.

The government's dilemma was clear. With no fiscal adjustment and growing deficits, it had to maintain relatively high interest rates in order to finance these in a noninflationary manner. But high interest rates themselves made government debt servicing expensive, thus increasing the difficulties of expenditure reduction and making it difficult to stimulate growth and consumption.

The ultimate success of the Real Plan basically depends on two factors. The most important is that the temporary fiscal adjustment obtained from the Fundo de Emergência Social would be made permanent through a constitutional amendment. Besides the immediate positive impact it would have on inflationary expectations, this is a necessary condition for long-term monetary control. Together with the constitutional amendment, the fiscal/monetary discipline also requires that the authorities be able to resist pressures from various sectors to settle distributional conflicts in an inflationary manner.

It is indisputable that the fiscal adjustment necessary for stabilization requires a complex political arrangement for its implementation. Throughout this chapter we have suggested that the successive economic plans devoted an increasing degree of attention to budget balancing as an anti-inflationary instrument. As this occurred, though, the difficulties this kind of reform faced in the political sphere became more evident.

Approaching this issue, some experts defend the necessity of a wide sociopolitical movement to trigger the institutional reforms that would lead to fiscal discipline. Also maintained is the need for all levels of public administration to act responsibly in order to achieve a balanced budget.

One cannot disagree with the desirability of a participant society and responsible political and public sectors. The question here concerns the timing involved in the process: will a new sociopolitical attitude lead to institutional reforms or a new institutional order mold different social, political, and economic behaviors? The assumption that this should all happen simultaneously would be an easy but very unrealistic one. Desirable widespread fiscal responsibility should be imposed from above, through a precursory reformed institutional order.

Only when the government is forbidden to finance new expenditures through money creation can a political process be developed to force the state to deny new expenditure demands, to bargain for reducing other expenditures, or to create appropriate new tax revenues. While it is possible to approve politically advantageous projects without specifying how they will be funded, it is naïve to expect any commitment to austerity from the public administration and from politicians in general.

As an illustration of this point, it is worth mentioning the scandal that broke out in October of 1993, involving several Brazilian congressmen, construction companies, and members of the public administration. A scheme was revealed in which congressmen received bribes to introduce and get approval for projects to be carried out by certain construction firms. Although these projects were mostly only of local interest, they were included as amendments to the federal budget. No source of funding was usually specified and prices were overstated. Investigators found evidence that the scheme had been in place at least since 1985 and involved billions of dollars. The congressmen involved lost their seats and had their political rights suspended for ten years.

Society's reaction to the episode and the measures taken against the people involved were satisfactory and seem to have reassured Brazil's democracy. One aspect that might have been overlooked in the midst of the indignation over this type of corruption was the legal channel that made the whole scheme possible: congressmen have the power to increase the federal government's expenditures almost indiscriminately. In most cases these projects were approved through negotiation in the congressional budget committee, not requiring discussion or a vote in the House of Deputies.

With respect to the federal budget, one other example of the lack of an adequate institutional structure to enforce austerity is that the 1994 federal budget was not approved until October 1994.

Among the reforms necessary for public sector austerity and stabilization to be achieved is a constitutional reform that would transfer obligations from the central government to states, to accompany the significant transfers of revenues in the same direction promoted by the 1988 constitution. This would make the central government's task easier and force local governments to use their resources in a more efficient manner than in the past.

Additionally, if the Central Bank is made more independent, this would also force the behavior pattern of local and state governments to change. For instance, in the 1980s many states used their commercial and development banks to make economically dubious but politically advantageous loans. The result was that many of these banks often faced the type of liquidity crisis that could undermine confidence in the banking system. This forced the Central Bank to rescue them and issue large quantities of money that had not been planned for, thus contributing to the rising rate of inflation. With an independent Central Bank and a higher risk of facing insolvency, these state banks would tend to act more responsibly. A more drastic measure to achieve such a goal would be the privatization of the entire state banking system.

Through new legal parameters it may be possible to change the behavior pattern of politicians and economic agents, who have traditionally avoided market forces through government favors. The fight for shares will have to be explicitly resolved, and not accommodated through monetary expansion and inflation. By subjecting economic agents (politicians and all levels of public administration included) to market forces and scarcity of resources, they will ultimately be forced to act in a way that could simultaneously increase efficiency and promote stability in the Brazilian economy.

Special Aspects of Brazil's Economy

Having concentrated on the growth, development, and stabilization policies of Brazil's economy, let us briefly examine some of the special institutional features that evolved over time.

Indexation

A very important characteristic of the Brazilian economy prior to the stabilization program of the mid-1990s was the indexation mechanism present in all of its sectors. It may seem intriguing to outside observers that Brazil lived relatively normally with such high and persistent inflation rates. The answer is found in the indexation practices developed in the country over many years.

In general terms, indexation means to peg (i.e., link) various prices, values, and contracts to an index that is adjusted according to the rate of inflation. In this way, for example, wages are periodically—and automatically—increased to compensate for increases in the cost of living; interest rates are expressed in real terms (i.e., a percentage to be added to the price index variation observed in the period of contract); most checking accounts have their balances updated daily, earning an interest rate that reflects the current inflation; prices are sometimes stated in terms of a particular indexer, instead of being expressed in the domestic currency, etc.

Practices like the ones described indeed helped the Brazilian economy and society to avoid some of the costs of hyperinflation. Nonetheless, indexation also has negative aspects. It is recognized by economists of various schools of thought that the degree of indexation encountered in Brazil makes stabilization a much harder task. This idea has been present in all stabilization plans implemented since 1986, which in one way or another tried to change or extinguish the economy's indexation mechanism (Baer 1995, ch. 7).

Structure of Production

As already mentioned, the growth and diversification that have taken place since the middle of the twentieth century have brought considerable changes to the productive structure of the Brazilian economy. In what follows we examine the evolution of the main sectors.

Agriculture. When examining the behavior of the agricultural sector since World War II, it is possible to identify two periods: the 1949–69 period of horizontal expansion and the period of conservative modernization, from 1970 to the 1990s (Mueller 1992). In the former the export sector relied heavily on coffee, but also on cotton, sugar, and a few minor commodities, while the domestic-oriented sector consisted of a few basic staple crops. ISI changed things drastically. Industrialization required critical tasks from the agricultural sector, especially that of generating most of the economy's foreign exchange, producing growing outputs of food and some industrial inputs, and transferring resources for ISI. The latter came from a tax on foreign exchange earned by coffee exports and from a persistent implicit taxation of agriculture. The virtual exclusion of many agricultural products from the world market caused by the highly overvalued cruzeiro resulting from the ISI strategy and the cheap domestic food policy that prevailed depressed prices in favor of the urban-industrial sector.

Paradoxically, the overall performance of agriculture in the same period was adequate. Agricultural GDP increased 4.2% a year between 1949 and 1969, a considerably higher growth rate than that of the population. A major factor in this performance was horizontal expansion (i.e., the incorporation of new land), especially along the agricultural frontier, made possible by an aggressive policy of road construction. The disincentives of the ISI policies were circumvented by maintaining ample access to land at concessionary terms for the landowning elite and for commercial farmers, reproducing a pattern established early in the colonial period. However, there was a neglect of technical change and of agricultural support policies.

By the late 1960s it was clear that horizontal growth of agriculture was rapidly reaching its limits and that increases in productivity would be essential for a continued expansion of production. This led to a conservative agricultural modernization strategy, which consisted of a program of technical change for a restricted number of subsectors and of incentives for the formation of agribusiness complexes.

Technical change involved the development and adaptation of green revolution technologies, geared mainly to large agricultural operations, with important roles for mechanization and for chemical inputs. Regarding agribusiness complexes, strong incentives were provided for the creation and expansion of processing industries and for the development and modernization of agricultural input industries. A number of processed agricultural products (soymeal and oil, instant coffee, processed beef, poultry, orange juice, textiles) were offered subsidized credit and guaranteed prices at the production end and received tax exemptions and subsidies when exported. Traditional unprocessed agricultural products, however, were subjected to heavy taxation and to price and other controls. As in the ISI phase, the production of cheap food was required and only recently have the policies applied to the sector changed in this respect (Mueller 1992).

The products benefiting from agricultural modernization responded well to the conservative modernization strategy and to opportunities arising from both the world and the domestic markets. They underwent considerable technical changes, and their production and yields increased substantially in the period. The products of the traditional sectors, however, had scant access to credit and to the support price policies and were frequently subjected to price controls and to a maze of regulations, export restrictions, and quotas and to the competition from subsidized imports when they failed to supply the domestic market adequately. It is no surprise that they failed to modernize and tended to perform poorly.

At the beginning of the 1990s the main crops of the modern sector of Brazil's agriculture were cotton, rice, sugarcane, oranges, corn, soybeans, and wheat; those of the traditional sectors included beans, manioc, bananas, peanuts, and to some extent coffee.

Brazil's livestock sector went through a similar process of selective modernization. Until the early 1970s it remained backward, and its expansion relied mainly on the incorporation of more land (and animals) into production. It also experienced a process of change in tandem with the expansion of agribusiness complexes. However, modernization has been concentrated in certain regions, and there are large differences between the modern and the traditional segments of the beef-cattle, poultry, and swine sectors—the country's main livestock subsectors.

Between 1970 and 1990 Brazil's beef-cattle herd grew at a 3.1% average yearly rate, from 78.5 to 147.1 million head, the slaughter of beef-cattle increased from 9.6 to 13.4 million head, and the carcass weight increased from 1.8 to 2.8 million tons. The beef-cattle industry in areas near the country's more developed areas experienced considerable modernization, interlocked with the expansion of a dynamic agribusiness sector, which supplies the industry with modern inputs and slaughters and processes its animals, for both the domestic and the world markets. As a result, Brazil's exports of beef have increased from 98.3 thousand tons of chilled beef and 15.8 thousand tons of processed beef, at a total value of US$298.6 million (in 1992 US$), to 196.8 thousand tons of chilled beef and 127.3 thousand tons of processed beef, at a total value of US$618.1 million in 1992. However, still substantial traditional beef-cattle zones can be found in frontier areas and in the more backward parts of Brazil, with low productivity and serious sanitary and management problems.

The poultry subsector experienced spectacular improvements in the 1970s and 1980s, changing from a small, backward sector into a modern industry. This is reflected by the fact that while the poultry herd increased 2.5 times between 1970 and 1990, from 214.3 to 545.2 million head, the total carcass weight of the birds slaughtered commercially increased 18.8 times, from 85.4 thousand to 1.6 million tons. Moreover, the export of poultry products, which was negligible in 1970, amounted to 378 thousand tons in 1992. This evolution was also achieved in the context of agribusiness complexes.

Industry.   As already noted, industrialization did not proceed with the same characteristics in the 1950–95 period. Focusing on the evolution and structural changes of the industrial sector, it is possible to identify four subperiods: until 1962 a phase of intense import substitution, especially of consumer goods, with basic industry growing at a significant but lower rate; from 1968 to 1973 a period of very rapid industrial expansion and modernization; from 1974 to 1986 a period of import substitution of basic inputs and capital goods and of expansion of manufactured goods exports; and from 1987 onward a period of considerable difficulties until 1993.

From 1949 to 1962 there was a considerable decline in the share of nondurable goods industries, from nearly 60% to less than 43%, and a sharp increase in that of consumer durable goods, from almost 6% to over 18%. The intermediate and capital goods groups experienced moderate increases, from 32 to 36% and from 2.2 to 3.2%, respectively.

A representative component of the nondurable group is the textile industry, the leading sector before World War II. Between 1949 and 1960 its share in the value added by industry as a whole declined from 20.1% to 11.6%. In the durable goods group, the component with the most significant change was transport equipment (automobiles and trucks), increasing from 2.3 to 10.5%.

The lower increases in the shares of intermediate and capital goods reflect the smaller priority given to them by the ISI strategy. In the early 1960s Brazil already had a fairly diversified industrial structure, but one in which vertical integration was only beginning. Thus, because of the limited degree of vertical integration in the industrial sector, the demand for imported industrial inputs more than offset the import savings of ISI.

The 1968–73 boom years still emphasized consumer goods, especially durables, but the capital goods industry also showed a significant expansion. The industrial sector not only experienced a significant expansion, but also underwent considerable modernization. This caused a sharp increase of capital goods imports and of basic and semiprocessed inputs. In those years the decline of the share of nondurable goods continued (especially of textiles and food products), while there was a considerable increase in the share of machinery, from 3.2 to 10.3%. There was also a notable increase in industrial exports. Their share of total exports rose from 5% in 1963 to 29% in 1974.

Import substitution cum exports began to be implemented in 1974, culminating in 1985. Contrary to the early ISI experience, it centered mainly on basic inputs and capital goods. Thus, over the long run, it genuinely contributed to the reduction of import requirements. However, during the phase of implementation, the strategy placed a heavy burden on the balance of payments, not only as a result of growing imports of inputs and capital goods, but also due to increases in the service of the foreign debt, stemming from the loans to finance the process.

The nature of the changes in the 1974–85 period can be better perceived by examining the evolution of the trade balance of three groups of manufactured products that contribute to the country's international trade. *Traditional manufactures* are composed of oils and fats, food products; beverages, tobacco; leather products; wood products, textiles and clothing; and hats and shoes. *Intermediate manufactures* include chemicals; pulp, paper, and cardboard; manufactures from non-metallic minerals; and metal products. And *technological manufactures* include plastic goods; ethers and esters from cellulose; artificial resins and resin products; rubber products; machinery and instruments; electrical material; transport equipment; arms and ammunition; and manufactures from precious metals and stones. In 1978 only traditional manufactures had a trade surplus. In 1984 traditional manufactures had a steady increase in their trade surplus. Intermediate and technological manufactures experienced a steady decline in their trade deficit, and after 1982 they continuously showed a surplus.

From 1987 onward some of the problems industry faced during the years of decline early in the decade were intensified, the macroeconomic conditions remained persistently adverse, and a stream of political troubles had negative effects on expectations. Until the end of the 1980s industry continued to rely heavily on protection and on government favors, but it also faced pervasive regulations and considerable governmental interference. These factors had a negative impact on industrial investment and on the productivity of several industrial subsectors, increasingly blunting the competitive edge they had struggled to achieve in the world market. Also, the fiscal crisis made it increasingly difficult for the government to continue to provide subsidies to industry and to maintain and expand the country's infrastructure (energy, transportation, and communications).

The administration inaugurated in 1990 introduced significant changes in Brazil's economic strategy. There were measures to eliminate regulations, to liberalize trade, and to markedly reduce governmental favors and subsidies. Also, several measures aimed at increasing industry's competitiveness were announced. The implementation of the first set of measures began early in the 1990s, but policies to promote greater industrial competitiveness proceeded at a much slower pace. Moreover, political and macroeconomic difficulties prevented the effective implementation of the new strategy, and the mounting fiscal crisis dampened efforts to rebuild and improve the badly deteriorated infrastructure. Thus an important part of the industrial sector failed to recover and to modernize. With stagnation, the domestic market could not provide a dynamic push to industry, and the reduction of investment and in modernization, coupled with deteriorating infrastructure, resulted in declines in competitiveness of industries that, in the previous period, had fared well in the world market.

The Service Sector. In 1950 Brazil's service sector was still small and, except for certain segments associated with international trade, quite backward. The urban-industrial sector was in an infant stage, and transportation and communications were still quite undeveloped. With industrialization the sector expanded and went through considerable changes; in the early 1990s it exhibited an important modern segment, mainly composed of parts of the subsectors of commerce, transportation, communication, finance, and professional services. However, other subsectors failed to develop adequately, the main instances being education and public administration at various levels.

Poverty, the rapid growth of the population, the inadequate provision of education, and the succession of economic troubles since 1980 induced the expansion of an informal sector, a large portion of which was located in the services sector. This can be seen by examining the sector's share of GDP and of employment over time. Between 1950 and 1980 the services sector generated around 50% of the country's GDP; in 1990 the share had increased to 55.9%, in part due to the poor performance of industry but, to the extent that the System of National Accounts captures its contribution, also due to the expansion of the informal sector. The share of the services sector in the absorption of labor also presents evidence of the recent growth of the informal sector. In 1950 the sector employed only 22.5% of the economically active population; this proportion rose to 33.3% in 1970, to 40.8% in 1980, and to 54.5% in 1990.

Distribution of Income

Brazil has always had a high concentration in the distribution of income, and this characteristic has worsened since the early days of ISI. This becomes clear from a glance at table 3.6, which shows that the Gini coefficient of concentration rose from 0.497 in 1960 to 0.630 in 1990, and the top 10% of income earners increased their share from 39.6 to 48.7%, while the share of the poorest 40% of the population was only 7.2%. The pattern of income distribution was similar in all of Brazil's five regions. In 1988 the lowest Gini coefficient was that of the South (0.58) and the highest that of the Northeast (0.64). Thus inequality was a generalized phenomenon.

Brazil's large population with a medium-range income per capita, together with a high degree of inequality, means that there are a substantial number of poor. Estimates based on the poverty line method indicate that 39.1 million persons, or almost a third of the population, were poor in 1990 (Rocha and Tolosa 1993). About half of the 1990 poor lived in rural areas. In relative terms, however, the proportion of the urban poor (22.5%) was substantially lower than that of the rural poor (50.1%). Although the rapid rural-urban migration of the last forty years substantially reduced the rural population, it did not improve the lot of those who remained on the land.

Substantial regional inequalities have existed in Brazil since the nineteenth century and the industrialization process has worsened them (Baer 1995, ch. 12). In 1991 the more developed Southeast and South,

Table 3.6. Income Distribution, 1960–90

Year	Lower 40%	Top 10%	Gini Coefficient
1960	11.3	39.6	0.497
1970	10.0	46.5	0.565
1980	9.7	47.9	0.590
1990	7.2	48.7	0.630

Sources: Perspectivas da economia brasileira 1994 (Brasília: IPEA, 1993), vol. 2, p. 480; O Brasil social: Realidades, desafios, opções, ed. Roberto Cavalcanti de Albuquerque (Rio de Janeiro: IPEA, 1993), p. 138.

which made up 17.6% of the country's territory, contained 58.7% of the population and it was responsible for 74.3% of the country's GDP in 1985. The Northeast, however, with 18.3% of the territory and 28.5% of the population, generated only 13.1% of the 1985 GDP. The enormous North and Center-West regions, with 64.1% of the territory, contained only 12.6% of the population and produced 12.6% of the 1985 GDP.

The rapid growth of Brazil's economy increased per capita income in 1992 dollars from US$1,691 in 1970 to US$3,041 in 1980; during the lost decade of the 1980s it declined to US$2,659 in 1983, and in 1992 it rose again to US$2,796. Although the five major regions of the country followed similar trends, regional disparities in per capita income deserve attention. In 1970 per capita income of the Southeast was 53.2% greater than the national average, while the Northeast's was 44.4% lower. This difference declined by only a small amount; in 1988 the per capita income of the Southeast was 43.6% greater than the national average, while the Northeast's was still 37.5% smaller (Cavalcanti de Albuquerque and Villela 1992).

It is possible that much of the concentration in the distribution of income is due to the lack of adequate investments in health and education, which has affected a large proportion of the population. This is partially confirmed by information contained in the United Nations Development Programme's *Human Development Report* and the World Bank's *World Development Report*. The latter's Human Development Index for Brazil is 0.739, compared to 0.976 for the United States and 0.982 for Canada. Expenditures on education at all levels of government were 4.3% of GDP in 1989, compared to 6.8% in the United States and 7.2% in Canada. Although 84% of primary school age children attended school, more than half failed to complete that school level; only 38% of secondary school age children are enrolled at that level, and only 11% are in institutions of higher education. Health expenditures amounted to 6.1% of GDP in 1989, compared to 12.9% in the United States and 18.3% in Germany (*World Development Report; Human Development Report*). When taking the average index of industrial countries at a base of 100, Brazil in terms of population per nurse stood at 12, in terms of scientists and technicians, at 36, and in terms of mean years of schooling, at 39. These numbers, of course, say nothing about the quality of education and health services received. Although adult literacy stood at 81% in 1990, the quality of that literacy for a large number was low, making a large share of the population functionally illiterate. Given the low remuneration of professionals in education and in the health services, a large proportion of the population is badly served in those areas and is therefore at a disadvantage in the marketplace.

Ownership

Three basic ownership sectors participated in Brazil's industrialization: domestic private firms, multinational corporations, and state enterprises (Baer 1995; Villela and Baer 1980). Table 3.7 gives an estimate of the relative share of each ownership category in some of the major sectors of the economy in 1992. It will be noted that agriculture, retail

Table 3.7. Share of Domestic, Foreign, and State Firms in Total Sales, 1992 (percentages)

	Domestic	Foreign	State	Total
Domestic dominance				
Agriculture	100	0	0	100
Retail trade	100	0	0	100
Construction	100	0	0	100
Auto distribution	100	0	0	100
Wood & furniture	97	3	0	100
Clothing	90	10	0	100
Hotels	85	15	0	100
Textiles	85	15	0	100
Paper & cellulose	81	19	0	100
Supermarkets	77	23	0	100
Wholesale trade	75	25	0	100
Fertilizers	75	7	18	100
Transport service	68	1	31	100
Electrical goods	67	33	0	100
Nonmet. min.	67	33	0	100
Food products	64	36	0	100
Steel	56	6	37	100
Transport products	46	45	9	100
Metal products	44	48	8	100
Foreign dominance				
Autos & parts	6	94	0	100
Hygienic products	12	88	0	100
Pharmaceuticals	18	82	0	100
Computers	33	65	2	100
Plastics & rubber	35	65	0	100
Beverage, tobacco	40	60	0	100
Gasoline distribution	12	55	33	100
Machines & equip.	50	50	0	100
State dominance				
Public utilities	0	0	100	100
Chem., petrochem.	13	21	66	100
Mining	32	7	61	100

Source: Melhores e Maiores, *Exame,* August 1993.
Note: Each sector includes the 20 largest firms.

trade, and construction are entirely in the hands of domestic private firms, while less exclusive but still dominated by domestic private firms are such sectors as clothing, textiles, hotels, electrical goods, and food products. Foreign firms are dominant in eight sectors, including such dynamic technology industries as automobile production, pharmaceuticals, and computers. It is difficult to present unambiguous information about the profitability of multinationals in Brazil and also about their impact on the balance of payments. The inflow of direct investments has been small relative to the balance of payments needs of the country. This is borne out by the fact that in the period 1977–86 the inflow of direct foreign investments fluctuated between 10 and 15% of the foreign loans obtained by Brazil. The balance of payments contribution of direct investment inflows is even smaller when one subtracts profit remittances. Reinvested earnings also represent a substantial sum of foreign direct investments. The rate of profit (reinvested earnings and remitted profits as a percentage of capital stock) of foreign firms in the 1971–90 period ranged from 16% in 1971 to 4.8% in 1980, while in the same period profit rates in the United States averaged about 12.8%.

State enterprises were dominant in public utilities, chemicals and petrochemicals, and mining. Comparing the performance of the three ownership sectors in terms of the rate of return on assets, it was found that the domestic private and multinational sectors performed much better than state firms, as shown by table 3.8 (see also table 3.9).

With the privatization process started in 1991, the ownership structure is undergoing a gradual transformation. For instance, steel used to be dominated by state enterprises, but with the privatizations of 1991–93 the sector became dominated by private domestic firms. Unlike in such countries as Chile, Argentina, and Mexico, privatization in Brazil was mainly restricted to the domestic private sector. Also privatized were various firms in the petrochemical sector. In 1994 plans were under consideration to privatize the state airplane manufacturing company (EMBRAER) and there were discussions about beginning to privatize public utilities. It thus seems that Brazil underwent a cycle: the private sector (mainly foreign) dominated public utilities prior to the 1950s,

Table 3.8. Return on Assets by Ownership, 1980–85

Ownership	1980	1981	1985
Private firms	19.1	11.1	13.1
Multinationals	15.6	18.2	16.4
State firms	2.3	10.6	2.5

Source: Melhores e Maiores, *Exame,* September 1982, p. 110; September 1986, p. 138.

Table 3.9. Stock, Flows, and Earnings of Foreign Capital, 1967–92 (US$ millions)

Year	Total Direct Investments	Direct Investments in Industry
1967	3,728	
1973	4,579	3,603
1980	17,480	13,005
1985	25,664	19,182
1990	37,143	25,729
1992	39,975	28,754

Year	Inflow of Direct Foreign Investments	Reinvestment of Earnings	Profit Remittances
1977	935		458
1978	1,196	975	564
1979	1,685	721	740
1980	1,487	411	544
1981	1,779	741	587
1982	1,370	1,557	585
1983	861	695	758
1984	1,123	472	796
1985	804	543	1,056
1986	-120	449	1,350
1987	669	617	909
1988	2,445	714	1,539
1989	678	531	2,383
1990	731	273	1,592
1991	1,185	365	665
1992	2,982	132	

Year	Rate of Profit*	Rate of Remittance**
1971	15.8	4.1
1980	5.5	3.1
1985	6.2	4.1
1986	6.0	4.5
1987	4.8	2.9
1988	7.0	4.8
1989	8.5	6.9
1990	5.0	4.3

Source: Carlos von Doelliger and Leonardo Cavalcanti, *Empresas multinacionais na indústria brasileira* (Rio de Janeiro: IPEA, 1975), pp. 89–90; Banco Central do Brasil, *Boletim*, various issues.
* Reinvested earnings + remitted profits as a % of capital stock.
** Remitted profits as a % of capital stock.

while in the ISI decades that sector was taken over by the state and the private sector (domestic and foreign) concentrated on manufacturing. As the result of the fiscal crisis of the 1980s and early 1990s, and the general world trend in diminishing the economic role of the state and maximizing the influence of market forces, Brazil was impelled to join the privatization trend (Baer and Birch 1992).

As the Brazilian state sheds its enterprises, market discipline will presumably force the private sector to increase efficiency, incorporate new technology, and refrain from monopolistic abuses. In fact, Brazilian governments have liberalized foreign trade policy, lowering tariffs, thus forcing many highly concentrated sectors to face international competition. One has to assume, of course, that in any future macroeconomic crisis the state will refrain from engaging in the type of price controls that were quite common in the 1970s and 1980s.

The issue of control, however, will come increasingly to the fore, as Brazil privatizes public utilities. These are natural monopolies, which in most countries are regulated. One of the major issues for the country's policymakers will therefore be the type of regulation that will be developed and the manner in which such regulation will be carried out. Regulation is not new to Brazil. It was prevalent in the 1930s when privately owned public utilities came under government regulation. This regulation was often applied in such a manner as to discourage investments and modernization, leading eventually to nationalization. Regulation was also responsible for the decadence of many public enterprises, as regulatory powers were used as instruments of macroeconomic policies.

As the state assumes the function of a regulator in a privatized economy, it will have to face such issues as (1) the impact of regulation on the distribution of income; (2) the extent to which regulation should take into account the need to set a price that will make it possible for the regulated firms to generate enough of a return to pay adequate dividends and to generate enough internal funds for expansion and modernization; and (3) who should do the regulating and how to avoid a situation where the regulating commission is captured by those firms that should be regulated. The answers to such issues are not easy within the institutional context of Brazil. The corporatist state that was created in the 1930s implied much regulation and control. In many cases, however, the control and regulation of specific sectors were left in the hands of institutes that came to be dominated by the groups that were supposed to be controlled. Over the decades since that time, it became obvious that in Brazil's mixed economy this access to government institutions for special favors (e.g., special credits) by the private sector was not evenly distributed. In fact, large oligopolistic groups have traditionally had special access to the state (Abreu in Baer and Conroy 1993, pp. 21–44).

Conclusion

In this chapter we have shown how periods of rapid economic growth were always led by industry after World War II. The state played a very important role in this process, both as a direct producer (through state enterprises) and by manipulating various instruments of economic policy to promote industrial growth. This strategy became known as ISI and was characterized by heavy protectionism: industry grew behind high tariff and exchange rate restriction walls. Individual sectors thus did not feel pressures to improve their productivity. Key industrial sectors also had the participation of foreign companies, attracted to Brazil by the ISI strategy and special advantages granted by the government.

In the early stages of ISI, agriculture and some other export activities were neglected. It was only later, in the late 1960s, that the government began to develop policies to diversify exports through special incentive programs and to develop programs to modernize agriculture, chiefly of crops destined for the external markets. Especially after the significant growth experienced in the 1970s, the general assessment is that ISI indeed succeeded in providing Brazil with a dynamic, diversified, though very closed, economy. As the negative aspects of the latter factor became overwhelmingly clear, Brazil began to liberalize and privatize its economy in the 1990s. The pace has been slow, but there is a definite trend to expose the economy to international market forces and thus to improve its efficiency.

We have also shown that through most of the years since World War II the Brazilian government has had difficulties in controlling government finances, resulting in recurring periods of inflation, which worsened from the 1970s on (see tables 3.10 and 3.11). Most stabilization plans until the mid-1990s failed because the government never succeeded in making the necessary fiscal adjustment. The Real Plan introduced in 1994 brought down the rate of inflation, but its continued success still depends at this writing (early 1995) on a permanent fiscal adjustment, which can only be achieved through constitutional amendments. If the liberalization and stabilization policies succeed, it is possible that the country will enter the twenty-first century as a major economic player on the world market.

It was still uncertain in the mid-1990s, however, whether a more efficient productive structure would also lead to a more equitable society. It remains to be seen whether, as a result of an extensive privatization process, the Brazilian government will have enough resources at its disposal (both financial and administrative) to make vast investments in health and education, which could lead to a more equitable distribution of the benefits of growth and development.

Table 3.10. Financing of the Public Sector, 1981–90

	1981	1982	1983	1984	1985	1986	1987	1988	1989	1990
Seigniorage (% of GDP)	1.7	1.9	1.3	2.3	2.3	3.7	2.8	3.6	5.0	4.8
Nominal net external public debt (in billions US$)	37.2	48.1	62.0	63.0	69.9	81.8	92.0	84.3	87.9	91.0
Index 1981 = 100	100	129	167	169	188	220	247	226	236	244
Real index, 1981 = 100	100	126	203	204	218	225	230	183	134	158
Net internal public debt	100	126	142	167	190	200	187	187	195	154
Real index, 1981 = 100 (excl. monetary base)	100	135	171	202	233	213	222	234	247	179
Real exchange rate	100	98	122	120	114	102	93	81	57	64

Source: Markwald 1991 , p. 118.

Table 3.11. Public Finances, 1970–90 (in % of GDP)

	1970/79	1980/82	1983/85	1986	1987/89	1990
Government						
Tax burden	25.4	24.9	23.1	25.3	22.4	28.1
Current expenditures	19.4	21.6	21.5	24.0	26.1	27.5
Personnel expenditures	7.3	6.6	6.4	7.5	8.5	10.5
Goods and services	2.9	2.9	2.9	3.5	4.6	5.1
Internal debt service	0.5	1.0	2.5	3.6	4.1	1.9
Social security	7.2	8.2	7.8	9.0	7.4	8.3
Subsidies	1.5	3.0	1.9	1.5	1.6	1.7
Current savings	5.4	2.1	0.6	-0.7	-1.1	3.5
Gross fixed capital formation	3.7	2.5	2.0	3.0	3.1	3.5
State enterprises						
Personnel	–	2.2	1.9	2.0	2.9	2.3
Investment	–	4.9	3.4	2.8	3.0	1.8
Financial needs of public sector						
Primary deficit(-) or surplus (+)	–	-2.5	2.8	1.6	-0.3	4.5
External and internal	–	-4.3	-6.6	-5.2	-5.5	-3.3
Interest payments						
Operational deficit (-) or surplus (+)	–	-6.8	-3.8	-3.6	-5.8	1.2

Source: Markwald 1991, p. 116.

Works Cited

Abreu, Marcelo de Paiva, ed. 1990. *A ordem do progresso: Cem anos de política econômica republicana, 1889–1989*. Rio de Janeiro: Editora Campus.

Baer, Werner. 1969. *The Development of the Brazilian Steel Industry*. Nashville, Tenn.: Vanderbilt University Press.

———. 1995. *The Brazilian Economy: Growth and Development*. 4th ed. Westport, Conn.: Praeger.

Baer, Werner, and Melissa Birch. 1992. Privatization and the Changing Role of the State in Latin America. *Journal of International Law and Politics* 25(1).

Baer, Werner, and Michael E. Conroy, eds. 1993. *Latin America: Privatization, Property Rights, and Deregulation I*. Special edition of the *Quarterly Review of Economics and Finance* 33.

Baer, Werner, and Claudio Paiva. 1994. Brazil's Drifting Economy: Stagnation and Inflation during 1987–93. Paper presented at the Montreal Conference on Latin America and the International Economic System in the 1990s: Macro-Level Adjustment Policies and Their Alternatives, April.

Baklanoff, Eric N., ed. 1969. *The Shaping of Modern Brazil*. Baton Rouge: Louisiana State University Press.

Barzelay, Michael. 1986. *The Politicized Market Economy: Alcohol in Brazil's Energy Strategy*. Berkeley: University of California Press.

Cavalcanti de Albuquerque, Roberto, and Renato Villela. 1992. Condicionantes econômicas e políticas. In João Paulo dos Reis Velloso, ed., *Estratégia social e desenvolvimento*. Rio de Janeiro: Jose Olympio Editora.

Conjuntura econômica.

Fishlow, Albert, 1972a. Brazilian Size Distribution of Income. *American Economic Review* 62(May).

———. 1972b. Origins and Consequences of Import Substitution in Brazil. In Luis E. Di Marco, ed., *International Economics and Development*. New York: Academic Press.

Furtado, Celso. 1972. *Formação econômica do Brasil*. 11th ed. São Paulo: Companhia Editora Nacional.

IGBE. 1990. *Estatísticas históricas do Brasil*. Rio de Janeiro: IGBE.

———. 1992. *Anuario estatístico do Brasil 1992*. Rio de Janeiro: IGBE.

Markwald, Ricardo A. 1991. Ajuste fiscal e estabilização. In *Perspectivas da economia brasileira 1992*. Brasília: IPEA.

Melhores e Maiores. August 1991, September 1982, September 1986. *Exame*.

Mueller, Charles C. 1992. Agriculture, Urban Bias Development and the Environment: The Case of Brazil. Paper presented at the conference Resources and Environmental Management in an Interdependent World, organized by Resources for the Future and held in San José, Costa Rica, January 22–24.

Paiva, Claudio. 1993. The Collor Plan: Two Alternative Interpretations. M.A. thesis. Champaign: University of Illinois.

Randall, Laura. 1993. *The Political Economy of Brazilian Oil*. Westport, Conn.: Praeger.

Rocha, Sônio, and Hamilton Tolosa. 1993. Metropolização da pobreza: Uma análise núcleo-periféria. In *Perspectivas da economia brasileira, 1994*, vol. 2.

Rio de Janeiro: IPEA.

Villela, Annibal V., and Werner Baer. 1980. *O setor privado nacional: Problemas e políticas para seu fortalecimento.* Coleção Relatórios de Pesquisa, 46. Rio de Janeiro: IPEA.

Villela, Annibal V., and Wilson Suzigan. 1973. *Política do govêrno e crescimento da economia brasileira, 1889–1945.* Rio de Janeiro: IPEA.

von Doellinger, Carlos. 1991. Reordenação do sistema financeiro. In *Perspectivas da economia brasileira, 1992.* Brasília: IPEA.

World Bank. Several years. *Human Development Report.* New York: Oxford University Press.

——. Several years. *World Development Report.* New York: Oxford University Press.

4.
Mexico

Miguel Ramírez
Trinity College, Hartford, Connecticut

The first section of this chapter gives an overview of the institutional origins and functions of the modern Mexican state. Particular emphasis is placed on the formal and informal mechanisms created by the state during the 1920s and 1930s to assist the process of private capital formation while, at the same time, legitimizing its policies to key sectors of Mexican society. The following section reviews the high rate of economic growth and performance achieved by the Mexican economy from 1940 to 1970 under the general strategy of import substitution industrialization (ISI). Section three examines both the nature of the interrelated economic and distributional problems arising from the excessive pursuit of ISI during the late sixties and seventies and how they manifested themselves in rising political discontent and a rapid polarization of society, thus paving the way for the pursuit of populist policies under the administration of Luis Echeverría Álvarez (1970–76) and, to some extent, that of José López Portillo (1976–82). The fourth section discusses the economic and social effects of the stabilization and adjustment program implemented during the 1983–88 period, with particular emphasis on the impact of the internal adjustment process on real minimum wages, employment creation, the distribution of income, public finances, and the rate and composition of capital formation.

The final section brings the chapter to a close by examining recent economic events, including a critical discussion of the growing macroeconomic imbalances that led to the economic and financial debacle of 1994–95. This section also examines the impact of privatization on public sector finances and the ownership structure of the banking sector; reviews how the liberalization of trade in basic foodstuffs may affect rural-urban migration; focuses on the problems associated with opening the economy to foreign capital, such as an overreliance on highly liquid foreign investment; and, finally, highlights the potential long-term costs associated with the unprecedented reduction in the nation's public investment in essential economic and social infrastructure.

Hermosillo

Chihuahua

MEXICO

Gulf of Mexico

Durango

Monterrey

Mazatlán

Tampico

Guadalajara

Mexico City

Mérida

Veracruz

Puebla de Zaragoza

Acapulco

Oaxaca

Pacific Ocean

| 600 | 0 | 600 | 1200 | Miles |

Capital
Major Rivers
Major Cities
National Boundary
Countries

N

W E

S

The Interventionist State: An Overview

The origins of active government participation in the Mexican economy can be traced to the triple alliance of the state, the landed elites, and foreign capital forged during the regime of military strongman Porfirio Díaz (1876–1911). The rapid economic growth the country experienced under a program of economic liberalism, however, came at a heavy cost in the form of growing inequality in the distribution of land ownership, mounting social problems, and foreign control of mining, banking, and basic industry.

Insofar as foreign ownership and control of basic industry are concerned, Mexican economist Miguel S. Wionczek observed that "in the last decades of the nineteenth century the British still held commercial and industrial pre-eminence in Mexico, and thus it was the British and the Canadians rather than the Americans who gave the initial impetus to the development of the country's power resources, while U.S. capital showed preference for mining and railroads. . . . By the end of the Porfirio Díaz era . . . the foreign companies controlled the most profitable concessions for hydroelectric power generation, having either received these concessions directly from the Díaz government or bought them from their domestic owners" (Wionczek 1964, pp. 22–23).

Similar foreign penetration and control of other key sectors of the economy such oil and refining (United States and Britain), railroads (United States and Britain), textiles (France and Spain), and copper and zinc mining (United States) gave rise to a popular saying among Mexicans at the time: "*Mexico*, mother of foreigners and stepmother of Mexicans." By 1910 the country's growing political instability and sharp polarization of income and wealth, coupled with a growing resentment and suspicion of foreigners, culminated in the 1910–17 Revolution (Keen 1992, pp. 214–20; Harber 1989; Ramírez 1989, ch. 2; Meyer and Sherman 1987). The reformist articles of the constitution of 1917 defined the modern Mexican state, reaffirming the state's role on behalf of the newly organized peasants, workers, and small businessmen (Meyer and Sherman 1987, pp. 542–45). This process was formalized during the late 1920s and the 1930s with the creation of peasant, labor, and popular sectors within the official party, the Party of the Mexican Revolution (PMR), as well as through the establishment of informal ties to business chambers such as the National Chambers of Commerce and Industry (CANACOMIN) (Cypher 1990, ch. 3; Maxfield 1990, chs. 2 and 3).

From an economic standpoint, the most significant development of the period was the creation of a highly pragmatic orientation toward the emerging private sector. First, primary reliance would be placed on the private sector, but the state stood ready to undertake those projects that the private sector was financially unable and/or unwilling to take on through the creation of state-owned firms. Second, the state would perform a leading role in financing and guiding the process of private capital formation via the establishment of key financial institutions such as the Banco de México, the agricultural development banks, and the country's first industrial development bank, Nacional Financiera, S.A. (NAFINSA) (Ramírez 1986; Aubey 1966; Brothers and Solís 1966; Bennet 1965). Finally, the state would reassert its sovereignty vis-à-vis foreign companies and nations that sought to intervene in the internal economic and political affairs of the nation.

At no time was the legitimating function of the Mexican state more in evidence than during the administration of Lázaro Cárdenas (1934–40). The Cárdenas regime used the institutional and legal apparatus of the state to consolidate its power base and mobilize the peasantry, the emerging industrial working class, and small businessmen against entrenched landed, commercial, and foreign interests that threatened to undermine the goals of the Revolution. The legitimation function was fulfilled via a far-reaching agrarian reform program that emphasized the ejido (a rural-based system under which the government owned land; the right to farm it often was given to indigenous communities that, in some cases, cultivated the land collectively, but more often than not parceled the communal holdings to individual families or *ejidatarios* for private cultivation) and the creation of the state oil monopoly, Petróleos Mexicanos (PEMEX), primarily designed to strengthen the economic and political power of the state (Hamilton and Harding 1986). With the election of Manuel Ávila Camacho to the presidency in 1940, the Mexican state aided private capital formation, forging an alliance with the nation's emerging capitalist class.

This class consisted of small and medium-sized businesses specializing in a wide variety of products ranging from electronic appliances and consumer durables to metal products, lumber, textiles, sugar, and cement. They were grouped under semiautonomous organizations such as the Cámara Nacional de Industria de la Transformación (CANACINTRA) and the Confederación Nacional de Cámaras de Pequeño Comercio. To a large extent, these businesses owed their very existence to the import substitution industrialization (ISI) policies pursued by the state during the forties, fifties, and sixties. These policies included extensive import licensing, quotas, overvalued exchange rates, subsidized long-term credit to selected industrial sectors, price supports, and high average tariff rates designed to channel resources in a different direction from that which would have occurred under a more market-based or laissez-faire strategy (Barkin 1990; Ramírez 1989, ch. 3).

Thus, as opposed to the more established and ideologically conservative segments of the business community, represented by the Confederation of Employers of the Mexican Republic (COPARMEX)—which represented "old" money in Mexico in the form of hacienda agriculture, commercial, and banking interests—the new groups thrived in highly protected markets that were guaranteed high profit rates through direct and indirect subsidies, protectionist policies, and the state's massive investments in infrastructure, basic industry, and capitalist agriculture. These investments generated substantial positive spillover effects for the emerging manufacturing sector by reducing its overall costs of transportation, communication, energy, capital inputs, and intermediate products; in the capitalist agricultural sector, on the other hand, public investments initially gave a boost to overall agricultural productivity by lowering its costs for fertilizers, hybrid seeds, irrigation networks, and marketing and distribution costs at the wholesale and retail level (Barkin 1990).

The Mexican government's commitment to the industrialization effort, via its support of gross capital formation, is clearly shown by table 4.1. For example, throughout the administrations of Ávila Camacho (1940–46) and Miguel Alemán (1946–52), the public sector's share of total gross investment expenditures averaged between 50.7% and 66%, even reaching a level of 70.7% in 1943—second only to the figure recorded in 1956. This initial phase in Mexico's industrialization also witnessed a significant increase in the growth of public enterprises as a result of the industrial promotional policies of NAFINSA. As the public sector's major industrial development bank, it financed enterprises in almost every sector of the Mexican economy, including the vast Altos Hornos steel complex, despite the fact that it faced determined opposition from powerful industrial groups such as the Monterrey-based Garza-Sada family (the most powerful and influential member of COPARMEX) (Luna et al. 1987).

Economic Growth and Performance of the Economy under ISI, 1940–72

Mexico in the post–World War II period continued its state-led strategy of establishing manufacturing sectors to produce what was formerly imported (see table 4.1). With the memory of the world depression of the 1930s still fresh on their minds, policymakers thought that import substitution industrialization would lessen the dependence of developing countries like Mexico on the markets and technology of the developed nations. In addition Mexican officials—who were influenced by the structuralist ideas of the Argentine economist Raúl Prebisch and the Economic Commission for Latin America (CEPAL)—subscribed to the notion that the use of primary exports to facilitate development was

**Table 4.1. Participation of the State in the Process of Capital
Formation, 1940–90** (as a percentage of total gross fixed capital
formation)

Year	Percent	Year	Percent	Year	Percent	Year	Percent
1940	49	1953	63	1966	31	1979	45
1941	42	1954	61	1967	36	1980	43
1942	65	1955	66	1968	36	1981	45
1943	71	1956	72	1969	36	1982	44
1944	61	1957	70	1970	35	1983	39
1945	50	1958	70	1971	27	1984	37
1946	37	1959	68	1972	34	1985	36
1947	40	1960	65	1973	39	1986	34
1948	42	1961	58	1974	37	1987	30
1949	44	1962	57	1975	43	1988	28
1950	58	1963	55	1976	41	1989	27
1951	64	1964	55	1977	41	1990	26
1952	64	1965	30	1978	46	1991	23

Period	Average Participation (in percent)
1940–49	50
1950–59	66
1960–69	46
1970–79	39
1980–85	41
1986–90	29

Source: Computed from NAFINSA 1978, pp. 19–45; 1986, tables 3.1 and 3.2, pp.
68–70; and 1992.

exhausted; therefore, they reasoned that import substituting industrialization was the only way to avoid the recurrent foreign exchange crises
brought about by the excessive fluctuation and long-term deterioration
in the country's terms of trade (the price of exports divided by the price
of imports) (Kay 1989, chs. 1–2). More important, Mexican policymakers
viewed ISI as an instrument to broaden the domestic market through the
creation of new industries, generate needed employment for the growing
number of rural migrants, and, ultimately, provide the basis for the
creation of a capital goods sector—the key element in the transition from
a peripheral to a semi-industrialized economy.

The initial, or "easy," phase of ISI (which lasted until 1954) began with
the administration of Ávila Camacho (1940–46) and consisted primarily
of promoting projects in the nondurable consumer goods industries
characterized by a high rate of return and a short-payout period. This

"take-off" into industrialization was facilitated by the high wartime demand in the United States for Mexican mineral products and strategic raw materials such as agricultural goods, petroleum, and rubber. It also received considerable impetus from the fact that the industrialized countries had redirected their output toward war production, thus enabling the Mexican state and domestic manufacturers to supply the consumer needs of a growing and captive domestic market (Hansen 1971a).

The industrialization process begun in 1940 resulted in rapid rates of economic growth that few countries in the world have been able to match. For example, during the 1940–46 period the country's real GDP (measured in pesos of 1960 purchasing power) grew at an average annual rate of 6.2%, while per capita output rose at an impressive rate of 3.3% (Nacional Financiera 1978, p. 1945) The performance of the industrial sector, particularly manufacturing and construction, was no less impressive, with an average yearly growth rate of 6.3%; and although agricultural output lagged behind, it was still a full 1.7 percentage points above the population growth rate. The high rates of economic growth and industrial output continued into the subsequent administrations of Miguel Alemán (1946–52) and Adolfo Ruiz Cortines (1952–58), with the added benefit of a significant improvement in the performance of the agricultural sector. The latter development was the result of the state's heavy investments in irrigation projects and social infrastructure to assist commercial farmers to cultivate thousands of acres of formerly desert land, mostly in the northern region of the country (Barkin 1987, pp. 271–97). As can be seen from table 4.1, this also explains the dramatic increase in the state's participation in the process of capital formation from 63% of the total in 1953 to 72% in 1956.

The Mexican economy experienced a substantial structural transformation of its various sectors, both during the initial phase of ISI (1940–54) and in the subsequent period, known as Stabilizing Development (1955–70). Table 4.2 shows that shifts in the composition of output and employment reflected the government's commitment to industrialization. In 1940 the agricultural sector employed 65.5% of the economically active population (EAP) and accounted for 19.4% of total output; by 1970 it employed no more than 37.5% of the economically active population and its output share had fallen to 11.6%. Meanwhile, the industrial sector's contribution to output rose steadily from 25% in 1940 to 29.2% in 1960 and 34.4% in 1970, while its share of the EAP increased from 15.5% in 1940 to 23.1% in 1970, which was not enough to provide employment opportunities for the majority of the people entering the labor force (Sassen 1992, pp. 14–20; Weintraub 1989, pp. 179–99). Productivity in this sector, as measured by the average product per

Table 4.2. Economic Indicators, 1940–90 (percentages)

	GDP by Sector			EAP by Sector		
Year	Agriculture	Industry	Services	Agriculture	Industry	Services
1940	19.4	25.0	55.6	65.5	15.5	19.0
1950	19.2	27.0	53.8	58.0	16.0	26.0
1960	15.9	29.2	54.9	54.0	19.0	27.0
1970	11.6	34.4	54.0	37.5	23.1	39.4
1980	9.0	35.2	55.8	26.3	23.5	50.1
1985	9.4	34.9	55.7	26.0	21.0	53.0
1990	8.0	36.4	55.6	25.4	22.4	52.2

Sources: Computed from NAFINSA 1978, pp. 33–34 and 44–45; NAFINSA 1986, p. 42, table 2.5; and OECD 1995, p. 176, table M.

person, gave further evidence of industry's dynamism, particularly manufacturing and construction, rising at a brisk average annual rate of 4.3% during the fifties and sixties. Finally, table 4.2 indicates that the output share of the services sector remained steady over the period under review, but the EAP employed in this sector of the economy rose dramatically, from 19% of total employment in 1940 to 39.4% in 1970, thus reflecting low overall productivity in this sector or disguised unemployment.

The rapid growth rate and structural transformation of the Mexican economy led to inflation that, as measured by the consumer price index for Mexico City, averaged over 14% during the six-year term of Ávila Camacho and continued to plague the subsequent administration of Miguel Alemán with close to double-digit levels (Nacional Financiera 1978, pp. 19–45). The inflationary pressures were fueled initially by high wartime demand; it was not until the government abruptly changed its monetary and financial policies in 1955 that the inflation problem was brought under control (Hansen 1971b, pp. 50–51).

Stabilizing Development, 1955–70

By the mid-1950s the Mexican state had shifted its emphasis in policy from capital formation to economic stability. The precipitating factor was a sharp devaluation of the peso in 1954, which resulted from the collapse in commodity exports during 1953 (the direct outcome of the end of the Korean War). The Mexican business elite, particularly those powerful groups affiliated with COPARMEX, viewed the devaluation as a sign of the government's inability to handle the economic crisis. The marked erosion in private sector confidence led to a fall in private sector investment, an increase in capital flight, and harsh and outspoken criticism of the government's policies by leading representatives of powerful and influential business associations such as the Confederación de Cámaras Industriales (CONCAMIN; large industrial capital), the Confederación de Cámaras Nacionales de Comercio (CONCANACO; large commercial and retail capital), COPARMEX, and the ABM (Mexican Banking Association) (Cypher 1990, pp. 59–73; Hansen 1971b). Interestingly enough, members of CANACINTRA refrained from criticizing the government's import substituting industrialization policies in public since they had benefited considerably from them during the first phase of industrialization (Mosk 1950, pp. 21–62).

In the wake of these criticisms, the administration of Adolfo Ruiz Cortines (1952–58) decided to grant a higher priority to price stability while at the same time maintaining its commitment to investments in social infrastructure and basic industry. However, rather than strengthening the country's public finances by overhauling its inefficient and regressive tax system (which would have further antagonized the private sector), the state decided to (1) compel private deposit banks and private development banks to supply the new financing required by the government and (2) increase the public sector's reliance on external funds. The former objective was achieved via the Banco de México's extensive control over the reserve requirements of the private banking system. Basically, it induced privately owned banks and other financial institutions (e.g., private *financieras*, or development banks) to meet their reserve requirement ratios by buying government bonds and/or issues of public enterprises. Failure to comply with these government-mandated requirements meant that any additional funds raised by the private banks were subject to a 100% legal reserve requirement (Ramírez 1986, pp. 103–11; Basch 1968, pp. 29–55).

The implementation of these policies led to remarkable price stability and economic growth. For example, during the sixties the country's inflation rate was brought below 3%, while industrial output accelerated to unprecedented rates of well over 8% (Nacional Financiera 1978, pp. 19–45). Domestic private capital formation also responded favorably to the Mexican government's tax exemptions, investments in economic infrastructure, and credit subsidies, as attested by the rise in its share in total output from 14.3% in 1955 to 23% in 1970. Last, Mexican policymakers maintained a low ratio of government budget deficits to total output during the stabilizing period, rarely exceeding 2.5%.

The reduction in the inflation rate, along with the extensive use of selective controls to finance the public sector deficits, drove up real interest rates as "free" loanable funds became scarcer. The higher rates not only stimulated domestic private savings, but also served to attract foreign financial capital in search of peso-denominated bonds, which, under the government's fixed rate of 12.5 pesos to the dollar, could be converted into dollars at any time. This helped to offset any "crowding-out" of private sector investment that might otherwise have taken place, and it was instrumental in financing the ever-growing current account deficits the country began to experience after 1962. In short, the pursuit of Stabilizing Development by the Mexican government enabled it to minimize the inflationary effects of deficit financing and avoid a direct clash with powerful factions of the private sector, who feared its inverventionist role (Solís and Ortiz 1977, pp. 518–48).

The Echeverría Years: The Reemergence of the Populist State

The administration of Luis Echeverría Álvarez (1970–76) had the unfortunate task of dealing with a number of interrelated economic, social, and political problems. The Stabilizing Development period (1955–70) did not produce a more equitable distribution of the benefits of growth, nor a balanced pattern of employment creation or sectoral productivity growth. On the contrary, the Mexican state by pursuing a development strategy that emphasized high rates of capital formation at the expense of redistribution and balanced agricultural development had generated social and economic problems such as rising unemployment and under-employment, highly uneven productivity levels between sectors of the economy, and chronic current account imbalances that could no longer be ignored by members of the ruling party, the Institutional Revolutionary party (PRI) (Purcell 1977, pp. 173–92). Chief among these structural problems was the country's significant deterioration in the share of income and wealth held by the poorest Mexicans. Table 4.3 shows that in 1963 the poorest 40% of the country's families received only 11.7% of the national income, while the upper 20% received 54.2% of the national income. By 1975 the already meager share of the bottom 40% of the families had fallen to 8.3%, while the upper 20%'s share had risen to 60%. Not surprisingly, the Gini coefficient rose from 0.534 in 1963 to 0.57 in 1975.

After 1975 the distribution of income in Mexico improved significantly, primarily as a result of the oil-induced boom of the late seventies and early eighties and agricultural development programs such as the Sistema Alimentario Mexicano (SAM), targeted to help the poorest segments of society. Table 4.3 shows that the share of income received by the bottom two quintiles increased from 8.3% in 1975 to 14.3% in 1984, while the upper 20%'s proportion of income actually fell to 49.5% in 1984—a drop of more than 10 points in less than a decade and the first time that the share of the top quintile had fallen below 50%. However, most of the improvement in the distribution of income during this period can be attributed to a redistribution of income within the upper

Table 4.3. Income Distribution by Quintile, 1963–92
(in percentage of total national income)

Household	1963	1968	1975	1984	1989	1992
I	4.6	3.5	2.0	4.8	4.4	4.3
II	7.1	7.3	6.3	9.5	8.4	8.4
III	11.9	11.5	11.8	14.3	13.2	12.8
IV	22.2	19.7	19.9	21.9	20.4	20.3
V	54.2	58.0	60.0	49.5	53.5	54.2

Sources: Obtained from Jesús Alejandro Cervantes, *México: Análisis de la distribución del ingreso, Comercio Exterior* 32 (1) (January 1982): 43 (table 1); Secretaría de Programación y Presupuesto (SPP), *La distribución del ingreso y del gasto familiar en México, 1977* (Mexico City: SPP, 1979); Instituto Nacional de Estadística Geográfica e Informática (INEGI), *Income and Expenditure Survey of Households (Encuesta nacional de ingresos y gastos de hogares)* (Mexico City: INEGI, 1992), p. 110, table 27; and *OECD Economic Surveys:* Mexico (Paris: OECD, 1995), p. 101, table 23.

and middle income families rather than a change in the overall trend toward income concentration. Between 1984 and 1989 the concentration in the distribution of income became increasingly skewed, reverting to its historical trend. For example, the share of the top 20% of Mexican families rose from 49.5% in 1984 to 53.5% in 1989. This marked reversal in the gains of the late seventies can be partially explained by the onset of the debt crisis and the implementation of austerity measures and neoliberal reforms whose burden has fallen disproportionately on the country's poor—the great majority of the Mexican people.

The excessive promotion of ISI accompanied by its capital-intensive pattern of industrialization, highly inequitable distribution of income and wealth, and limited employment opportunities was aggravated by a number of policies.

1. The emerging industrial sector enjoyed high rates of effective protection. By 1960 the Mexican state had erected a tariff structure with a pronounced antiexport bias that provided consumer goods with the greatest level of effective protection, followed by intermediate inputs and capital goods. During the sixties the manufacturing sector received nominal protection (for the finished good) of 35% and effective protection of 74%; these figures compared favorably with the level of protection between 3.9 and 6.7% received by the agricultural sector (Villarreal 1977, pp. 67–108).

2. Overvalued exchange rates made dollars and imports inexpensive.

The government's policy of fixing the exchange rate at 12.5 pesos per dollar during the 1954–76 period acted as a de facto subsidy for the importation of capital-intensive goods in the emerging industrial sector.

3. Extensive import permits also played an important role in biasing enterprises toward imports of capital inputs and intermediate products. The percentage of total imports subject to import permits rose from 25% in 1956 to 60% in 1965, 80% in 1970, and 100% in 1975 (Zabludovsky 1990, pp. 173–202)!

4. Cheap credit policies implicitly subsidized the importation by Mexican businesses and their foreign associates of state-of-the-art capital goods and equipment. They incorporated capital-intensive technologies, and their importation took place at the expense of domestic labor and capital. Ann D. Witte has estimated that these policies led the effective price of capital in Mexico relative to labor to decline at an average annual rate of 5% during the fifties and sixties, and the share of total income going to owners of capital averaged 69% during the 1955–70 period, while that received by labor averaged only 31% (Witte 1971).

Despite the sought-after reduction in import growth from 1950 to 1970, the antiexport bias of the government's policies led to an even greater reduction in exports, so the country began to experience ever-growing current account deficits from the mid-sixties onward (see table 4.4; Nacional Financiera 1978, pp. 397–98). In part, this was a direct outcome of the end of the so-called easy phase of ISI, viz., the disappearance of high-yield, short-payout projects in the nondurable consumer goods industry. As the country began to replace imports of intermediate and durable consumer goods with domestic products, the higher capital-output ratios of the new projects set a limit to the further reduction in the ratio of imports to GDP. The extent of this dependence was so pronounced that by 1970 four-fifths of Mexican imports were intermediate or capital goods (Reynolds 1970, p. 190; Villarreal 1977, pp. 71–73). Moreover, the structural inability and/or reluctance of the state to raise needed revenues for the industrialization effort drove it to a greater reliance on external sources of funds to cover its rapidly growing current account imbalances during the sixties (Hansen 1971b, pp. 50–51).

ISI was supposed to decrease the economic dependence of Mexico on the industrialized countries. Instead, it only altered the nature of the dependency toward technologically sophisticated imports of machinery and equipment that could only be supplied by relatively few and large foreign firms (mostly U.S. in origin). Moreover, many of the domestic managers of the ISI enterprises in the higher stages of manufacturing lacked the necessary experience, organizational skills, and technological background to start and sustain these complicated types of production processes—not to mention their relative inability to advertise and

Table 4.4. Selected External Indicators, 1940–80

Item	1940	1950	1960	1970	1975	1980
Shares (%)						
Exports/GDP	6.3	9.7	6.1	4.3	4.3	9.1
Imports/GDP	8.8	11.8	9.8	7.8	10.0	14.3

Growth rates (average annual rates, %)					
	1940–50	1950–60	1960–70	1970–75	1975–80
Exports of goods and services	12.3	4.5	6.7	12.7	12.2
Imports of goods and services	8.2	6.0	8.7	15.9	14.0

Growth Rates (average annual rates, %)					
	1955–60	1960–65	1965–70	1970–75	1975–80
Total imports	6.8	5.7	8.3	7.9	16.0
Consumer goods	11.8	7.5	9.6	8.0	23.1
Intermediate goods	4.7	6.7	7.2	11.4	15.0
Capital goods	8.7	5.1	9.0	7.3	15.1

Source: Computed from NAFINSA 1978 and 1986.

market the respective products generated from these processes. Foreign firms were therefore encouraged, under a variety of state-sponsored financial and economic incentives, to supply these essential services by entering into joint ventures with domestic private partners and the state. In so doing, state policy actually increased Mexico's economic vulnerability vis-à-vis the industrialized nations by extending foreign control over the production process of the more dynamic branches of domestic industry (Bennett and Sharpe 1982, pp. 169–211). If the problems enumerated above were not enough, the Echeverría administration faced a legitimation crisis stemming from the political conflict that had engulfed the nation following the 1968 Tlatelolco student massacre at the hands of government troops—a few days before the start of the Olympic Games. It must be remembered that Echeverría himself, who had been secretary of the interior in the previous administration, was directly involved in the events leading up to October 2, 1968. To make matters worse, the rising political discontent and sharpening social conflict that emerged in the aftermath of the crisis of 1968 also manifested itself in "the possibility of a [rural] guerrilla movement developing at a time when leftist ideology was significantly more important in Latin America than it is today" (Bazdresch and Levy 1991, p. 237). The Echeverría administration was thus under immense pressure to find a negotiated solution to the political and social crisis confronting the nation (Barkin 1985, pp. 106–27).

Rather than deciding between promoting industrialization or redistributing the country's wealth, the Echeverría administration decided to do both at the expense of monetary and financial stability. Beginning in 1972 it embarked upon a populist program designed to increase the "social wage" (i.e., housing, health, and education) while, at the same time, accelerating the process of state-assisted import substitution in the core or strategic sector of the economy. "Shared growth" had arrived with its twin objectives of diminishing the country's political and social tensions while also fostering rapid economic growth and profits. To accomplish these objectives the state's role and size in the economy increased dramatically. For example, its share in total investment rose from 27% in 1971 to 43% in 1975 (see table 4.1; Bazdresch and Levy 1991, p. 283).

The 160 public enterprises created during the six-year term of Echeverría was greater than the 103 established between 1952 and 1970 (Bazdresch and Levy 1991, p. 242). The total number of public enterprises (including those with a minority participation by the state and public trust funds) rose sharply from almost 300 in 1972 to over 600 in 1977—a level that would not be surpassed until 1981 (Cypher 1990, p. 97; Ferrer 1990, p. 40).

The sheer number of state enterprises created during the Echeverría regime suggested a clear shift toward statism, and it was so perceived by powerful business associations such as COPARMEX (the coordinating body of the Monterrey-based industrialists and financiers), CONCAMIN (large industrial capital), CONCANACO (large commercial capital), and ABM (Cypher 1990; Hamilton 1984, pp. 148–74). They interpreted the administration's pursuit of a "shared growth" strategy, along with its stern criticisms of the business community, as an attempt to break the implicit political pact that had been forged between the government and business during the Stabilizing Development period. Only the moderate segment of the business community, primarily the owners of small and medium-sized businesses grouped under CANACINTRA, CNPP (National Confederation of Small Property Owners), and CNPC (National Confederation of Chambers of Small Commerce) welcomed, if not publicly, the government's increased participation in the economy (Luna and Valdés 1987, pp. 13–43).

A careful reading of the investment data also suggests that the business sector as a whole initially responded favorably to the state's increased rate of investment in infrastructure and basic industry. These investments lowered the overall transportation, distribution, and marketing costs of the private sector (Ramírez, 1991, pp. 425–38). For example, the growth rate in real private investment expenditures rose from 2.5% in 1972 to 3% in 1973 and 11.4% in 1974, before falling to 2% in 1975. In absolute terms, total real private capital formation increased from 64.7 billion pesos in 1972 to 77.6 billion in 1975 (Bazdresch and Levy 1991, p. 243). These figures suggest that, despite the business sector's growing criticism of the regime's populist policies, it was not until after 1974, when inflation was becoming a serious problem, that business-state relations began to deteriorate significantly.

Perhaps no single factor contributed more to straining business-state relations than tax reform legislation. As early as 1970 the Echeverría administration had tried—and failed—to implement a small tax reform bill in the form of a 1% increase in the sales tax rate. President Echeverría himself was reprimanded by the then leader of COPARMEX, who "called on the president to say that this was not the way policy was done, and that tax matters had to be negotiated directly with the private sector" (Bazdresch and Levy 1991, p. 239). Subsequent attempts by the administration to reform the tax system in 1972 and 1975 by increasing and/or placing taxes on high-income groups were roundly defeated. If the government could increase its revenue base, then it could pursue its program of "shared development" without being constrained by the implicit veto of powerful domestic creditors represented by the ABM. From this perspective, it is perfectly understandable why the Echeverría regime, unable to secure a reliable and steady stream of domestically generated revenues via tax reform and unwilling to increase its rate of domestic indebtedness to powerful banking groups, turned to foreign borrowing. Fortunately for the administration, the emergence of the Eurocurrency market and the 1973 oil shock led to capital markets flush with petrodollar deposits in search of willing borrowers (Cypher 1990, p. 100).

Nonetheless, government deficits rose beyond the capacity of the government to cover them via increased external indebtedness, so the Banco de México supplied the public sector's ever-growing need for financing. During the last three years of the Echeverría administration inflation averaged 20.4% and real yields on long-term bonds became negative, which, in turn, discouraged private domestic saving and encouraged capital flight (Nacional Financiera 1978, pp. 19–45). As a result, the peso became increasingly overvalued, contributing to a pronounced deterioration of the country's current account balance beginning in 1974.

Despite Mexico's growing internal and external deficits, the Echeverría administration could not abandon its strategy of shared development. Having lost considerable support in the business community and among certain segments of the middle class that were hurt by inflation, it would have been political suicide for the government to alienate its base of support in organized labor and the peasantry through drastic spending cuts and devaluation. Consequently, in order to finance its various programs, the public sector increased its rate of external indebtedness.

During the last year of the Echeverría administration the economic and political situation of the country took a turn for the worse, as inflationary pressures intensified, the growth rate in GDP fell, capital flight skyrocketed, and the country's major business associations mounted, through the creation of a new umbrella organization, the Consejo Coordinador Empresarial (CCE), a concerted offensive against the state's populist policies. The strained relations between the government and powerful factions of the private sector generated an increasingly acrimonious public debate that descended to the level of unprecedented personal attacks on the president. For his part, Echeverría lashed back at his critics in the business elite by calling them "questionable Christians and profound reactionaries who are the enemies of the people" (Cypher 1990, p. 106). He even ordered the state to expropriate large tracts of fertile agricultural land belonging to members of COPARMEX in the northern state of Sonora. By the third quarter of 1976, it became apparent to government officials that export revenues had failed to increase as expected and that the Central Bank's reserves were depleted. Increasing speculation against the peso and led to a flight of capital from the country, which reached a level of $4 billion during 1976 (Solís 1982, p. 344). Faced with no alternatives, the Echeverría administration devalued the peso in September of that year to 19.95 pesos per dollar from 12.5 pesos—a rate that had been nominally fixed since 1954—and signed a three-year austerity agreement with the IMF in exchange for a stabilization loan of $1.2 billion (Street 1978, p. 102).

The López Portillo Years

The López Portillo administration had the difficult task of implementing the IMF-sponsored stabilization and adjustment program. It called for a sharp decrease in the public-sector deficit to 6% of GDP, an overall ceiling on annual wage increases of no more than 10%, systematic devaluations of the peso to maintain domestic prices in line with external ones, and trade liberalization in the form of a replacement of quantitative restrictions and permits with tariffs. The administration sought to restore the confidence of the business sector by publicly condemning the profligate ways of the previous regime and supporting legislation and policies that directly benefited the private sector.

These measures generated the usual deflationary results, namely, a drop in the rate of real GDP growth to 3.4%—barely ahead of the population growth rate of 3.1%; a sharp decrease in the government's deficit to a level well below that targeted by the IMF; a reduction in the rate of inflation in 1977 to 20.7% (from 27.2% the year before); and an increase in the international reserves of the Central Bank to over $500 million, from $320.9 million the previous year. As is often the case with these programs, the burden of the adjustment fell most heavily on the working class and poor. Real minimum wages, which had risen steadily between 1972 and 1975, experienced a sharp cumulative drop of 12.2% in 1976–77 (Ramírez 1989, pp. 85–86). To make matters worse, the urban unemployment rate jumped from 6.7% in 1976 to 8.3% by the end of 1977.

Beginning in 1978, the IMF stabilization program was shelved by the López Portillo administration. The discovery of vast oil and gas reserves in southeastern Mexico and their rapid exploitation increased government revenues and reduced the financial constraint on state spending and thus had the effect of postponing or canceling the implementation of structural reforms. President López Portillo and his advisors saw in oil a historic opportunity for the state to secure a reliable source of revenues with which to reaffirm its leading role in the economy. They felt relatively immune to the vagaries of private investment and therefore in a position to pursue their ambitious policy objectives without facing "the same kind of blackmail (through capital flight) experienced by Echeverría" (Bazdresch and Levy 1991, p. 248).

The process, which had already been well under way during 1979, was formalized in the first quarter of 1980 with the administration's Global Development Plan. It called for massive investments by the state in the petroleum, steel, chemical, and capital goods industries and for sustained increases in employment and income for Mexico's rapidly expanding population. Real government spending on economic projects rose at an average annual rate of 28% during 1979–81, compared to a rate of 14.3% in 1978–79, and the state increased its entrepreneurial role (Nacional Financiera 1984, pp. 236–40). Between 1977 and 1982 the number of newly created enterprises in which NAFINSA participated with its own risk capital grew from 74 to 94 (Ramírez 1986, p. 135).

Initially, the boost to aggregate demand induced by the sharp increase in state expenditures generated impressive rates of real GDP growth of better than 8% annually between 1978 and 1981, and in favored sectors such as industry it even led to an unprecedented increase in output of 10.8% during 1979 alone. Real minimum wages, which had fallen during two consecutive years, experienced a net increase of 2.5% between 1978 and 1981, while employment growth averaged close to 6% per year in 1979–81 (Nacional Financiera 1984, pp. 30–51). Last, Mexico recorded its largest increase in agricultural output in more than a decade during the 1980–81 period because under the government's rural development program, known as the SAM (Mexican Food System), the land dedicated to the production of staples such as corn and beans was increased dramatically from 5.6 million hectares in 1979 to 8.2 million hectares in 1981 (Austin and Esteva 1987; Spalding 1984, pp. 17–32).

On the other hand, Mexico increasingly depended on foreign exchange earnings derived from oil exports, particularly from 1979 onward. Between 1979 and 1981 the value of oil exports jumped from US$3.9 to 14.5 billion, while the oil share in total exports increased from 43.9 to approximately 75% (Nacional Financiera 1984, p. 262). Despite public assurances by the government that the country would avoid the inherent vulnerability associated with relying on a single export, it rendered such an outcome inevitable when it imposed a high rate of taxation on PEMEX. During the 1977–81 period the portion of taxes contributed by PEMEX averaged close to 25% of the total revenues generated by the federal government (Inter-American Development Bank 1984, p. 176).

The country's ever-growing public sector deficits were a major problem. After registering a low of 7.4% of GDP in 1978, they rose to an all-time high of 17.9% by the end of 1982 (Nacional Financiera 1986, pp. 261–68). As in the past, the deficits were financed by Central Bank purchases of government debt, which increased the money supply, and, given the newly found creditworthiness of the nation due to its vast oil reserves, by borrowing heavily from external sources. The response of inflation was not immediate (thus allowing for temporary increases in real GDP), but when it came it was devastating in its impact: the rate of inflation accelerated from 20.3% in 1979 to 98.2% in 1982; and real minimum wages, which had grown in 1980–81, fell by 9.6% in 1982 alone (Nacional Financiera 1986, pp. 291–311).

Developments in the external sector mirrored the country's growing structural problems and the fiscal crisis of the state. The trade deficit in the balance of payments almost doubled between 1980 and 1981. The imbalance in the current account was even more severe, primarily owing to interest payments on the growing external debt. In this connection, the share of total interest payments in the value of exports rose from 33.7% in 1979 to 61% in 1982, which left insufficient foreign exchange to pay for needed imports (Inter-American Development Bank 1983, 1984).

The economic and political situation of the country took a turn for the worse in the second half of 1981 when, as a result of the weakening of oil prices and the massive overvaluation of the peso, the rate of capital flight accelerated to unprecedented levels of an estimated $15 billion (Cypher 1990, p. 7). During the 1980–82 period, the rate at which Mexico's "dollar plunderers" transferred funds outside the country—in the form of private deposits in U.S. banks—increased from an annual rate of 2% in 1980 to 38% in 1981 (FitzGerald 1985, pp. 210–40). In early 1982 the continuing fall in oil prices, the U.S. recession, which decreased the demand for Mexican exports, and the steep rise in real interest rates, which increased the cost of servicing the debt, left Mexico with insufficient foreign exchange. On February 18, 1982, the Central Bank withdrew its support of the peso, and the currency plunged in value by more than 70% to 44.64 pesos per dollar (from 26.23) (IMF 1993; Secretaría de Programación y Presupuesto 1981, p. 184).

Massive as the devaluation was, along with a makeshift contractionary package that included cuts in public investment, food subsidies, and a 40% increase in the prices of government-controlled commodities such as gasoline and electricity, it failed to stem capital flight. By August 5, 1982, the drain on reserves became unsustainable, so the administration once again massively devalued the peso to 104.0 pesos to the dollar and took the unprecedented action of suspending dollar payments and declaring a temporary moratorium on external debt payments.

Several days later foreign exchange markets were reopened, and the government announced that it had begun negotiations with the IMF for a structural adjustment loan that would enable Mexico to draw on IMF lines of credit totaling $3.9 billion in 1983–85. Despite these efforts to manage the crisis, the escalation of capital flight continued unabated. The outgoing López Portillo administration first imposed exchange controls on September 1. It nationalized the country's banking system on September 10. The decision to nationalize was taken because members of the nationalist sector within the government blamed the banking community for an estimated capital outflow of over $9 billion from Mexico in 1982 alone.

The banking system had become increasingly concentrated. For example, "in 1950, 75% of total banking assets were spread among forty-two banking companies. By 1981 only six banks remained to control the same share of assets. The top four banks controlled 60% of all bank assets" (Tello 1984, p. 29). Carlos Tello Macías, then director of the Bank of Mexico, argued that these banks were using their power and international connections to channel profits out of the country from the productive sectors of the economy, saying that the "Banco Hipotecario de Crédito had sent $300 million out of the country in a single day" [Hamilton 1984, p. 17). These public revelations were all that was needed by the beleaguered López Portillo, who declared "that in recent years a group of Mexicans, led, counseled, and supported by private banks, have taken more money out of the country than all the empires that have exploited us since the beginning of our history" (López Portillo 1982).

The nationalization of the banks was important even though the assets of the 56 institutions nationalized by the government amounted to only 10% of the total value of assets of the 500 largest firms in Mexico. According to Mexican specialist James Cypher, this misses the point because "the private banks that were nationalized either controlled or participated in the management of nearly 1,000 firms . . . [and] the assets held by the banks constituted funds that . . . could be utilized to control very large amounts of capital that were lent by banks" (1990, p. 122).

Moreover, the largest banks (such as Banamex and Bancomer) had played a prominent role in securing loans for the Mexican government (via their extensive connections with transnational banks), as well as refinancing the government's internal domestic debt.

The conflict that erupted between the state and economically powerful factions of the private sector in the aftermath of the nationalization decision marked the end of the political pact that had been forged over the previous decades. Ex-bankers and powerful business associations affiliated with the CCE campaigned to reverse the government's actions, calling for a general strike of the business community to paralyze the state. These and other actions would eventually lead to the partial reprivatization of the assets of the banking community under the administration of Miguel de la Madrid (1982–88) and, as we shall see, the complete reversal of the nationalization decision in the subsequent administration of Carlos Salinas de Gortari (1988–94).

The Resurgence of Neoliberalism, 1983–93

Upon taking office in December 1982, President Miguel de la Madrid faced the most serious economic and political crisis the nation had faced since the 1930s. Inflation was running at an annualized rate of 100%; unemployment was rising; real minimum wages had undergone drastic reductions; and large and growing fiscal deficits reduced the state's ability to manage the crisis. In addition, the actions of his predecessor further undermined business "confidence" because they suggested that the new regime might also pursue policies designed to minimize the impact of the stabilization program on the poor (FitzGerald 1985, pp. 210–40).

The new president—a former secretary of the budget with close ties to the private banking community—announced his IMF-sponsored economic program, Programa Inmediato de Reordenación Económica (PIRE). Its emphasis on draconian cuts in government expenditures, widespread elimination of subsidies for food and transportation, and the rapid liberalizing and restructuring of the economy along market lines indicated a reversal of many, if not all, of Carlos Tello Macías's nationalist measures. Before outlining the program, it is important to point out that, with or without IMF conditionality, many, but not all, of the plan's key elements for stabilizing the economy would eventually have been adopted and implemented by government officials because of the country's severe economic and financial difficulties. But, as argued below, the sequencing, timing, and particularly the relative burden of the stabilization (expenditure-changing) and adjustment (expenditure-switching) program on the poor could have been implemented in a less ruthless fashion by first targeting the most pressing economic constraints and then adjusting the appropriate policy instruments. Instead, the Mexican government, under pressure from IMF officials, pushed ahead simultaneously on all fronts, forgetting that you need at least as many policy instruments as economic targets, and adopted policies that generated huge dislocations and hardship for workers, peasants, and owners of small and medium-sized businesses (Taylor 1991, chs. 2 and 3).

To illustrate the dangers of such a strategy, consider the following example: if the most immediate and pressing constraint (target) is a current account deficit that cannot be financed with a net inflow of funds, then it is advisable to devalue the currency gradually and then implement a crawling-peg system to control the rate of further currency depreciation. The reason why it is best to devalue gradually rather than abruptly—as the Mexicans did—is because in a country like Mexico, where nearly 80% of imports are in the form of intermediate goods and capital inputs (often denominated in dollars), a sharp devaluation of the domestic currency will increase the unit costs of domestic producers prohibitively. Producers in monopolistic and/or oligopolistic industries will react by raising their prices to maintain or even increase their short-run profits. The inflationary pressures generated by such a policy may then undermine the objectives of the original devaluation. If, in addition, government expenditures are cut across the board, with little regard to the adverse long-term effects this might have on overall investment, as happened in Mexico during the 1982–84 period, then stagflationary pressures are likely to be generated as the economy's capital stock per worker is lowered, thereby reducing the overall productivity of labor. Rather than pursue this shortsighted policy, government policymakers could have altered the *composition* of government spending, shifting it toward infrastructure, health, and education—investments that generate substantial spillover benefits to the private sector—while at the same time reducing both the rate of government spending on other items and money creation to reduce inflationary pressures, thus encouraging private sector agents.

It is somewhat ironic that almost a decade after the imposition of the IMF's stabilization program in Mexico many IMF and World Bank officials themselves now recognize that a necessary condition for the long-term success of structural reform programs such as privatization and liberalization in the region (notably in Chile and Mexico) is adequate infrastructural support in a noninflationary environment (Ramírez 1993a, pp. 1015–40; Meller 1991, ch. 8).

In any event, the main features of the austerity program called for (1) reducing aggregate spending via sharp reductions in the public-sector deficit and restrictive credit policies; (2) reducing the value of the real exchange rate by devaluing the peso at rates equal to or greater than the rate of inflation and increasing the prices of government-controlled goods and services; (3) liberalizing the tradable sector by eliminating licensing agreements, removing quotas, lowering tariffs, and eventually seeking membership in the GATT; (4) renewing efforts to promote nonpetroleum exports via the further promotion of *maquiladoras* or assembly-line operations along the U.S.-Mexico border; (5) encouraging foreign investment and technology through a more flexible interpretation of the 1973 Foreign Investment law; and (6) "disincorporating" or privatizating state-owned enterprises.

The new administration also reassured the business community of the government's shift in policy by replacing the nationalist Carlos Tello as head of the Central Bank with the far more conservative Miguel Mancera and purged Tello's associates from key government agencies. It then compensated ex-bankers quickly and at a rate higher than the stock market value of banks' shares before nationalization (Elizondo n.d., pp. 1–27). This was followed by the passage of a bill authorizing the government to sell up to 34% of the total assets of the nationalized banks to ex-bankers, as well as permitting them to sit on the boards of director of the public banks (Cypher 1990, pp. 163–64). In order to prevent a concentration of financial assets in relatively few hands the bill stipulated that no single individual or institution could own more than 1% of these assets; yet many long-time observers of the Mexican economy correctly noted that since the bank stocks were being offered in large indivisible portfolios the measure amounted to no more than a scheme for former bank owners and wealthy Mexicans (mostly operators in the stock exchange) to reassert as well as gain new influence and control (Hamilton 1986, pp. 167–68).

The Impact of the Austerity Program

The government's orthodox stabilization program during the 1983–85 period generated some encouraging results at first. The public-sector deficit as a proportion of GDP was reduced from a high of 17.6% in 1982 to 8.5% in 1984, primarily as a result of reductions in public investment and social expenditures. The smaller deficit enabled the monetary authorities to reduce the rate of growth of the money supply. The inflation rate fell from 98.8% in 1982 to 59.2% in 1984.

The stabilization program improved the current account balance. It went from a $6.1 billion deficit in 1982 to a $5.4 billion surplus in 1983, and a $4.1 billion surplus the following year. Most of this improvement, however, was the result of a sharp drop in imports, primarily intermediate and capital goods; there was only a very slight increase in total exports. Finally, the sharp decrease in overall aggregate demand brought about by the expenditure-reducing policies of the government came at a heavy price in terms of reductions in real GDP per capita and real minimum wages—earned by close to two-thirds of the Mexican labor force.

Unforeseen events had an impact on the stabilization program in 1985, and many of its positive gains were completely reversed during the 1986–88 period. The combined effect of the government's stabilization program, the earthquakes of 1985, and the precipitous fall in oil prices during 1985–86 (not to mention the Mexican stock market crash of 1987) sent the economy into a downturn as severe as the one experienced in 1982–83. The recession-induced shortfall in revenues led to an overall deterioration in the finances of the public sector, with the deficit rising from 8.7% in 1984 to 16.1% by 1987. The rate of inflation accelerated from 63.7% in 1985 to 105.7% in 1986 and an unprecedented 159.2% in 1987. Capital flight increased dramatically as a result of negative yields on 28-day government treasury bills (CETES) and the repercussions of the stock market crash—again emphasizing the extreme vulnerability of the Mexican economy to movements in short-term capital flows.

A result of the government's efforts to enhance the competitiveness of exports by deliberately holding increases in money wages below the rate of peso devaluation was that the real minimum wage plummeted by more than 27.2% between 1985 and 1988 while the real effective exchange rate rose 32% (see table 4.5).

Policymakers were aware that in a structurally dependent economy such as Mexico's a real devaluation of the domestic currency would increase the domestic currency costs of dollar-denominated imports. If money wages and the general price level were then allowed to increase as rapidly as the exchange rate, the price of exports in foreign currency would not decrease (assuming no changes in the productivity of labor). Thus, even though export receipts would not increase, the rise in the domestic currency price of imports would increase the rate of inflation. When the currency was allowed to appreciate in real terms, as in the 1983–85 period, both inflation and the rate of decrease in real minimum wages were brought down, but when it was allowed to depreciate after 1985 the inflation rate and the rate of decrease in real minimum wages

Table 4.5. Selected Economic Indicators, 1982–92 (annual growth rates, in percent)

Item	1982	1983	1984	1985	1986	1987	1988	1989	1990	1991	1992
Real GDP	-0.5	-5.3	3.6	2.6	-3.8	1.5	1.1	2.9	4.0	3.6	2.6
Real GDP/capita	-3.3	-8.1	0.9	-0.2	-6.5	-1.1	-1.5	0.7	1.7	1.4	0.4
Gross domestic investment	-28.7	-24.9	6.1	10.3	-22.6	2.3	13.3	3.5	9.4	5.1	7.0
Public sector deficit (% of GDP)	17.6	9.0	8.7	10.0	16.3	16.1	12.3	6.0	3.5	1.3	-1.0
Rate of inflation[a]	98.8	80.8	59.2	63.7	105.7	159.2	51.7	19.7	30.0	18.8	11.9
Real minimum wage	-9.6	-18.0	-7.4	-1.3	-8.5	-6.3	-11.1	-7.9	-7.3	-6.5	-7.2
Real avg. wage	0.9	-21.0	-7.3	1.5	-5.8	-0.5	0.6	4.8	3.5	3.7	—
Real interest rate	-25.2	-3.8	1.1	9.9	14.1	-2.9	28.4	30.0	8.4	4.6	6.1
Interest payments[b]	5.3	8.5	8.0	8.5	13.6	17.6	15.2	11.4	8.5	5.0	—
Domestic	4.1	6.4	6.2	6.6	10.9	14.5	12.4	9.0	6.1	2.9	—
External	1.1	2.2	1.9	1.9	2.7	3.1	2.5	2.5	2.4	2.1	—
Real effective exchange rate (1980 = 100)	115.3	123.7	102.9	98.5	145.2	158.1	130.2	118.3	114.4	109.9	102.5
Trade balance ($B)	6.5	13.7	12.9	8.5	4.6	8.4	1.8	-0.7	-4.4	-11.3	-20.7
Current acct. bal. ($B)	-6.1	5.4	4.1	1.1	-1.6	3.9	-2.4	-4.0	-7.5	-14.6	-24.4
Foreign investment ($B)	—	—	—	—	1.5	3.2	2.6	3.5	4.6	12.2	8.3
Debt service ($B)	16.3	13.6	15.9	14.5	12.3	11.4	14.7	14.3	13.1	13.5	20.7

Sources: IDB 1989–94; ECLAC, Economic Survey of Latin America and the Caribbean 1991–92, pp. 473–88; ECLAC 1991–93; Mexico Business Monthly 1(12) (January 1992): 23; and Pinheiro and Schneider 1993, table A.2.1.
[a] Percentage variation from December to December.
[b] As a percentage of GDP.

shot up (Sheahan 1991, p. 10). The Mexican Workers' Confederation (CTM) therefore pressured the government to allow the peso to appreciate in real terms vis-à-vis the dollar.

Organized labor's efforts were partially rewarded when the de la Madrid administration, under threat of a general strike by the CTM in late 1987 and with an eye to the upcoming presidential elections of 1988, in December 1987 implemented a solidarity pact designed to eliminate inflationary pressures through moderate price increases, nominal wage readjustments, and controlling the rate of peso depreciation. The plan, which amounted to an incomes policy, was subsequently renamed the Pact for Stability and Growth (PECE) under the Salinas administration (1988–94), and it brought the inflation rate down from 159.2% in 1987 to 18.8% in 1991 and 8% in 1993.

The rate of peso devaluation was eased substantially during the Salinas administration, reflecting the government's stubborn commitment to containing inflationary pressures, even at the expense of further gains in exports of manufactured goods and a deterioration in the overall rate of economic activity in the nontradable sector (Ramírez 1993b, pp. 173–90). The government's anti-inflationary policy was facilitated by the massive inflow of foreign investment and the attendant increase in international reserves during the 1989–93 period. However, the economic price of this policy was a steep rise in the country's trade and current account deficits, an associated increase in real interest rates to attract and/or prevent capital from leaving the country, and a greater than anticipated slowdown in the rate of economic growth during 1992–93, well below the country's population growth rate of 2.2%.

The Waning Years of the Salinas Administration and the Beginning of the Zedillo Term

The slowdown in economic activity experienced by the Mexican economy in 1992 degenerated into a fullblown recession in 1993, only to be followed in 1994 by several destabilizing political developments such as the armed rebellion in the state of Chiapas by the Ejército de Liberación Nacional (EZLN) and the assassinations of the PRI's presidential candidate, Luis Donaldo Colosio, and the PRI's secretary general, José Francisco Ruiz Massieu. The incoming administration of Ernesto Zedillo Ponce de León (1994–2000) thus inherited a number of intractable political and economic problems that seriously undermined the public's confidence in the government's ability to maintain the peso's value without risking complete depletion of its foreign reserves. The government's earlier attempt to attract funds to finance its ballooning current account deficit via the introduction of short-term instruments known as Tesobonos (discussed in more detail below) had backfired, because $9.9 billion were expected to mature in the first quarter of 1996 alone and the government's reserves, amounting to a mere $6.3 billion in December 1994 (down from close to $30 billion in February 1994), were insufficient to cover them. Only a few days after Zedillo's inauguration on December 1, 1994, the EZLN threatened to walk out of the peace talks and resume its warfare against the government, a politically explosive situation that further destabilized international bond markets and confidence in the peso. The hemorrhage of capital from the country accelerated and the pressure on the highly overvalued peso became irresistible (see table 4.6), particularly in view of a current account deficit that had reached close to $30 billion in 1994. On December 20, 1994, the Zedillo administration was forced to devalue the peso by 15% (in real terms) and then, a few days later, under intense pressure from speculators, to allow the peso to float freely against the dollar. By month's end the value of the peso had dropped by more than 30% and the country had lost between $7 and $8 billion in foreign exchange reserves (ECLAC 1995).

The severity with which the market reacted to the government's decision to abandon its previous commitment to maintaining a strong currency—the centerpiece of the previous administration—quickly led the government to introduce an austerity program on January 4, 1995. The program called for fiscal stringency, tight monetary policy, and strict guidelines with respect to wage and price increases. These measures, however, failed to reassure markets and as the secondary effects of the peso's depreciation came into effect, particularly on the Mexican stock market and the fragile banking system, a widespread perception arose that the government was not in control of the economic crisis. In order to prevent further financial speculation and a total loss of investor confidence, the Clinton administration engineered at the end of January a $52 billion international financial rescue package that called on the Zedillo administration to furnish foreign investors and officials with timely and accurate economic data and to guarantee the repayment of the loan with their oil revenues (Cypher 1996, pp. 451–62).

The international aid bailout, although welcomed by the government and foreign investors, was not capable of preventing interest rates from soaring to over 70% and the real economy from rapidly deteriorating during the month of February. The worsening economic downturn put severe pressure on borrowers' ability to service their debts, which, in turn, added to the financial woes of the commercial banking system (discussed below). On March 9, 1995, the Zedillo administration introduced yet another austerity program, the Acuerdo para Superar la Emergencia Económica (AUSEE), in order to reduce the current account deficit,

Table 4.6. Selected Economic Indicators, 1989–95

Item	1989	1990	1991	1992	1993	1994	1995
(percent change)							
Real GDP	2.9	4.0	3.6	2.6	0.3	3.0	-6.9
Real GDP/capita	0.7	1.7	1.4	0.4	-1.9	0.8	-9.0
Consumer prices	19.7	30.0	18.8	11.9	8.0	7.0	52.0
Real minimum wage	-7.9	-7.3	-6.5	-7.2	-5.6	-5.0	-21.0
Urban unemployment	2.9	2.7	2.7	2.8	3.4	3.9	6.4
(percent of GDP)							
Fiscal deficit	6.0	3.5	1.3	-1.0	-0.2	0.5	0.0
Domestic investment	17.2	18.6	19.5	22.0	20.5	20.8	19.1
National savings	16.2	15.5	14.1	13.8	14.0	13.5	16.2
Current acct. bal.	-2.8	-3.2	-4.8	-6.8	-6.4	-8.1	0.0
Public investment	4.7	5.0	4.5	4.3	4.0	4.0	—
Private investment	12.5	13.6	15.0	17.7	16.5	16.8	—
Public external debt	32.5	31.7	26.1	31.0	31.1	29.8	41.1
Real effective exchange rate (1990 = 100)	103.2	100.0	91.1	83.8	78.0	85.7	115.0

Source: ECLAC 1995, 1996; and IDB 1990–96, various reports.

prevent the development of a wage-price spiral, and address the growing difficulties of the banking system (Ramírez 1996–97, pp. 129–56).

The draconian measures included in the latest austerity package have led to a sharp decline in the level of economic activity, imports, investment, and the standard of living of millions of Mexico's poor. Table 4.6 shows that after recording anemic increases during 1993 and 1994 real GDP is estimated to have fallen by an unprecedented 6.9% (-9.0% in real per capita terms) during 1995 (*Latin American Economy and Business* 1994, pp. 4–5)—the worst single drop in real GDP since 1932! Table 4.6 also reveals that the peso's steep fall in value vis-à-vis the dollar unleashed strong inflationary pressures during 1995, with a year-end inflation rate of 52%–second only to Venezuela's 57% rate of inflation (December to December) and more than 10 points higher than Mexican officials had predicted (IDB 1996, pp. 50–51, fig. 56).

On a "positive" note, the peso's plunge in value has stimulated an increase in Mexico's exports of 28.7% in 1995, particularly in the *maquiladora* (assembly-line) sector, which, in conjunction with a 28% drop in imports (approximately $8 billion), had virtually eliminated the country's current account deficit at the end of 1995 (-$700 million). On the negative side of the ledger, the sharp decline in imports has fallen disproportionately on essential intermediate goods and capital inputs used by the country's manufacturing firms. This, in turn, produced an unprecedented drop in real gross fixed capital formation of 39.5% during 1995, thus inducing a decline in the investment ratio from 20.8% in 1994 to just over 19% in 1995 (see table 4.6). In view of the well-established fact (at least among economists) that future sources of income growth and employment creation depend on vigorous and sustained levels of real investment spending, one cannot avoid concluding that the ill-advised stabilization policies implemented by the Zedillo administration have attained "external balance" at the cost of jeopardizing the country's long-term economic growth potential.

On a sectoral basis, real output in manufacturing fell by 6.4% in 1995, while construction and mining registered drops of 22 and 2%, respectively. Not surprisingly, the unprecedented downturn in economic activity has generated a dramatic increase in the country's unemployment rate. For example, the official unemployment rose from 3.4% in 1993 to an estimated 6.4% by the end of 1995. More important, the unofficial unemployment rate, long considered a more accurate gauge of the extent of labor underutilization in Mexico because it includes those individuals who are officially unemployed *plus* those working less than 15 hours a week at less than the minimum wage, rose from 14% during 1993 to 27% in October 1995 (ECLAC 1995, p. 59, table 3). Three million workers out of Mexico's 24 million labor force were unemployed or underemployed.

Real minimum wages, which serve as an important benchmark for wage settlements throughout the country, fell continuously during the Salinas administration, culminating in a drop of 21% during 1995 (IDB 1996, p. 47, fig. 48). The sharp drop in the real purchasing power of the Mexican people can be gauged from the following figures released by the Banco de México. In December 1988 the minimum wage could buy approximately 56% of the basic food basket for a family of five. The 1994 minimum wage could buy only 38% of the same basic food basket (*Latin American Economy and Business* 1994, p. 5). In the past year and a half since the economic crisis set in, Banamex—Mexico's leading private bank—reports that "the cost of the basic food basket has surged by 64%, while average [nominal] wages have risen only 18%. Consumption of basic grains by the average Mexican has declined by 29% in that same period" (*Latinamerica Press* 1996, p. 1). It goes on to report that "fully one-half of Mexico's estimated 92 million people consume less than the minimum daily requirement of 1,300 calories, most as a direct result of the worst economic downturn since 1932."

The almost continuous decrease in real minimum wages and related social services that the Mexican people have had to endure since the onset and aftermath of the debt crisis in 1982 has undoubtedly contributed to the marked reduction in the share of income received by the country's middle and lower sectors, displayed in table 4.3. For example, the income share of the top quintile rose from 49.5% in 1984 to 54.2 in 1992, while the cumulative income share of the "bottom" 80% of the Mexican population fell from 50.5 to 45.8% over the period in question. Perhaps not surprisingly, the functional distribution of income also become highly unequal over the past decade (Martínez 1995). Only the very rich and powerful were able to escape the painful adjustment costs borne by the rest of the population and, in many instances, even increase their income and wealth as a result of market-oriented reforms such as the privatization program. Thus, the share of national income received by capitalists increased from 48% in 1982 to 57.1% in 1994, while that going to labor fell from 41.7% in 1982 to 30.9% in 1994 (the residual share is absorbed by indirect taxes) (OECD 1995, pp. 34–35, fig. 12 and table 11).

The government's almost single-minded strategy of stabilizing prices via tight monetary policy (the average cost of funds was 20.8% in 1993, 24.74% in 1994, and over 50% in 1995) has hit small and medium-sized businesses in manufacturing especially hard. For example, manufacturing output as a whole is estimated to have fallen by 1.5% in 1993, with textiles and electrical machinery (where small and medium-sized firms predominate) registering a steep fall of 7.4 and 10.1%, respectively (*Latin American Economy and Business* 1994, p. 4). To compound matters, the economic crisis unleashed by the 1994 peso devaluation was expected to bankrupt more than 20% of the nation's 1.5 million registered small businesses, thereby costing hundreds of thousands of jobs in the sector that employs the majority of Mexicans.

The primary sector (which includes agriculture and lumbering) has been mired in a deep economic recession since early 1992, and the figures for 1993 show that it was the economy's worst performer with a growth rate of -4.0%. Critics of the government's stabilization program and the accompanying market-oriented reforms point out that the economic slowdown in this sector can be attributed, in large measure, to the modifications of Article 27 of the 1917 constitution in late 1992, which empowered the government to redistribute land to petitioning peasants and ejidos (indigenous communities that hold land in common). They contend that the liberalization of farming and ownership practices in the traditional ejido sector, allowing *ejidatarios* for the first time to sell, lease, sharecrop, or mortgage their tiny plots of land to large farmers and agribusiness concerns, has disrupted and inhibited the production of basic foodstuffs such as beans, maize, and wheat—consumed in large measure by poor rural households, which, according to the government's own estimates, represent close to 43% of total rural homes (Barkin 1994, pp. 29–34; Barkin 1990, ch. 11).

The passage of the North American Free Trade Agreement (NAFTA), in the eyes of these critics, promises to accelerate further the stagnation, displacement, and marginalization of peasants in the basic foodstuffs sector. They contend that the elimination of tariff and quota barriers to highly subsidized agricultural products from the United States and Canada will harm or wipe out the 2 million small growers of corn and beans (out of a rural labor force of 6 million) who do not have the resources, access to credit, and technological know-how to compete effectively. A recent study estimates that full liberalization in basic grains such as wheat, corn, and beans would lead to more than 800,000 peasants leaving the rural sector because of their inability to compete. More than 600,000 would migrate to the United States within the first year. The critics also report that the cumulative rural-urban migration over nine years would be close to 2 million. This compares with 1 million peasants migrating if there is no full trade liberalization (Hinojosa-Ojeda and Robinson 1992, pp. 69–108).

If we add the estimated 1 million to 1.5 million Mexicans who enter the labor force every year to these increased migratory flows, the supply of unskilled labor in Mexico will increase at a much faster rate than any NAFTA-induced employment opportunities—the most optimistic forecast is for approximately 600,000 additional jobs generated over the next three to five years, mostly in the assembly-line or *maquiladora* industry (Hufbauer and Schott 1992, p. 56). Obviously, the country's employment situation has deteriorated dramatically as a result of the current economic depression and the austerity measures incorporated in the AUSEE. According to CANACINTRA, an additional 1 million Mexicans lost their jobs during 1995 alone. The open unemployment rate rose from 3.2% in December 1994 to 6.7% in October, only to stabilize around 6.4% in December 1995 (IDB 1996, p. 45, fig. 41). This means that close to 3 million workers in the formal sector were unemployed at that last date. If we add to these figures those individuals who work fewer than 35 hours a week, almost 13 million people were not fully employed in late 1995.

The only sector of the Mexican economy that performed relatively well over the two years leading up to the 1994 economic crisis was the financial and banking services sector. In 1992 it grew by 3.9%, and it is estimated to have grown by a robust 4.9% in 1993 (*Latin American Economy and Business* 1994, p. 4). The healthy expansion of this sector can be attributed to the heavy investments made in the recently privatized and highly profitable banking system. However, much of the economic activity in this sector is associated with relatively unproductive operations such as the reallocation of profits, flight capital, and managerial resources to acquire and preserve *existing* income and wealth—i.e., these financial maneuvers are not associated with the creation of *new* sources of employment and income in the form of additional investments in plant, machinery, equipment, and new factories.

Meanwhile, during the same period, the banking system's overdue loans as a percentage of total loans rose from 3.25% at the end of 1991 to 5.5% in 1992, then to 8% in 1993, and finally to over 10% by the end of 1994, and an unprecedented level of 17% in 1995 (Cypher 1996, p. 454, fig. 1). The banking system's problems can be traced to the debt-led nature of the 1989–92 recovery and to the economic slump of 1993. James Cypher comments that "the bulk of these loans were for consumer credit, including auto loans, mortgage loans, and credit card loans, and secondarily to the business sector to finance real estate and construction activities (which were primarily linked to speculation activities in office buildings and shopping centers). Conspicuous for its absence was any mention of the credit explosion being linked to industrial activities or to any other economic activity that would point to the expansion of the productive base of the economy" (1996, pp. 456–57).

Turning to the government's finances, Mexico had considerable success during the Salinas administration in reducing the fiscal deficit, but the greater part of the improvement in the fiscal position of the state is the direct result of the draconian cuts in public investment in infrastructure and the government's privatization program. Tables 4.5 and 4.6 show that the deficit, as a proportion of GDP, fell from 16.1% of

GDP in 1987 to an estimated surplus of 0.2% in 1993. A small part of this reduction can be attributed to the recovery-induced increase in government revenues, but the greater part of the improvement in the fiscal position of the state stems from cuts in public investment and the privatization program. With regard to the latter's impact on public revenues, it is important to note that between 1989 and May of 1992 total revenues from privatizations amounted to 6.3% of GDP or, in absolute terms, in excess of $19.5 billion. Only the United Kingdom and New Zealand have accumulated greater privatization proceeds relative to average annual GDP (for further details, see OECD 1992, p. 85, table 19).

The rationale for privatizing state-owned firms is usually couched in terms of its capacity to increase competition and efficiency in the long run for affected industries, but in practice its most immediate and valued effect—from the standpoint of government officials—has been to generate much-needed revenues to bring down public-sector deficits. For example, in 1991 the government's public-sector deficit without privatization income was 1.3%, while it became a surplus of 2.4% with privatization revenues (*Latin American Economy and Business* 1992, pp. 4–5). Critics, however, contend that in exchange for a lump-sum infusion of cash privatization often leads to a long-term loss in government revenues, which are often replaced by a smaller, and more variable, stream of future tax revenues from the privatized firms. In this connection, the Salinas administration eliminated limits on the amount of profits or dividends repatriated (*Business Latin America* 1992, pp. 44–45; Baer and Birch 1991, pp. 1–39). The deficit-reducing effects of privatization may be offset completely when one includes the government's efforts to "sanitize" the public enterprises in order to render them more salable by transferring the company's liabilities to the state, closing portions of parastatal operations, reneging on existing labor contracts (Baer and Birch 1991), and changing tax and tariff structures so as to minimize the company's role as a provider of government revenues. Finally, critics of the privatization program contend that it leads to the withdrawal of the state from key sectors of the economy, thus leading to unemployment, a concomitant loss of income and purchasing power among the poor, and the weakening of unions and hard-won labor rights.

The trend toward economic concentration was most evident in the reprivatization of the nation's eighteen commercial banks. Despite the Finance Ministry's stated goal of distributing the country's financial power more equitably by prohibiting individual investors from owning more than 5% of a privatized bank's shares, ex-bankers and other business and financial leaders have created new financial holding companies that can obtain up to 100% of shares of the newly privatized banks. This has enabled some of the same prominent families that dominated the banking system before the 1982 nationalization to reassert their control over the banking system along with powerful industrialists and new financiers. The latter are mainly owners of stock brokerage houses who "knew how to profit from the stock market much better than former bankers" (Elizondo n.d., p. 15).

In view of the above, the "improvement" in the fiscal position of the state during the Salinas years was achieved at a heavy economic and social price. Moreover, it was completely undone by the imbalance in the country's private sector as measured by the gap between its gross national savings and gross domestic investment. National savings declined from 16.2% of GDP to 13.5% in 1994, while investment, after increasing during the 1989–92 period and falling in the recession year of 1993, flattened out at slightly above 20% of GDP during the final year of the Salinas administration. The drop in the national savings rate can be explained in part by the overvalued exchange rate and the debt-led nature of the recovery in consumption that took place in the early 1990s, much of it financed with large inflows of short-term capital. It can also be explained by the expectation, widespread throughout 1992 and 1993, that the passage of NAFTA would lock in the country's market-oriented reforms and lead to a significant increase in the nation's future wealth and income. Under such circumstances, Mexican consumers engaged in a massive intertemporal substitution of present consumption for future consumption (Edwards and Cox Edwards 1987, ch. 7).

Not surprisingly, Mexico's macroeconomic imbalance in the private sector—due to spending in excess of its domestically generated income—was reflected in a dramatic increase in the current account deficit as a percentage of GDP. By the end of 1994 the deficit in the country's current accounts had reached an unprecedented level of 8.0% of GDP (close to $30 billion).

At the time, the Salinas administration did not consider the financing of these deficits to be too problematic because of the massive inflow of capital the nation had attracted since 1989 (Baer and Birch 1991, p. 77). Contributing to the net inflow of capital were the relatively low real interest rates in the United States and the prospects that the passage of NAFTA would lock in the market-oriented reforms pursued by the Mexican government. For example, $21.7 billion in private foreign investment was received during 1993 (much of it in anticipation of the passage of the NAFTA accord). The lion's share of it, however, was in the form of highly liquid portfolio investments in the Mexican stock market—not long-term investments in plant, machinery, and equipment (*Latin American Economy and Business* 1994, p. 5). For example, of the total private foreign investment flows coming into the country in 1993, only $4.9 billion was in the form of direct investment in new plant machinery and equipment, while $17.0 billion, or approximately 78.3%, was invested in the form of portfolio or indirect investments such as 28-day CETES, BONDES, and stockmarket issues (OECD 1995, p. 19).

The problem with this strategy is that aside from exposing the structural overreliance of the economy on foreign capital it also rendered the Mexican government highly vulnerable to economic and financial decisions taken outside the country. For example, in 1994 political instability forced the Mexican government to introduce Tesobonos, which were a new risk-free short-term debt instrument (a year or less), in order to prevent apprehensive investors from transferring their money out of the country. This transferred the default (devaluation) risk from the investor to the Mexican government because the principal (in pesos) was indexed to the value of the dollar. The dramatic switch in the government's debt structure is revealed by the following figures. In 1993 CETES or nonindexed instruments held by the public represented 63% ($24.3 billion) of the total debt of the government, while Tesobonos accounted for only 4% ($1.6 billion) of the outstanding debt. One year later, Tesobonos represented 74.3% ($22 billion) of the government's debt, while nonindexed bonds such as CETES, BONDES, and Ajustabonos accounted for only 7.6% ($7.6 billion). Moreover, 75% of the Tesobonos were in the hands of nonresidents (OECD 1995, p. 26). Even though Mexico had accumulated an impressive level of reserves during the last three years of the Salinas presidency, when both the stability of the country's political institutions and the availability of dollars came into question in late 1994, the attempt by foreign and wealthy domestic investors to convert their massive stock of Tesobonos into dollars became a major contributor to the crisis.

Before concluding, it should be mentioned that the collapse of public investment in economic and social infrastructure during the Salinas years may be very costly in terms of the country's prospects for future economic growth. Public investment in roads, bridges, ports, and dams fell in both relative and absolute terms, reaching a post–World War II low of 4.0% of GDP in 1994—practically a third of the level recorded in 1981 (see tables 4.1 and 4.6). The modest recovery in the rate of private capital formation that took place from 1989 to 1992 ended, beginning with the recession of 1993 and culminating with the severe economic downturn of 1995. In 1993 the rate of total capital formation rose by less than 1%, with public investment actually registering a negative growth rate of 2.5%, and in the depression year of 1995 gross fixed capital formation fell by an unprecedented 40% (ECLAC 1996, p. 58, table 2; IDB 1996, p. 37, table 29)!

The underinvestment in economic infrastructure thus threatens to undermine both the trade liberalization and privatization programs; any economic efficiency gains obtained via trade liberalization and/or privatization may be entirely offset by a lack of adequate infrastructure in the form of product-to-market roads, dams, irrigation networks, ports, airport fields, water treatment plants, sewage facilities, and adequately housed and trained workers (Nazmi and Ramírez 1997; Ramírez 1994, pp. 1–17). The financing of Mexico's expenditures on economic and social infrastructure will require the rapid expansion of markets for equity and debt and a tax reform aimed at broadening the tax base in an efficient and equitable fashion.

Works Cited

Aubey, Robert T. 1966. *Nacional Financiera and Mexican Industry*. Los Angeles: Latin American Center, University of California.

Austin, James E., and Gustavo Esteva, eds. 1987. *Food Policy in Mexico*. Ithaca: Cornell University Press.

Baer, Werner, and Melissa Birch. 1991. *Privatization and the Changing Role of the State in Latin America*. Bureau of Economic and Business Research, Faculty Working Paper 92-0123. Champaign: University of Illinois.

Barkin, David. 1985. Mexico's Albatross: The U.S. Economy. In Nora Hamilton and Timothy F. Harding, eds., *Modern Mexico*. New York: Sage Publications.

———. 1987. The End to Food Self-Sufficiency in Mexico. *Latin American Perspectives* 14(3).

———. 1990. *Distorted Development: Mexico in the World Economy*. Boulder: Westview Press.

———. 1994. The Specter of Rural Development. *NACLA: Report on the Americas* 28(1).

Basch, Antonin. 1968. *El mercado de capitales en México*. Mexico City: Centro de Estudios Monetarios Latinoamericanos.

Bazdresch, Carlos, and Santiago Levy. 1991. Populism and Economic Policy in Mexico, 1970–1982. In Rudiger Dornbusch and Sebastian Edwards, *The Macroeconomics of Populism in Latin America*. Chicago: University of Chicago Press.

Bennet, Robert L. 1965. *The Financial Sector and Economic Development: The Mexican Case*. Baltimore: John Hopkins University Press.

Bennett, Douglas, and Kenneth Sharpe. 1982. The State as Banker and Entrepreneur. In Sylvia Ann Hewlett and Richard Weinert, eds., *Brazil and Mexico: Patterns of Late Development*. Philadelphia: ISHI.

Brothers, Dwight S., and Leopoldo Solís M. 1966. *Mexican Financial Development*. Austin: University of Texas Press.

Business Latin America. 1992. February 10.

Cypher, James M. 1990. *State and Capital in Mexico*. Boulder: Westview Press.

———. 1996. Mexico: Financial Stability or Structural Crisis. *Journal of Economic Issues* 30(2) (June).

de Murguia, Valdemar (1986). *Capital Flight and Economic Crisis*. San Diego: Center for U.S.-Mexico Studies, University of California.

Economic Commission for Latin America and the Caribbean (ECLAC). 1991–93, 1995, 1996. *Economic Panorama of Latin America*. Santiago de Chile: United Nations, ECLAC.

Edwards, S., and A. Cox Edwards. 1987. *Monetarism and Liberalization: The Chilean Experiment* (chapter 7). Cambridge, Mass.: Harper and Row Publishers.

Elizondo, Carlos. N.d. The Making of a New Alliance: The Privatization of the Banks in Mexico. *CIDE*, Documento de Trabajo 5. Mexico City: CIDE.

Ferrer, Oscar Humberto. 1990. The Political Economy of Privatization in Mexico. In William Glade, ed., *Privatization of Public Enterprises in Latin America*. San Francisco: ICS Press.

FitzGerald, E. V. K. 1985. The Financial Constraint on Relative Autonomy: The State and Capital Accumulation in Mexico, 1940–82. In Christian Anglade and Carlos Fortin, eds., *The State and Capital Accumulation in Latin America*, vol. 1. Pittsburgh: University of Pittsburgh Press.

Hamilton, Nora. 1984. State-Class Alliances and Conflicts. In *Latin American Perspectives* 11(4).

———. 1986. Mexico: The Limits to State Autonomy. In Nora Hamilton and Timothy F. Harding, eds., *Modern Mexico: State, Economy, and Social Conflict*. London: Sage Publications.

Hamilton, Nora, and Timothy F. Harding, eds. 1986. *Modern Mexico: State, Economy, and Social Conflict*. London: Sage Publications.

Hansen, Roger D. 1971a. *Mexican Economic Development: The Roots of Rapid Growth*. Washington, D.C.: National Planning Association.

———. 1971b. *The Politics of Mexican Development*. Baltimore: Johns Hopkins University Press.

Harber, Stephen H. 1989. *Industry and Underdevelopment: The Industrialization of Mexico, 1890–1940*. Stanford: Stanford University Press.

Hinojosa-Ojeda, Raúl, and Sherman Robinson. 1992. Labor Issues in a North American Free Trade Area. In Nora Lustig et al., eds., *North American Free Trade: Assessing the Impact*. Washington, D.C.: Brookings Institution.

Hufbauer, Gary, and Jeffrey Schott. 1992. *North American Free Trade: Issues and Recommendations*. Washington, D.C.: Institute for International Economics.

Inter-American Development Bank (IDB). 1983, 1984a, 1989–94, 1996. *Economic and Social Progress in Latin America*. Washington, D.C.: IDB.

———. 1984b. *External Debt and Economic Development in Latin America*. Washington, D.C.: IDB.

International Monetary Fund. 1993. *Direction of Trade Statistics*. Washington, D.C.: IMF.

Kay, Cristobal. 1989. *Latin American Theories of Development and Underdevelopment*. London: Routledge.

Keen, Benjamin. 1992. *A History of Latin America*. 4th ed. Boston: Houghton Mifflin Company.

Latin American Economy and Business. 1992 (1); 1994 (3, 4).

Latinamerica Press. 1996. 28(34), September 19.

López Portillo, José. 1982. *State of the Union Message*. September 1.

Luna, Matilde, Ricardo Tirado, and Francisco Valdés. 1987. Businessmen and Politics in Mexico. In Sylvia Maxfield and Ricardo A. Montoya, *Government and Private Sector in Contemporary Mexico*. San Diego: Center for U.S.-Mexican Studies, UCSD.

Martínez, Ifigenia. 1995. Desarrollo sustentable sectorial y regional. Un proyecto alternativo. *Problemas del Desarrollo* 26(100).

Maxfield, Sylvia. 1990. *Governing Capital*. Ithaca: Cornell University Press.

Meller, Patricio, ed. 1991. *The Latin American Development Debate*. Boulder: Westview Press.

Meyer, Michael C., and William L. Sherman. 1987. *The Course of Mexican History*. 3rd ed. New York: Oxford University Press.

Mosk, Sanford. 1950. *Industrial Revolution in Mexico*. Los Angeles: University of California Press.

Nacional Financiera, S.A. (NAFINSA). 1978, 1984, 1986, 1992. *La economía mexicana en cifras*. Mexico City: NAFINSA.

Nazmi, N., and Miguel D. Ramírez. 1997. Private Capital Expenditures, Public Investment and Economic Growth in Mexico. *Contemporary Economic Policy* 15 (January 1997).

Organization for Economic Cooperation and Development (OECD). 1992. *OECD Economic Surveys: Mexico*. Paris: OECD Publications.

———. 1995. *OECD Economic Surveys: Mexico*. Paris: OECD.

Pinheiro, Armando C., and Ben R. Schneider. 1993. The Fiscal Impact of Privatization in Latin America. Paper presented at *Latin America 2000 Conference*, University of Texas at Austin, Nov. 4–5, 1993.

Purcell, Susan Kaufman. 1977. The Future of the Mexican System. In José Luis Reyna and Richard S. Weinert, eds., *Authoritarianism in Mexico*. Philadelphia: ISHI.

Ramírez, Miguel D. 1986. *Development Banking in Mexico*. New York: Praeger Publishers.

———. 1989. *Mexico's Economic Crisis: Its Origins and Consequences*. New York: Praeger Publishers.

———. 1991. The Impact of Public Investment on Private Capital Formation: A Study Relating to Mexico. *Eastern Economic Journal* 17(4).

———. 1993a. Stabilization and Adjustment in Latin America: A Neostructuralist Perspective. *Journal of Economic Issues* 27(4).

———. 1993b. Stabilization and Trade Reform in Mexico: 1983–1989. *Journal of Developing Areas* 27(2).

———. 1994. Private Capital Formation in Mexico, 1950–90: An Empirical Analysis. *Southern Economic Journal* 61(1).

———. 1996–97. The Latest IMF-Sponsored Stabilization Program: Does It Represent a Long-term Solution for Mexico's Economy? *Journal of Interamerican Studies and World Affairs* 38(4).

Reynolds, Clark W. 1970. *The Mexican Economy*. New Haven: Yale University Press.

Sassen, Saskia. 1992. Why Migration? *Report of the Americas* 26(1).

Secretaría de Programación y Presupuesto. 1981. *Diez años de indicadores económicos*. Mexico City: Secretaría de Programación y Presupuesto.

Sheahan, John. 1991. *Conflict and Change in Mexican Economic Strategy*. San Diego: Center for U.S.-Mexican Studies, University of California.

Solís M., Leopoldo. 1982. Reflexiones sobre el panorama general de la economía mexicana. In Héctor Gonzales, ed., *El sistema económico mexicano*. Mexico City: Real Jonas Premia Editora.

Solís M., Leopoldo, and G. Ortiz. 1977. Mexican Financial Structure and Exchange Rate Experience, Mexico 1954–77. *Journal of Development Economics* 6(4).

Spalding, Rose J. 1984. *The Mexican Food Crisis: An Analysis of the SAM*. San Diego: Center for U.S.-Mexican Studies.

Street, James H. 1978. Mexico's Development Crisis. *Current History* 86(518).

Taylor, Lance. 1991. *Varieties of Stabilization Experience*. Oxford: Oxford University Press.

Tello, Carlos. 1984. *La nacionalización de la banca en México*. Mexico City: Siglo XXII Editores.

United Nations Development Programme. 1992. *Human Development Report*. New York: Oxford University Press.

Villarreal, René. 1977. The Policy of Import-Substituting Industrialization, 1929–1975. In José Luis Reyna and Richard Weinert, eds., *Authoritarianism in Mexico*. Philadelphia: ISHI.

Weintraub, Sidney. 1989. Implications of Mexican Demographic Developments for the United States. In Frank D. Bean, Jurgen Schmandt, and Sidney Weintraub, eds., *Mexican and Central American Population and U.S. Immigration Policy*. Austin: Center for Mexican American Studies.

Wionczek, Miguel S. 1964. Electric Power: The Uneasy Relationship. In Raymond Vernon, ed., *Public Policy and Private Enterprise in Mexico*. Cambridge, Mass.: Harvard University Press.

Witte, Ann D. 1971. Employment in the Manufacturing Sector of Developing Economies: A Study of Mexico, Peru and Venezuela. Dissertation. Raleigh: North Carolina State University.

Zabludovsky, Jaime. 1990. Trade Liberalization and Macroeconomic Adjustment. In Dwight S. Brothers and Adele E. Wick, eds., *Mexico's Search for a New Development Strategy*. Boulder: Westview Press.

5.
Argentina

Robert McComb
Texas Tech University

Carlos E. J. M. Zarazaga
Federal Reserve Bank of Dallas

At the end of World War II, per capita income in Argentina was third in the Americas. By 1990 Argentina ranked about seventieth in the world. This chapter describes the Argentine economy during the post–World War II period and the events contributing to its poor performance.

Historical Overview

The colonial experience of present-day Argentina differed from the experience of the rest of the Spanish colonial empire in the Americas. Unlike Mexico and Peru, the region of present-day Argentina was not endowed with precious metals and thus was of little economic interest to the Spanish. After independence, important technological advances were made in food processing and maritime transportation. The elimination of the hostile Indian threat in the late 1870s led to substantial inflows of foreign capital and labor. The extension of railroads and infrastructure connected Argentina to the world market through the coastal ports and enabled a rapid expansion in agricultural output and livestock production in the Pampa region, as well as in the transport, processing, distribution, and export of the agricultural output. There was virtually no development of heavy industry, however, and only limited development of production of intermediate goods.

Foreign ownership was characteristic of Argentine industry during this period. Tariff structures tended to favor agricultural interests and light industry, which were dominated by native-born Argentines. Nevertheless, the outbreak of World War I and the resulting shortages of imported goods provided effective protection and an additional impetus for growth in domestic production of otherwise importable goods. Argentina was largely a full-employment economy in the years prior to 1929 (see table 5.1).

Prior to the Great Depression, the financial system of Argentina had thrived in a very unregulated environment. The depression, however,

Pacific Ocean

Córdoba • Santa Fe
    •   •Rosario
Mendoza

Argentina
Buenos Aires

• Bahía Blanca

• Comodoro Rivadavia

Atlantic Ocean

• Río Gallegos

900   0   900   1800 Miles

⊛ **Capital**
/\ **Major Rivers**
• **Major Cities**
▓ **National Boundary**
☐ **Countries**

N
W   E
S

Table 5.1. An Overview of Argentine Policies

Political-Economic Policies	Financial Market Policies
1853–1930: Free market	Free market
1930–45: Great Depression	Move toward a more regulated financial industry. Complete statization of financial industry ("nationalization of deposits").
1945–55: Military coup ousts President Ramón S. Castillo (6/4/43). Colonel Juan D. Perón is inaugurated as president on 6/4/46. He is reelected for a second term in 1952.	
1955–66: Military coup ousts Juan D. Perón. Peronist party is banned. Limited democracy with weak civilian presidents controlled by the military. President Arturo H. Illia, elected in 1963, deposed by military in 1966.	Deposits are denationalized in 1957. Rest of the regulatory measures introduced by the Peronists persist until 1977. Financial repression reduced by lax interpretion and enforcement of the law.
1966–70: Military government headed by General Juan C. Onganía implements economic plan masterminded by minister of finance, Adalbert Krieger Vasena.	
1970–73: Onganía replaced by General Roberto M. Levingston (6/18/70), who is in turn removed on 3/23/71 by General Alejandro A. Lanusse. Free elections held.	Tighter implementation of the law and interest rate caps. Financial repression increases. Financial and monetary policies similar to those of 1945–55. Nationalization of deposits. Heavy controls on the price and allocation of credit.
1973–76: Héctor J. Cámpora inaugurated as president on 5/25/73. Political anarchy forces the resignation of Cámpora on 7/13/73. Raúl Lastiri calls general elections. Perón wins, but dies on 7/1/74. His constitutional successor is his wife. The escalation of urban guerrilla activities against military targets and inflation rates of 50% a month create the conditions for the military coup of March 24, 1976.	Complete liberalization of financial markets in June 1977. Creation of the Monetary Regulation Account, source of significant "quasi-fiscal" deficits throughout the 1980s. Attempts to alleviate private sector debt and to restore free-market policies fail, in part because of the Malvinas/Falkland wars.
1976–81: Military government of General Rafael Videla attempts free-market reforms under the intellectual guidance of the minister of finance, José Alfredo Martínez de Hoz.	
1981: General Roberto Eduardo Viola becomes president on 3/29/81.	Financial counterreform of July 1982. Imposition of interest rate caps.
January–June 1982: Populist General Viola replaced by General Leopoldo Fortunato Galtieri on 12/22/81. Malvinas/Falkland Islands war from April 2 to June 10.	
July 1982–83: Defeat in the Malvinas/Falklands war brings down Galtieri, who is	Heavy regulation of the financial industry through 1989. The hyperinflation of February–July 1989 leads to stabilization attempts

Table 5.1. Continued

Political-Economic Policies	Financial Market Policies
replaced by General Reynaldo Benito A. Bignone on 7/1/82. *1983–89:* The Radical party wins in free general elections. President Raúl Alfonsín inaugurated on 12/10/83. *1989–95:* The Peronist party wins in May 1989. The hyperinflation forces the transfer of power on 7/8/89 to President Carlos Saúl Menem. The devaluation of the Mexican peso on December 20, 1994, brings about a speculative attack against the Argentine peso and a severe financial crisis. By the end of 1995 Argentina seems to have successfully surmounted this "tequila effect."	that fail. Default on the quasi-fiscal domestic debt in December 1989 and partial confiscation of time deposits in January 1990. On April 1, 1991, the "Convertibility Plan" establishes a currency board system, privatizes almost all state-run enterprises, reforms the tax system, enforces prosecution of tax evasion, and creates the most liberal conditions for the financial system since 1935. It also removes barriers to trade and capital flows.

prompted a wave of regulation that, with brief interludes, would last until almost the end of this century. The most important development was the creation of the Central Bank, Banco Central de la República Argentina, on March 28, 1935, as a mixed ownership firm, with 33% of the capital subscribed by the government. The main goal of the institution was to preserve the stability of the domestic currency and the financial system.

Special interest groups increasingly controlled the Central Bank in their own interest. For example, in 1937, with the official blessing of the Central Bank, a group of private banks reached an agreement on a floor for interest rates on loans. When the Peronist party came to power ten years later, the Central Bank channeled transfers to politically influential constituencies at the expense of the rest of society.

Post–World War II Political Economy

The postwar Argentine economy's declining average growth rates have been highly variable (see chart 5.1 and table 5.2). Changes in the level of GDP and the rate of inflation usually have moved in opposite directions. Although the economy continuously expanded during 1963–74, brief periods of rapid expansion have been followed by sharp contractionary bouts. After 1975 lower average growth rates accompanied an increased frequency in the stop-go cycles during which inflation rates tended to ratchet upward (see chart 5.2).

Chart 5.1. Real GDP Growth Rates, 1952–94 (1990 Prices)

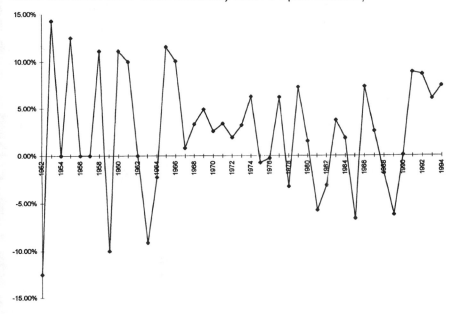

Chart 5.2. Real Per Capita GDP, 1951–93 (1990 Prices)

Table 5.2. Real GDP, 1945–94

Year	Millions of 1960 Pesos At Market Prices	Index (1950 =100)	Index (1970 =100)	Year	Millions of 1970 Pesos At Market Prices	Index (1970 =100)
1945	5,883	77.9	38.1	1970	87,746	100.0
1946	6,373	84.4	41.2	1971	91,050	103.8
1947	7,247	95.9	46.9	1972	92,940	105.9
1948	7,334	97.1	47.4	1973	96,420	109.9
1949	6,998	92.7	45.3	1974	101,630	115.8
1950	7,553	100.0	48.9	1975	101,030	115.1
1951	7,846	103.9	50.8	1976	101,020	115.1
1952	7,451	98.6	48.2	1977	107,470	122.5
1953	7,846	103.9	50.8	1978	104,000	118.5
1954	8,170	108.2	52.8	1979	111,217	126.7
1955	8,747	115.8	56.6	1980	112,919	128.7
1956	8,990	119.0	58.2	1981	105,471	120.2
1957	9,456	125.2	61.2	1982	100,259	114.2
1958	10,033	132.8	64.9	1983	103,279	117.7
1959	9,385	124.3	60.7	1984	106,015	120.8
1960	10,124	134.0	65.5	1985	101,405	115.6
1961	10,843	143.6	70.1	1986	107,210	122.2
1962	10,671	141.3	69.0	1987	109,534	124.8
1963	10,418	137.9	67.4	1988	106,658	121.6
1964	11,491	152.1	74.3	1989	101,864	116.1
1965	12,544	166.1	81.1	1990	102,296	116.6
1966	12,625	167.2	81.7			

Year	Millions of 1990 Pesos At Market Prices	Index 1990 =100
1967	12,959	171.6	83.8
1968	13,516	178.9	87.4
1969	14,670	194.2	94.9
1970	15,459	204.7	100.0
1971	16,198	214.5	104.8	1990	68,922	100
1972	16,705	221.2	108.1	1991	75,059	109
1973	17,720	234.6	114.6	1992	81,554	118
1974	18,874	249.9	122.1	1993	86,474	125
1975	18,625	246.6	120.5	1994	92,891	135

Source: As reported in *Evolución económica;* World Bank 1993; and Banco Central de la República Argentina; for 1990–94, International Financial Statistics.

Imports grew more than two and one-half times the accompanying rate of growth in aggregate output. Import substituting activities in finished goods and the addition of some new basic industries (petroleum and petrochemicals, for example) provided net savings in foreign exchange, but new domestic production of final consumer goods caused an increase in imported raw materials and intermediate inputs.

Argentine manufactured goods never became price competitive in world markets due to high costs arising from inefficient production and inadequate scale that continued because of excessive protection. Argentine exports remained agricultural. When output expanded, demand for imports and domestic consumption of exportables—particularly beef—increased, provoking an exchange crisis.

Argentine policymakers' response to foreign exchange crises typically entailed devaluation of the peso, increased quantitative import restrictions, and policies to reduce real incomes and output. This increased domestic prices even as output contracted; the devaluation consequently could not produce a trade surplus.

Table 5.3 indicates Argentina's inability to achieve higher rates of growth despite the relatively large share (20%) of investment in national output in the 1980s. This figure is misleading, because the domestic price of capital goods relative to other goods in the economy is higher in Argentina than in the developed countries. Moreover, private sector real investment was stunted by the climate of uncertainty. Funds that could have been invested in machines and equipment were instead spent on financial speculation and on influencing government policy to increase favored sectors' income via tariffs, tax concessions, and similar measures. By the 1980s the process culminated in a sharply declining standard of living.

Anti-inflation and exchange rate stabilization policies were doomed to failure as long as the fiscal deficits were unchecked. Argentina came to depend on inflation, taking advantage of negative real interest rates, reduced real tax burdens, and attractive returns to financial speculation. When workers' purchasing power lagged as inflation proceeded, organized labor responded by bringing the economy to a standstill. Efforts to control output prices led to shortages. Staunch adherence to a fixed exchange rate led inevitably to overvaluation, balance of trade difficulties, and an unavoidable and inflationary devaluation. The ever-recurring stabilization imperative, coupled with regime changes, led to a monotonous repetition of policies chosen by successive governments.

The Rise of Peronism, 1945–55

During Juan D. Perón's presidency, Argentine society was reorganized into a corporatist structure, grouped by labor, business, and agriculture. Perón reorganized and integrated labor unions into a social and political force he could control. Only one government-sanctioned union per industry was allowed, strikes required governmental authority, and the industrial unions were organized under the General Confederation of Labor (CGT). Perón enforced an attractive minimum wage and wage scales and improved the conditions for labor. Perón's supporters were placed at the heads of the individual labor unions. Health care and

Table 5.3. Gross Domestic Capital Formation, 1945–94 (indices and percentage shares)

	1945	1946	1947	1948	1949	1950	1951	1952	1953	1954	1955	1956	1957	1958	1959	1960	1961
Index 1970 = 100																	
GDP	38	41	47	45	49	51	48	51	53	57	58	61	65	61	65	70	69
GDCF	33	43	65	67	57	34	42	37	37	35	41	44	42	52	41	62	73
Percentage shares																	
GDP	100	100	100	100	100	100	100	100	100	100	100	100	100	100	100	100	100
GDCF	19	22	30	30	27	15	18	17	16	14	16	16	15	17	15	21	22

	1962	1963	1964	1965	1966	1967	1968	1969	1970	1971	1972	1973	1974	1975	1976	1977	1978
Index 1970 = 100																	
GDP	67	74	81	82	82	84	87	95	100	104	106	109	116	115	115	122	118
GDCF	66	56	62	65	67	71	78	95	100	408	108	101	105	105	116	138	122
Percentage shares																	
GDP	100	100	100	100	100	100	100	100	100	100	100	100	100	100	100	100	100
GDCF	21	18	18	17	18	19	19	22	21	22	22	20	19	19	21	24	22

	1979	1980	1981	1982	1983	1984	1985	1986	1987	1988	1989	1990	1990	1991	1992	1993	1994
Index 1970 = 100																	
GDP	126	127	119	113	116	119	114	122	125	122	116	116	100	109	118	126	135
GDCF	127	132	109	82	82	74	67	69	78	66	48	41	90	112	146	168	200
Percentage shares																	
GDP	100	100	100	100	100	100	100	100	100	100	100	100	100	100	100	100	100
GDCF	21	22	19	15	15	13	13	12	13	12	9	8	14	16	20	21	19

Sources: BCRA as reported in *Evolución económica*; Díaz Alejandro 1970; Agencia 1987; and World Bank 1993.
a Imported share was actually 0.3%.
b 1960–65 domestic/imported shares from Díaz Alejandro; D/I shares by category all from Díaz Alejandro; otherwise, from *Evolución económica* before 1970.
c Adapted from table 14 of Díaz Alejandro.
d GDP in 1960 pesos for 1945–65.
e GDP in 1970 pesos for 1966–94.
f GDP in 1990 pesos, 1990 = 100 (from International Financial Statistics).

Chart 5.3. Changes in Consumer Prices, 1949–74 (percentage)

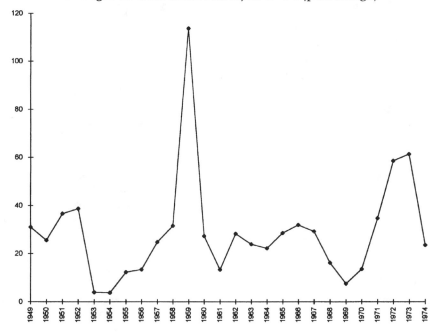

Chart 5.4. Changes in Consumer Prices, 1975–95 (percentage)

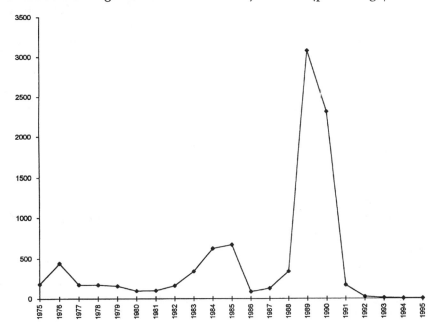

recreational amenities were organized through the unions. By 1954 union membership stood at 2.3 million, a fivefold increase over membership in the early 1940s (Manzetti 1993).

Perón redistributed real income to the urban working classes. By use of a state monopoly in the purchase of agricultural commodities for export, the state decreased the price of agricultural goods relative to industrial goods, thereby boosting the real wages of urban residents and increasing demand for and domestic production of consumer goods. Subsidized credit—often at negative real interest rates—was granted to urban activities. It was expanded through the newly nationalized banking system.

Perón increased the role of the state in an increasingly autarkical economy. Nationalization with indemnity of the banks, railroads, telephone, utilities, and other foreign-owned infrastructure increased state sector employment. The expanded government activity contributed to large and increasing public sector deficits that were financed through the banking system and social security funds.

The Central Bank was to guarantee "a high level of employment." This clause was similar, in letter and spirit, to the National Employment Act that the United States enacted in 1946. Government control of the economy was increased when the Central Bank nationalized the financial services industry by taking over all assets and liabilities of the financial institutions on March 25, 1946. Deposits in the financial institutions were considered deposits in and liabilities of the Central Bank of Argentina. They implicitly were covered 100% by cash reserves, since the Central Bank could honor them by printing money. Private financial institutions obtained funds by rediscounting with the Central Bank. Thus, the financial intermediaries simply "rationed" the funds provided by the Central Bank following the strict guidelines dictated by that institution. Financial institutions had no incentives to screen borrowers since their income depended on commissions for their services rather than earnings from their portfolio of assets and liabilities.

In 1949 the government shut down all savings and loans and replaced them with the state-owned National Mortgage Bank. Long-term lending to the industrial sector was put under control of the Industrial Credit Bank. The provinces also created their own banks, which enabled them to create money indirectly to spend on their own needs. Though this was a benefit to the individual provinces, the inflation thus generated burdened the entire nation.

The Peronist redistributive policies were not sustainable. Public enterprise prices increased after those in the rest of the economy; their costs rose more rapidly than their receipts. This contributed to a continuously expanding public sector deficit as the decade closed. Rapid depletion of the substantial postwar coffers of foreign exchange occurred as a consequence of the nationalizations, economic expansion, and anti-export policies. Efforts at external stabilization were necessary. After 1949 policies favored expansion of private sector activity and agricultural output to increase exports and boost foreign exchange earnings. Real wages declined in 1952 and 1953. Nevertheless, by the time the military coup occurred in September 1955 the economy had begun to recover.

The Military Intervention, 1955–66

Under the military regimes, the enhanced role of the state in the economy remained largely intact. The goal of economic policy was to increase exports and deepen the capital stock. The peso therefore was devalued in 1956 and exports increased less than anticipated, in part because of a rise in protectionism in the world marketplace. At the time of the 1955 military coup, the loans in the Central Bank's portfolio were of poor quality. In 1957 the military government assumed responsibility for a large portion of the losses on loans, thus transferring the burden of promotional and subsidized credit from the beneficiary special interests to the entire population. Although deposits were returned to the financial system, substantial elements of the preceding regime remained in place. The new Central Bank charter specified that the primary goal of the Central Bank was to provide a "reasonable degree of liquidity in line with the need of businesses." The Central Bank remained under the jurisdiction of the Treasury; it was allowed to make temporary advances of funds to the Treasury for an amount of up to 30% of the fiscal revenues of the federal government during the previous twelve months and was authorized to hold in its portfolio a stock of government bonds of up to 25% of the total deposits in the financial system. This created the money the government used to finance its deficit.

In order to circumvent heavy Central Bank controls, financial institutions operated under names designed to disguise their real character. In 1961, however, the government required such firms to register in order to operate legally. In 1964 new legislation enabled the government to regulate the interest rate these intermediaries could pay for deposits and charge on loans.

In 1958 the elected president, Arturo Frondizi, had turned his attention to developing a long-term economic program intended to effect structural changes in the Argentine economy. Renewed emphasis on import substitution favored the development of petroleum extraction and refining, coal and iron ore extraction, petrochemicals and chemicals, steel, and automobile production.

The substantial investment required for these industries exceeded domestic savings. Therefore, foreign direct investment was actively courted and foreign firms were permitted entry into import substituting activities, including petroleum exploration and production. Import restrictions were relaxed, although a system of differential tariffs was put in place under which capital equipment received favored treatment.

Frondizi was confronted with a seriously deteriorating balance of payments. A 1959 stabilization created a favorable environment for investors (Petrecolla 1989). Following a sharp drop in output in 1959, and a resulting increase in foreign exchange reserves, an investment-led expansion continued through 1961. A new foreign exchange crisis in 1962 brought the expansion to a halt. Productive capacity increased significantly as a result of liberalizing imports of capital goods, while foreign exchange savings from the expansion in domestic petroleum production were quite substantial.

Following the brief tenure of Dr. José María Guido in the presidency, President Arturo Illia reversed Frondizi's course by stressing short-term stabilization policies over structural change. Foreign-owned firms in the petroleum industry were bought out and oil contracts annulled. Petroleum production stagnated. Nevertheless, in 1964 the economy entered its longest postwar period of growth. World market prices for Argentine exports were high; agricultural output expanded, reflecting technological improvements and use of more capital per unit of output in agricultural production, which had been taking place for more than a decade. Manufacturing growth reflected increased industrial capacity, which enabled continuous growth in manufacturing output without importing capital equipment.

In the previous period, inflows of foreign capital had financed the import boom. By 1965 debt repayment represented 40% of exports (Guadagni 1989). Furthermore, frequent and small devaluations limited the problems that overvaluation presented for the current account. Last, limitations were placed on writing new foreign debt.

Inflation continued. The share of credit allocated to the private sector decreased; restrictive fiscal and monetary policies were combined with an incomes policy that attempted to restrain real wages. In the end, political support for the Illia administration evaporated and the military returned to power by coup d'état in 1966.

The 1966–73 Military Regime

The 1966–73 military government immediately devalued the peso 30%. Efforts to control inflation centered on restraints on wage growth; agreements with large corporate producers to restrict price increases while credit facilities to private business were expanded; a decrease in the fiscal deficit; and a reduced share of government borrowing needs met through the commercial banking sector. The impact of the devaluation on domestic prices was mitigated by reductions in import tariff rates and increased export taxes. By the end of the decade, inflation was reduced to single digits. Both aggregate output and real wages rose as existing idle production capacity was brought on line.

Nevertheless, inflation reappeared because beef prices increased by about 75% from late 1969 through early 1971. Workers demanded compensating increases in wage rates. Moreover, wage increases in the public sector increased public expenditures and led to a deterioration in the fiscal accounts.

Union activity had been instrumental in triggering the 1966 coup that brought the military back to power. At the outset, Juan Carlos Onganía attempted to make a deal with organized labor. However, a division in union leadership led to a general strike and a repressive military response. Onganía moved against unfriendly unions, jailing their leaders, depriving them of financial resources, and finally taking over the CGT.

The regime's free market orientation reduced both the Central Bank's allocation of credit through the discount window and its management of reserve requirements, as well as its extension of temporary credit to the Treasury. A lower inflation rate led to real interest rates that adequately reflected the relative scarcity of credit.

By 1972, however, the fiscal deficit had risen to 4.9% of GDP. The monetary authorities offset the potential expansion in money supply by increasing the minimum reserve requirements. Moreover, with increased inflation, interest rate ceilings interfered with the allocation of credit. The government responded by issuing very detailed regulations on how credit should be allocated, which led to the most regulated environment since 1957. Thus, the effort to free the market stumbled to its end.

A Return to Peronism, 1973–76

The success of the Peronist candidate for president, Héctor Cámpora, in the 1973 elections fueled a sharp increase in inflation as producers attempted to get ahead of the expected return to price controls. In response, the government based its stabilization efforts on an agreement between business and the labor unions to hold wages and prices at recent averages while allowing a one-time increase in the real wage. On the supply side, a land tax was levied against potential rather than actual output in order to elicit technological advances in production techniques. All agricultural exports were channeled through marketing boards. New restrictions were placed on foreign investment and profit remittances. The state increased its control of credit allocation and of prices and a value added tax was introduced.

The social pact, a compromise incomes policy, coupled with favorable external circumstances, had led to a decrease in inflation and vigorous economic growth. Nevertheless, the government sharply increased public sector employment and expenditures. Despite improved flows of tax revenues, the increased deficit led to excessive money creation and political chaos. To restore political order, Perón was allowed to return, winning the presidency in the election held in September 1973.

In Perón's third presidential term, almost every economic decision of consumers and businesses was again subject to the close scrutiny, when not direct control, of the government. Although economic growth was relatively high, it took place without the unusually favorable international economic conditions that had prevailed in 1945–55. This explains why the predictable adverse consequences of so much intervention came much sooner than they had twenty years earlier. In 1974 price controls led to scarcities, wages were adjusted, and an overvalued peso complicated external balance.

When Juan Perón died in July 1974, he was succeeded in the presidency by his wife, Isabel Perón. She sought a constituency among the conservatives by using "unofficial" paramilitary squadrons to eliminate suspected radicals. Economic policy at first continued its moderate yet distributionist course. The social pact incorporated increased price and wage flexibility. Restrictive monetary and fiscal policies were introduced. Nevertheless, adverse terms of trade and the overvalued peso provoked a peso devaluation in March 1975. In mid-1975 efforts to clip the power of the labor unions were complemented by price adjustments that resulted in a sharp decline in labor's purchasing power.

The financial system deposits had again been "nationalized" by the Peronists. The government relied more heavily on temporary advances from the Central Bank to finance its deficits, thus reducing availability of Central Bank loans (by rediscounting) to the private sector. This led to a severe recession and escalating inflation, which reached 50% per month in March 1976 and led to a military coup on March 24, 1976, that overthrew the democratically elected Peronist government once more.

Return to Military Government, 1976–83

The 1976 military government under General Jorge Rafael Videla and finance minister José Martínez de Hoz pursued policies that reduced real wages 30% from their 1975 level, failed to slow inflation, and culminated in a new crisis in 1978. A January 1979 stabilization plan involved using predetermined exchange rates (the *tablita*) in conjunction with liberalized foreign trade, unrestricted capital flows, and fiscal reforms to combat inflation and to realign the relative prices of goods traded in the domestic market.

Only the *tablita* and liberalization of capital flows were fully implemented. The domestic rate of inflation was not consistent with the scheduled devaluations in the *tablita* and resulted in increasing overvaluation of the peso.

The inflation rate was in part the result of the serious moral hazard features associated with the 1977 deposit insurance scheme. (Moral hazard refers to a situation in which economic agents [such as banks] are induced to take actions in their favor to the detriment of others, because the full consequences of such actions are not borne by the agents responsible for them. For example, banks will take riskier loans with deposit insurance than without it, because even if the loans are not repaid they will be able to pay the deposits with the taxpayers' money that the government makes available to them through the deposit insurance system.) The Central Bank was required to administer a system of deposit insurance that was free and that insured 100% of all deposits. Depositors, free of the risk of losing their savings, placed their money in whatever institution offered the higher interest rates without regard to the financial stability of the institution. This period therefore witnessed the appearance and survival of numerous financial institutions of dubious solvency. In 1978 the military government "denationalized" and progressively deregulated financial services.

In an attempt to correct the deposit insurance system, it was replaced on November 18, 1979. Deposits in domestic currency were covered in full only to $650. The insurance coverage was 90% for larger deposits in domestic currency. Deposits in dollars were not covered.

The removal of full insurance triggered the financial crisis that it was meant to prevent. Deposits were withdrawn from institutions of questionable solvency. In March 1980 the largest bank and the next largest nonbanking financial institution were unable to honor withdrawals of deposits. The Central Bank was forced to liquidate these institutions, whose deposits represented about 10% of the monetary base at that time. This resulted in monetary expansion because the Central Bank was responsible for the payment of at least 90% of those deposits.

Depositors' fears that this would lead to an inflation-devaluation spiral triggered a massive chain reaction. Because the new insurance system did not cover deposits in dollars, investors withdrew their funds from the banks and bought dollars, forcing the Central Bank to provide them with a special line of credit through Repurchase Agreements for loss of deposits.

Three major banks had to be foreclosed as a result of overexposure in questionable loans to firms belonging to holding companies to which they themselves belonged. In a further attempt to restore confidence, the deposit insurance was modified once more by raising the deposit limit for 100% coverage to $56,000. But, in an unprecedented step, the new limits applied retroactively to November 18, 1979, and were applicable to deposits in dollars as well.

These retroactive revisions created the expectation that the Central Bank would act similarly in the future, thus defeating the purpose of the reform of the insurance system, and were partly responsible for the almost endless succession of financial crises that took place into the mid-1990s. Despite Central Bank efforts to rescue weak banks, the share of total deposits in private national banks fell from 45% in December 1979 to 35% in June 1980. There were corresponding gains in the share held in government-owned and foreign banks.

At the beginning of 1981 international reserves were depleted. On April 1 the domestic currency was devalued by 30% and once again "temporary" capital controls were introduced, which lasted until 1990. The government opened another special line of credit (through its rediscounting operations) on April 24, 1981, to refinance private sector

---

The Monetary Regulation Account

A major feature of the 1977 financial reform was the Monetary Regulation Account (CRM), which was intended both to restore the profitability of domestic financial intermediaries and to replace temporary advances to the government of funds from the Central Bank. The CRM financed the ever-increasing government deficit. The CRM was set up as an account of the Treasury in the Central Bank. The financial intermediaries paid a tax on their demand deposit balances and deposited the proceeds of the tax in that account. At the same time, the Treasury paid the financial intermediaries a subsidy for the amount of reserves they had to immobilize in the Central Bank. The tax and subsidy rates were set by the Central Bank. The deficit increased to such a level that, in 1990, the government was compelled to confiscate the time deposits that gave rise to the large government payments to the CRM, thus defaulting on its debt.

The deficits of the CRM were often referred to as "quasi-fiscal" deficits and represented a substantial part of the overall fiscal deficit during the 1980s.

debt under favorable conditions. In particular, the goal was to transform its short-term to longer-term debt, under the supervision of the Central Bank, which tightened credit.

In the meantime, the continued erosion of international reserves and the increasing difficulties of rolling over private and public sector debts with foreign creditors forced another devaluation of 30% on June 1, 1981. The Central Bank compensated losses caused by the devaluation and offered exchange rate insurance on foreign loans to private sector firms. In practice, the system yielded a large subsidy, because 180 days later the exchange rate had fallen 20% more than the guaranteed premium. By the end of 1982 the implicit subsidy was equal to 16% of GDP, and the government was unable to honor these exchange rate insurance contracts.

In order to stop capital flight, the financial institutions were offered a government bond for the equivalent of the amount of the loans they refinanced. Their worst loans were refinanced at the Central Bank, which ended up a few years later "owning" a wide range of bankrupt firms, ranging from hotels to soap factories. The Central Bank payments on these bonds contributed to the ever-growing fiscal deficits that continued to crowd out the private sector from the shrinking capital markets. Under pressure from that sector, the government took the first steps in November toward placing a ceiling on interest rates and improved the terms of exchange rate insurance. Far from restoring the confidence of investors, these measures frightened them. They stayed away from the domestic capital markets.

The army removed General Roberto Viola at the end of 1981 and replaced him with General Leopoldo Galtieri, who vowed a return to more free-market policies. On December 24, 1981, the new minister of finance, Roberto Alemann, announced a stabilization strategy based on strict control of the expansion of the money supply rather than on fixing the exchange rate.

The Falklands War worsened the economy and in July 1982 led the military to dismantle the financial reform of 1977 and return to the financial and monetary policies it had promised to eliminate in 1976. The defeated General Galtieri was replaced in the presidency by General Reynaldo Bignone, whose new economic team created inflation and impaired the ability of market participants to index financial assets and liabilities, thus reducing the real value of domestic debts by 30 to 40% by the end of October. The counterpart was, of course, a comparable decline in the real value of deposits in the financial system, but this occurred at the expense of capital flight and, consequently, insufficient funds to finance investment. The Central Bank therefore imposed mandatory renewal of some of the contracts and paid the exchange rate difference for the rest with yet another bond (Monetary Absorption Bond).

The government requested financial assistance from the IMF. It was not able to carry out either its commitments with the IMF or the deeper structural reforms the Argentine economy needed.

Output fell 11% from 1980 to 1982. The resulting fall in imports led to a trade surplus in 1983. Following steep decreases in real wages due to the devaluations and public enterprise price increases, labor demanded and won significant wage increases. Inflation reached annual rates of 400% by the end of 1983, and real per capita income fell 15% from 1978 to 1983.

Alfonsín and the Return to Democracy, 1983–89

The severe recession and failed invasion of the Falklands/Malvinas Islands led the public to elect the centrist Radical party candidate Raúl Alfonsín 1983. The new government wanted to withhold any important changes in domestic policies until the government's foreign debt was refinanced. But it was precisely this unwillingness to reform the public sector that worried foreign creditors the most. A financial crisis followed. In May 1985 the Central Bank foreclosed the Banco de Italia and Río de la Plata, a bank that ranked third, with 10.4% of the total volume of deposits in dollars. This triggered a run against deposits in dollars throughout the system, which the Central Bank confronted by suspending payment of such deposits for 180 days. The resulting flight out of the domestic currency and into goods and dollars put additional upward pressures in the general price level and pushed the monthly inflation rate above 30% in May 1985.

On June 14, 1985, the government adopted a heterodox stabilization plan—the Plan Austral I. Later two more plans were introduced and abandoned. In February 1989 predictions that the Peronist party would win the presidential elections scheduled for May 1989 prompted massive capital outflows. Following the presidential election in which the Peronist candidate, Carlos Menem, was elected, public confidence disintegrated and a flight from the austral fueled hyperinflation, which reached 200% a month in July. Rioting and looting of supermarkets made it clear that Alfonsín's administration could not govern. The presidency was transferred to Menem in July instead of December 1989, as originally planned.

Although Menem had campaigned on a traditional populist Peronist platform, he pursued a program of economic reforms aimed at restoring a market-oriented economy with a limited role for the central government. Output had been falling for a decade; hyperinflation peaked at

20,000% in early 1990, and tax administration broke down completely. Menem had little choice but to abandon his campaign promises. He instead reformed the public sector by privatizing most of the public firms, by transferring broad fiscal responsibilities and employment to provincial government, and by improving tax collections and design.

Menem's first economic plan was just a repeat of the fixed exchange programs and therefore failed. As a consequence, on December 10 the government defaulted on the domestic debt voluntarily held by the public and rescheduled it unilaterally. Repayment of the principal was suspended for two years. A massive withdrawal of funds followed the rumors and financial markets went into a tailspin. The government appointed a new minister of finance, Ermán González, on December 15. He moved to a dirty float, but the withdrawal of deposits continued and on January 1 the "Plan Bonex" imposed the "restructuring" of the deposits of the financial system by exchanging all time deposits, bankers' acceptances, and similar financial instruments whose face values exceeded approximately 1 million australs for long-term government bonds payable in dollars (Bonos Externos—BONEX). The BONEX bonds were deeply discounted. On the first business day of 1990 this implied a capital loss of 57% with respect to an original deposit. The Plan BONEX reduced the quasi-fiscal deficit that had originated in the interest payments of that debt, but did not reduce the deficit excluding interest payments. The deficit was financed by money creation and resulted in higher inflation: in March 1990 the Consumer Price Index increased 96%. The government delayed payments on government contracts, pensions, and even wages of public workers until enough revenues were collected.

These failures led Menem to announce policy measures—designed by the new economics minister, Domingo Cavallo—that were intended to reduce the public sector and to restore the market process for resource allocation in Argentina. Sharp reductions in public sector employment, divestiture of public enterprises, expenditure cuts, and other fiscal reforms in conjunction with increased tax revenues led to a rapid reduction in the fiscal deficit. Elimination of quantitative controls on imports (except automobiles) and drastic reductions in import tariffs from 22.3% in October 1989 to 9.1% took place in April 1994. Moreover, export taxes were eliminated and foreign direct investment was once again welcomed.

The most important measure was the Convertibility Act, which declared the austral to be fully convertible at a fixed rate to the dollar. The law requires that the monetary base be fully backed by gold and hard-currency reserves and eliminates indexation of wages and other contracted prices.

The "Convertibility Plan" lifted all interest rate caps. The financial system again operated under a fractional reserve regime, with relatively high reserve requirements for demand deposits and none on time deposits. A minimum maturity of thirty days was applied to time deposits. The lending capacity of the financial system would be determined by mandatory reserve requirements. Loan policies were set by the financial institutions.

The main goal of the 1992 Central Bank was the preservation of the value of the currency. Congress, however, is given the power to establish and modify exchange rate policy in a separate Convertibility Law. The Central Bank cannot grant transitory advances to the Treasury, implement any form of deposit insurance, or act as lender of last resort on a large scale, although it can still buy limited amounts of government debt from the Treasury.

Discount window loans must be backed by securities valued at their market price; therefore, the fiscal deficit of the provinces could not be financed by such loans. The provinces thus were unable to meet their payroll commitments. This led to political and social unrest in several provinces, particularly in Córdoba (the second richest province of Argentina), Tucumán (one of the poorest), and Río Negro.

The result of the reforms was a dramatic decline in the inflation rate to 30% by early 1992, 7.4% in 1993, and 3.9% in 1994. Annual growth of GDP in 1986 pesos was 8.9% in 1991, 10.8% in 1992, 10.3% in 1993, and 10.6% in 1994. This was interrupted in 1995 owing to the "tequila effect" produced by the Mexican financial crisis that began in December 1994. Fear that Argentine banks were exposed to Mexican public debt led to a banking panic. By the end of April 1995 Argentina's financial system had lost 18% of the deposits it had before the Mexican peso devaluation, forcing many banks to suspend withdrawals of deposits. As a result, gross domestic product contracted and the unemployment rate reached an all-time high of 18.6% in May 1995. Argentina nonetheless did not devalue its currency. Moreover, during the 1991–94 period, real investment averaged about 22% of GDP per annum. Widespread deregulation of industry and eliminations of distortions in the allocation of credit were undertaken at the national level. By the end of 1993 the government had obtained about US$20 billion from the sale of its assets, roughly 30% of the country's public external debt at the time, some of which was paid off. The reduced interest payments on the smaller foreign debt and the elimination of deficit-ridden public firms contributed to the reduction of the government fiscal deficit. On January 1, 1995, the Common Market of the South (MERCOSUR), which includes Argentina, was established. It was expected that the enhanced profits that would be available from a larger common market, in contrast to a national market alone, would increase investment in each of the member nations of the market.

Table 5.4. Public Sector Expenditures and Revenues, 1961–92 (percent of current GDP)

	1961	1962	1963	1964	1965	1966	1967	1968	1969	1970	1971	1972	1973	1974	1975	1976
Public sector																
Revenues	31.4	27.6	27.3	25.5	25.3	26.8	30.3	30.2	29.7	29.5	26.5	25.0	26.5	32.3	24.0	27.9
Expenditures	34.7	33.8	32.7	30.6	28.3	31.6	31.6	31.6	30.5	30.4	30.0	30.2	33.8	41.7	39.1	39.4
Balance	-3.3	-6.2	-5.4	-5.1	-3.0	-1.8	-1.3	-1.4	-0.8	-0.9	-3.5	-5.2	-7.3	-9.4	-15.1	-11.5
State enterprises and binational entities																
Revenues	9.6	9.9	9.7	8.6	7.7	8.0	8.7	9.0	8.6	8.1	7.4	7.7	7.9	10.2	7.7	9.8
Expenditures	14.8	15.0	14.4	12.1	10.6	10.4	10.6	10.5	9.8	10.0	10.2	10.7	10.7	14.4	11.9	14.6
Balance	-5.2	-5.1	-4.7	-3.5	-2.9	-2.4	-1.9	-1.5	-1.2	-1.9	-2.8	-3.0	-2.8	-4.2	-4.2	-4.8

	1977	1978	1979	1980	1981	1982	1983	1984	1985	1986	1987	1988	1989	1990	1991	1992
Public sector																
Revenues	32.9	37.0	34.4	35.4	34.1	34.1	33.2	33.1	36.8	33.9	31.0	32.3	31.0	26.7	28.8	32.3
Expenditures	37.7	43.9	41.7	43.8	48.2	46.9	48.9	44.5	46.4	43.1	46.1	48.1	40.7	40.0	39.1	38.2
Balance	-4.8	-6.9	-7.3	-8.4	-14.1	-15.5	-15.7	-11.4	-9.6	-9.2	-15.1	-15.8	-10.7	-13.3	-10.3	-5.9
State enterprises and binational entities																
Revenues	10.2	11.3	8.9	8.9	10.5	9.9	10.7	10.5	13.6	12.1	11.8	12.8	12.8	8.8	6.7	6.0
Expenditures	13.0	14.5	12.8	12.4	15.0	15.6	15.9	13.5	15.5	12.9	13.5	16.3	14.7	9.5	8.0	5.7
Balance	-2.8	-3.2	-3.9	-3.5	-4.5	-8.7	-5.2	-3.0	-1.9	-0.8	-1.7	-3.5	-1.9	-0.6	-1.3	0.3

Sources: 1961–83 as reported in World Bank 1985 and credited to IMF; Dirección Nacional de Programación Presupuestaria, Secretaría de Hacienda, *Sector Público*; Esquema de Ahorro, Inversión y Financiamiento, 1961–79; IMF Staff Estimates, 1990–92; World Bank 1994.

By the end of 1995 capital inflows had slowly started to resume and deposits in the financial system had almost completely recovered their pre–Mexican crisis levels at the same time that the number of financial institutions shrank, falling from 205 at the end of 1994 to 153 a year later. Thus, in 1995, by force of circumstance, Argentina started to implement the much needed and often postponed structural reform of its financial sector.

The fiscal deficit, although smaller, remained intractable. Efforts to reduce the deficit by reducing spending on welfare provoked a general strike by the unions, the traditional Peronist base. In order to appease them, President Menem replaced Domingo Cavallo as minister of the economy with Roque Fernández in June 1996. Renewed efforts to cut overall spending have so far met with stiff resistance and little success.

The Argentine Public Sector

Increased state penetration of the economy began in the immediate post–World War II period as a consequence of Perón's nationalization of large enterprises. Growth and diversification in central and provincial administration and productive activities expanded, while the use of state sector employment at all levels of government for political purposes swelled the rolls of civil servants and public sector employees. Interest groups used the state apparatus to assure themselves economic rents through an array of explicit and implicit subsidies. Direct subsidies, subsidized credit, tax exemptions, low public enterprise output prices, and high input prices, to name a few, represented roughly 8% of GDP in 1987–89.

Fiscal deficits have been a chronic problem. Deficits reached 5 to 14% of GDP in the 1970s and over 15% in the 1980s. If one also includes Central Bank losses, the quasi-fiscal deficit, the combined public sector deficit probably exceeded 20% of GDP in the 1980–83 period (World Bank 1993). The public sector also assumed the private sector's external debt in 1980–82. Foreign loans were not available to Argentina in the early 1980s. Menem's reforms led to a sharp increase in revenues and a significant decrease in noninterest expenditures. By 1992 the fiscal deficit was converted into a surplus.

The Structure of the Argentine Public Sector

The Argentine public sector is composed of the federal government, twenty-two provincial governments, Tierra del Fuego, the federal district of Buenos Aires, the financial public sector, and separate health funds. The federal government consists of the national administration, public enterprises, and the national social security system. The provincial governments include administrative machinery, public enterprises, social security systems, and, for purposes of this study, municipalities. The financial public sector contains the Central Bank, twenty-three provincial banks, and, until recently, four nationally administered commercial banks.

Nonfinancial public sector expenditures averaged approximately 35% of GDP over the course of the 1960s, 45% in the seventies, and more than 55% by 1983; they declined somewhat following public sector reforms in the nineties. Since the mid-1970s the national administration's expenditures have represented approximately 20% of nonfinancial public sector expenditures. Prior to the privatization programs in the 1990s, public enterprise expenditures contributed about one-third of total public sector expenditures. Divestiture of public enterprises more than halved expenditures from this source, declining to about 5–6% of GDP by 1992. Social security expenditures grew sharply as the number of beneficiaries expanded, amounting to more than 12% of GDP in 1985 and covering more than 99% of the population sixty years old and older. Provincial governments' expenditures more than doubled between 1960 and 1993, representing more than 12% of GDP.

Total expenditures on health care increased from about 7% of GDP in 1970 to about 10% in the 1990s. Of the 60% spent through the public sector, about one-third is in the form of central and provincial government expenditures. The remainder consists of obligatory health insurance funds. As a result of the transfer of expenditures, hospitals and clinics, and other social welfare programs to the provincial governments, the central government's share of health expenditures has dwindled significantly. Two-thirds of the Ministry of Health and Social Action's spending is primarily utilized to support provincial governments' subsidized housing programs.

The Argentine system of public education has performed poorly and demonstrated further declines in quality over the course of the 1980s. The low quality of instruction has been exacerbated by declining salaries of teachers, who have reduced the hours spent teaching in order to pursue supplemental employment. The low instructional quality probably contributes to very high dropout rates at both primary and secondary levels (World Bank 1993).

Argentine military expenditures as a share of GDP have decreased substantially in the last decade, from the high point of approximately 6% of GDP in the early 1980s—the time of the Malvinas/Falkland Islands War—to 2% in the mid-nineties. This resulted from resolution of border disputes with Chile, improved relations with Brazil, and a diminished internal threat that accompanied the dissolution of Communist governments that provided support to Argentine insurgents. The total number of military personnel was roughly halved between 1984 and 1991. Prior to the privatization programs pursued by the Menem administration, a large number of public enterprises producing both military and civilian goods were attached to the military. These enterprises were established in the 1940s and employed more than 30,000 workers in the early 1990s.

There was a slight downward trend in public sector investment in terms of shares in both GDP and total investment in constant pesos over the course of the fifties and sixties while total investment oscillated for the most part between 15 and 20% of GDP (see table 5.3). Public sector investment attained its maximum as a percentage share of GDP during the 1977–78 period. A dramatic decrease in public sector investment in the 1980s resulted from the suspension of foreign capital inflows. By the end of the eighties, public sector investment had fallen below 2% of GDP and represented less than one-fifth of total gross fixed capital formation, and it fell further after 1990, as the program of divestiture of public enterprises proceeded.

Public sector employment in 1947 accounted for 9.5% of the economically active population. During Perón's first presidency, it rose to 17.8% by 1951. After 1960 this share varied from 16.3% in 1970 to 19.3% during the Isabel Perón administration in 1975.

Central government employment (national administration, public financial sector, and public enterprises) was about the same in 1985 as it had been in 1960, but this is misleading. The transfer of health, sanitation, and education services from the central government to the provincial governments after 1980 helps to explain a rapid growth in provincial employment, because employment of teachers was transferred.

The Public Enterprise Sector

Argentine public enterprises are found primarily in capital-intensive activities, such as utilities, air transport, and exploitation of natural resources, as well as in petroleum refining, chemicals, and iron and steel, which were viewed as essential to a process of industrialization and economic independence. Prior to the privatizations of the early 1990s, public enterprise output accounted for approximately 6–8% of GDP, 20% of investment expenditures, and some 7% of total employment.

In 1970 the public enterprise sector output accounted for 7.4% of GDP, producing 36% of total mining output, 77% of total electricity, gas, and water, 34% of transportation and commercial services, and 2% of manufacturing output. Between 1950 and 1980 the relative importance of the national railroad (nationalized in 1947) dwindled from over

43% to about 14% of sectoral output as trucks replaced trains, although the national airline company (established in 1950 by merger) expanded significantly. In the energy sector, the share of output produced by Gas del Estado (established by nationalization in 1945) and Servicios Eléctricos del Gran Buenos Aires (created in 1958) grew rapidly.

As a share of GDP, total expenditures of the public enterprise sector declined from slightly more than 16% in 1960 to about 11% in 1965, remaining at that level until 1974 and rising to a high point of 18.2% in 1985, because of the high prices paid by the public enterprises as a result of the requirement that they buy from Argentine suppliers (Agencia 1987).

Public enterprise sales revenues were quite variable over the period 1961–81. Upon inauguration of a new stabilization policy package, public sector relative prices were increased in order to reduce financing needs of the sector and to restore output prices that appropriately reflected production costs. Later, public enterprise prices were restrained in order to curb inflation and, as anti-inflation policies were largely unsuccessful, public enterprise relative prices deteriorated until a new cycle was begun.

The public enterprise sector was in deficit every year from 1961 through 1991. The need for financing varied from 1.7% of GDP in 1969 to 6.9% in 1982. The total accumulated public sector financial transfers to the thirteen largest public enterprises from 1965 through 1987 were equal to the stock of external debt acquired by Argentina (World Bank 1993; Porto 1992).

The Argentine tax system performed very poorly from 1970 to 1990, because of the high variability in tax receipts as a percentage of GDP and the increased resort to inefficient but easily collectible taxes, such as stamp taxes and forced savings. Furthermore, tax collections showed a tendency to decrease over the decade of the 1980s owing to the inflationary loss in real value of delayed tax receipts and more widespread tax evasion.

Reform of the Public Sector

Between 1980 and 1981 external debt roughly doubled from 18 to 37% of GDP and increased rapidly relative to exports (see table 5.5). A symptom of the need for economic reform was the fact that by 1981 both public and private debt service were in arrears.

The foreign debt owed was restructured in 1985 and again in 1987. However, the continuing deterioration of the public sector accounts necessitated a suspension of interest payments from 1988 to 1990. The public enterprise sector's deficit was on the order of US$5 billion per year

Table 5.5. External Debt, 1970–94 (millions of US$)

Year	Total (1)	GDP (2)	Exports (3)	Reserves (4)	(1)/(2)	(1)/(3)	(4)/(1)
1970	3,876	23,150	1,773	759	.17	2.19	.20
1971	4,525	23,688	1,740	374	.19	2.60	.08
1972	5,092	21,628	1,941	541	.24	2.62	.11
1973	4,986	35,657	3,266	1,462	.14	1.53	.29
1974	5,514	48,934	3,931	1,411	.11	1.40	.26
1975	8,085	45,381	2,961	620	.18	2.73	.08
1976	9,738	46,288	3,916	1,812	.21	2.49	.19
1977	11,761	49,251	5,666	4,039	.24	2.08	.34
1978	13,663	64,083	6,400	6,037	.21	2.13	.44
1979	19,035	104,284	7,810	10,480	.18	2.44	.55
1980	27,162	153,348	8,021	7,684	.18	3.39	.28
1981	35,671	95,794	9,143	3,877	.37	3.9	.11
1982	43,634	66,469	7,624	3,206	.66	5.72	.07
1983	45,087	74,000	7,836	3,470	.61	5.75	.08
1984	46,903	80,000	8,107	3,734	.59	5.79	.08
1985	48,312	69,370	8,396	5,471	.70	5.75	.11
1986	51,422	–	6,852	–	–	–	–
1987	58,324	103,754	6,360	3,734	.56	9.17	.06
1988	58,303	121,370	9,134	5,158	.48	6.38	.09
1989	65,511	70,220	9,573	3,217	.93	6.84	.05
1990	62,974	135,150	12,353	6,222	.47	5.10	.10
1991	65,229	189,600	11,978	8,975	.34	5.45	.14
1992	68,339	228,800	12,240	12,445	.30	5.58	.18
1993	70,566	255,600	13,100	17,382	.28	5.39	.25
1994	77,388	280,200	15,800	16,003	.28	4.90	.21

Source: World Bank 1993, BCRA, FIEL, World Debt Tables.

by the end of the 1980s. Argentina began an ambitious and rapid program of divestiture of state enterprises in 1990. The sale of these enterprises generated needed cash receipts and enabled the state to reduce foreign debt by swapping equity in privatized enterprises for Argentine government debt held by foreigners. After 1990 proceeds from the privatization program permitted significant reductions in commercial bank debt. As early as mid-1992 the sales of the national telephone company, the national airline, and some railway lines enabled foreign debt to be cut by about US$7 billion. Negotiations in 1993–94 led to a major restructuring of Argentine debt. New bond issues for the principal and initial interest payments were collateralized by United States Treasury bonds. The agreement provided for issuing bonds worth US$25.1 billion and DM564 million.

Purchase of the state enterprises was not restricted to Argentine nationals. In June 1993 Argentina sold a 45% stake in the state petroleum company, Yacimientos Petrolíferos Argentinos (YPF), for slightly more than US$3 billion and opened the petroleum industry to foreign firms. In 1989 only four foreign oil firms were active in Argentina. By 1993 there were more than forty such firms.

By 1995 Argentina had either already divested itself of or was in the process of selling virtually the entire national public enterprise sector. Provincial governments have been slow and, in some cases, unwilling to pursue similar policies. Beginning in 1991, the fiscal accounts have been roughly balanced on average, as a result of increases in tax revenues, proceeds from privatization, and, to a lesser degree, through expenditure restraint. In the 1990s increased reliance on the value-added tax, initially set at 18%, led to sharp increases in real tax revenues. Moreover, personal income and corporate profits taxes have been reinforced and a tax on personal assets has been introduced. Through simplification of the tax system, distortions were reduced, equity was enhanced, and collections were facilitated.

The Agricultural Sector

The agricultural sector generates the lion's share of foreign exchange and produces nearly all of the food consumed in Argentina. Agriculture in the Pampas has represented about 80% of the area under cultivation and accounted for roughly an equivalent share of export earnings. Non-Pampean agriculture is significantly more diverse and oriented toward the domestic market.

The 1945–70 period was marked by relatively stagnant Pampean output and productivity and declining export performance relative to both Argentine GDP and world trading volume. In the post-1970 period Argentine agriculture adjusted to significant changes in export demand by shifting land-use patterns and more rapid adoption of modern agricultural technologies. While increased protectionism in the Common Market resulted in sharp reductions in traditional exports to Western Europe, the United States' embargo of grain exports to the Soviet Union provided new export opportunities for Argentina.

Crop production in 1970 was approximately the same as it had been during World War II; crop output per hectare fell sharply. Total agricultural production did not regain its 1940–44 levels until the early 1960s and was not sufficient to maintain export levels in the face of rising domestic consumption. As a result of higher profits in cattle production, more land was devoted to pasturage, at the expense of grain production. Given the growth in domestic and export demand for traditional Argentine agricultural exports in the immediate postwar period, Argentine agricultural production performed disappointingly.

Prices for agricultural output relative to nonagricultural goods and land tenure practices help to explain this puzzle. Export taxes and an overvalued peso reinforced the deterioration in the international terms of trade for traditional Argentine agricultural exports in the early postwar years. Nevertheless, in 1952 relative agricultural prices began to recover, nearly attaining their prewar levels by 1962, before declining again over the latter half of that decade. However, these prices fluctuated widely; consequently, agricultural output was slow to change in response to changing relative prices. Moreover, in cattle production, herds represent both capital stock and potential output. When suppliers expect increased relative prices for cattle, they hold cattle from slaughter in order to increase herd size and future output. This short-term reduction in supply itself causes an increase in cattle prices. When herds reach desired levels, the market process is reversed and falling prices induce a reduction in herd size and an increased supply of cattle. This was increasingly important. Argentina shifted land use from crops to cattle as a result of the rural to urban migration of labor and new rural wage and tenancy regulations that established minimum wage scales for rural laborers, froze rural rents—reducing landowners' rental income to 10% of its prewar level by 1955—and established a basis for permanent tenancy by restricting landowners' rights to force tenant farmers from their holdings in the 1940s. Production shifted toward less labor-intensive outputs, such as cattle ranching and wheat, from 1940 to 1953.

Increases in agricultural output due to technological improvements can be obtained by increased use of machinery as well as by application of new hybrid seeds and animal breeds, fertilizers, and pesticides. Some 30,000 tractors were in use at the end of the war, and almost 200,000 more powerful tractors were in use by 1969. They replaced both laborers and horses, releasing land devoted to grazing horses for either cattle grazing or crop production.

Diffusion of improved seeds and use of chemical fertilizers, pesticides, and herbicides were hampered by the near absence of extension services. A surprisingly slight use of chemical fertilizer resulted from its high price (relative to the price of fertilizer in the United States), which, given a paucity of research as to effectiveness in the Pampean context and low output prices, made its application financially unattractive.

The period beginning in the early to mid-1970s has been called the "second agricultural revolution of the Pampas." The area under cultivation of cereals and oilseeds expanded. Their output increased more rapidly as a result of impressive increases in yields. Aggregate production of wheat, corn, soybeans, sunflower seeds, and sorghum tripled from the 1960s to the early 1980s. The introduction and expansion of soybeans and sorghum production in the sixties and seventies were particularly striking. By the beginning of the eighties, these five crops accounted for 95% of all crop exports but only 77% of area under crop cultivation nationally. The volume of crop exports grew 7.5% per year. Livestock exports *decreased* by slightly more than 2.1% annually.

The crop production increases were achieved as a result of a tariff reduction on imported fertilizers at the end of the 1970s that reduced domestic fertilizer prices and resulted in wider and more intensive application of chemical fertilizers during the eighties. Use of early maturing wheat varieties made double cropping with soybeans possible, while new seed varieties of sunflowers and sorghum boosted their yields.

The mechanization of Pampean zone agriculture was complete by 1970. The high cost of machinery has led to the extensive use of contracting for machinery services. This has enabled Argentina to increase the level of machinery utilization well above the levels found elsewhere in temperate zone agriculture. For example, the average annual area harvested by a combine in Argentina in 1982 was 549 hectares compared to an average of 160 hectares in the United States. The share of total area organized in farm groups working 200–1,000 hectares—the size that would be likely to support increased mechanization—increased quite substantially in the postwar period (Agencia 1987; World Bank 1985).

Farm size distribution remained fairly stable, with the exception of very small-scale farms that are of little importance in aggregate output. Between 1947 and 1974 the share of land held by owner-operators more than doubled, from 36% to 74%. Land held by tenants and sharecroppers declined from 24% to 13%, as tenants either purchased their land or were bought out by landowners, who increasingly used contractors. This contributed to increasing the area worked by a single management. In the 1970s, as a result of reduction in regulatory obstacles, small-scale farms tended to be leased to larger operators.

The Industrial Sector

Growth in industrial output was the principal source of economic growth before the mid-seventies, and contraction in industrial activity was the primary cause of the sharp declines in overall economic activity and employment at the end of the decade. The crisis of the eighties brought gross domestic investment in plants and equipment to a near standstill while net capital formation was negative. Deterioration in the industrial fabric and a widening technological lag between Argentina and the advanced economies were natural consequences of disinvestment.

By 1950 only 15% of the total domestic supply of industrial goods was imported. During the 1950s emphasis was placed on the replacement of imports in the supply of consumer durables. This prompted high rates of growth in machinery and vehicles, electrical machinery and appliances, and metals. Policy shifted in the 1960s, leading to high rates of growth in iron and steel, petroleum and its derivatives, chemicals, and synthetic fibers. Continued high growth rates in the domestic automobile industry and the requirement that it increase purchases from domestic suppliers prompted rapid growth in the production of selected automobile components.

These industries share certain characteristics. First, their technology requirements are more sophisticated than those that characterized traditional lines of Argentine manufacturing. The acquisition and application of more technologically advanced products and production methods were brought about by an increasingly large foreign presence, which took the form of foreign subsidiaries. Second, they had increasing returns to scale; their output was increasingly concentrated among a few large firms. Third, their production is relatively intensive in the use of capital and skilled labor. The increased share of industrial output produced by these industries was thus accompanied by a reduction in their share of total manufacturing employment even while the rest of Argentine industry increased output at roughly constant employment levels prior to 1980 (Mallon and Sourrouille 1975).

Between 1950 and 1974 the industrial sector grew about 4.5% per year, compared to an average growth rate in gross domestic product of 3.4%. Despite this generally impressive performance, doubts about the sustainability of ISI were voiced during the mid-1960s, because imports still were required for growth. The high prices of Argentine manufactures made them difficult to export. Therefore, measures to promote nontraditional manufactured exports were introduced in the late 1960s. Export subsidies were to offset the relative price disadvantages of Argentine manufacturers, and a more realistic exchange rate policy was to be pursued. The manufacturing sector responded to these incentives and its exports increased by 125% between 1970 and 1974. However, there was a sharp drop in manufactured exports in 1975 when a reorientation of export policies took place (World Bank 1985).

Industrial output rose from 27% of output in 1970 to 28.3% in 1974. After 1980, however, manufacturing's share of GDP began a decade of sharp decline (Agencia 1987; see table 5.6). By 1990 its share of GDP had fallen to 20.7%. During the 1980–85 period real GDP fell 2.1% per year. The contraction in industrial output contributed 42.5% of this decline. The greatest declines were registered in production of consumer goods, "light" intermediate goods, and machinery and transport equipment.

Following the military coup in 1976, the policy of ISI was abandoned. In 1979 protection of domestic industry was sharply reduced as trade was

Table 5.6. Sectoral Shares of GDP, 1945–92

	1945	1950	1955	1960	1965	1970	1975	1980	1985	1990	1990*	1992
Agriculture	23.0	18.0	19.3	16.6	16.6	13.2	13.1	12.6	15.8	16.7	8.9	7.8
Mining	0.8	0.5	0.7	1.1	1.1	2.3	2.2	2.5	2.7	2.9	2.7	2.3
Manufacturing	30.4	27.9	29.2	31.1	31.1	27.0	27.8	24.6	22.5	20.7	26.6	27.0
Construction	3.5	4.8	3.8	4.0	4.0	6.5	5.9	6.5	3.2	1.9	4.5	5.6
Electricity, gas, and water	0.8	0.9	1.1	1.2	1.2	2.3	2.9	3.5	4.6	5.4	2.1	1.9
Commerce[a]	6.7	19.5	18.6	18.9	18.9	15.2	15.0	16.2	14.0	13.0	15.5	16.7
Transport and communications[a]	16.5	8.5	8.0	7.9	7.9	11.3	10.7	10.6	11.7	12.2	5.0	5.0
Banking	3.9	4.1	4.1	4.0	4.0	7.6	7.1	8.9	7.8	12.2	15.0	15.7
Public and private services	14.5	15.8	15.2	15.2	15.2	14.6	15.4	14.6	17.7	8.4	20.2	17.0
TOTAL	100	100	100	100	100	100	100	100	100	100	100	100

Note: Sectoral shares of GDP for the years 1945–69 are measured in 1960 pesos, for the years 1970–90 in 1970 pesos.

[a] Data for 1945–49 from BCRA reported in Díaz Alejandro 1970, table 17; data for 1950–69 from BCRA, *Origen del producto y distribución de ingreso, años 1950–1969*, reported in Randall 1978—clearly there is a difference in definition of the commerce sector and transport and communications sector between the two series; data for 1970–90 from BCRA reported in World Bank 1993; data for 1990* and 1992 from BCRA, reported in the *Anuario estadístico de la República Argentina*, vol. 9, 1993.

liberalized, import tariffs were reduced, and the peso was allowed to become increasingly overvalued. Although Argentine firms reduced labor redundancy in an effort to reduce costs, the currency overvaluation narrowed export possibilities and introduced intense foreign competition in the domestic market for firms producing tradables. Rising real rates of interest increased the relative attractiveness of financial investment as opposed to real investment and led to a drop in investment in plant and equipment (World Bank 1985).

Following the 1991 economic reforms, industrial activity increased. Quantitative restrictions on imports were eliminated and tariffs were sharply reduced, leading to greater competitiveness.

The structure of Argentine industry has undergone rapid change over the last fifty years. The production of heavy intermediate goods, as a share of total industrial value-added, increased quite significantly between 1970 and 1985. This increased share came largely at the expense of declining shares of "light" intermediate goods and capital goods production and resulted from absolute declines in the other sectors' outputs, rather than from a significant absolute increase in output of "heavy" intermediate goods. The share of consumer goods remained roughly constant.

Although Argentine industry was significantly more diversified by 1970 than it was in the prewar period, foodstuffs and beverage industries still accounted for the largest share of output, followed by chemical products, petroleum products, and metals, which together represent nearly 37% of total manufacturing production. Those four industries account for nearly 60% of manufacturing output. Capital goods production, after enjoying a period of expansion, declined to earlier production levels in the decade of the 1980s. The textiles and clothing industries saw their share of output fall quite significantly after 1975.

Over 80% of manufacturing employment and value-added is concentrated in Buenos Aires and the surrounding region. Two-thirds of manufacturing employment and 65% of manufacturing value-added are located in the federal capital and greater Buenos Aires. Heavy industry is located primarily within the Pampean region, principally the area of Buenos Aires. Regional resource endowments determined the location of other industries. For example, foodstuffs, beverages, and tobacco dominated production in Entre Ríos, Tucumán, Jujuy, Salta, Corrientes, Santa Cruz, and La Pampa. Textile, clothing, and leather goods production accounted for the largest share of manufacturing activity in Chaco, while metals and machinery represented nearly three-quarters of the value of manufacturing in Tierra del Fuego.

In 1984 small business establishments (employing 50 or fewer persons) accounted for 88.5% of the total number of registered establishments and 18.2% of total manufacturing value while employing 28.0% of the labor force. Medium-sized firms (with 51 to 200 employees) accounted for 27.4% of employees and 25.6% of production. Large firms (with more than 200 employees) had 44.4% of the labor force and produced 56.2% of total manufacturing output, while only representing 2.7% of the total number of establishments. Nearly a third of the total number of business establishments were sole proprietorships, while slightly more than 28% were organized as corporations. In terms of total value of production, the sole proprietorships held only a 2.5% share compared to nearly 80% for corporate entities. State-owned or -controlled enterprises contributed slightly more than 8% of the total value of production.

Income Distribution

Incomes in Argentina have traditionally been high because its highly productive agriculture supported the development of a predominantly urban society with low unemployment rates. The percentage of individuals in poverty was lower in Argentina in 1980 than in any other Latin American country, and extreme poverty was nearly nonexistent (Psacharopoulos et al. 1992). However, the percentage of the rural population in poverty more closely approximates the average percentage for the populations in the rest of Latin America. The dispersion of incomes has been relatively slight across a wide middle group of households (3rd–7th deciles), although there has been concentration of total income at the upper end of the scale (see table 5.7). Increased concentration since the mid-seventies has accompanied a decline in per capita real income. Whereas inequality in income distribution in Argentina was perhaps moderate over the first three decades of the post–World War II period, increasing inequality over the last twenty-five years has placed Argentina among the group of countries with greatest concentration of income. By 1990 absolute income levels in Argentina were in a much less favorable position relative to the other countries of the region than they had been at the outset of the post–World War II period.

In 1953 and 1961 the lower-income groups' primary incomes came mainly from wages and salaries. Two-thirds of the heads of households in the upper decile of the income distribution derived their income from self-employment. Rural entrepreneurs represent only a small fraction of this group. Those whose income comes from property are found primarily in the upper-income decile. Yet this group captures only a small portion of total income and has little effect on overall inequality. Within-group income distributions also differ. Within the wage and salary group, the top 10% received only 27% of total wage and salary

Table 5.7. CONADE-CEPAL Estimates of the National Distribution of Income, 1953–89 (income shares)

| | By Total Household Income | | | | | | By Per Capita HH Income | |
Percentile	1953[a]	1959[a]	1961[a]	1969/70[b]	1975[c]	1980[c]	1980[c]	1989[c]
1–10	3.2	3	2.9	2.3	2.2	2.0	1.9	1.4
11–20	4.3	3.8	4.1	3.9	3.7	3.0	3.4	2.7
21–30	5.0	4.4	4.8	5.1	5.1	4.2	4.6	3.8
31–40	5.7	5	5.5	6.0	6.3	5.3	5.7	4.8
41–50	6.4	5.8	6.1	7.2	7.5	6.7	6.9	6.0
51–60	7.2	6.5	7	8.5	9.0	8.2	8.3	7.3
61–70	8.3	7.6	8.0	10.1	10.5	10.0	10.1	9.3
71–80	9.9	9.1	9.6	12.0	12.8	12.8	12.5	12.0
81–90	13.0	12.5	12.9	15.7	16.2	16.9	16.6	16.7
91–100	37.0	42.3	39.1	29.2	26.7	30.9	30.0	35.9
Top 5%	27.3	32.1	29.4					
Top 1%	13.1	15.6	14.5					
Gini coef.	.413	.463	.435	.373	.361	.416	.4081	.4759

[a] Survey: CONADE-CEPAL, reported in *Economic Development and Income Distribution in Argentina.*
[b] Survey: *Encuesta de presupuestos familiares;* covers Greater Buenos Aires only.
[c] Survey: *Encuesta permanente de hogares;* covers Greater Buenos Aires only.

income, while the top 10% of the self-employed group received 49% of total self-employment income. This distinction between wages/salaries and self-employment incomes is more important than sectoral, regional, or urban-rural differences in explaining overall income distribution (Altimir 1986).

Urban-rural and interregional household income differences were less significant in Argentina than in other countries in the region. Average sectoral incomes in 1961, as a percentage of the national average, were 85 in agriculture, 100 in industry, and 105 for services. Although the average rural income in Argentina was not substantially lower than in the other sectors, income within that sector exhibited more inequality than income in nonagricultural sectors. In the 1980s the percentage of the rural population in poverty was roughly four times as great as the percentage of the urban population in poverty.

Stabilization policies and redistributive policies aimed at influencing income shares between the urban and rural sectors, and between wages/salaries and profits, have had a substantially greater impact on Argentine income distribution than the underlying structural changes occurring in the economy. The burden of stabilization was placed on urban wage earners and benefited the rural self-employed as well as many urban entrepreneurs.

Fiscal policies prior to the 1980s were progressively redistributive in Argentina: in 1961 the education and public health services received from the public sector augmented the poorest 20% of the population's money income by nearly one-sixth, so that their real income—which includes these services—was higher than their money income. Simultaneously considering tax burden and benefits received by income group indicates that in 1961 real income shares for the lower half of income recipients were greater than money income shares. However, public expenditures allocated to basic social services as a share of GDP fell beginning in the mid-1980s and fell further by 1990. Nevertheless, Argentine social indicators continue to rank favorably in comparison to other countries of the region with the exception of Uruguay. Urban illiteracy rates are low even among the lowest-income groups, averaging around 4% for the four lowest income deciles, while net primary school enrollments exceed 95%.

Conclusion

Argentina's experiment with import substituting industrialization has come to a close. The Argentine economy is once again pursuing an export-led growth strategy within the context of an increasingly open and deregulated economy. The economy withstood the impact of the "tequila effect" and benefited from the creation of the MERCOSUR.

Nonetheless, many tasks remain. The provincial governments have been slow to adopt the fiscal discipline essential to overall public sector equilibrium. Fundamental reforms in labor regulation encounter stiff union resistance. While goods markets are liberalized and Argentine producers are increasingly subject to the discipline of world markets, inflexibilities in labor contracting place them in disadvantageous positions. And, most important, promising as the new initiatives are, including the MERCOSUR, unless the benefits of reform and economic growth are equitably distributed, political support for reform will subside and Argentina will again find itself dogged by shortsighted policymaking and excessive state intervention.

Works Cited

Agencia de Cooperación Internacional del Japón. 1987. *Estudio sobre el desarrollo económico de la República Argentina: Informe final.* Tokyo: Agencia de Cooperación Internacional de Japón.

Altimir, Óscar. 1986. Estimaciones de la distribución del ingreso en la Argentina, 1953–1980. *Desarrollo Económico* 25 (100) (January–March).

Díaz Alejandro, Carlos. 1970. *Essays on the Economic History of the Argentine Republic.* New Haven: Yale University Press.

Di Tella, Guido, and R. Dornbusch. 1989. *The Political Economy of Argentina, 1946–83*. Pittsburgh: University of Pittsburgh Press.

Guadagni, Alieto Aldo 1989. Economic Policy during Illia's Period in Office, 1963–66. In Guido Di Tella and R. Dornbusch, *The Political Economy of Argentina, 1946–83*. Pittsburgh: University of Pittsburgh Press.

Mallon, Richard D., and Juan V. Sourrouille. 1975. *Economic Policymaking in a Conflict Society: The Argentine Case*. Cambridge, Mass.: Harvard University Press.

Manzetti, Luigi. 1993. *Institutions, Parties, and Coalitions in Argentine Politics*. Pittsburgh: University of Pittsburgh Press.

Petrecolla, Alberto. 1989. Unbalanced Development, 1958–62. In Guido Di Tella and R. Dornbusch, *The Political Economy of Argentina, 1946–83*. Pittsburgh: University of Pittsburgh Press.

Porto, A. N.d. Una revisión crítica de las empresas públicas en la Argentina. In P. Gerchunoff, ed., *Las privatizaciones en la Argentina*. Buenos Aires: Instituto Torcuato Di Tella.

Psacharopoulos, George, et al. 1992. *Poverty and Income Distribution in Latin America: The Story of the 1980s*. Report no. 27, Latin America and the Caribbean Technical Department. Washington, D.C.: World Bank.

Randall, Laura. 1978. *An Economic History of Argentina in the Twentieth Century*. New York: Columbia University Press.

World Bank. 1985. *Argentina Economic Memorandum*. Washington, D.C.: World Bank.

——. 1993. *Argentina from Insolvency to Growth*. Washington, D.C.: World Bank.

6.
Peru

Efraín Gonzales de Olarte
Instituto de Estudios Peruanos and
Pontificia Universidad Católica del Perú

Since the 1950s Peru has transformed its economy while failing to develop. A period of high economic growth in the middle of the seventies preceded a period of decline and crisis that reached its nadir in 1990. Peru lost its gains from the first phase of the cycle during the second, declining phase. Per capita gross domestic product is back to its level in the mid-sixties (see chart 6.1). Peru's income distribution remained unequal throughout, and poverty worsened during its economic cycle's declining phase.

Peruvian history resembles that of other Latin American nations, which also saw the income levels and well-being they achieved in the middle of the seventies dissipate in the following twenty years (Balassa et al. 1986).

Development theories explain why countries grow. They do not sufficiently analyze why countries fall back after an initial spurt of growth. In Latin America, the current explanation is that the import substitution model of industrialization (ISI) failed, in tandem with the failure of a Keynesian-structuralist state interventionism exacerbated by populism. However, the problem is more complex. Each country's separate history requires a separate explanation. We must analyze what in particular broke down in Peru. The external context? The economic model? Economic policies? Political styles? This chapter attempts to explain Peru's scanty economic development in the last forty years as due to the combination (or ineffective combination) of these several conditions and policies.

The Peruvian Pattern of Growth

Peru's economy and society dramatically changed in the postwar period. The changes in Peru's economic policies, which continued until the eighties, and the population increase from 4.85 million in 1920 to 6.1 million in 1940 largely explain these changes.

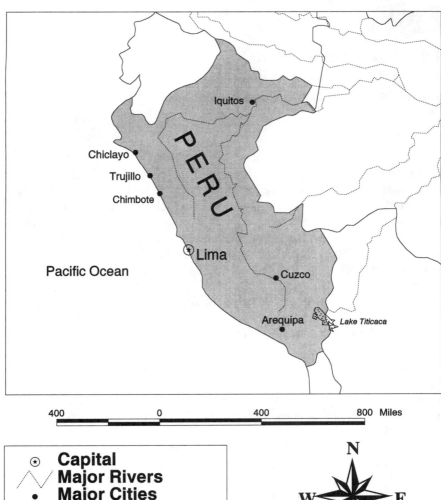

PERU

Iquitos

Chiclayo

Trujillo

Chimbote

Lima

Pacific Ocean

Cuzco

Arequipa · Lake Titicaca

400   0   400   800   Miles

⊛ Capital
Major Rivers
• Major Cities
National Boundary
Countries

N
W   E
S

Chart 6.1. Gross Product and Investment Per Capita, 1950–94
(constant 1979 prices)

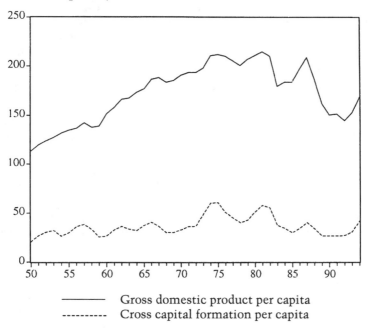

Gross domestic product per capita
Cross capital formation per capita

A growth model provides an overview of the way in which an economy normally functions. It shows how the dynamism of one or more productive sectors causes growth, how growth in turn configures the distribution of income, and, consequently, how growth generates the conditions for a specific process of capital accumulation. The functional relation between financing, production, and distribution constitutes the axis of the growth model, which holds that the functional relation's variations from nation to nation explain the difference in growth between nations.

The postwar world economy's reconfiguration and recuperation created favorable conditions to expand both production and export of raw materials. General Manuel Odría's military government (1948–55) simultaneously created a liberal institutional and legal framework favorable to foreign investment. Its major incentives for investment were tax stability, tax exemptions, free entry and repatriation of capital, and laws to promote the mining and petroleum industries.

Historically, foreign investment had represented less than 10% of total investment in Peru. Odría's policies raised the proportion of foreign to total investment to 13% in the 1950–60 period. American capitalists invested $418 million in Peru in those years, especially in the export-driven mining and petroleum sectors.

The export sector's changing composition caused important transformations in Peru's economic policies during the next thirty years. Foreign savings financed the growth of the economy's new sectors. First by mining and later by fishing Peru consolidated the foundations of its primary-export growth model. Future growth would depend on these sectors' ability to provide the foreign exchange needed to buy the imports necessary for development.

In 1950 agricultural exports were Peru's main source of foreign exchange. New investments through the decade progressively changed the composition of the nation's exports. Minerals took first place by 1960, while livestock-related exports were relegated to a secondary position.

Growth also gave rise to important spatial changes, including accelerated urbanization, rural-urban migration, and the shaping of economic regions (Gonzales 1982).

Peru's population began to grow rapidly. Rising from an annual population growth rate of 1% during the thirties, the population grew at an annual rate of 2.3% between 1940 and 1960, while its urban population grew at 3.7%. Later population growth rates were even higher. Urban demand for consumption goods increased at a greater rate than domestic production could supply. Imports made up the difference. This imbalance was one of the main reasons why Manuel Prado's government (1956–61) initiated the import substitution industrialization policies at the end of the fifties that aimed to obtain more foreign exchange for Peru and to improve Peru's international terms of trade (Beaulne 1975; Torres 1975). These policies included general incentives for industrial investment, the creation of the Banco Industrial (Bank for Industry), and protective tariffs.

Peru consolidated a semi-industrial dependent primary-export growth model (PESID) in the sixties and retained it until the end of the eighties. Peru established an economy with two dynamic axes, albeit with one sector dependent on the other. The export sector of mining and fishing was the principal axis, which earned the foreign exchange then used to create the middle-sized industrial sector. This industrial sector, directed toward the domestic market, came to constitute the second axis of the Peruvian economy.

Domestic savings invested never surpassed 70% of total domestic investment; per capita investment grew in 1950–75, but fell in 1976–93 (Gonzales 1994b; see chart 6.1). Peru always depended on some external savings to finance its growth, as much by foreign enterprises' direct investments as by indebtedness to the international financial system.

PESID generated a distributive structure with three particular characteristics. The inequality of personal income distribution was cyclic:

income inequality decreased when the economic cycle was at its high point, but returned to its initial inequality at every balance of payments crisis (Gonzales and Samamé 1994). Counterintuitively, the declining investment rate (see chart 6. 2) increased the share of profits in income (see chart 6. 3), which in turn caused the investment profit ratio (I/P) to decline. Finally, since Peru's "trickle down" mechanisms were very weak, the least competitive and capitalist sectors, such as the peasants, were excluded from the fruits of growth. The peasants' limited ties to markets decreased the "trickle down" effects, but also later protected them from the full effects of external crises, compared to those that the other social sectors endured (Gonzales 1994b, ch. 5).

The PESID economic policy began to demonstrate its two basic limitations by the middle of the sixties: dependence on external constraints and an inability to redistribute the fruits of Peru's growth stably, so that income distribution did not oscillate. Belaúnde's first government (1963–68) paid great attention to these problems. Belaúnde's main policies were to increase public investment in the basic infrastructure of education, health, housing, and roads, to create the Bank of the Nation (Banco de la Nación), and to institute a semiliberal macroeconomic policy. However, these policies did not address the problems of dependence and income distribution. His economy minister at the time, Manuel Ulloa, proposed structural adjustment policies in 1967 to reduce dependence and improve income distribution. The economic and political crises of 1967–68, followed by the coup d'état of 1968, prevented Ulloa's policies from going into effect.

The new "revolutionary" military government (1968–75), under General Juan Velasco Alvarado, "solved" the lack of foreign exchange through foreign borrowing. Peru's foreign debt increased from $788 million in 1968 to $6,257 million in 1975, 21% private and 79% public.

Institutional and property reforms addressed Peru's distribution problems. These reforms included land reform, nationalization (defined here as both the replacement of firms' foreign owners with domestic owners and the conversion of foreign firms into state enterprises such as the International Petroleum Company), and the creation of Labor Communities representing all the workers from the principal industrial, mining, and fishing enterprises. Peru gave these Labor Communities shares in the new state firms. Collectively, the military government's reforms changed the property ownership structure, redefined the social classes, and altered income distribution.

Peru increasingly relied on import substitution policies. Around 1970 the government instituted a tariff system highly protective of industry, based on the Registry of Manufactures. Tariffs varied according to the strategic importance of each sector, and Peru entirely prohibited the

Chart 6.2. Investment/Profits, 1950–94 (percentage)

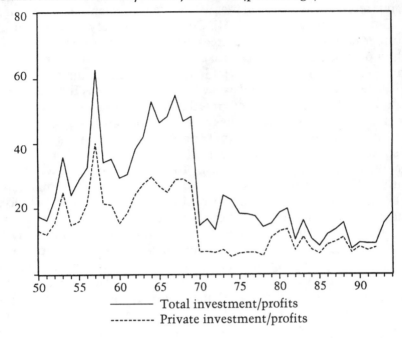

——— Total investment/profits
--------- Private investment/profits

Chart 6.3. Functional Distribution of Income, 1950–92 (percentage)

——— Profits   --------- Wages   – – – Independent

import of several categories of goods. It maintained a constant sol/dollar exchange rate for seven years (1969–76). Furthermore, Peru increased credit to its industrial and domestic commerce sectors.

Taken together these policies changed Peru from a primary export economy to a mixed primary export and semi-industrial economy. This new mixed economy was uncompetitive and depended on imported inputs and technology.

The PESID economic policies changed both the productive structure and the employment structure of Peru. In 1950 agriculture produced 24% of the GDP and employed 59% of the labor force. In 1990 agriculture only produced 13% of the GDP and employed just 34% of the labor force. Peruvian industry went from 19% of GDP and 13% of the labor force in 1950 to 22% of GDP and 11% of the labor force in 1990 (see table 6.1).

Agricultural and industrial employment growth both failed to match the growth of the labor force, while Peru's sectoral productivity differentials simultaneously increased. Mining and fishing produced between 9 and 10% of GDP, but provided only 3% of total employment. The heterogeneous service sector increased from 38 to 41% of the GDP during those forty years, but its labor force grew from 23 to 49% of the total. The service sector became Peru's "adjustment sector" for employment. The service sector possessed the greatest degree of informality and heterogeneity. It included professional, personal, productive, and social services; trade; transport; banking; and communications. These different subsectors had high productivity differentials. The least efficient service subsectors were roughly as productive as Peru's highland peasants.

These shifts in Peru's economic structure took place during a business cycle with two highly distinct periods. From 1950 to 1975 GDP grew at an annual rate of 5.4%, with a sufficiently rapid growth of production in the dynamic sectors of mining, fishing, and industry to sustain development. In contrast, from 1975 to 1990 the GDP grew at an annual rate of 0.3%, while Peru's "dynamic" sectors grew very little, or even shrank (see table 6.1). The gains in per capita income during the business cycle's expansion were lost during the ensuing crisis.

The most disquieting aspect of this evolution was Peru's continuing inability to make employment growth match production growth. We will return to this theme of Peru's structural difficulty generating employment (Verdera 1995; Gonzales 1994c).

PESID's economic policies simultaneously led to the nation's uneven regional development and to economic and governmental centralization. Peru's backward sectors, such as traditional agriculture, remained concentrated in the highlands. The dynamic export sectors, such as fishing, industry, and mining, established themselves on the coast. Tax receipts from fishing and mining and private and commercial and

Table 6.1. Production and Employment, 1950–90

	1950	1960	1970	1975	1980	1985	1990	1993	Rates of Growth		
									1950–75	1975–90	1950–90
Gross domestic product (millions of 1979 soles)	865.6	1,504.7	2,518.6	3,213	3,646.6	3,573.9	3,243.8	3,464.7	5.4	0.3	3.5
% of GDP											
Agriculture	23.8	17.1	14.2	11.5	9.9	11.6	13.4	12.7	2.4	1.2	2.0
Fishing	0.2	0.9	1.9	0.5	0.5	0.8	1.3	1.4	11.8	8.7	10.6
Mining	7.6	10.3	9.1	7.2	12.9	12.7	9.6	9.6	5.8	2.9	4.7
Manufacturing	19.0	23.6	24.9	25.1	23.8	21.8	22.1	22.6	6.6	-0.3	4.0
Construction	5.9	5.4	5.3	6.7	5.5	4.6	5.9	6.7	6.5	-0.1	4.0
Government	5.9	5.5	5.7	5.9	6.4	7.8	6.7	6.1	5.4	1.1	3.8
Services[a]	37.6	37.2	38.9	43.1	41.0	40.7	41.0	40.9	6.0	1.0	3.6
Employment (thousands of workers)	2,410	3,055	4,081	–	5,587	6,531	7,573	7,110	2.8	3.1	2.9
% of total											
Agriculture & fishing	58.9	52.8	48.0	–	39.8	36.6	34.0	–	1.5	1.4	1.5
Mining	2.2	2.2	1.5	–	2.1	2.2	2.4	–	1.7	5.5	3.1
Manufacturing	13.0	13.5	12.5	–	11.6	10.4	10.5	–	2.7	1.8	2.4
Construction	2.7	3.4	4.2	–	3.9	3.7	3.7	–	4.6	2.2	3.7
Government & services[a]	23.2	28.1	33.8	–	42.6	47.1	49.4	–	4.9	4.9	4.9

Sources: Instituto Nacional de Estadística: *Perú: Compendio estadístico 1988* (Lima: Dirección General de Indicadores Económicos y Sociales, 1989); Instituto Nacional de Estadística e Informática: *Perú: Compendio estadístico 1994–1995* (Lima: Dirección Técnica de Indicadores Económicos, 1994); Cuánto S.A., *Perú en números 1991* (Lima 1992).
[a]Includes electricity, water, and housing.

financial flows from these sectors went to Lima. These sectors' influence in regional development has been small, since their capital-intensive technology has not generated development in the "hinterland." Peru's resulting economic and political centralization is characterized by conflicts over resource assignment and income redistribution (Gonzales 1982, 1991).

At the same time that changes in the production and employment structures took place, Peru's ownership structure also changed. Although some former landowners successfully converted their wealth into ownership of agro-industry, fishing, industry, and banking, the agrarian oligarchy generally declined. Peruvian capitalists tended to invest in non-capital-intensive enterprises directed to the country's domestic market. Businessmen in various economic sectors competed for favorable treatment from the government. Foreign investors began to dominate mining, industry, and banking. Domestic and foreign investors desired different governmental policies, particularly in regard to public finance and international trade. National investors in the industry and service sectors demanded controlled exchange rates, as well as subsidies, while foreign investors (particularly investors in the export sectors) preferred free exchange rates and low tariffs. The policies desired by capitalists in traditional agriculture differed from those wanted by capitalists for modern industry (Cotler 1978; Thorp and Bertram 1978). Moreover, a capital goods industry was not created, so that the production of consumer goods depended on the availability of foreign exchange and imported technology. The process of accumulation depended on the association of national and foreign capital, a relationship that was cooperative or conflictive, depending on the stage of the business cycle.

As urbanized production expanded, a progressively unionized working class composed of laborers and employees took shape. These new unions decisively influenced salary determination and income distribution and in consequence acquired political importance. However, the unions grew weaker during the crisis of the eighties.

The agrarian reform of 1969–75 eliminated the landowning, agrarian oligarchy's remaining hold on the land. The reform created a new agrarian and social structure in the countryside, composed of cooperatives, small and medium owners, sharecroppers, and peasants. From 1980 on this structure changed so much as to reduce and divide the cooperatives' landholdings. The reform endowed Peru with an agrarian structure composed of peasants and small to medium-sized proprietors, with one of the least-unequal landholding structures in Latin America.

Peru categorizes latifundia as landholdings of more than 500 hectares, middle-sized properties as 50 to 500 hectares, small properties as 5 to 50 hectares, and minifundia as under 5 hectares. In 1961 individual owners held 73% of the land, while 27% belonged to peasant communities. The latifundia, 1.2% of the agrarian units, held 52.3% of the land, while minifundia, representing 84.6% of owners, accounted for 40.8% of the land. Obviously, land ownership was highly unequal.

By 1984, 51% of the land belonged to individuals, 29% to peasant communities, and 20% to agrarian cooperatives. Agrarian cooperatives with large landholdings, 1.9% of all landowners, owned 53.9% of the land. Middle-sized farmers increased their share of agricultural units from 14.2% to 25.6%, while their landholding share rose considerably, from 6.9% of the total to 34.1%. Today most agrarian cooperatives have been divided into parcels and distributed among their members. The successive changes in the rural area did not affect the rest of the economy and society. These changes did, however, affect political violence after 1980.

The heterogeneous, independent sector of microenterprises and family businesses engaged in small industry, commerce, and services is the newest ownership sector in Peru. The unemployed's struggle to survive (and not the demand for services by the rapidly growing industrial sector) generated this sector's enormous growth.

Peru failed to create an autonomous national bourgeoisie, although the social structure continuously changed over forty years (Thorp and Bertram 1978). The nation also failed to create a large working class. Peasants continued to live in conditions of poverty and remained socially and politically marginalized. Peru's independent self-employed were preoccupied with the search for a better socioeconomic situation. The social organization has been most characterized by fragmentation.

The Peruvian state therefore constituted itself as an organizer of the fragments of society (FitzGerald 1979; Cotler 1978), as an arbitrator of economic and social conflicts, and as a promoter of development. The state's size and functions grew: the government's contribution to GDP rose from 7.8% in 1955, to 11.4% in 1970, and, at its highest level, to 21.4% in 1975, after which the government contribution significantly fell (see table 6.2). The same evolution occurred in regard to investment. The government invested only 3.9% of GDP in 1955, while its investment grew to 8.8% by 1975. By then the government was Peru's principal investor, particularly via the substantial increase of public enterprises. The state likewise became the principal employer, with nearly 1 million employees by 1989, representing 13% of the labor force.

The structure of government finances deteriorated. The tax structure became regressive, as consumption taxes and indirect taxes grew from 54% of tax income in 1955 to 77% of tax income in 1985. The government ran up a chronic deficit whose levels increased with each external crisis. Starting in the seventies, Peru partially financed its government

Table 6.2. Economic Participation of the Goverment, 1955–90

	1955	1960	1967	1970	1975	1980	1985	1989	1990
Value added by the public sector (% of GDP)	7.8	8.8	10.6	11.4	21.4	12.6	19.8	15.0	12.0
Fixed investment (% of GDP)	3.9	2.3	4.0	4.5	8.8	5.8	5.2	4.0	3.9
Gross capital formation (% of total)	21.0	14.0	27.0	36.0	51.0	35.0	24.0	24.0	19.0
Employment									
Government	140.0	168.0	251.0	220.0	355.0[a]	385.0[b]	482.0[c]	693.0[d]	693.0
Other institutions	8.0	11.0	19.0	84.0	208.0	208.0	212.0	284.0	284.0
Total	148.0	179.0	270.0	304.0	563.0	593.0	694.0	977.0	977.0
Taxes (% of GDP)	6.4	6.5	12.5	12.0	12.3	17.1	13.5	7.0	9.4
Direct (% of total)	40.1	41.9	32.7	34.6	34.4	34.8	20.0	14.0	14.0
Indirect (% of total)	53.9	53.1	57.2	52.0	56.4	64.7	77.0	76.0	63.0
Expenditures									
Current (% of total)	76.9	91.4	88.7	76.5	76.4	77.3	85.7	86.4	89.7
Investment (% of total)	15.8	8.6	11.3	23.5	23.6	22.7	14.2	13.6	10.1
Economic deficit (% of total)	-0.6	1.3	-3.3	-1.2	-4.6	-2.4	-2.1	-4.5	-2.6

Sources: Banco Central de Reserva del Perú: *Cuentas nacionales*, several years; *Compendio del sector público no financiero 1968–1984* (Lima, 1985); Instituto Nacional de Estadística. *Perú: compendio estadístico 1989* (Lima, 1990); Instituto Nacional de Estadística e Informática, Dirección Nacional de Cuentas Nacionales,1991; FitzGerald, 1979; Gonzales and Samamé 1994.

[a] 1976.
[b] 1981.
[c] 1984.
[d] 1990.

expenditure with debt. During the eighties debt service became the principal pressure on the government deficit. Paradoxically, the growth of the state accompanied a declining capacity of the state to collect taxes, and, consequently, a declining capacity to maintain itself. This governmental evolution gave rise to the emergence of populism.

From Growth to the Crisis and Hyperinflation

The PESID economic policies generated both long- and short-term economic crises. The short-term crisis and its solutions came from variations in foreign demand for Peruvian goods (Thorp and Bertram 1978). The long-term crisis consisted of continuingly insufficient private investment (and hence a shortfall in total investment) in relation to Peru's demographic growth. Among other reasons, private investment fell because of the changing rates of profit from alternate economic activities. The consequently uncertain outlook encouraged investment in land, inventories, foreign exchange, and foreign investment opportunities, instead of investment in productive activities in Peru.

Foreign trade has been the motor of Peruvian economic growth. The external sector's characteristics included a proclivity (provoked by foreign shocks) to disequilibrium in the balance of trade (Pinzás 1993; Herrera 1989; see chart 6.4). The explosive character of these disequilibria arose from exchange rate policies that fostered a declining tendency in the real exchange rate (see chart 6.5). These policies were accentuated starting in the late sixties. Peru's strategy of import substitution was in part responsible for these policies. Political reasons, however, were paramount, inasmuch as the exchange rate has a decisive influence on both real salaries and the level of employment and therefore has an equally decisive influence on the government's popularity (Gonzales and Samamé 1994).

Peru had a multiple exchange rate system. The export exchange rate (soles per dollar) was higher than the import exchange rate in the midsixties. This explains the then-lower levels of external disequilibrium. Peru's export exchange rate was below that for imports by the midseventies, which generated a larger trade deficit. Later, the nation had an unstable exchange rate.

Short-term crises had the following sequence: a diminution of exports led to a balance of payments deficit, which led to devaluation, which led to inflation accompanied by a fiscal crisis. The sequence came to an end either with the increase of some mineral and fishmeal prices, with an orthodox fiscal adjustment, or with both. These crises occurred in 1948–51, 1957–59, 1967–68, 1983–85, and 1988–92. The last crisis was characterized by three years of hyperinflation (1988–90), which marked the end both of the PESID model and of the long business cycle.

Chart 6.4. Balance of Trade, 1950–94 (millions of dollars)

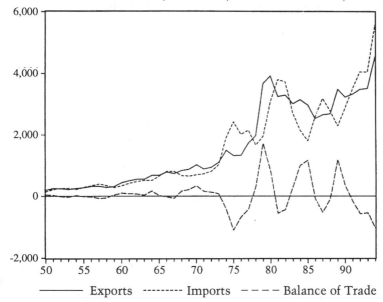

Exports ········ Imports − − − − Balance of Trade

Source: Banco Central de Reserva del Perú, *Memoria* (annual publication).

Chart 6.5. Real Exchange Rate, 1950–93 (index 1979 = 100)

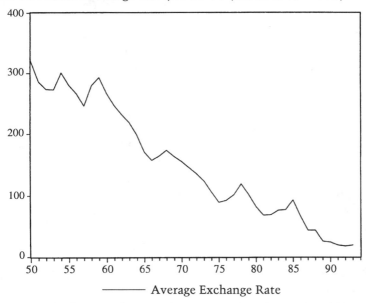

———— Average Exchange Rate

Source: INEI, *Compendio estadístico, 1992–1993, 1994, 1995.* Author's calculation.

Beginning in 1976, Peru added an increasing debt service burden to its traditional balance of trade deficit, thus revealing the economy's structural weaknesses. The problems included insufficient savings, resulting from insufficient investment in relation to population growth, from the growing gap between domestic savings and investment, and from increasing use of capital-intensive technology. These factors generated a combined unemployment and permanent underemployment level of more than 50% of the labor force.

The economy also continued to depend on exports. The productive export and industrial sectors generated more economic links with other nations than with the Peruvian economy's other sectors and regions (Gonzales 1991; Torres 1975). Moreover, the intersectoral relations depended on foreign exchange availability (Pinzás 1993; Herrera 1989).

Peru's unequal income distribution (unchanging between 1950 and 1972, and worsening after 1976) is the result of the nation's economic policies and of the power structure as it is reflected in these economic policies (De Habich 1989; Glewwe 1987; Figueroa 1982; Webb 1977; Webb and Figueroa 1975). It is also the result of the limited effectiveness of redistributive policies and of the inability of institutions such as trade unions and chambers of commerce to maintain salary agreements over long periods.

Peru's demand structure derived from the nation's income distribution. The high-income sectors, small in number, consumed large amounts of imports. Real income increases, moreover, owing to the low income elasticity of national supply in relation to that of imported supply, resulted in large increases in the consumption of imported goods, but only small increases in national production (Herrera 1989). The larger low-income sectors' small total demand imposed another limit on Peru's industrial growth.

The Alan García government's (1985–90) hyperinflation (the inflation rate rose from 63% in 1986, to 115% in 1987, and finally to an annual rate of 4048% in 1988–90) combined three crises: the foreign sector crisis, the savings crisis, and the governmental crisis. The foreign sector crisis combined a trade crisis and a foreign debt crisis. The savings crisis paralyzed productive investment. The governmental crisis consisted of the rise of populism and an extremely interventionist state. The overall impact of this triple crisis generally weakened Peru's economic and political institutions. This general impact requires an understanding of how the nation's economic cycle related to its political cycle during forty years of populism.

The Peruvian economy's long cycle began at the end of the forties, reached its height in the mid-seventies, and reached its end at the end of the eighties (see chart 6.1). During these forty years Peru underwent five

Table 6.3. Evolution of the Economy, 1950–93

Period	GDP	GDP Per Capita	Rates of Growth (%) Investment	Investment Per Capita	Remuner-ations	Inflation
1950–53						
Average	3.41	0.83	5.65	3.00	1.42	309.71
Standard deviation	5.12	4.91	19.56	19.06	12.09	1,216.28
Variation rate	1.50	5.95	3.46	6.34	8.49	3.93
1950–75						
Average	5.42	2.57	8.77	5.82	6.23	9.55
Standard deviation	2.69	2.63	18.00	17.53	3.35	5.23
Variation rate	0.50	1.02	2.05	3.01	0.54	0.55
1976–93						
Average	0.62	-1.59	1.31	-0.91	-5.64	743.27
Standard deviation	6.26	6.17	20.77	20.36	16.15	1,816.04
Variation rate	10.07	-3.87	15.85	-22.36	-2.86	2.44
Governments						
M. Odría 1950–56	5.88	3.19	13.68	10.79	7.73	6.87
M. Prado 1956–62	5.88	3.01	2.74	-0.05	5.58	8.76
F. Belaúnde 1963–68	4.63	1.69	1.14	-1.70	5.19	11.90
J. Velasco 1968–75	4.96	2.07	15.25	12.08	6.26	11.46
F. Morales 1976–80	2.59	-0.08	4.03	1.34	-1.25	55.66
F. Belaúnde 1981–85	-0.18	-2.47	-9.33	-11.41	-1.62	108.10
A. García 1986–90	-1.54	-3.57	6.71	4.50	-8.91	2,464.94
A. Fujimori 1991–93	2.29	0.64	5.50	3.81	-18.53	78.47

Sources: INEI, *Compendio estadístico 1992–93, 1993–94* (Lima, 1993, 1994); Cuánto, *Perú en números 1990, 1992* (Lima, 1991, 1993).
Note: The growth rate of remuneration covers 1951–92. Inflation includes 1950–93. Investment corresponding to gross capital formation.

medium cycles of seven to eight years, each starting with an export surge, generally caused by exogenous forces, and each ending with a crisis in the foreign sector (see chart 6.4 and table 6.3). During this period a succession of civil and military governments applied alternating liberal and interventionist policies. Peru had twenty-one years apiece of military and civilian government after 1948 and, by 1990, eighteen years of predominantly liberal policies, twelve of liberal-interventionist policies, and twelve of interventionist policies (see table 6.4).

Each government enjoyed some years of expansion and then faced a crisis in the external sector. The connections between the political and economic cycles were determined by the foreign sector's behavior. Neither economic expansion nor economic recession correlated with government type (military or civilian); instead, they depended on the foreign sector's evolution and on macroeconomic policies.

PESID's long economic cycle was one of the bases for the establish-

Table 6.4. Governments, Economic Policies, and Business Cycles, 1948–95

Government	Type	Years	Economic Policy	Business Cycle Long-Term	Crisis Short-Term
Odría 1948–56	Military	8	Liberal	Expansion	1948–51
Prado 1956–62	Civilian	6	Liberal/ interventionist	Expansion	1957–58
Pérez/Lindley 1962–63	Military	1	Liberal/ interventionist	Expansion	
Belaúnde 1963–68	Civilian	5	Liberal/ interventionist	Expansion/ crisis	1967–68
Velasco 1968–75	Military	7	Interventionist	Crisis	1971–72
Morales B. 1975–80	Military	5	Liberal	Crisis	1977–78
Belaúnde 1980–85	Civilian	5	Liberal	Recession	1983–84
García 1985–90	Civilian	5	Interventionist	Recession/ hyperinflation	1988–90
Fujimori 1990–95	Civilian	5	Structural adjustment	Recession/ growth	1990–92

Source: Compiled by author.

ment of populism as a political style from the seventies until 1990. General Odría's military government (1948–56) helped create the economic prerequisites for the appearance of populism. During this period, the primary-export economy's rapid expansion generated large amounts of government income. The primary-export economy also concentrated income and created a greater distributive inequality that excluded important parts of Peru's growing population from the benefits of growth. This increased pressure on the state to redistribute export sector profits, since the market had not done so.

Popular Action (Acción Popular), Christian Democracy (Democracia Cristiana), and the Social Progressive Party (Partido Social Progresista), leftist and/or populist parties, were created in the mid-fifties in an attempt to mediate the various claims made on the state. From 1963 to 1990 populists of every variety governed Peru: civilians and military men under Velasco, liberals under the Partido Acción Popular of Belaúnde or under General Francisco Morales Bermúdez's military government, and social democrats under Alan García's APRA. Populism, with its nationalist, redistributionist, and developmentalist message, did much in the beginning of the seventies to bring about Peru's adoption of the import substitution model of industrialization.

Populism functioned well in periods of economic expansion, when foreign exchange and government income could finance state expenditures. But rejection of populism during each balance of payments crisis led to "the Peruvian pendulum" (Gonzales and Samamé 1994): "stop-go" policies that swung the nation from orthodox policies to interventionist ones, and back again, throughout the last forty-five years.

Peru's continuing private investment gap (chronic since the sixties) and persistent income distribution inequality together brought the political system to a profound crisis by the end of the eighties. Falling private investment induced both Fernando Belaúnde's and General Juan Velasco's governments in the mid-sixties and early seventies to resort to public investment to finance growth. The ensuing diversion of government funds to service Peru's foreign debt reduced the amount of money available for governmental domestic spending in the following decade and also reduced the nation's capacity for investment, growth, and job creation. These events cast doubt on the effectiveness of the PESID economic policies. Falling income led to the political violence that Peru suffered from the beginning of the eighties, when the Sendero Luminoso's attacks disrupted the nation. In formal terms, Peruvians began to seek economic solutions outside the legal system, either by informalizing vast sectors of the economy (De Soto 1986; Matos Mar 1984) or by terrorist violence.

The PESID economic policies had failed after forty years to provide stable bases for the political system, which remained dependent on great distributive inequality and could not channel social demands into state action. Each economic crisis therefore led to a concomitant political crisis, which only laid bare Peru's social fragmentation and deepened the distributive inequality. The military always had a pretext to stage a coup d'état when the combined economic and political crisis became acute.

The dominant classes' political fragmentation and dependence on the state (Cotler 1978), the political and labor organizations' lack of ties to other groups and internal conflict, and the difficulty peasants and informal urban groups had in expressing themselves politically were all factors conditioning Peru's political system and economic policies. Economic booms diluted the political fragmentation, but recessions accentuated it. The combination of short-term (hyperinflation) and long-term (low investment) crises in 1988–90 practically pulverized Peru's fragile political system and gave rise to the so-called Fujimori phenomenon. Alberto Fujimori, an independent political outsider, came to power and found an institutional near-vacuum. This gave him an enormous opportunity for political manipulation. Fujimori carried out a drastic stabilization policy and put Peru through a profound structural adjustment. Faced with resistance from the then-stronger labor unions and political parties, preceding governments had been unable to undertake these policies.

From Hyperinflation to Structural Adjustment:
The Fujimori Government

In 1990 the long-term PESID cycle ended, and a new cycle began. A new pattern of growth had not yet been defined by 1996. The Fujimori government (1990–) began with a drastic stabilization program, known as "the Fujishock," whose objectives were to reinsert Peru into the international financial community and to abate the nation's hyperinflation. The program relied on the approval both of international organizations (the International Monetary Fund, the World Bank, and the Inter-American Development Bank) and of the military. These organizations' combined support for President Fujimori overcame the fragility of his political movement and made it possible for Peru both to obtain a bridge loan and to gain institutional stability.

Fujimori's economic reforms began in 1991: liberalization of foreign trade, privatization, deregulation of markets, and reform of fiscal administration. Peru ultimately responded to its profound short- and long-term economic crises of the late 1980s by implementing structural adjustment based on the "Washington Consensus" (Williamson 1990).

Six years after structural adjustment began, the Peruvian economy was in transition toward a different pattern of growth. The results achieved do not yet permit us to say that Peru has passed from stabilization to growth; the nation's stability was still fragile and its reforms incomplete and unequal in their effects. Peru had controlled its inflation rate, reinserted itself into the international economy, and reestablished confidence in its economy, but the mechanisms and institutions that sustained these results were still weak (Gonzales 1993).

Prices relative to those in other nations (the exchange rate appreciation, high interest rates, low salaries, and high-priced public goods and services) failed to promote dynamism in either the export or domestic sectors. For the time being, Peru had converted itself into an import economy that financed part of its growth with foreign savings. This import economy allowed the nation to maintain two fundamental disequilibria: savings that were less than domestic investment and imports that were greater than exports. Moreover, the current account deficit rose to 6% of GDP. These disequilibria led Peru to adopt a new economic correction program in 1996.

Commercial and financial liberalization and market deregulation have been the most radical and rapidly carried out economic reforms. The hurried nature of these reforms, and their inappropriate sequencing and programming for a policy of structural adjustment, decisively contributed to the above-mentioned problem of hobbling relative prices, as well as to the disequilibria in foreign trade and growth finances.

Given Peru's international image, privatization has yielded better-than-expected results. Privatization has helped close Peru's fiscal gap, has substantially increased its net international reserves, and has attracted foreign capital. It is unclear, however, whether privatization had made the economy more efficient or more equitable by 1996. The relative prices of the privatized enterprises' goods and services have increased, without a proportionate increase in income. Moreover, the government was still unable to use the greater part of its income from privatization, since so great an income expenditure would risk inducing both a large fall in the exchange rate and a rise of inflationary pressures.

The reform of fiscal administration has been a success and can be used as a model to reform other parts of the Peruvian government. The fiscal structure has not yet been reformed. Consumption taxes still exceed taxes on earned income or rent. Thus, the tax structure still does not meet this minimum criterion of equity. It gives greater emphasis to rapid tax collection, among other reasons, to pay the foreign debt.

The Economy's Changing Owners, Property Rights, and Income Distribution

The oligarchy's century-long domination of Peru came to an end in the fifties. The decline of the oligarchy is a major factor in the institutional instability that has troubled the nation from the fifties onward. Another major factor has been property-right instability, occasioned in part by neighboring Bolivia's example of land reform. Peasants on the Bolivian side of the border received land when their relatives, friends, and neighbors in Peru could not. The armed forces' revolutionary government instituted land reform at the end of the sixties. A counterrevolution occurred from the second half of the seventies to the beginning of the eighties. From 1990 on Alberto Fujimori's government extensively privatized government enterprises.

Reforms in the Structure of Ownership

Property Redistribution, 1968–75. Peru's ideological, political, and cultural traditions encourage a view of property rights that favors property redistribution to aid national development. Thus, General

Velasco's military government in the seventies statized, nationalized, and redistributed agricultural, industrial, fishing, and mining property to the workers and the government. Twenty years later, Alberto Fujimori's neoconservative government privatized the same enterprises. In both cases governmental arguments that the reigning property structure impeded economic development justified governmental action.

The Agrarian Reform. Peru's agrarian reform from 1969 to 1980 was one of the most radical in Latin American history. The reform affected 64.5% of agricultural land on the coast and 36.7% of agricultural land in the highlands, redistributed 8.3 million hectares of cultivable land and natural pastures, some 28.5% of Peru's total cultivable land, and benefited 359,600 heads of families (Caballero and Álvarez 1980, p. 34). The reform reduced properties of more than 100 hectares from 36% of the land to 16.9% and converted the former haciendas into collectively owned cooperatives.

The agrarian reform's beneficiaries—day workers, sharecroppers, and peasants—did not become free individual landowners capable of disposing of their own land. The reform instead transformed them into members of cooperatives, unable to sell or rent the cooperatives' lands. Moreover, since latifundia-cooperatives replaced latifundia-haciendas, the agrarian reform failed in one of its main aims, to change Peru's income distribution. The effects of the agrarian reform led to the significant conclusion that land redistribution alone was an insufficient policy. The reform also needed to give land to individuals.

However, the agrarian reform's objective was more political than economic. The Peruvian government designed the reform to change the countryside's social structure, to eliminate the exploitative *hacendados* and their latifundias, and to distribute the *hacendados'* lands to their workers and the workers' families. In the highlands the reform also distributed land to the peasant communities surrounding the haciendas. The reform defined the working family, as represented by the family's male or female head, as its intended beneficiary.

The agrarian reform took into account the substantial differences between the coastal and highland haciendas. The reform expropriated the coastal sugarcane haciendas in their entirety. This included the technological stage of sugar production, the haciendas' sugar and molasses factories, along with the sugar fields. The reform followed different policies in its treatment of the cotton haciendas and of the haciendas devoted to other crops. In the highlands, also for technical reasons, the reform created huge cattle cooperatives that sometimes exceeded in size the haciendas that preceded them. These new cooperatives were differently organized from the coastal cooperatives. The highland cooperatives included peasant communities as collective members and gave the peasant communities the right to share in the cooperatives' profits. Most important, the cooperatives agreed to give preference to laborers from the peasant communities when they hired temporary labor.

The reform organized cooperatives in new agrarian entrepreneurial units, the intended basis for Peru's new agrarian structure. Although the cooperative consisted of worker-members, the government guided the cooperatives' organization, intervened in their administration, and set their production and investment goals. The reform divided the cooperatives' lands into two parts: a demesne of cooperative enterprise under centralized administration, and the private lands of the cooperatives' members, which were worked autonomously and individually. This division became the main cause of the cooperatives' later failure. The division made the cooperatives' members simultaneously bosses and workers, and so created a kind of schizophrenia among them. The cooperatives' members finally chose to be workers. Their choice weakened the cooperatives' entrepreneurial aspect, decapitalized them, and finally brought them to bankruptcy.

Changes in Industry Ownership. Peru's industrial sector appeared toward the end of the fifties. Although primarily dependent on national capital, the industrial sector required foreign capital to undertake the import substitution process. Various transnational corporations (Bayer, Lever, Bata, Westinghouse) formed associations with national capital. According to E. V. K. FitzGerald (1979), in 1968 some 200 firms owned 80% of the Peruvian industrial sector's assets and also controlled 65% of the industrial sector's sales. Foreign capital controlled 100 of the 200 firms. The Peruvian government also began to create industrial firms from the fifties onward, in steel, electricity, and fertilizers. As a result, diversified ownership and a varied scale of operations characterized the industrial sector.

Because the military government's economic model focused on strengthening industrial development through import substitution, the government initially did little to change industrial property ownership in the sector, making exceptions only for those firms tied to economic sectors such as sugar production or electricity generation. The government's basic idea was that private Peruvian industrialists should become the axis of Peru's new development model. In the mid-seventies the government controlled almost 25% of industrial production, with ownership concentrated in the strategic sectors of steel, cement, paper, petrochemical products, and fertilizers. Private Peruvian and foreign capital owned the rest of the industrial sector and controlled the production of industrial goods for final consumption.

Changes in Ownership of Fishing.   In its first years, in the mid-fifties, the fishing sector largely belonged to Peruvian owners. This pattern of ownership changed notably, beginning with Peru's first overfishing crisis in 1963–65. A third of the fishing sector's capital passed into foreign hands, the Banchero group took control of another third, and the remaining third remained controlled by a handful of small owners. Sectoral ownership became highly concentrated. In 1973, faced with the second overfishing crisis, the military government nationalized the entire sector into two government-owned enterprises: Empresa Pesquera del Perú (PescaPerú) for production and Empresa Peruana de Comercialización de Harina de Pescado (EPCHAP) for sales. The sector's ownership change failed to solve the private firms' capitalization problems and failed to improve management of Peru's maritime biomass.

Changes in Ownership of Mining and Oil.   In the mid-sixties an oligopoly of three U.S. "great enterprise" mining firms completely owned Peru's mining sector: the Cerro de Pasco Corporation, the Marcona Mining Company, and Southern Peru. The International Petroleum Company dominated Peru's oil production and distribution.

The military government nationalized the Cerro de Pasco Corporation in 1973 and converted it into a state firm, called Centromín. The government similarly nationalized the Marcona Mining Company in 1975 and converted it into HierroPerú. Refining and international trade passed into the hands of another state firm, MineroPerú (FitzGerald 1979). Southern Peru was the only mining firm to remain under private ownership.

One reason Belaúnde's government fell was a scandal over oil concessions. Belaúnde's government granted concession agreements without a clear policy and designed them to favor some U.S. companies. General Velasco used the ensuing scandal as one of the pretexts for his military coup. The new military government then nationalized the American-owned International Petroleum Company (IPC) and merged the IPC with the government firm Empresa Petrolera Fiscal. The merged firms became the state enterprise PetroPerú, which in turn absorbed the Lobitos, Gulf, and Conchán firms, converting them into an integrated monopoly that is to this day one of Peru's largest firms.

The military government also instituted other property changes in the industrial, fishing, and mining sectors. The state took over part of the large enterprises, PetroPerú, HierroPerú, AeroPerú, SiderPerú, MineroPerú, and Centromín. Elsewhere, the state organized communities of workers into collective partnerships that partly owned and managed their firms. Property socialization had little impact on income distribution (Webb and Figueroa 1975). After 1980 these communities began to disappear, and the government began to liquidate various state enterprises.

Creation of New Enterprises. The military government had created 174 public enterprises by 1975, which produced 21% of GDP, employed almost 200,000 workers, and accounted for approximately one-third of Peru's total imports and exports. These firms existed in every economic sector. They produced 35% of mineral production and 33% of transport services and controlled 100% of production in sectors such as electricity, drinking water, and communications.

According to FitzGerald, the state percentage of GDP rose from 11% in 1968 to 21% in 1975, while foreign enterprises' percentage of GDP fell from 22% to 11%, private domestic firms' percentage of GDP fell from 34% to 27%, and the cooperatives' percentage of GDP rose from 0% (they did not exist in 1968) to 8% of GDP (FitzGerald 1979, table 19).

Thus, the military government created a kind of state capitalism whose ownership pattern reflected a distinct economic and political power structure in which the state controlled the economy by participation in production and by economic policy.

The new property rights structure did not greatly change Peru's unequal personal income distribution. "The reforms' total redistributive effect from 1968 to 1973 was very modest. Estimates in this work show that the reforms transferred between three to four per cent of national income in patrimonial and liquid form" (Webb and Figueroa 1975, p. 162). Obviously, Peru needs to do more than just change its ownership structure if it wants to improve its income distribution.

Between 1975 and 1980 the military government's "second phase" progressively undid its previous reforms. The reformed ownership structure remained untouched until after 1980. In 1980 Fernando Belaúnde's second government returned various nationalized enterprises (among them the *El Comercio* and *El Expreso* newspaper companies) to their prior owners and promulgated Law 002. Law 002 ended the agrarian reform and gave cooperatives' members permission to dispose freely of the cooperatives' land. In effect, the law allowed the members to parcelize the cooperatives, converting the parcel's new owners into small farmers. Belaúnde's government did not privatize the biggest of the public enterprises, such as PetroPerú, Centromín, Compañía Telefónica del Perú, AeroPerú, and ElectroPerú.

Alan García's government (1986–90) maintained Peru's ownership structure, although it unsuccessfully attempted to nationalize privately owned banks in 1987. In 1989 the Peruvian central government transferred control of the Tintaya Mining Company, the regional electricity companies, as well as the National Coca Company to Peru's regional governments.

Privatization and Economic Reforms, 1990–95. In 1990 Alberto Fujimori's government returned Peru to the private ownership philosophy of the fifties. Fujimori's government also initiated massive privatizations of public enterprises as part of the nation's structural adjustment.

The Fujimori government began to privatize public enterprises in June 1991. The privatization process had not been completed by 1996, although by then the government had sold almost 80 of 186 state enterprises. By December 1995 Peru's receipts from the sale of public enterprises were $3.5 billion, approximately 7% of its GDP. Peru received more money for the privatized firms than the base price that the government had set for bidding, but less than the various enterprises' real value (Seminario 1995). Nevertheless, the influx of privatization income has allowed the government to accumulate significant reserve funds and has allowed Peru's net international reserves to rise to previously unattained levels.

The main firms sold (each worth more than $50 million) were Hierro-Perú, Refinería de Ilo, Cía. Minera Tintaya, Cementos Lima, Cementos Yura, Refinería de Cajamarquillo (mining industry), Entel CPT (communications), Empresas Eléctricas del Sur y del Norte (electric power distribution), Interbanc, Banco Continental (finance), and Petromar and Refinería de la Pampilla (oil).

Both the statist and the privatizing ownership reforms, in the seventies and since 1990, have increased Peru's functional income distribution concentration (see chart 6.3). The reforms also increased profits' share of national income, each time at the expense of salaries. Even more important, Peru's private domestic investment has not risen with the rise of absolute and relative increase in profits. Income concentration (which the Fujimori government hoped would promote domestic saving) has not played its expected role. The responsibility for this outcome lies with Peruvian entrepreneurial decisions and not with any inefficiency of income concentration as a tool toward saving.

The Different Kinds of Owners

National and foreign private firms, the government, and organizations (cooperatives, peasant communities, and agrarian enterprises with collective partners) have owned Peru's factors of production. Each of these entrepreneurial forms has its own economic rationale, its own economic objective, its own behavioral functions, and its own rules. Foreign capital and foreign enterprises have played a particularly important role during these last forty years. Their absolute contributions of capital have not been very large, but foreign decisions to invest in particular sectors of the Peruvian economy and foreign association with domestic capital have strongly influenced the formation of business expectations. Thus, foreign investment in the fifties decisively reoriented the nation's economic policies to favor mining and fishing exports (Thorp and Bertram 1978). Foreign investment in import substitution industries was equally important in the sixties in its effect on economic policies. Foreigners' repatriation and reduction of their capital during the seventies following Peru's nationalization of foreign enterprises in turn contributed to the general reduction of private investment.

The Peruvian state increased its ownership role from the sixties on, reaching its height in 1970–90. State capital replaced private capital when the latter withdrew. The state's access to foreign savings, and the initial success of its government enterprises, facilitated this replacement process. Later, the government enterprises' administration in unfavorable and unstable macroeconomic contexts and the politicization of their management brought the enterprises to a condition of permanent deficit. By 1990 the government enterprises' deficit led Peru to begin their privatization.

Thereafter foreign capital regained its prominent role in Peru, as European, Asian, and U.S. investors became the principal purchasers of the nation's privatized public enterprises. This influx of foreign capital is significantly changing Peru's economic power structure and has broadened the range of investment finance sources.

The Personal Distribution of Income

Table 6.5 shows Peru's personal income distribution in 1961, 1971, and 1986. Distributive inequality did not vary substantially. Peru's two poorest population deciles never received more than 3% of total income, while the richest population decile continued to receive around 45% of total income. Ownership reforms in the seventies did not substantially change this distribution. However, it should be noted that Peru's six poorest deciles saw their combined share of national income rise from 17.9% in 1971 to 20.9% in 1986. The two richest population deciles simultaneously saw their share of national income drop from 62.6 to 60.3%.

Peru's substantial ownership changes from 1961 until 1986 do not appear to have affected the unequal personal income distribution. Several reasons explain this distributive immobility. Ownership redistribution mainly shuffled assets among the richest deciles, while the poorest sectors, such as the peasants, did not receive substantial transfers of property (Webb and Figueroa 1975). Ownership concentration failed to improve Peruvian productivity or to win greater political power, the two methods of advantageous participation in income distribution.

Table 6.5. Personal Distribution of Income, 1961–86 (%)

Deciles of Population	1961 (Webb)	1971 (FitzGerald)	1986 (de Habich)
I & II	2.5	1.8	3.0
III & IV	5.5	5.5	6.8
V & VI	10.2	10.6	11.1
VII	7.6	8.1	8.0
VIII	9.8	11.4	10.8
IX	15.2	17.5	15.7
X	49.2	45.1	44.6
Gini	0.572		

Sources: Webb and Figueroa (1975, p. 29); FitzGerald (1979, table 22); de Habich (1989).

Finally, ownership changes have failed to replace Peru's rentier economy with a production-oriented economy, and the rentier economy remains the essential determinant of unequal income distribution (Webb 1989).

Peru's enormous economic growth in 1993–94 (when the GDP grew 20% and social expenditure increased for political reasons) improved the personal income distribution (see table 6.5).

Peruvian personal income distribution fluctuated with the business cycle, improving in expansionary phases and worsening during recessionary phases. Inflation, and the subsequent stabilization policies, concentrated income distribution during recessionary phases.

On the other hand, redistributive policies acting by means of subsidies, temporary employment, controlled prices, and transfers had a limited impact, which only lasted as long as the policies were in force (Gonzales and Samamé 1994; Figueroa 1982).

Income distribution remained a structural problem, which would change only with a shift in economic policy. Peru's new policy would have to be maintained for several years and would have to include support of stable property rights.

Sources of Economic Growth

There are two ways to analyze the determinants of economic growth. Supply side analysis uses production functions, aiming to measure the individual contribution to the economy of each factor of production (capital, labor, natural resources, and technological progress). Demand side analysis explains economic growth as a function of changes in supply (income) and demand, which act through the determinants of saving and investment, in relation to capital utilization.

Analysis using both approaches permits an overall glimpse of Peru's growth process. I attempt to provide such an overview in this section. The reader should be warned that this presentation is very simple and that the theme of determinants of growth is theoretically and empirically complex. For example, several factors seem to stimulate growth, while other factors retard growth.

In Peru, investment was the main source of growth, while excessive population growth acted as a brake on growth. Technological progress, usually defined as the third source of growth, decisively shaped the production and employment structures and, to a lesser degree, shaped the structure of growth (Gonzales 1994b; Vega-Centeno 1983). Taken together, these factors do not by themselves explain either the growth toward the middle of the seventies or the later decline. We must also take into account the international macroeconomic and institutional context of the economy's dynamics.

Determinants of Growth

Production-function models assume that growth results from investment, labor, and a residual factor of technological progress, which, for some authors, is an exogenous variable (Solow 1994). Scarcity of capital and an abundance of labor characterize underdeveloped nations like Peru, where the residual factor usually is neither small nor exogenous. In order to explain the role of each factor determining economic growth, I have formulated a simple, computable growth model. The inclusion of economic and institutional factors inherent in small economies leads me to maintain that investment is converted into the principal factor of growth only when certain conditions obtain (Gonzales 1995).

I assume that the following function explains growth:

$$y_t = y_t(IF_t, IP_t, \alpha K^*_t, \lambda WL^*_t, \rho dp_t, \beta(X-M)_t, \ddot{a}d(e/p)_t, \ddot{i}RP_t, \eta Pe_t, \mu) \ (1)$$

where:

y_t = annual rates of growth of GDP

IF_t = fixed annual investment in year t

IP_t = private annual investment in year t

K^*_t = capital stock in year t

WL^*_t = remuneration of workers in year t

dp_t = change in the rate of inflation p from year $t = t1 - t0$

$(X-M)_t$ = trade balance in year t

$d(e/p)_t$ = change in the real exchange rate from year t

RP = political regime (civil or military government) (dummy)

Pe = type of economic policy, interventionist or orthodox (dummy)

$\alpha, \beta, \lambda, \rho, \ddot{a}, \ddot{i}, \eta$ = parameters

μ = residual variable, technological progress

Table 6.6 shows my estimates. The combination of variables that best explains Peruvian GDP growth from 1950 to 1992 includes total fixed investment, workers' remunerations, a low inflation rate, economic policy stability, installed capacity's utilization level, a negative-signed exchange rate (i.e., the change in how fast the exchange rate was changing fell when growth increased), and a positive trade balance. Investment explained only 40 to 45% of Peru's GDP growth rate, requiring me to incorporate other factors into my analysis. The other factors explained the remaining 55 to 60% of the GDP growth rate.

The exchange rate and the foreign trade balance are used to estimate the effect on Peruvian growth of the external context. They have a positive influence on growth. Lagged two years' fixed investment and salaries have a negative sign, reflecting their limited period of impact.

I obtained different results when I divided the period between the two phases of Peru's long cycle, 1950–68 and 1968–90 (see table 6.6). In the 1950–68 period fixed investment did less than wages to propel growth, and domestic economic stability, defined as the change in the rate of inflation, mattered more than in the following period. From 1968 to 1990 fixed investment played a larger role in Peruvian growth, due above all to the weight of public investment financed with foreign loans. Salaries played a secondary role then, and external stability (the real exchange rate) affected economic growth more than domestic stability did.

These results indicate that private investment was necessary, but not sufficient, to spark economic growth (King and Levine 1994). Investment did not automatically generate growth unless Peru possessed domestic and foreign economic stability. The residual growth factor, attributable to technological progress and the improved education of the population, oscillated around 10% (Gonzales 1994b; Vega Centeno 1989).

Private and Public Investment

Foreign investors and the state, in their roles as owners, have most influenced Peruvian growth and investment. During the fifties and the middle sixties foreign investors sparked private investment's dynamism. From the late sixties to the middle eighties state capital replaced foreign capital as the motor of private investment. From 1991 on, as Peru faced a reduction in domestic savings because of the crises of foreign public debt, foreign capital once again became the key to the nation's investment process.

Private and public investment evolved in different directions between 1950 and 1993. Private investment generally increased, marked by a few

Table 6.6. Determinants of Long-term Growth, 1950–92

Variable	50-92 (1)	50-92 (White) (1')	50-92 (2)	50-92 (White) (2')	50-68 (3)	50-68 (White) (3')	68-90 (4)	68-90 (White) (4')	68-92 (5)	68-92 (White) (5')	70-90 (6)	70-90 (White) (6')
Constant	-20.790 (-2.6827)	-20.790 (-2.8418)	-12.548 (-2.1175)	-12.548 (-2.9199)	7.357 (3.2407)	7.357 (3.9551)	-1.604 (-0.2244)	-1.604 (-0.2334)	-3.784 (-1.2347)	-3.784 (-1.5423)	2.335 (0.3507)	2.335 (0.6877)
Fixed investment	0.018 (2.3914)	0.018 (2.4506)	0.020 (3.9909)	0.020 (3.7875)	0.014 (1.0660)	0.014 (1.1038)	0.024 (3.7457)	0.024 (3.0626)	0.025 (4.1186)	0.025 (3.3716)		
Fixed investment (t-1)	-0.027 (-4.9025)	-0.027 (-4.6298)	-0.030 (-5.5361)	-0.030 (-5.4900)	-0.044 (-2.9867)	-0.044 (-2.8276)	-0.031 (-4.7288)	-0.031 (-3.9832)	-0.032 (-5.6191)	-0.032 (-4.6043)		
Private investment											0.029 (2.7584)	0.029 (2.9443)
Private investment(t-1)											-0.036 (-3.5723)	-0.036 (-3.4863)
Remunerations	0.014 (2.8676)	0.014 (3.3923)	0.015 (3.0665)	0.015 (3.7460)	0.082 (2.6720)	0.082 (3.3945)	0.018 (2.8272)	0.018 (4.0635)	0.018 (3.7027)	0.018 (4.5236)	0.018 (2.2639)	0.018 (4.6879)
Remunerations (t-1)	-0.013 (-2.5151)	-0.013 (-2.8471)	-0.010 (-2.1029)	-0.010 (-2.9506)	-0.073 (-2.4276)	-0.073 (-3.2328)	-0.012 (-1.8432)	-0.012 (-2.0817)	-0.010 (-1.9550)	-0.010 (-2.5604)	-0.016 (-2.0053)	-0.016 (-2.8973)
d|Inf| (change in rate of inflation)	-0.001 (-2.9749)	-0.001 (-4.7547)	-0.001 (-3.2064)	-0.001 (-5.8564)	-0.207 (-2.3714)	-0.207 (-2.8177)	-0.001 (-1.0234)	-0.001 (-1.2700)	-0.001 (-3.3059)	-0.001 (-8.3631)	-0.001 (-1.5158)	-0.001 (-3.0290)
Economic policy	2.132 (2.0626)	2.132 (2.3461)	2.301 (2.7315)	2.301 (2.5640)			2.994 (2.8322)	2.994 (2.5540)	2.994 (2.9876)	2.994 (2.7030)	2.431 (1.812)	2.431 (2.0272)
Real exchange rate	-0.015 (-0.8908)	-0.015 (-0.8246)					0.011 (0.5014)	0.011 (0.5316)	0.015 (1.0414)	0.015 (1.4532)		
UPOT (potential product)	30.511 (2.6407)	30.511 (2.3898)	16.959 (2.7466)	16.959 (3.5872)								
Trade balance	0.004 (1.0479)	0.004 (1.2443)										
R²	0.8607	0.8607	0.8489	0.8489	0.6745	0.6745	0.8997	0.8997	0.8997	0.8997	0.8701	0.8701
R² adjusted	0.8215	0.8215	0.8178	0.8178	0.5389	0.5389	0.8528	0.8528	0.8558	0.8558	0.8101	0.8101
Durbin-Watson	1.9311	1.9311	2.0073	2.0073	2.4632	2.4632	2.1901	2.1901	2.1819	2.1819	2.8260	2.8260
F statistic	21.9726	21.9726	27.2884	27.2884	4.9742	4.9742	19.2122	19.2122	21.7862	21.7862	14.5073	14.5073

Note: t statistics in parentheses; t - 1 refers to prior year. The notation (') indicates a matrix consistent with covariance under White's heteroscedasticity criterion.

explosive short-term periods and by a declining growth rate in the late sixties. Private investment recovered from 1978 to 1981, but then decreased again (see chart 6.6). Public investment remained low until the middle sixties. Public investment's growth rate increased in the early seventies, but then fell without pause, in great contrast to the trends of private investment.

Private investment oscillated between 15 and 20% of GDP until 1963, fell to around 10% thereafter, and then increased again from the eighties on. Public investment stayed above 5% from 1970 to 1986, peaking at 9% between 1974 and 1976 and in 1983. Private investment has represented around 80% of total investment in Peru. Therefore, it has been decisive in explaining the evolution of the economy.

When I added labor and investment to the regression equation, they explained 72% of Peruvian growth, while domestic stability (the change in the rate of inflation), external stability (the real exchange rate), and the institutional variables (the kind of economic policy utilized) explained the remaining 28% of Peruvian growth.

In chart 6.7 I have estimated the trends of private and public investment as a share of Peruvian GDP for the 1950–93 period. Private investment equaled around 15% of Peruvian GDP until the sixties, fell to an average of 10% of the GDP in the next two decades, and returned to the 15% level from the mid-seventies on, with a tendency to increase. In contrast, public investment was less than 5% of the GDP until the seventies, but rose to an average of 7 to 8% of the GDP from the military government up to 1985.

The principal determinants of private investment in Peru are the economic cycle, domestic credit, the political cycle, and the amount of prior investment. The most important variable is the economic cycle, since private investment is larger when Peru is near full capacity. Domestic credit has an elasticity with respect to investment greater than one and doubtless constitutes the most important exogenous variable. In contrast, profits do not seem to be an important variable, since their elasticity with respect to investment is low. This coincides with the investment/profit ratio's tendency to fall (Gonzales de Olarte 1996).

Public investment did not have a linear relation to private investment, since it had a crowding-out effect during the expansion phase of the cycle and a crowding-in effect during the recession. The crowding-in occurred because public investment did not compete in sectors of the Peruvian economy where private firms invested, but rather invested in Peruvian infrastructure. State infrastructure investment itself was an incentive to private investment.

Chart 6.6. Total Public and Private Investment, 1950–93 (millions of soles, 1979 prices)

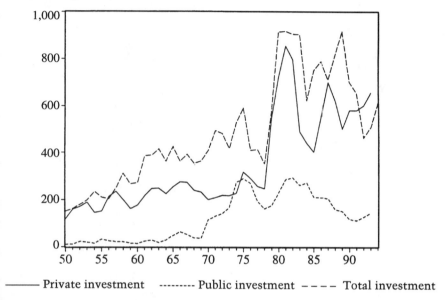

———— Private investment ········· Public investment – – – – Total investment

Chart 6.7. Public and Private Investment as a Share of Gross Domestic Product, 1950–93 (percent)

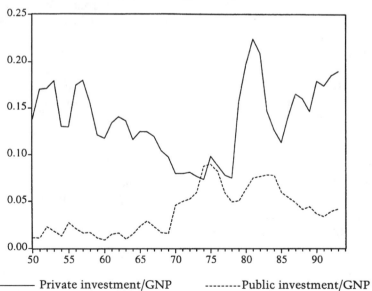

———— Private investment/GNP ········Public investment/GNP

Chart 6.8. Private and Foreign Investment, 1970–92
(millions of dollars)

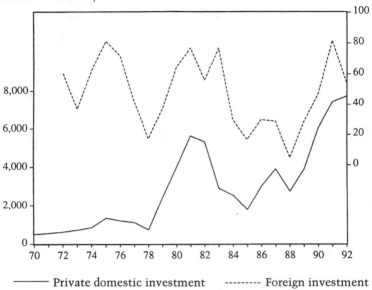

——— Private domestic investment   -------- Foreign investment

Foreign and Domestic Investment

Foreign investment, concentrated in the primary-export sector, has played an important part in the Peruvian savings process and in shaping the economic structure. Foreign investment has had important macro-economic repercussions on Peru's balance of payments. It has also played an important role in sparking structural adjustments, since foreign investors provide signals for national investors (who possess limited information on risk and uncertainty) to follow (Gonzales 1994a; Thorp and Bertram 1978) and because foreign and domestic investors formed joint ventures on various occasions. Thus, the trend of domestic private investment followed, with slight variations, the trend of foreign investment (see chart 6.8). This causal relationship is statistically significant for the 1970–92 period. Direct foreign investment fell in relative terms in the 1968–74 period (though there was no absolute capital outflow from Peru), increased in the early eighties, fell during Alan García's government, and rose drastically beginning in 1991, immediately after Peru's new structural adjustment began.

The Accumulation of Capital

The accumulated capital stock and its relation to production, the labor force, and income distribution constitute the axis of growth and development. My estimate of Peruvian capital stock in comparison with product and population shows some characteristics of capital accumulation.

Between 1950 and 1990 total capital stock (K) sextupled, while capital per capita (K/N) only doubled (see chart 6.9). If we add to this the fact that the growth rate of Peru's economically active population exceeded the growth rate of the total population, the amount of capital in relation to the labor force has increased even less. Capital stock grew at an annual rate of around 4.5% in 1950–92: at a stable rate until the seventies, more quickly from 1975 to 1985, and increasingly slowly thereafter. This behavior raises the following question: how did capital stock increase when Peru's crisis began, yet fail to serve as a way out of crisis?

An explanation may lie in the variations of Peru's dependency ratio, defined as the economically inactive population divided by the economically active population (those older than fifteen and younger than sixty-five). If we compare the 1981 and 1993 censuses, we see that this ratio fell from 2.42 to 2.18. This appears to have been due to the increase in the rate of activity of workers and to the simultaneous diminution of the Peruvian population under fifteen years of age. This diminution in turn is due to the falling urban fertility rate (the rural fertility rate has been static) and to improved education.

Peru's capital/output ratio (K/Y) rose from 2.3 in 1950 to 3.8 in 1990 (see chart 6.9). This ratio exceeded the average ratio of the six largest Latin American nations, which rose from 1.9 to 2.8 during the same period (Hofman 1992, p. 387). This growth suggests that the Peruvian economy became inefficient from the early eighties, since the nation's increasing capital stock produced a declining GDP. Although Peru possessed little capital per capita, it underutilized what capital it had. Chile, in contrast, preserved a stable capital/output ration of around 2.5. Peru's problem lies in the fall in its production in relation to capital, which has grown stably.

The K/Y ratio oscillated as a function of the economic cycle, falling in expansive phases (1973–75, 1979–81, and 1986–87) and increasing during the recessive phases. Economic growth depends not only on capital accumulation, but also on the degree of capital utilization (see chart 6.9).

The capital growth rate exceeded the labor growth rate (of the estimated economically active population) until the beginning of the seventies. The capital growth rate increased in the seventies, but then declined from the middle eighties. In contrast, the economically active population grew in a stable manner until the beginning of the seventies, but its growth rate then increased considerably. This suggests that the growth of the labor force (economically active population: EAP), greater than the population's growth rate, has created a strong need for an increase in Peru's investment rate: an unfulfilled need. Therefore,

Chart 6.9. Capital/Output Ratio and Capital Per Capita, 1950–93

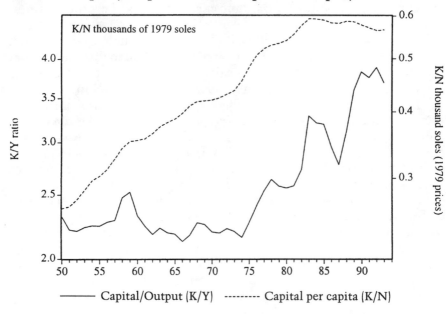

Chart 6.10. Private and Public Capital Stock, 1950–93 (millions of 1979 soles)

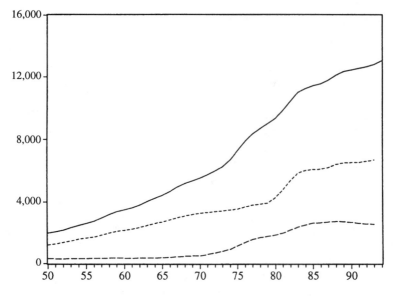

unemployment and underemployment have grown to dramatic levels (Gonzales 1994b; Verdera 1995).

Foreign debt plays an important role in Peru's capital accumulation process, since it reduces the number of economic growth policy options that are available. The Peruvian foreign debt's growth rate has been greater than its capital accumulation rate, above all because high international interest rates dramatically increased the weight of debt service in the eighties. Peru used part of its debt for investment purposes, but it used the remainder for military spending and current expenditures. My overall judgment is that Peru's debt has made no positive contribution to capital accumulation, since the ensuing requirements to service that debt reduced the amount of domestic savings Peru could use for investment.

Comparing Peru's foreign debt to its capital stock in constant 1979 prices, we find that the debt increased in value during the stabilization processes (1976–79, 1984–85), when Peru carried out major devaluations, although its debt did not increase during the 1990–91 stabilization. This trend suggests that foreign debt and foreign investment played different roles. Peru's debt did not much affect capital stock created from private investment. The debt reduced public investment levels (and, therefore, total investment levels) by reducing the amount of domestic savings available for purposes other than payment of the debt service.

The Harrod Domar model analyzes economic growth from the point of view of supply (income) and demand, incorporating population as an exogenous variable. The model provides a theory that allows us to make the desired rate of economic growth compatible with the "natural rate" of growth imposed by population increases. This allows us to estimate how much investment is needed for growth for each given population.

The model then requires a savings level compatible with investment, taking the existing capital stock into account (the required savings is lower if existing capital is underutilized). The famous equation of equilibrium growth is:

$$g = \{ (sn + sf) / (ICOR + \emptyset) \} - n$$

where:

g = desired rate of growth per capita

sn = share of domestic saving in GDP

sf = share of foreign saving in GDP

$ICOR$ = new investment per additional unit of output

$\emptyset$ = correction coefficient, indicating that the observed amount of investment needed for additional output may differ from theoretical estimates. This can be due to strikes, lockouts, and other factors limiting or enhancing the use of capital. The correction coefficient sometimes is referred to as "labor productivity" or as the "residual factor."

n = population growth rate

Table 6.7. Indicators of Harrod Domar Growth, 1950/60–81/90
(period averages)

Years	g	sn	sf	ICOR	e	n
1950–60	2.4	18.9	3.1	3.8	0.5	2.7
1961–70	2.9	19.6	1.5	4.4	-0.8	2.9
1971–80	0.9	15.8	2.8	6.3	-1.3	2.8
1981–90	-1.9	21.7	2.7	-3.6	44.3	2.5

Source: Based on data from Instituto Nacional de Estadística e Informática, *Compendio estadístico,* 1981, 1991–92; Dirección Tecnicade Indicadores Económicas, Lima, 1982, 1992.

Peru's economic growth has depended on the net savings rate and on increases in labor productivity and income. Two influences have reduced Peruvian economic growth: the increase in the *ICOR* due to Peru's reduction in production (that is to say, its increasingly inefficient capital use) and the nation's population growth rate, still very high despite recent reductions.

Peruvian economic growth has been largely based on domestic savings (foreign savings have been complementary in character, not supplementary), and, except during the 1970s, it has been fairly stable. The savings rate increase in the 1980s was one of the factors that made the *ICOR* grow. But, although Peru's residual factor is very high, it has not been reflected in the growth rate, as one would hope on the basis of theory.

The fall in the Peruvian population's natural growth rate depends in part on the fall in the per capita economic growth rate. However, exogenous factors such as health policies, preventive health programs, and provision of food for children also affect the population growth rate (see table 6.7).

According to theory, Peru's observed savings rate should have resulted in higher growth than actually occurred. The Harrod Domar model does not provide more explicit explanations and must be supplemented by another analytical framework in the following sections.

Restriction on Growth: The Three Gaps

Many theorists have indicated that factors particular to Latin America restrict economic growth. The first two factors that theorists advanced as "gaps" that limited Latin American development were lack of savings and hard currency and external constraints. Theorists added government inability to obtain adequate tax revenues as a third gap that inhibited growth after Latin American governments indebted themselves hugely in the seventies, since the ensuing need to service their debt reduced government spending levels and in consequence reduced savings, investment, and possibilities of increased exports.

In Peru, scantily endowed with capital and relatively overpopulated, effective savings were not sufficient to finance the levels of private and public investment needed to employ the unemployed and underemployed population. Moreover, investments in the export and industrial sectors did not adequately increase, since foreign enterprises repatriated profits and domestic investors engaged in capital flight. These investments therefore could not supply sufficient total savings and foreign exchange for Peru. Public foreign indebtedness simultaneously solved the problems posed by these multiple gaps. Since Peru's foreign debt was almost entirely governmental, its debt has strongly influenced its fiscal gap, directly affecting Peruvian public investment and providing a strong indirect influence on private investment.

In the long run, private investment basically has depended on private domestic savings. Public investment provided a small, complementary effect on Peruvian growth (crowding-in), though as much through the business sector as through the public sector. Foreign savings have also had a positive effect on Peruvian growth.

The external gap has moderately limited private investment during this long period. Peru's limited foreign exchange supply and its public sector's high marginal propensity to import capital goods (albeit reduced during each fiscal crisis) have both contributed to this result. Foreign debt's role as regards Peru's foreign exchange supply is ambiguous. Peru's indebtedness provided it with foreign exchange during several periods of trade crisis, but the foreign exchange supply decreased when the weight of Peru's debt service increased from 1984 on.

Finally, the governmental budget deficit affected growth by means of its influence on private investment. Private investment fell when Peru possessed a fiscal surplus and grew when it possessed a deficit and when Peru's positive or negative public savings were greater than the sum of savings from private and foreign sources together.

Growth without Development

I have shown that from the fifties on Peru grew without developing. To better explain this phenomenon, we must move to a less conventional micro- and macroeconomic focus. Amartya Sen (1984) has contributed a suggestive conception of development, which allows us to move between micro- and macroeconomic processes and between the economy and politics.

According to Sen (1984), economic development not only expands the people's capabilities to produce goods and services, but also expands their ability to emancipate themselves. This process should simultaneously broaden the people's entitlement to the combination of goods and services required to satisfy their needs and improve their standard of living. Sen defines "capabilities" as the people's inherent abilities to produce, while he defines "entitlements" in terms of the institutions needed to give the people access to increasing income, property rights, and public goods.

Following this definition, I hypothesize that the Peruvian people's capabilities have increased slowly, in a badly distributed pattern, that the people's entitlements have increased even more slowly, and that the imbalance between the growth in capabilities and entitlements made Peru grow economically without being developed. The results of growth without development are largely reflected in the imbalanced evolution of Peru's productive factors, such that the quality of the labor force improved more rapidly than that of capital and natural resources. This imbalance underlines the fact that Peru's possibilities of achieving development depend on the human factor, since its endowment of capital and natural resources per capita is very small.

The Slow and Unbalanced Creation of Capabilities and Entitlements

Peru's economic transformations have been mirrored in its population, since the population's size, location, education, and aspirations to social mobility have all depended on the amount and kind of access individuals and families have had to available economic resources.

The changes the economy has undergone in the last thirty years can be evaluated in terms of the population's changing amount of access to Peru's capabilities, as represented by economic resources. Increased access to these resources has allowed the population to satisfy its basic needs, to improve its standard of living, and to create aspirations toward social mobility. Yet Peru's organization of its national economy to create, increase, and distribute economic resources has only been spottily effective in fulfilling individuals' aspirations.

Peru's principal capabilities are its people and their skills, which neoclassical theorists call "human capital," and the natural and created resources on which the people can rely. Peru's global capabilities increased steadily from the fifties to the end of the seventies, when they stagnated (table 6.8).

Peru's natural resources (lands, pastures, and woods) did not qualitatively improve, but their quantity increased. Cultivated land increased most of all, in the great coastal irrigation systems and in the small and medium highland irrigation systems. Cultivable land per capita fell from

Table 6.8. Evolution of Capabilities, 1961–93

	1961	1972	1981	1990	1993
POPULATION					
Total (thousands)	9,907	13,538	17,031	21,379[a]	22,128
Annual growth rate	2.25	2.88	2.57	2[a]	2.2
% urban population	47.7	59.5	65.1	70.1[a]	70.4
Annual growth rate	3.6	5.0	3.6	2.8[a]	2.9
% in cities > 20,000	3,804	6,794	9,678	–	–
% of total population	38.4	50.2	56.9	–	–
% of urban population	80.9	84.3	87.3	–	–
CULTIVATABLE LAND					
(1,000 hectares)	3,897.4	3,691.4	2,720.8	2,561[b]	[b]
Hectares per capita	0.39	0.27	0.16	0.12	–
Hectares per rural population	0.75	0.67	0.46	0.4	–
INSTALLED ELECTRIC POWER					
(Mw)	779	2,108	3,238	4,143.3	4,113[c]
Mw per capita	0.08	0.16	0.19	0.19	0.19
EDUCATION					
Infrastructure					
No. of ed. centers	–	22,795	29,620	47,751	–
No. of government ed. centers	–	19,774	25,247	41,314	–
No. of private ed. centers	–	3,021	4,373	6,437	–
Personnel					
No. of students (thousands)	–	4,465	5,779	7,973	–
No. of teachers (thousands)	–	138	182	307	–
Student pop./total pop.	–	32.9	33.9	37.3	–
Students per teacher	–	32.4	31.8	25.9	–
Educational attainment of those 15 years and older					
Primary (%)	46.3	47.7	41.3	31.5[a]	–
Secondary (%)	11.1	20.4	30.7	35.5[a]	–
Literacy rate					
Total	38.9	27.5	18.1	12.8[a]	–
Men	25.6	16.7	9.9	7.1[a]	–
Women	51.7	38.2	26.1	18.3 [a]	–
Educational spending (% of GDP)	–	19.6	8.8	6.6	–
University graduates	1,710	4,756	8,930	14,714	–
Accounting/education/law (%)	42	64.9	40	27.7	–
Engineering	17.1	16.0	19.9	17.7	–
Health sciences	29.3	8.3	14.8	18.5	–
University graduates/students (%)			0.18	0.20	–
HEALTH					
No. of hospital beds	–	28,550	29,345	32,434	38,910[d]
No. of government hospital beds	–	22,992	23,559	26,088	31,701
No. of private hospital beds	–	5,558	5,786	6,346	7,209
HOUSING					
No. of occupied houses (thousands)	1,942	2,687	3,303	4,428[a]	–
With water (%)	21.1	29.6	38	38[a]	–
With power (%)	26.3	32.1	45.0	45.7[a]	–
With sewers (%)	14.6	23.3	29.0	30.1[a]	–

Table 6.8. Continued

	1961	1972	1981	1990	1993
CAPITAL					
Stock (millions of 1979 soles)	4,008,555	6,181,692	9,928,451	12,499,095	12,742,390
Stock per capita	404.6	456.6	583.0	584.6	575.8
OUTPUT PER CAPITA					
In 1979 soles	158.1	193.4	214.9	153.0	–
In 1979 dollars	703.7	860.7	954.3	681.0	–

Sources: INEI: Compendio estadístico 1991–1992, 1992, 1993 (Lima: Dirección Técnica de Indicadores Económicos, 1992, 1993); Cuánto, S.A., *Perú en números: Anuario estadístico, 1991, 1992, 1993.*
[a] Census 1993.
[b] Cuánto 1989.
[c] Cuánto 1991.
[d] Cuánto 1992.

1961 on. Today Peru has barely 0.12 hectares (1 hectare = 2.471 acres) to feed each inhabitant. Capital stock in the form of construction, machinery, and equipment per capita increased from S/. 254 (US$1,230) in 1950 to S/. 404 (US$ 1,958) in 1961 and to S/.583 (US$2,595) in 1981 (US$2,595), but then stagnated. The nation's installed electric capacity also grew until the early eighties but then also later stagnated. Peru's problem is that its capital stock is geographically concentrated. For example, although installed electric capacity increased substantially between 1961 and 1981, only 45.7% of the population had access to it in 1981 (see table 6.8).

Most likely, Peru's greatest achievement during the last thirty years was the great improvement in quality of life in regard to education and health. Male and female illiteracy both decreased greatly. The educational infrastructure, the proportion of the population in school, and the annual number of professionals granted university degrees have all increased. However, educational quality and spending both fell or stagnated with the crisis, beginning in 1981. Mortality and infant morbidity both fell, and the health infrastructure significantly improved. For example, the number of hospital beds, hospitals, and other kinds of health centers has increased. On the other hand, their availability per person has fallen.

This process of creating capabilities, which means improving the population's well-being and ability to create income, has had various common characteristics. The capabilities created have followed the long economic cycle. Peru accumulated more capabilities in the late seventies. Then came stagnation and, in some cases, regression, through infrastructure deterioration and through terrorist destruction of physical capital during the eighties.

Although Peru's absolute capability total increased, individual capabilities did not follow suit, except in the realm of education. The long-term disequilibrium between supply growth and labor demand resulted from an inadequate system of resource assignment by the state-dominated economy. For example, the number of matriculated students increased from 1972 to 1981 at an annual rate of about 3.6%, while the capital stock growth rate increased at about 2.6% and the installed electric energy capacity increased at about 2.8%. Education thus improved quantitatively and qualitatively, but Peru created insufficient demand to absorb its educated population at salary levels that would allow them to satisfy their basic needs. Hence the nation suffers from structural problems of underemployment and unemployment (Verdera 1983; see table 6.8).

The number of professionals granted university degrees increased at a steady annual rate of 6.4% between 1972 and 1990, while capital stock grew at only 3.9%. This disequilibrium had a double effect. Peruvians entered professions related to those sectors that improved their educational capacity: education and health (see table 6.8). Second, professionals who could not find work in the domestic labor market emigrated. Between 1980 and 1988 alone, 23,300 professionals and 36,870 students left Peru (Senado de la República 1992).

These changes are mirrored in other changes in Peru's labor force and employment. While the population growth index rose from 100 in 1961 to 223 in 1993, the labor force index increased only from 100 to 137. This disequilibrium reflects Peru's demographic structure, which includes a large juvenile population. The unemployment rate has been constantly increasing, as has the underemployment rate. Both unemployment and underemployment have become especially acute in the metropolitan Lima area during the last decade.

The central reason Peru has grown without development is that it created more human capacity through educational improvements (labor supply) than it could create adequately remunerated jobs (demand for labor).

The Institutional System and Peru's Inadequate Conversion Mechanisms of Entitlements and Capabilities

There were basically four solutions to these unemployment and underemployment problems. Peruvians could acquire government jobs through the "political market," by clientelism. They could become self-employed in various rural and urban goods and services sectors that were characterized by small-scale investment and underutilization of educational skills. This mechanism of creating entitlements has been classified as informality, because it generally exists at the margin of the legally supervised economy. Peruvians could also emigrate to other countries. More than 1 million Peruvians are estimated to live abroad (Altamirano 1992), roughly 5% of the total population. Finally, Peruvians found employment and income by illegal activities, principally in the production of coca leaves and their derivatives.

These experiences indicate that when capabilities are created means are always found to transform them into entitlements, including at the margins of the law and the margins of the country. In Peru, since neither the formal market economy nor the state could absorb the total labor supply, social conflict arose. The final result of this disequilibrium was to increase Peru's unemployment and underemployment until 81% of the economically active population fell into one of the two categories. In 1995 less than 40% of the economically active population had salaried employment.

The conversion of capabilities into entitlements in the market has had two characteristics. There are two ways to increase or maintain real incomes: increase productivity or attain a degree of monopoly in the market. Monopoly or oligopoly enterprises, and labor unions able to fix prices unilaterally or by negotiation, have gained the most entitlements. Peruvians participating in competitive markets have converted their capabilities into entitlements as a function of their productivity. The highlands peasants, who participate in competitive markets and who have low family productivity, have the lowest incomes. State intervention to control or fix prices by market regulation has also been a way to influence the conversion and transference of entitlements.

State intervention to convert capabilities into entitlements has run into two main types of problems. First, Peru lacks adequate "intermediaries" between the state and those who aspire to obtain entitlements. Political parties, which represent fragmented social interest, have proved incapable of acting as major intermediaries (Gonzales and Samamé 1994; Cotler 1990). Other intermediaries, such as the unions or social organizations, were also unable to become stable intermediaries. Second, short-term, medium-term, and long-term political shifts have all made Peru subject to a continual modification of the "rules of the game." Moreover, shifts in short-term economic policies, as Peru created and then suppressed subsidies, price controls, and regulation, made access to the most important (if limited) long-term entitlements uncertain. The politico-institutional system has failed, in the matter regarding entitlements.

Final Thoughts

Peru is a typical Latin American case of growth without redistribution. The government failed to readjust its economic policies at the right time, in the mid-sixties. Subsequently, populist economic policies and great population growth frustrated development. Political instability limited private investment. Peru's political instability was reflected in its shifting economic policies and was itself at bottom a reflection of a social fragmentation that was reinforced by distributional inequalities.

Peru's primary export and semi-industrial economic policies (PESID) functioned well until the early seventies, when lack of investment and foreign exchange revealed the long-term structural disequilibria the growth model had generated. The military government financed these policies for several more years by means of foreign borrowings. However, the military government achieved neither a large increase in exports nor a large increase in import substitution. Peruvian growth depended on private investment. The nation's level of economic activity depended on its economic policies. Workers' remunerations depended on political conditions and domestic economic stability. When these factors combined harmoniously, Peru grew; when they were out of phase with each other, Peru suffered crises. At different stages, foreign investment and state intervention in turn served as the main promoters of growth. Foreign investment played a crucial role by giving adequate economic signals to information-short private domestic investors. The national entrepreneurs' lack of information gave them a subordinate role in the capital accumulation process.

However, there are indications of a change in Peru's pattern of growth since 1990. PESID is being transformed by neoliberal reforms and structural adjustment and appears to have initiated a new long-term economic cycle. The Peruvian economy has become more open and its economic policies less interventionist.

Changes in income distribution depended on economic growth and on political and institutional factors. Incomes were linked more to power or to differential rents than to productivity. Peru's personal income distribution did not vary substantially in the forty years studied and remained throughout one of the most unequally distributed national incomes in Latin America. Even during the government of Alberto Fujimori, there do not seem to have been changes in Peru's income distribution, despite economic growth. Profits tended to increase as a share of Peru's functional income, even though investment underwent a proportional decline.

Peru's growth and distribution processes generated a small accumulation of capital stock per capita, which only doubled in forty years, along with increasingly inefficient capital use and a high rate of unemployment and underemployment in the labor force.

The state was a fundamental actor during the 1950–90 period. It had its own cycle: it grew in the sixties, attained its greatest influence in the seventies, and declined into crisis in the eighties. The PESID economic policies could not have been enacted without the military government's decision to intervene in the economy by means of state capitalism (1968–75), when the state acted simultaneously as the economy's regulator, producer, and redistributor.

During these forty years of government intervention, Peru's various governments maintained questionable relative prices, which were probably unpropitious for development, by systematically overvaluing the exchange rate, by letting real salaries tend to decline, and by allowing great interest rate instability. In combination with the concomitant political instability, these relative prices resulted in a falling investment rate, relative both to profits and to the slow improvement of income levels.

Peru's major disequilibrium of underdevelopment has been to create an educated and skilled class, for whom it has not created sufficient demand and whom it could not pay according to their qualifications. Low and inefficient Peruvian saving, combined with rapid population growth, caused massive unemployment and underemployment.

When the long-term crisis arrived, the disequilibrium between capabilities and entitlements deepened, and part of the population emigrated from Peru.

Growth without redistribution, if it did not bring development, transformed Peru and the Peruvians on at least three levels. Growth homogenized the people's average education. Though the educational quality is not excellent, the educational capabilities are more equitably distributed today than they were forty years ago. This provides a base for development and for democracy that Peru can use in the future. Second, the economic culture was transformed, as Peruvians' expectations changed from dependence on the state to self-reliance. Finally, Peru learned that when the market and the state do not cooperate, growth and distribution fail to lead to development. Today the nation needs to design new institutions, new roles, and new rules of the game so that the public sector can cooperate with the private sector in such a way that the state and the government will promote development without direct intervention in the economy. In this way Peru could create more capabilities and entitlements, and create them by stable means, so that created and accumulated capabilities and entitlements would not later be lost.

Note

My thanks to Laura Randall, Julio Cotler, Javier Iguiñiz, Francisco Verdera, and two anonymous referees for their valuable commentaries on a preliminary version of this article. I also thank Pedro Llontop for his collaboration. Obviously, everything I have written is my responsibility.

Works Cited

Altamirano, Teófilo. 1992. *Éxodo: Peruanos en el exterior.* Lima: Fondo Editorial, Pontificia Universidad Católica del Perú.

Balassa, Bela, Gerardo Bueno, Pedro-Pablo Kuczynski, and Mario Henrique Simonsen. 1986. *Toward Renewed Economic Growth in Latin America.* Washington, D.C.: Institute for International Economics.

Banco Central de Reserva del Perú. *Memoria.* Annual publication. Lima.

Beaulne, Mary. 1975. *Industrialización por sustitución de importaciones: Perú 1958–69.* Lima: Campodónico Editores.

Caballero, José María, and Elena Álvarez. 1980. *Aspectos cuantitativos de la reforma agraria (1969–79).* Colección Mínima 12. Lima: Instituto de Estudios Peruanos.

Cotler, Julio. 1978. *Clases, estado y nación en el Perú.* Serie Perú Problema 17. Lima: Instituto de Estudios Peruanos.

——. 1990. Partidos políticos: Inestabilidad democrática en el Perú. Report presented at the seminar Parties and Party Systems in Latin America, Helen Kellog Institute. MS.

de Habich, Midori. 1989. Un análisis exploratorio de la distribución del ingreso en el Perú. Lima: Banco Central de Reserva del Perú. MS.

de Soto, Hernando. 1986. *El otro sendero: La revolución informal.* Lima: Editorial El Barranco.

Figueroa, Adolfo. 1982. El problema distributivo en diferentes contextos sociopolíticos y económicos, Perú, 1950–80. *Revista de Desarrollo Económico* (Argentina) 22.

FitzGerald, E. V. K. 1979. *The Political Economy of Peru, 1956–78: Economic Development and the Restructuring of Capital.* Cambridge: Cambridge University Press.

Glewwe, Paul. 1987. The Distribution of Welfare in Peru 1985–86. LSMS Working Paper 42. Washington, D.C.: World Bank, Population and Human Resources Department.

Gonzales de Olarte, Efraín. 1982. *Economías regionales del Perú.* Serie Estudios Económicos. Lima: Instituto de Estudios Peruanos.

——, ed. 1989a. *Economía para la democracia: Siete conferencias.* Serie Análisis Económico 13. Lima: Instituto de Estudios Peruanos.

——. 1989b. Underaccumulation and Disintegration in Peru: Economic and Political Crisis. *International Conference Economic Crisis and Third World Countries: Impact and Response, Kingston, Jamaica.* Geneva: UNRISD.

——. 1991. Hacia la reestructuración económica del Perú. Instituto de Estudios Peruanos. MS.

——. 1993. Economic Stabilization and Structural Adjustment under Fujimori. *Journal of Interamerican Studies and World Affairs* 35(2).

——. 1994a. *En las fronteras del mercado: Economía política del campesinado en el Perú.* Serie Análisis Económico 16. Lima: Instituto de Estudios Peruanos.

——. 1994b. Peru's Difficult Road to Economic Development. In Joseph S. Tulchin and Gary Bland, *Transformación sin desarrollo.* Current Studies on Latin America. Washington, D.C.: Woodrow Wilson Center.

——. 1994c. Transformación sin desarrollo: Perú 1964–94. In Julio Cotler, ed., *Perú 1964–94: Economía, sociedad y política.* Serie Perú Problema 24. Lima: Instituto de Estudios Peruanos.

——. 1996. *Inversión privada, crecimiento y ajuste estructural en el Perú 1950–95.* Documento de trabajo 81. Lima: Instituto de Estudios Peruanos.

Gonzales de Olarte, Efraín, and Lilian Samamé. 1994. *El péndulo peruano: Políticas económicas, gobernabilidad y sub-desarrollo.* 2nd ed. Serie Análisis Económico 13. Lima: Instituto de Estudios Peruanos.

Herrera, César. 1989. Restricción de divisas: Efectos macroeconómicos y alternativas de política. Documento de trabajo 229. Lima: Instituto de Estudios Peruanos.

Hofman, A. A. 1992. Capital Accumulation in Latin America: A Six Country Comparison for 1980/89. *Review of Income Wealth* (December) 38(4).

King, Robert G., and Ross Levine. 1994. Capital Fundamentalism, Economic Development and Economic Growth. Policy Research Working Paper 1285. Washington, D.C.: World Bank.

Matos Mar, José. 1984. *Desborde popular y crisis del estado: El nuevo rostro del Perú en la década de 1980.* Perú Problema 19. Lima: Instituto de Estudios Peruanos.

Pinzás García, Teobaldo. 1993. Relaciones entre el sector externo y la economía global. Documento de trabajo 46. Lima: Instituto de Estudios Peruanos.

Seminario, Bruno. 1995. Notas sobre el crecimiento económico del Perú. Consorcio de Investigación Económica y Red Macroeconómica Latinoamericana, Cochabamba. MS.

Sen, Amartya. 1984. *Resources, Values and Development.* Cambridge, Mass.: Harvard University Press.

Senado de la República. 1992. Violencia y pacificación en 1991. Comisión Especial de Investigación y Estudio sobre la Violencia y Alternativas de Pacificación, Lima.

Solow, Robert. 1994. Perspectives on Growth Theory. *Journal of Economic Perspectives* 8(1).

Thorp, Rosemary, and Geoffrey Bertram. 1978. *Peru 1890–77: Growth and Policy in an Open Economy.* London: Macmillan.

Torres, Jorge. 1975. *Estructura económica de la industria peruana.* Lima: Editorial Horizonte.

Tulchin, Joseph S., and Gary Bland. 1994. Transformación sin desarrollo. In Efraín Gonzales de Olarte, *Inversión privada, crecimiento y ajuste estructural en el Perú 1950–95.* Documento de trabajo 81. Lima: Instituto de Estudios Peruanos, 1996.

Vega Centeno, Máximo. 1983. *Crecimiento, industrialización y cambio técnico en el Perú 1955–80.* Lima: Fondo Editorial, Pontificia Universidad Católica del Perú.

———. 1989. Inversiones y cambio técnico en el crecimiento de la economía peruana. *Economía* 12(24) (Departamento de Economía, Pontificia Universidad Católica del Perú, Lima).

Verdera, Francisco. 1983. *El empleo en el Perú: Un nuevo enfoque.* Serie Análisis Económico 7. Lima: Instituto de Estudios Peruanos.

———. 1995. El estancamiento de la economía peruana: Los límites del desarrollo capitalista en el Perú 1950–90. Lima: Instituto de Estudios Peruanos. MS.

Webb, Richard Charles. 1977. *Government Policy and the Distribution of Income in Peru 1963–73.* Harvard Economic Studies 147. Cambridge, Mass.: Harvard University Press.

———. 1989. Los problemas de redistribución en contextos democráticos. In Efraín Gonzales de Olarte, *Economía para la democracia: Siete conferencias.* Serie Análisis Económico 13. Lima: Instituto de Estudios Peruanos.

Webb, Richard, and Adolfo Figueroa. 1975. *La distribución del ingreso en el Perú.* Serie Perú Problema 14. Lima: Instituto de Estudios Peruanos.

White, Halbert. 1980. A Heteroskedasticity–Consistent Covariance Estimator and a Direct Test for Heteroskedasticity. *Econometrica* 48.

Williamson, John, ed. 1990. *Latin American Adjustment: How Much Has Happened?* Washington, D.C.: Institute for International Economics.

Sources of Statistical Data

Banco Central de Reserva del Perú, Lima. *Boletín semanal.* Various issues.

———. *Cuentas nacionales del Perú.* 1950–65, 1960–67.

———. *Memoria anual.* Various years.

Instituto Geográfico Militar del Perú. 1989. *Atlas del Perú.* Lima.

Instituto Nacional de Estadística e Informática, Lima. *Censos nacionales de población y vivienda,* 1961, 1972, 1981, and 1993.

———. *Cuentas nacionales del Perú,* 1950–80.

———. *Perú: Compendio estadístico,* 1988, 1990, 1991–92, 1993–94, and 1994–95.

Cuánto S.A. (Richard Webb and Graciela Fernández Baca), Lima. *Perú en números: Anuario estadístico,* 1991, 1992, 1993, 1994, and 1995.

7.
Ecuador

Joan B. Anderson
University of San Diego

Physically, Ecuador is one of the smallest countries in South America. It has 283.6 thousand square kilometers, an area slightly smaller than the state of Nevada. The country is situated on the west coast of South America between Colombia on the north and Peru to the east and south. It has three distinct regions: the coastal plains, where most of the agri-export business is; the central sierra (mountain region), where, until recently, the majority of the population resided; and the Oriente (eastern region), which has oil, but is just beginning to be settled by people other than the small native population.

Historically, the high mountain range that runs the length of the country made communication between cities difficult. Each city in the sierra was isolated within its own area and the mountain region was completely separated from the coastal plains, lacking permanent roads. Rather than being a unified country, Ecuador was a collection of separate regions. The construction of the Pan American highway and the highway to the coast facilitated unification, though strong regional interests remain. The coastal road also opened up the central coastal zone to agriculture, primarily involving export crops.

This regional split, with agribusiness and commerce centered on the coast in Guayaquil and the traditional oligarchy and the capital, Quito, located in the sierra, has prevented the high population concentration and political centralization in the capital city found in many other Latin American countries. On the other hand, the strong regional interests have contributed to the country's political instability. The most unstable period occurred between 1929 and 1947, when Ecuador had nineteen presidents in nineteen years (Benalcázar 1989).

During colonial times Ecuador exported livestock products, crude textiles, and some gold. During the mid-nineteenth century a boom in cocoa began, with smaller booms in coffee and palm nuts. These were the first in a series of commodity booms. The cocoa boom ended in the late 1920s, due to disease on the cocoa plantations and then the Great

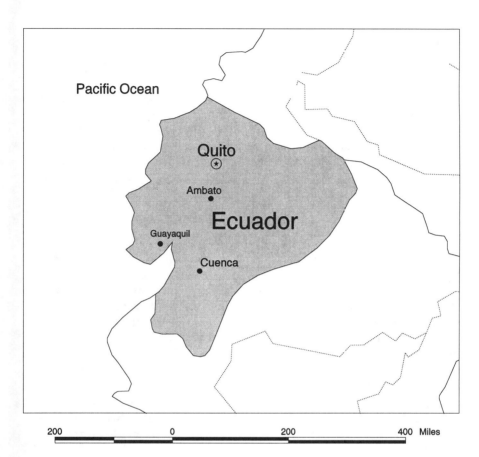

Pacific Ocean

Quito
⊛

Ambato
•

Ecuador

Guayaquil
•

Cuenca
•

| 200 | 0 | 200 | 400 Miles |

⊛ **Capital**
Major Rivers
• **Major Cities**
National Boundary
Countries

N
W   **E**
S

Depression. Export revenue fell from $15 million in 1928 to $7 million in 1931. Booms in bananas and then oil followed (Corkill and Cubitt 1988).

These commodity booms and busts have had a distorting effect on growth, a so-called Dutch disease effect (Cardoso and Helwege 1992). The economic success of the single commodity draws resources away from competing activities and tends to prevent the economy from developing a diversified economic base. The gains from the single commodity trade are often limited in distribution. Further, the extreme dependence on one commodity leaves the economy very vulnerable to shifts in supply and demand. A bust in the single commodity is a bust for the whole economy. This certainly has been true in the case of Ecuador.

Overview of Ecuador's Political Economy, 1950–90

In 1950 Ecuador had a population of 3 million, 59.5% of which was concentrated in the sierra, 40.5% on the coastal plain, and 1.4% in the Oriente (eastern jungle area). The majority of the population, 71%, lived in rural areas. Agricultural production was the primary economic activity, constituting one-third of total production and 90% of all exports (see table 7.1). Petroleum and mining represented less than 2% of production and a negligible proportion of exports. The currency is called the sucre and in 1950 the exchange rate was 16 sucres to the U.S. dollar. Gross national product was 7 billion sucres ($438 million). The annual per capita income in U.S. dollars was $140, compared to an average per capita income for all of Latin America of $245. Income distribution was highly unequal (see table 7.2), so average per capita income is not a very representative figure. (Unless otherwise stated, statistics are from the Banco Central del Ecuador.)

The oil boom of the 1970s raised Ecuador from a low to a median income country, with respect to Latin America. By 1990 per capita income had increased to $940. The distribution of income by type of activity is also important. Using 1990 data, the distribution of value added by major economic sector has the industrial sector (manufacturing, oil refinery, and electricity) at 20% of value added, commerce at 21%, other services, construction, and transportation combined at 27%, agriculture at 13%, and the petroleum and mining sector at 15% (see table 7.1). Population had shifted from rural to urban, with 56% living in urban areas. It had also shifted toward the coastal plain, with half of the population living there.

Ecuador's post–World War II economic history is similar to that of other Latin American countries in many ways. It has had an annual real growth rate (measured in 1975 sucres) of 5.3% between 1950 and 1990. Its population grew from 3 million in 1950 to slightly over 10 million and

Table 7.1. Major Sectors of the Economy as a Percentage of GDP, 1950–90

Sector, % of GDP	1950	1965	1970	1975	1980	1985	1990
Agriculture	32.17	27.19	23.95	17.94	12.13	13.33	13.41
Petroleum, mining	1.20	2.21	1.55	11.59	12.17	17.07	14.58
Manuf., oil refining	13.79	17.18	18.19	15.97	17.66	18.94	19.68
Electricity	0.41	0.93	0.95	0.75	0.83	0.31	0.13
Construction	2.41	2.08	3.93	5.56	7.41	4.38	3.76
Restaurants, hotels	9.22	14.97	14.56	15.73	14.57	15.62	21.34
Transport, communication	4.06	4.05	6.74	5.73	7.89	8.55	8.59
Finance	1.26	12.16	10.85	10.43	11.67	7.56	6.08
Social, personal services	8.69	7.75	6.25	4.19	4.95	4.22	4.01
Government services		6.87	8.59	8.95	9.06	7.79	4.75
Domestic services		1.09	0.76	0.52	0.59	0.39	0.23
Value added		95.01	94.51	95.43	95.90	96.21	94.49
Other		4.98	5.49	4.09	4.09	3.79	5.51
GDP	100%	100%	100%	100%	100%	100%	100%
GDP (millions of sucres)	7,068	20,721	35,019	107,740	293,337	1,109,940	8,160,080

Source: Banco Central del Ecuador (several issues), Memoria anual.

Table 7.2. Income and Land Distribution, 1970–87

% of EAP Population	Year	Low 20%	2nd 20%	3rd 20%	4th 20%	5th 20%	Gini Ratio
% of income	1970	2.9	4.7	6.4	16.5	69.5	.625
% of income	1987	5.4	9.3	13.7	21.0	50.5	.445
Size of farm (in hectares)		0–5	5–20	20–100	100–500	500+	
Number of farms (as a percentage)	1954	73.1	16.7	8.1	1.7	0.4	
% of farmland	1954	7.2	9.4	19.0	19.3	45.1	
Number of farms (as a percentage)	1974	66.7	18.6	12.6	1.8	0.3	
% of farmland	1974	6.7	11.7	33.5	21.1	27.0	
% of farm income	1974	38.8	17.6	12.7	10.5	20.4	

Source: Income distribution: Wilkie, Lorey, and Ochoa 1994 and Psacharopoulos et al. 1993. Land distribution: Benalcázar 1989.

real per capita growth had a mean annual increase of 2.3% during that period. As in other Latin American countries, foreign debt began increasing rapidly during the last half of the 1970s and inflation began to rise. The 1980s represented a period of negative growth rates and rising inflation.

Politically, Ecuador has vacillated between military and democratic rule, and in the periods of democratic rule vacillated between liberal and conservative leadership. Democracy prevailed in the 1950s. After a long period of political instability, dictators, and military rule, the election of Galo Plaza Lasso in 1948 ushered in twelve years of democracy, called the "democratic parenthesis" in Ecuador's history (Corkill and Cubitt 1988). Galo Plaza, a U.S.-educated economist and a liberal, began a process of state-led "modernization," emphasizing state-led economic development and a set of political reforms aimed at creating political stability. His emphasis on infrastructural investment, especially in support of the banana industry, resulted in a rapid expansion of roads and ports (financed mainly by loans from the United States and the World Bank), colonization projects, and development of natural resource use. Liberal credit was made available to banana plantations. He greatly increased and strengthened the economic role of the government (Corkill and Cubitt 1988, p. 18).

Plaza's term began with the "Banana Boom." A combination of rising European demand for bananas and Ecuador's substantially lower production costs caused export earnings to triple between 1948 and 1960, with two-thirds of those earnings from bananas. By 1960 bananas grown in the coastal regions of Ecuador supplied 30% of all banana exports in the world.

Following Galo Plaza's four-year term, two more elected presidents, both conservative, completed four-year terms, José María Velasco Ibarra and Camilo Ponce Enríquez. For Velasco, it was his third (out of five) times as president and the only time that he completed his four years without being forcibly removed. Known for his oratory and demagoguery (he was called the great *balconista*), he ran on a populist platform. Though he described himself as opposed to government intervention in the economy, he significantly increased public works and government bureaucracy (Schodt 1987, pp. 73–76).

In 1955 the dramatic growth in export earnings leveled off as the international banana market became saturated. However, earnings levels never reversed. This slowing in the growth rate provided incentives for the country to move toward industrialization. In 1957 Ponce initiated an import substitution industrialization (ISI) strategy, already being widely used in Latin America. This economic development strategy, derived from theories of development economists, especially the Argentine economist Raúl Prebisch and the Economic Commission for Latin

America (ECLA), sought to use government intervention in the economy to initiate and/or speed up industrialization. As a result, manufacturing, which was 15.5% of GDP between 1950 and 1960, increased to 18% by 1970 and to almost 20% by 1990.

In 1960 Velasco was elected for a fourth term as president, but was forced to resign after only one year and replaced by his vice-president, Carlos Julio Arosemena Monroy. Targeted by conservative elites and the U.S. Central Intelligence Agency, Arosemena was removed from office in 1963 by a military junta (reputedly because of his out-of-control alcoholism). The military government initiated a series of reforms aimed at speeding up the industrialization process with more centralized state planning and control. They centralized the tax system, initiated a personal income tax, and instituted a weak agrarian reform that only succeeded in dividing up a few southern haciendas and ended the *huasipungo* feudal, indentured servant agricultural labor system. It was the first government since World War II to allocate more funds to education and public works programs than to the Ministry of Defense (Schodt 1987, pp. 84–86).

In 1966 there was a return to civilian presidents following the military junta's resignation. Otto Arosemena Gómez became the interim president until the 1968 election put Velasco in office again, for his fifth and last term. Facing a faltering economy and huge trade and budget deficits and frustrated with a Congress that resisted financial austerity, Velasco assumed dictatorial powers in 1970. He then stabilized public finances by devaluing the sucre by 28%, introducing a uniform sales tax, and abolishing half of the autonomous public institutions.

Large deposits of oil were discovered in the late 1960s in the mostly unpopulated Oriente region. The first major oil exports began in 1972. A year later Ecuador joined the Organization of Petroleum Exporting Countries (OPEC) and oil prices doubled. The military, afraid that the civilian government would squander the country's rich oil resources, took over again in 1972, intending to transform oil returns into reform and development. They nationalized four million hectares of oil holdings by forcing companies to renegotiate concession contracts and buying a 25% share of the Texaco-Gulf consortium. The government then received revenue from oil directly, increasing its power and control. Export earnings rose rapidly between 1972 and 1975, but imports, after a short lag, rose even more. Ecuador sustained substantial deficits financed through bank borrowing. Foreign debt increased sharply from half a billion dollars in 1975 to over six billion dollars in 1982 (Corkill and Cubitt 1988, pp. 19–20).

The oil boom brought significant changes to the economy. Per capita income rose from 60 to 70% of the Latin American average, raising Ecuador from a low- to middle-income country. The military government's Industrial Development Plan, supported by oil revenues, resulted in the quadrupling of the value of output of manufacturing. Major infrastructure development of roads and communication increased the connections between the diverse regions of the country. Increasing investment in education and health decreased illiteracy from 25% in 1974 to 16% in 1982 and increased life expectancy from fifty-six to sixty-six years. Those with access to safe water expanded from 12% to 59% of the population and the percentage of dwellings with electricity improved from 32% to 63% over the same period (World Bank 1987). However, lack of sufficient reform in the highly unequal income distribution during this period seriously limited the internal market (Corkill and Cubitt 1988).

In 1979 the government returned to civilian rule with the election of Jaime Roldós Aguilera. A new constitution granted illiterates the right to vote, expanding the voting proportion of the population from its previous average of about 15% to 21% in 1979 and 31% in the 1984 election (Schodt 1987, p. 71). World oil prices soared in 1979 and 1980, but world interest rates also began to rise. Roldós used the extra oil revenue to raise wages and increase protectionism for industry. By 1981 oil prices began to drop, never again reaching their 1979 and 1980 levels, while debt service payments increased sharply due to the higher interest rate. The combination of falling export revenues and increased debt service, followed by a general drop in foreign investment, led to increased borrowing. This resulted in even larger debt service payments. The "growth-led debt" of the 1960s and 1970s was borrowing used to finance capital for industrial expansion. After 1982 the borrowing, which financed debt service payments, was "debt-led debt." The economy slumped into a period of low to negative growth rates.

In 1984 a conservative president, León Febres Cordero, took office and adopted the "Chicago Boys' free market" approach to the economy. With the philosophy of "keeping prices right" the exchange rate was devalued and many state regulations and controls eliminated. He opened up oil exploration to foreigners and established incentives to attract private capital. Tariffs and quotas on a large number of manufactured goods were reduced. He cut subsidies on basic foodstuffs and limited increases in the minimum wage to far less than the inflation rate. His approach pleased the IMF, which granted additional loans. The debt, whose growth had leveled off between 1982 and 1984, increased from less than seven billion dollars to over nine billion during his tenure. The abrupt reduction in protection for local manufacturers and rising interest rates caused a slowdown in production and rising unemployment. General strikes in 1986 and 1987 and a major earthquake in 1987 shook the economy. The earthquake ruptured the oil pipeline, interrupting the export of oil. The country temporarily suspended all debt service payments. Inflation increased and income distribution became more unequal.

With the election of Rodrigo Borja in 1988, policy moved away from the conservative, monetarist policies of Febres Cordero back toward a view of more active government intervention in the economy. However, despite growing exports and substantial trade surpluses on goods and services, excluding interest payments, the drain of debt service on the economy and net capital outflow left few resources for social programs. Austerity programs mandated by the IMF continued as the primary guide for economic policy.

In 1992, in the fourth consecutive democratic election, Sixto Durán Ballén, a conservative, became president, promising to further decrease the role of the government in the economy by reducing cumbersome regulations and encouraging foreign investment and free trade. He developed a radical program for privatizing state enterprises, including telecommunications, oil, highways, and social security. As with the previous two presidents, he has had sharp resistance to his proposals from the Congress (Busey 1995). With the 1990s economic growth rates returned to being slow but positive. They did not remedy the inequality of income distribution. There was inadequate provision for the investment in education and infrastructure that is essential for long-term development.

Microeconomic Bases for Growth

This section describes the basic composition of Ecuador's economy at a micro level. It first examines the issues of income and wealth distribution, which have an important impact not only on "who gets the production," but also on the structure of demand, affecting the "what" and "how" questions as well. Second, each major sector of the economy is presented and its basic composition is described, along with an examination of how factors within each of these sectors contribute to or hinder overall growth. Finally, this section describes the development of human resources, including health, education, and the labor force. It explores how each affects the possibilities of growth.

Income and Wealth Distribution

The highly unequal income and wealth distribution has had a predominant effect on the shape and progress of Ecuador's economic development. For growth to translate into economic development, the benefits of growth need to be widespread. Too high a degree of inequality can hamper the development process. Choices such as the type of industry to be developed, what government infrastructure development should be given priority, the type of legal structure (determining what and who should be protected), and the focus of the educational system (defining the kind of education and to whom it should be directed) are all affected by the distribution.

According to several theories of savings (e.g., John Maynard Keynes, Milton Friedman's permanent income hypothesis, Hendrik Houthakker, Nathaniel Leff), the higher the income, the higher average propensity to save. It has then been argued that a highly unequal distribution of income should be an advantage for generating the domestic savings needed for development. On the other hand, there are several reasons why too unequal an income distribution can retard economic development. One is that wealthy elite classes in Ecuador (and other parts of Latin America) have tended to align themselves with developed country interests. They tend to prefer U.S. and European goods to those domestically produced and often invest their savings abroad, especially when the domestic economy is looking shaky.

A second reason is that culturally elite interests were not directed toward supplying an entrepreneurial class for industrialization. Furthermore, the goal of maintaining a large cheap labor supply and exploiting cheap materials to help maintain their lifestyles shapes the policies that they support with their power. Monopoly control over labor resources, including the system of indentured servitude in agriculture that persisted until the mid-1950s, permitted the wealthy to pay labor less than its contribution to production (i.e., less than the value of its marginal product). New industries tended to be capital intensive, despite labor being relatively cheaper than capital. This approach further awarded the owners of capital at the cost of the rest of society. Development was slowed to the extent that scarce capital generated less output and employment than it could have.

Another way in which the inequality hampers growth is in the resulting limitation of market size. Ecuador is already a small country with a limited potential market. When a high proportion of that population is too poor to participate in the market, the domestic market is limited even further. The distribution also affects the nature of the goods demanded. The market basket of goods demanded by wealthy consumers, who spend a high proportion of their income on luxury goods, is very different from that demanded by middle and lower classes, who spend a much higher proportion on basic necessities. Another problem limiting domestic demand is that the consumption patterns of the wealthy have a much higher import content than is true for poorer classes, who consume primarily domestically produced (nontradable) goods.

In summary, too much inequality is detrimental to development and growth. In order to generate savings that will be used for increasing the capital stock and to supply an entrepreneurial class that will combine the land, labor, and capital to meet development requirements, an economy appears to need a strong middle class. Inequality that is derived from paying more for higher productivity stimulates development. Inequality derived from inheritance and monopoly power functions as a hindrance.

Individual Distribution of Income

Ecuador's national income accounting data use the methodology established by the United Nations. This does not elaborate data in a way that permits an analysis of the distribution of income by percentiles. The data that exist come from special studies. There are two such studies for Ecuador, one by the International Labor Office in 1970 and a second in 1987 by Ecuador's census bureau, Instituto Nacional de Estadística y Censos (INEC). Estimates for income distribution in 1970 yielded a Gini ratio of .625, one of the highest in all Latin America. In 1987, following the oil boom growth spurt, the Gini ratio was estimated to have fallen to .445, suggesting a marked improvement in income distribution. These data, presented in table 7.2, indicate that the proportion of income rose in the four lowest quintiles, at the expense of the highest quintile. The poorest quintile of the population accounted for 2.9% of income in 1970, rising to 5.4% in 1987. The second quintile's share rose from 4.7% to 9.3%, while the third quintile increased from 6.4% to 13.7%, The fourth quintile increased from 16.5% of income in 1970 to 21.0% in 1987. The richest fifth claimed 69.5% of income in 1970, falling to 50.5% in 1987. The richest 10%'s share of income, less affected by the shift, accounted for 37.5% of the income in 1970, falling to 34.6% in 1987. A study by Ecuador's census bureau, INEC, in 1975, following the oil boom, suggests that this improvement in the distribution happened soon after this spurt of industrialization. It estimates a Gini ratio of .469 in 1975 (Villalobos 1985). Since these data come from different sources, one must use caution in the comparison. Nonetheless, the evidence indicates that increased industrialization helped to substantially reduce inequality. A 1989 Encuesta nacional de hogares shows that the medium income of the richest one-fifth is 4.8 times greater than the medium income of the poorest one-fifth nationally (Dávalos 1993).

Functional and Structural Distribution of Income

The distribution of income by type of activity is also important. Using 1990 data, the distribution of value added by major economic sector is as follows: agriculture is 13.4% of value added, the industrial sector, including manufacturing and oil refining, is 19.8%, petroleum is 14.6%, commerce is 21.3%, and other services, construction, and transportation together are 27.4% of value added (see table 7.1).

Another measure of distribution is the proportion of gross domestic product that goes to wages. In general, the higher this proportion, the more equally distributed is income. Between 1950 and 1990 on average about one-quarter of Ecuador's GDP was in the form of wages. (In the United States and other developed countries this proportion is between two-thirds and three-fourths.) In 1950, 26% of Ecuador's GDP was in wages. This proportion reached a peak of 32% in 1980 and then fell dramatically to 24% in 1984. By 1989 that proportion had declined to 14%. With the decrease in national income due to the debt crisis, the decline in wage earners' incomes was disproportionately large and suggests that income inequality increased during that period.

By region, Xavier Dávalos (1993) used calculations of income variances from a 1989 Household Survey as an index of distribution. He found that income is most unequally distributed in Quito, the capital city, located in the sierra. Overall he also found more inequality in the distribution in the sierra, where members of the oligarchy reside, than on the coast, the center of agribusiness and export.

Distribution of Land and Wealth

From other data on agriculture and industry, there is indirect evidence that income distribution corresponds closely with the size of landholdings in agriculture and with size of enterprise in industry. The elite class, the oligarchy, historically was the large landholders, mainly in the sierra. Agricultural land distribution is extremely unequal, as shown in table 7.2. According to the agricultural census of 1974 (the most recent), two-thirds of the farms are 5 hectares or fewer, accounting for 6.7% of the total cultivated land area and 39% of farm income. On the other hand, 2.1% of the farms have over 100 hectares of land and account for 48.1% of farmland area and 20.4% of agricultural income. A third of the land area is in medium-sized farms, ranging from 20 to 99 hectares. These earn 23% of agricultural income. In 1974, when average per capita income was slightly over $320 (based on an exchange rate of 25 sucres per U.S. dollar), average per capita income on farms of under 5 hectares was $132, for farms from 5 to 10 hectares, $180, for farms from 10 to 20 hectares, $196, for farms from 20 to 50 hectares, $368, for farms from 50 to 100 hectares, $936, and for farms over 100 hectares, $3,264. Incomes for farms larger than 100 hectares are more than 25 times the incomes for farms of fewer than 5. This parallels the high degree of concentration in the industrial sector. In that sector the 98 largest firms account for two-thirds of total industrial output. This high concentration in wealth translates into a high concentration in power that has shaped policy to

its own advantage, perhaps at the cost of more rapid economic development (Benalcázar 1989).

Key Economic Sectors

This section examines how the principal economic sectors—agricultural, private industrial, public, petroleum, and foreign—have developed
and the contributions each has made to the general economic growth and
development. Ecuador's economy has always had a strong agricultural
base and a relatively small but growing industrial sector. Until the
petroleum boom that began in 1972, agricultural products accounted for
almost all of Ecuador's exports. Agriculture as a proportion of gross
domestic product fell from 32% in 1950 to 13% in 1990. Mining, mainly
petroleum (including petroleum refining), rose from less than 2% in
1950 to 15% of the economy in 1990. Over the same period, industry rose
from 16% to 24% and services ranged from 46% to 40% of the economy.
In this small open economy, trade represents about 30% of GDP.

Agricultural Sector

Though agriculture is still the most important economic activity next to
oil, it has declined in importance as economic development has proceeded over the postwar period. Until the mid-1980s over half of the
population resided in rural areas. In 1950, 71% of the population was
rural. By the 1982 census, the continual rural-urban shift had decreased
that proportion to 51%, and by 1990 the majority resided in urban areas,
with the rural population down to 44% of the total.

As reported above, Ecuador's agricultural sector is marked by a high
degree of inequality in income and land distribution resulting in a sharp
division in types of crops, farming methods, productivity, and income
between the large and small farms. Land is worked much more intensively on small farms, where 85% of the surface area is under cultivation.
Small farms account for the almost 40% of farm income derived from
just under 7% of the cultivatable land. The richest 2.1% account for 20%
of the income. But, two-thirds of the income for farms of fewer than 5
hectares comes from sources other than agricultural activity, mainly
wage income, since these farms are too small to support a family. Much
of the rural-urban migration is due to the fact that incomes for farmers
with fewer than 20 hectares were less than the national average income.
Rural dwellers are attracted to the cities by the potential of higher wages,
along with more available services, such as water, health, and education.

Agrarian problems of a perennial shortage of basic foods, inefficient
production in the small land plots, and a large surplus of landless
peasants have led to land reform. The first attempt at agrarian reform was

in 1964, when the Ecuadorean Institute for Agrarian Reform and Colonization (IERAC) was formed. This attempt was met with strong opposition by landowners and little of substance was accomplished. In 1973 a new Agrarian Reform Law was passed. Under the strong lobbying of the large landowners this law emphasized "efficient production" and government-provided credit to farmers, rather than land redistribution. Two million hectares of land were supposed to be redistributed, but in fact fewer than half a million hectares in total were involved, aiding only 79,000 people. Twenty percent of the land redistributed was church land. Less than 15% of total agricultural land was affected by land reform and less than 20% of the peasants benefited. In 1994, representing the interests of twenty large landowners, a new "free market" agrarian law was passed, which eliminates the reforms carried out under the two previous laws and returns land "given" to indigenous populations. The power of the landowners, using a combination of political pressure, economic sabotage, and violence, including the murder of peasant union leaders, has been enough to forestall any meaningful land reform. In addition, most of the government monies made available in the form of credit assistance and technology to increase efficiency were co-opted by the large landowners (Corkill and Cubitt 1988, pp. 33–37; *Latinamerica Press*, June 9, 1994, p. 7). Small and many medium-sized farms grow basic crops, such as corn, rice, wheat, and potatoes. Farm productivity per hectare for these basic crops is higher for medium (50 to 100 hectare) than for small farms. According to 1974 census figures, yields for corn are 30% higher on medium-sized farms, 20% higher for potatoes, and 25% higher for wheat. Rice yields are virtually the same. Large farms produce the export crops and commercial livestock. Agricultural exports remain an important source of foreign exchange to use for development. In 1990 agricultural exports represented 40% of the total. Major export crops are mainly grown on large plantations in the coastal region of the country.

The banana boom began toward the end of the 1940s. While the rapid growth in banana exports leveled off by 1958, they never declined, and bananas still represent about 20% of export earnings. Bananas receive protection in the form of a legislated minimum price, set by the Ministry of Agriculture and Livestock, which exporters must pay to growers. The up and coming export is shrimp, which was Ecuador's fastest-growing export during the 1980s, rising from 2% of total exports in 1980 to 17.5% by 1992. Coffee and cocoa are the third- and fourth-largest export crops. In addition to traditional export crops, the African oil palm and soy beans have been introduced and are becoming more important.

René Benalcázar (1989) estimates that the supply of foodstuffs grew at the rate of about 3% per year in the 1950–85 period, a rate below that of other economic sectors. At the same time the demand for food (based on population and income increases) grew at the rate of slightly over 4% per year. Market share shifted from carbohydrate foods toward protein foods and fruits. Production of wheat, corn, and barley actually fell, partly due to government-controlled prices that were set below the costs of production and also due to competition from imported wheat and barley from the United States at subsidized prices.

As is true of many of the Latin American countries, Ecuador's economic development policies have had an urban bias. First, farm prices were controlled to keep food prices low for the urban workforce. Second, urban industrial firms were given credit at preferential rates while credit for agriculture was not only costlier, but also less available. For the small farmer it was (and is) virtually nonexistent. Third, most of the government infrastructure investment was done in urban areas, directed toward developing urban industry. Fourth, throughout the 1960s and 1970s the sucre was overvalued. This worked against the competitiveness of agricultural exports in favor of capital imports for urban industry. These policies contributed to the fact that the agricultural sector has grown more slowly than other sectors of the economy, even though in many respects it remains the core of the economy. In addition these policies accelerated the rural-urban migration.

The growth of Ecuador's major agricultural export sector in the coastal plain has caused a shift in population and economic power from the sierra to the coastal region. With most of the export agriculture being located on the coastal plain, population migrated from the sierra to the coast. The coastal city of Guayaquil grew to be the commercial center, with power rivaling that of the capital city, Quito, located in the sierra. By 1980 Guayaquil was the largest city in Ecuador.

Industrial Sector

Manufacture of artisan goods in Ecuador dates back to pre-Incan times, when the manufacture of textiles, garments, tools, ceramics, and gold and silver was developed for both utilitarian and artistic purposes. After the conquest food processing, textiles, leather goods, and straw hat manufacturing were further developed both for domestic use and for export to Lima and Nueva Granada. This continued until the end of the eighteenth century, when these activities were prohibited by the Spanish Crown. After independence, some of this small artisan manufacturing reestablished itself, especially in textiles and food processing (Schodt 1987).

From 1910 to 1950 industrialization grew slowly and diversified somewhat into such goods as powdered milk, silk, petroleum products, cement, chemicals, and pharmaceuticals. By 1950 manufacturing represented 14% of the economic output. Within manufacturing 61% of the employment, almost 70% of value added, and 66% of the invested capital were in foods, beverages, tobacco, and textiles. By 1990 manufacturing represented 20% of the economy (construction and electricity, another 4%) and was much more diversified. The food, beverage, tobacco, and textile categories had fallen to 40% of value added with chemicals, nonmetallic minerals and metallics, machinery, and equipment rising to half of the valued added in manufacturing.

A development strategy of import substitution industrialization (ISI) was adopted in 1957 under President Ponce to increase industrial production and to compensate for the leveling off of banana revenues. ISI's aim was to promote economic development by creating domestic industry to produce consumer goods to replace those that were being imported, thereby saving foreign exchange for the importation of capital goods. It was also hoped that the new industry would generate employment, improve utilization of Ecuador's natural resources, transfer technology, and avoid a deterioration in the terms of trade.

To stimulate industrialization via ISI, the government began to take a more active role in the economy. In 1949 a state enterprise, the Development Corporation, was established with the mission of creating and promoting industries in strategic areas for development, especially in electricity generation. In the following years state-owned enterprises such as Chimborazo Cement, Miraflores Electric Company, and Tourist Hotel of Ibarra were established. Protection for industry, especially new industry, increased. The Laws for Industrial Development of 1957 increased tariffs, established quotas to protect domestic production, eliminated taxes on new industry, dispensed technical assistance, subsidized the costs of imported machinery and raw materials, and provided credit at preferential rates. Through much of the period the currency, the sucre, was overvalued. This cheapened the price of imports, including imported capital and raw materials. High tariffs and quotas somewhat controlled the importation of consumer goods.

From 1956 through 1971 the industrial sector grew faster than the real gross domestic product. After that, with the increase in oil production, growth in GDP outstripped growth in the manufacturing sector. In 1970 Ecuador's manufacturing sector was one of the smallest in Latin America. Between 1970 and 1976 output in this sector quadrupled, and hundreds of new firms were formed. Between 1972 and 1980 manufacturing averaged a real growth rate of 10% per year, but this growth was brought to a sharp halt with the crisis of the 1980s. Throughout the period from 1950 to 1990 capital investment in manufacturing fluctuated between 20 and 25% of value added.

Under the ISI approach to development, subsidies on importation of capital and primary goods led to the creation of an industrial structure where capital goods and primary goods were imported and domestic industry was mainly assembly and final production stages. Imports of primary materials for industry remained at approximately 30% of total imports between 1950 and 1980. After the debt crisis in 1982 the proportion rose to 40%, but this was due more to a rapid decrease in final goods imports than to an increase in primary goods imports. Imports of capital goods fluctuated trendlessly around an average of 13% of total imports over this period. Dependence on foreign inputs did not decrease during this period of industrialization.

As is true in many developing countries, capital was relatively scarce and has become much more so as a result of the heavy debt service payments. Though theoretically banks will make loans of up to ten years, credit is highly restricted and often unavailable. Until 1985 the government controlled interest rates, so that real borrowing rates were low to negative, but credit was tightly rationed. Since the freer market regime of Febres Cordero, interest rates are no longer set by government. While capital is scarce, unskilled and semiskilled labor is plentiful and cheap. However, skilled and semiskilled technical and managerial labor is also scarce, expensive, and often lacks sufficient education, a direct result of the low proportion of the population with higher education.

Industrial production in Ecuador, reflecting the overall inequality in income and wealth distribution in the economy, is highly concentrated. According to the 1984 Manufacturing and Mineral Industrial Census, the *gran industria*, the 98 largest firms, employing 200 or more, produces two-thirds of the total production in mining and manufacturing and employs 45% of the workforce in this sector. At the other extreme, 905 firms, employing 50 or fewer workers, produce 11.7% of the output and account for 21% of the employment. Ownership is even more concentrated than industrial concentration ratios might indicate, given the economic organization of *grupos económicos*. These are conglomerates of a range of firms, whose ownership tends to be family based or in a long-term partnership between families. *Grupos'* monopolistic market power gives them a competitive advantage that allows them to maintain control of much of the private sector of the economy. They tend to maintain overcapacity, which they use as a barrier to entry. *Grupos'* ownership in a bank guarantees adequate credit for the group and scarce to nonexistent credit for would-be competitors, especially medium-sized and small businesses. Under the group system government-controlled interest rates on deposits meant that depositors received low interest rates on accounts, subsidizing borrowers. Overall the system represented a transfer from the public at large (who received below market rates on their savings) to the owners of the *grupos* (Comard 1990).

At the other extreme from the large groups are the small industrial and artisan firms. These are defined as firms employing 7 or fewer persons or producing 180,000 sucres or less by the 1980 census. According to that census there were 32,320 such establishments, employing 45,436 persons. They accounted for 2% of the economically active population, 40% of employment, and 10% of manufacturing output. Much of this sector consists of what is often referred to as the informal sector. Many of the firms are single, self-employed workers. One-third of the economically active population has been classified as self-employed throughout the 1950 to 1990 period (Benalcázar 1989). Within these establishments there is a scarcity of both human and physical capital. There is almost no availability of credit, nor of other forms of protection available to the *gran industria*. Output per worker in these enterprises is on average about one-quarter of that in the large firms. At the same time these enterprises actually subsidize the large firms in that they provide cheap goods and services that serve as inputs into the larger firms.

With respect to the legal environment for business, Ecuador has long had reasonable industrial and intellectual property protection laws. Contracts are regarded as secure. Patents, trademarks, copyrights, and industrial designs and models are recognized and enforcement is improving. As of January 1994 Ecuador, as an Andean Common Market (ANCOM) country, began to implement the Andean Pact Decisions 344 and 345 on patents, trademarks, and copyrights. Penalties for violation include fines and prison terms. Enforcement is under the Ministry of Industry, Trade, Integration, and Fishing (Business International 1993, pp. 12–13). Labor laws are detailed and complex, with government establishing minimum wages, a complex system of bonuses and fringe benefits including social security, and rules for termination of employees, including severance pay. Environmental laws are weak and there is not much enforcement. There is no general pollution control legislation, except in mining and oil, but there is legislation for consumer protection that sets standards and labeling requirements. The Consumer Protection Law does allow government to set maximum prices for some basic consumption goods and minimum prices for agriculture and livestock products. The number of goods whose prices are actually controlled has been limited. Currently, prices are controlled for sugar, milk, rice, flour, soft drinks, beer, pharmaceuticals, bottled gas, public services, and a few other goods (Price Waterhouse 1992, pp. 41–47).

In summary, the industrial sector is characterized by a duality of a large number of small-scale artisan producers and a small number of large modern industrial firms. The large firms are capital intensive, resulting in low employment creation. Besides the low credit and other preferential treatment of large firms, the concentration in production can be attributed to the need for efficient size due to economies of scale. Ecuador is a small country whose market is made even smaller by the large poor population with limited market participation.

Public Sector

Ecuador's oil boom had a side effect of dramatically increasing the public sector's role in the economy. The relative size of the nation's consolidated public sector spending grew to a peak of 34% of the gross domestic product in 1982. Then, with the debt crisis, the role of government began to decline, falling to 27% by 1990. The decline, brought on by financial necessity, was accompanied by a shift in development philosophy from one favoring strong government intervention to one favoring a freer market approach. With a limited capacity to cut current expenditures, much of the decrease in government spending came at the expense of public investment, especially infrastructure investment. In relative terms, gross fixed capital investment of public administrations fell from 5.7% of GDP in 1980 to 2.8% in 1991. This slowing of infrastructure investment has a long-run detrimental effect on private industrial growth. Despite its decline the public sector continues to account for over half of the country's wage bill. Of the total wages paid in 1989 (which were only 14% of value added), 56% were represented by public sector wages (Banco Central, *Memoria anual*, 1992).

Ecuador's public sector is fairly decentralized, with much of it outside of the control of the state budget. Outside the budget are special agencies, state-owned enterprises, and local governments. In 1991 the state budget represented 52% of public sector expenditures, falling from 61% in 1987. The large amount outside the budget process makes it difficult to control public sector deficits. The breakdown of the state budget is 10% for military and security expenditures, 20% for education, 7% for health, 10% for transportation and communication expenditures, slightly over 20% for general services, and an enormous 28% of the budget for debt servicing.

Public sector income is highly dependent on oil and varies with its price. Based on 1991 figures, oil revenues represented 51% of the state budget's income. The 10% value added tax on all sales and transactions represents another 20%. Income tax, the only progressive tax, represents a little over 6% of the budget. The corporate tax rate is 25%. Until 1993 there was an additional 11% tax on repatriated profits for foreign investors. Tax evasion is a large problem in Ecuador. It is estimated that evasion of the value added tax is over 60%, of income tax around 50%, and of corporate tax about 80%. Import and export taxes have been an important source of revenue, but with the new strategy of more open markets these revenues have been cut. By 1992 they represented slightly less than 10% of income (Banco Central, *Memoria anual*, 1992).

Despite its relatively large size, until 1972 Ecuador's public sector was concentrated in traditional government roles of providing services, public works, the military, and education. Accompanying Ecuador's adoption of an import substitution industrialization strategy, in 1957, was the notion of "state-led development." Primarily this meant increased public works and special protection of and concessions to private-sector industry. There were few public enterprises, and those had been created to take care of special needs. For example, during World War II a shortage in fertilizer led to the creation of a state fertilizer factory, Fábrica de Abonos del Estado. In 1972 all public enterprises combined contributed less than 2% to GDP.

During the oil boom years, supported by petroleum revenues, the role of government expanded into a more activist one, extending its participation into direct production. In the seven years from 1972 to 1979 fifteen additional state-owned enterprises were established and existing ones enlarged. From 1973 to 1982 the nonfinancial public sector increased 12% per year and went from 22% to 34% of GDP. Public sector employment grew at a rate of 8.8% per year, expanding from 150,552 employees in 1975 to 271,966 in 1982. Public enterprises accounted for 12% of GDP by 1983 (Schodt 1987, pp. 108–17). Not only did the government create new enterprises, but it also nationalized bankrupt private enterprises (for example, Ecuatoriana Airlines). By 1992 there were 163 enterprises with public investment, about half of them wholly owned by the state, the rest public-private joint ventures.

Public financial institutions were also expanded during this period. In 1968 public financial institutions accounted for 26% of total deposits and 36% of total domestic credit supply. By 1981 public-sector deposits had expanded to 40% of the total and these institutions supplied 55% of domestic credit. This growth was largely due to petroleum revenue deposits in public-sector institutions and increased public-sector borrowing requirements. Government restrictions on interest rates and credit also retarded growth in private bank deposits (Schodt 1987, p. 117).

During the 1980s and into the 1990s the military, seeking to preserve its power and looking for ways to maintain its financing, has moved into industrial operations. Engineering companies and the military airline, Transportes Aéreos Militares Ecuatorianos (TAME), which is the largest domestic transport airline, began to compete directly with the private sector. By the early 1990s it had interests in at least twenty-eight companies in mining, tourism, manufacturing, and energy. It has a hold on air, ground, and oil transport businesses through ownership of the firms TAME, FLOPC (Flota Petrolera Ecuatoriana), and TRANSNAVE (Transportes Navieros Ecuatorianos). These holdings are administered under the army's industrial holding company, Dirección de Industrias del Ejército (DINE). Following the model of the private *grupos*, it operates a bank, giving it access to the use of capital from private depositors. Many private-sector businesses complain of unfair competition with military-owned enterprises. An example of the military's aggressive move into this competition is its joint venture with the U.S.-based Marriott International hotel chain to build a new $100 million, 250-room luxury hotel in Quito (*Latinamerica Press*, October 1994, p. 8).

Ecuador is moving more slowly than many of the other Latin American countries toward restructuring and privatization, but it is moving in that direction nonetheless. Heavy debt payments, amounting to a quarter of the budget, have spurred this move. The administration of León Febres Cordero, elected in 1984, began shifting toward a more market-oriented economy and with the election of Sixto Durán Ballén in 1992 there was a new dedication to decreasing the role of government. As part of a deficit reduction and inflation control plan, he reduced government subsidies for a broad range of goods and services and dramatically decreased the number of public sector employees.

To carry out privatization of state-owned enterprises, the National Council to Modernize the State (CONAM) was formed at the end of 1992. Its first job was to review the financial status of all 163 public firms and decide which should be targeted for privatization, which should be liquidated, and which should remain in the public domain. In January 1994 the legislature approved the State Modernization Law, which allows the government to divest itself of all but a few "strategic" enterprises. Among its first sales were Fertiza, the state's fertilizer plant, and 51% of the state cement factory. The state railroad is slated for liquidation, because it is judged too costly to sell. Services such as water and sewage operations, previously operated by the state, are being contracted out to be run by private firms.

The privatization of the "strategic" enterprises, the natural monopolies of gas, electricity, and telephones, is hotly debated within the country. The myth that private is identical with efficient and public is inefficient ignores the fact that it is not being private per se that creates efficiency; rather, it is competition. With a natural monopoly the economies of scale are such that the existence of more than one firm raises costs more than is gained from efficiency and competition. Privatizing a natural monopoly then either is controlled by attempting to regulate a price and output close to the competitive solution or is left unregulated, guaranteeing a monopoly price/output solution. The latter may be far more expensive than even an inefficient state-owned solution. The use of controls can be complicated, costly, and political. It almost always falls short of an efficient competitive solution to price and output (as U.S. experience with the Public Utilities Commission, for example, shows).

The Petroleum Sector

Ecuador's oil boom that began in 1972 was responsible for a major spurt of income growth and infrastructure development. Until that discovery, the government had provided very liberal concession terms for foreign oil companies. In 1917 a British-owned oil company, Anglo-Ecuadorian Oilfields, Ltd., began to produce oil from fields on the coastal plain. However, the quantity remained small, less than 1% of the total production of South America. It was not until 1967, when a consortium of Texaco-Gulf discovered large deposits of high-quality petroleum at Lago Agrio, in the northeastern corner of the country, that oil exploration and development became a major activity. In 1972, in an attempt to reassert national control of oil, a new decree was issued bringing the majority of oil exploration concessions back under Ecuador's control. Oil companies were forced to renegotiate contracts, increasing royalties paid to the state, decreasing the size of the territory over which the companies had control, and shortening the time of that control. It also required the oil companies to develop roads and airports into the region. Texaco-Gulf financed the construction of an oil pipeline from Lago Agrio to the coast at the Esmeraldas (north of Guayaquil). Completion of the oil pipeline, which allowed Ecuador to begin exporting large quantities of oil, coincided with the increase in world prices in 1972. By 1973 it was shipping 195,000 barrels per day (Schodt 1987, pp. 99–105).

At the same time a state-owned oil corporation was formed, the Ecuadorean State Petroleum Corporation (CEPE), and was given responsibility for marketing, exploration, refining, and eventually production. In negotiation with Texaco-Gulf CEPE was given the right to buy a 25% share of that consortium. Other oil companies failed to find additional rich oil deposits and, as a protest against increasing state control of the oil, exploration and production stagnated during the 1970s. Production hit a peak in 1973 of 75.3 million barrels, falling to 63.8 million barrels the following year and not recovering to that level again until 1979, when production went up to 78.3 million barrels. Exports stagnated even more as domestic demand for oil grew rapidly, in part due to very low internal prices. For example, in 1978 gasoline at the pump sold for $0.18 per gallon at a time when production costs were estimated to be $0.43 per gallon. The number of automobiles increased from 82,000 in 1970 to

223,000 in 1977 (Schodt 1987, p. 110). Despite stagnating production, oil revenues grew due to the rapidly increasing price of oil. With the formation of OPEC the world price of oil went from $3.97 per barrel in 1973 to a high of $35.20 per barrel in 1980. Ecuador joined OPEC in November 1973 and Ecuador's oil minister, Gustavo Jarrín Ampudia, became OPEC's president, pushing for higher prices and greater state participation in production. Oil revenues grew at the rate of 35% per year between 1973 and 1982. After that oil prices declined, falling to a low of $9.70 per barrel in June 1986 and remaining under $20 through most of the last half of the 1980s and first half of the 1990s (Corkill and Cubitt 1988, pp. 26–29).

In 1992 Ecuador withdrew from OPEC (the first nation ever to do so), hoping to increase oil revenues by 41% through increased production. As a member of OPEC Ecuador was too small to have sufficient bargaining power and never was able to get what it considered to be an adequate production quota. Along with the withdrawal from OPEC, the state petroleum company, CEPE, was reorganized into Petroecuador. The new organization was charged with increasing exploration, drilling, refining, and distributing the oil. It also has more powers to contract with private domestic and foreign firms to participate in exploration and production (Business International 1993, p. 7).

Petroleum revenues supported the most rapid economic growth period of Ecuador's history. During the five years 1970 to 1975 real output grew at an average rate of 11.4% per year. Unlike the earlier cocoa and banana booms, which were led by the private sector, oil revenues went directly to the government, fundamentally changing its role in the economy. The government became a much more active player in the economy, using the oil revenues to invest heavily in infrastructure and also in the development of industrial production.

In spite of the rapid influx of revenue in the early years of the oil boom, the government managed to increase expenditures even faster, running substantial deficits after 1975, which it financed through foreign borrowing. Ecuador is a typical "Dutch Disease" example with oil increasing the inflation rate and becoming the central activity of the economy at the expense of other sectors. The economy became highly dependent on oil, which accounted for 10% of Ecuador's economic production and two-thirds of its export earnings in the 1980s, falling to 45% of exports in the early 1990s (Banco Central, *Memoria anual*, 1992, pp. 130–31). This high dependency creates instability in the economy, especially since oil prices fluctuate dramatically. For example, in March 1993 they fell to below $13 per barrel, creating a fiscal crisis in Ecuador. By the second quarter of 1994 prices had recovered to over $20 per barrel, improving the internal situation for the time being. This type of fluctuation makes development planning difficult. Income that comes in spurts

is difficult to channel into the type of long-term infrastructure investment needed for growth.

Trade and Foreign Investment

As a small economy, Ecuador has always been dependent on trade. In
1950 exports were 18% of GDP and imports 14%. By 1990 they were 28%
and 20%, respectively. Its exports are mostly primary goods, with 85%
concentrated in five products: petroleum, bananas, shrimp, coffee, and
cocoa. Petroleum alone accounts for between 45% and 50%, depending
on the price of oil in a given year. From 1950 to 1980 exports averaged an
annual growth rate of 6.9% and imports averaged 8% per year. Much of
the increase came in the five years between 1970 and 1974, when exports
increased by 27.6% per year and imports by 15.6%. In the last half of the
1970s growth of exports fell to an average of 1.7% per year, but imports
continued to grow at an average rate of 5.3% per year. The debt crisis
created a pressure to increase exports and decrease imports in order to
meet debt service payments. Exports grew an average of 5.4% per year
between 1980 and 1984 and 6% between 1988 and 1992, despite the fall
in the price of coffee, Ecuador's fourth largest export. Imports decreased
at an average rate of 4.1% per year in the crisis years of the first half of
the 1980s. Between 1988 and 1992 they averaged 4.9% annual growth.

Between 1965 and 1990 industrial goods exports have averaged slightly
over 11% of total exports (they were 11% in 1966 and 9% in 1990).
Despite policies and special concessions to encourage industrial growth,
they have not increased as a share of exports. Since 1968, 82% of imports
have been in raw material and capital goods. Using 1992 figures, 55% of
total imports were industrial inputs: 33.5% were industrial raw materials and 22% were capital goods for the manufacturing sector. The
manufacturing sector accounted for $1.3 billion in imports and $274
million in exports. This large trade deficit and high proportion of raw
materials and capital imports is, in part, the result of the ISI trade policies
followed through most of this period. Ecuador's small market size, along
with the high levels of protection under these policies, meant that many
market goods were inefficiently produced, selling at high prices relative
to the international market.

The United States is Ecuador's most important trading partner,
accounting for 47% of its exports and 33% of its imports (Banco Central,
Memoria anual, 1992). It runs a significant trade surplus with the United
States ($595 million in 1992). Its other exports are spread out; Chile, with
5%, is the second largest. For imports, Japan is the second largest,
representing 13% of imports, and is the country with which Ecuador
runs the largest trade deficit ($266 million in 1992).

Ecuador's commercial trade balance has consistently maintained a positive balance over the 1950–90 period, with exports of goods exceeding imports by an average of 20%. However, the negative balances of services, transportation, and interest payments have resulted in a deficit in the total current account balance and balance of payments since 1955. The annual deficits increased steadily until 1982 and have fluctuated since. Service on the foreign debt has been a major contributor to the negative balance. Between 1950 and 1986 cumulative interest payments on the foreign debt equalled $4.8 billion. Over that same period the total sum of the negative balance on current account was $8.9 billion (Benalcázar 1989, pp. 389–91).

As is true of most other Latin American countries, Ecuador is moving in the direction of opening up its economy through lowering tariffs and nontariff barriers and through seeking regional trade agreements. It has been a member of the Andean Pact since its formation in 1969. Historically, this has been a very weak agreement, and the total amount of trade between those countries has remained small, accounting for 5.8% of Ecuador's exports in 1992. With the world trend toward regional trading blocs in the 1990s, these countries began to strengthen their alliance and turn it into a common market, ANCOM. In January 1992 they established a free trade zone involving Colombia, Venezuela, Bolivia, and Ecuador, with a common tariff against outside nations, ranging from 0 to 20% except for autos, where the tariff is 35%. Rules of origin require 60% ANCOM content for the good to pass regional borders tariff free. At the same time Ecuador is talking about free trade agreements with Chile and with the Group of Three: Colombia, Venezuela, and Mexico. Ecuador is also in the process of joining the General Agreement on Tariffs and Trade (GATT).

Before the oil boom that started in 1972, Ecuador was of very little interest to foreign investors. In 1952 its annual net direct foreign investment was $4.7 million. With the oil boom, foreign investment jumped rapidly from $38 million in 1969 to $88 million in 1990 and to $162 million in 1971, its historical peak. By 1976 transnationals owned or controlled fourteen of Ecuador's largest firms (Corkill and Cubitt 1988, p. 31). Overall, direct foreign investment is a fairly small proportion of total investment. For example, in 1990 it was just under 7% of total investment and less than 1% of GDP. In the forty years from 1952 to 1992 total cumulative net foreign direct investment was $1.6 billion. To put this in perspective, export earnings of oil exports alone for the single year of 1992 were $1.25 billion.

Over this forty-year period two-thirds of foreign investment expenditures were in manufacturing and one-fifth in financial institutions. Another 6% was directed toward agriculture. Within manufacturing, one-third went into chemicals and another third into food processing. As to country of origin, 60% comes from the United States, Caribbean countries, and Panama. The latter countries are used to channel investment as a way of reducing taxes. European countries account for about a third of the foreign investment. Other countries in the Andean group constitute approximately 3%. The rate of return on U.S. direct investment in Ecuador was estimated to be 10.1% in 1991 and 15.8% in 1992, considerably higher than the average rate of return on all U.S. direct foreign investment of 7.3% and 6.5%, respectively, for those two years (Viteri 1992 and *Survey of Current Business*, August 1994).

In the 1980s Ecuador shifted its stance from trying to regulate and control direct foreign investment to trying to stimulate and encourage it. During the 1950s and 1960s Ecuador required prior approval of detailed investment plans by the Monetary Council. With approval, the foreign investment had to be registered at the Central Bank. There were no limits on the amount of profit that could be repatriated. However, capital goods could not be re-exported for five years from the time of registration. In December 1970, as part of the Cartagena accord, the Andean Pact countries signed the "Common Regulation" for the treatment of foreign capital, trademarks, patents, licenses, and gifts. This regulation tried to control and direct foreign investment into sectors of highest priority and to avoid competition between the countries in attracting foreign investment through special concessions.

While Ecuador stated that foreign capital was welcome, it did increase its regulation (1) for both investment and reinvestment, a requirement of prior authorization and registration of the investment; (2) a requirement of progressive national participation in the enterprise until 51% was nationally owned; (3) rules on the importation and production of technology; (4) rules on the use of internal credit and authorization and control over interest payments on foreign credit. This included limitations on the accessibility of foreign exchange. There were still no limits on repatriation of profits, but an additional 11% tax was added to profits that were repatriated.

In the 1980s, with the need for capital after the debt crisis, foreign investment rules were liberalized with the aim of attracting more foreign capital. In 1987 new rules were adopted that gave foreign investors national treatment, except in a few key industries; eliminated the need for authorization prior to investment; allowed for free convertibility of currency, full repatriation of profits, funds from selling stocks, and liquidation of capital; eliminated the additional 11% tax on repatriated profits; and gave foreign investors access to the same concessions designed for export promotion as national firms. The limit of 49% foreign ownership was eliminated except for the fishing industry. Intellectual property rights are protected under the Andean Pact Decision

291. Patents, trademarks, copyrights, and industrial designs are legally recognized and are increasingly well enforced. There is a special *maquiladora* law for export processing. Firms coming under this classification have more flexible labor contracts and exemptions on import and export licenses. With the more liberal investment laws and gradual improvement in the economy, net foreign investment has increased steadily since 1984, though it remains small as a source of income into the country.

Development of Human Resources: The Labor Force, Health, and Education

Human resources are an essential component of economic development. The development of human capital through investment in health and education of the labor force is at least as important as physical infrastructure investment. Edward F. Denison (1962) in a study of economic growth in the United States concluded that human capital contributed substantially more to that growth than did the increase in physical capital. In Ecuador, as in the rest of Latin America, trends in health and education over time show improvement.

The dissemination of improved health and education throughout the population is closely related to income distribution. In general, countries with highly unequal distribution also tend to have less human capital. The United Nations Development Programme uses the Human Development Index, an index that ranks a country's development according to a combination of life expectancy (a proxy for health), literacy, and per capita income, to measure the level of development. While Ecuador has a plentiful supply of unskilled labor, human capital is scarce. Its Human Development Index ranking in 1990 was 74, placing Ecuador below most South American countries, including Colombia, Venezuela, and Brazil, but above Paraguay, Peru, and Bolivia and all the Central American countries, except Costa Rica and Panama. The high inequality of income distribution in Ecuador, effectively limiting access to health, nutrition, and education for the majority, is one of the major factors limiting improvements in this area. Even more important is its low income level. Ecuador's Human Development Index ranking is 28 points higher than its per capita income ranking (United Nations Development Programme 1994).

Health

Health and education affect the quality of the labor force and its level of productivity, as well as the quality of life in general. Overall, though Ecuador's health and nutrition have shown improvement, the provision of health care services remains inadequate. These services tend to be directed toward urban rather than rural regions and directed toward curative rather than preventive activities, such as safe drinking water and sanitation. In short, health care, including publicly subsidized health care, tends to be directed toward the wealthier rather than poorer classes.

There have been significant improvements in birth and death rates, but they are still high relative to other Latin American countries and life expectancy is relatively low. Life expectancy rose from an average of 48.4 years in 1950 to 64.2 years in 1990. Infant mortality rates fell from 139.5 per 1,000 live births in 1950 to 51.7 in 1990 and the crude death rate from 18.9 per 1,000 population to 8.1. The population growth rate declined from an average annual rate of 2.95% between 1950 and 1962 to 2.25% between 1982 and 1990. Rural areas are far behind urban areas with respect to health indicators. In 1990 life expectancy in rural areas was 60.73 years, while in urban areas it was 67.6 years. The rural infant mortality rate was 67.05 per 1,000 live births compared to 37.89 in urban areas and the crude mortality rate per 1,000 population was 9.95 in rural areas compared to 6.63 in urban. The rural fertility rate was 5.7, while the urban rate was 2.53. The considerably worse statistics for rural areas, with infant mortality rates and fertility rates almost twice as high, are striking demonstrations of the effects of rural poverty.

Falling birth and death rates affect the age distribution of the population. This in turn affects the proportion of the population that is potentially productive (i.e., of working age). The dependency ratio, a ratio of those too young to be in the labor force (fifteen and younger) and those too old (seventy and over) to those of working age, for Ecuador was .47 in 1974, falling to .42 in 1990. The decrease is mainly the result of falling birth rates, lowering the proportion of children in the economy. With respect to caloric intake, over half of the population falls below the United Nations standard for minimum daily caloric requirement of 2,300 calories per day.

Education

As Ecuador's development has proceeded and the amount of industrialization has increased, so have the needs for a well-educated labor force. Even unskilled labor in the industrial sector needs a minimum of basic literacy skills to perform productively. As in health, the trend in education shows improvement, but not enough improvement. Illiteracy has fallen from 43.7% of the population over ten years old in 1950 to 11.7% of the population over six years old in 1990. Illiteracy in rural areas is still 20.5%. Illiteracy for women remains higher than for men, but the gap is closing. In 1970 female literacy was 91% that of males. By 1992 it was 95% (United Nations Development Programme 1994).

The education system in Ecuador consists of six years of primary education followed by six years of secondary school. In theory six years of primary education, starting at age six, are obligatory. In practice many children never enroll and almost half of those who do drop out before the end of primary school. The reasons given for the high dropout rates are learning difficulties, often associated with overcrowded homes and poor study facilities; malnutrition, which affects mental development and learning; and, as children get older, the expense of attending school and the pressure to leave and join the work force (Corkill and Cubitt 1988, p. 64).

Between 1974 and 1982 the proportion of population that had no formal education fell from 26% to 17%. At the other extreme, the proportion of population with at least one year of higher education increased from 2.1% to 4.6%. In 1982, 21.5% of the population had one to three years of primary education; another 30.7% had three to six years. Twenty-three percent of the population had more than a primary education, up from 16.5% in 1974.

There is a close correlation between levels of income and education. This correlation works both ways in that those born into families with higher incomes have much more opportunity for education and those with education can earn higher incomes. Education, even publicly supported education, is much more available in urban middle and upper class areas than in rural and poor urban areas. Even though education is "free," it is still expensive for poor families. Books, supplies, and uniforms must be supplied by parents. In addition there is an opportunity cost for the children to be in school rather than either helping at home so other members of the family can work or going out into the workforce themselves. The vicious cycle of the poor being too poor to acquire education and being poor for lack of education remains in Ecuador. To counter it would require a shift in policy toward funding more educational facilities directed toward poor and rural areas, adjustment in curriculum to meet the needs of this population, and educational grants to some children to cover the costs of books, supplies, and uniforms.

The Labor Force

The proportion of Ecuador's population over eight years of age that was in the labor force was 47% in 1974 and 43% in 1990. Regionally, it was 46% in the sierra and 42% on the coast. The labor force participation rate for men over eight years of age was 65.5% and for women, 23%. Of those not in the labor force, slightly over half were students, and another 44% were homemakers. The rest were categorized as retired, disabled, or other.

Over the postwar period labor has shifted out of agriculture and into services. In 1974, 46% of the labor force was engaged in agriculture and 42% in services. By 1990 the proportions were 31% and 58%, respectively. The industrial sector's proportion of the labor force remained relatively constant, 11.7% in 1974, 12.2% in 1984, and 11% in 1990. While value added in manufacturing increased at an annual rate of 9.4% between 1955 and 1984, employment in manufacturing grew at an average of only 4.1% per year. Production became increasingly capital intensive over this period, in spite of relatively low labor costs. This was in part due to government policies that favored capital investment and capital-intensive production. Such policies included subsidized interest rates and an overvalued currency to make capital cheap, as well as labor laws that required significant fringe benefits and made firing workers difficult, to increase the cost of labor. Also contributing to excessive capital intensity was the tendency of multinational subsidiaries to use the capital-intensive methods of their parent companies and of local firms to copy production methods used in developed countries, where capital is the relatively cheap input. The result is the use of more capital-intensive methods than the relative labor/capital prices would warrant. As a consequence, industrial growth has not been adequate to absorb the increasing urban labor supply and the service sector, especially the informal service sector, has grown rapidly.

Highly skilled labor is scarce in Ecuador, while unskilled and semi-skilled labor is plentiful and low cost. Managers and other skilled labor, including technicians, are in short supply and on average, given the low percentage of population with higher education (less than 5%), the educational levels tend to be deficient. The shortage of skilled labor relative to unskilled increases the earnings differentials between the groups. On average, within the industrial sector managerial incomes are 50 to 60 times higher than those of unskilled labor.

The government has a very detailed and complicated Labor Code whose purpose is to protect workers' rights. It institutes a forty-hour work week and a national minimum wage, as well as establishing legally required fringe benefits such as social security and certain bonuses. For example, in September at the beginning of the school term there is a bonus to help parents pay for school supplies. It is referred to as the fourteenth salary and is equal to two minimum monthly salaries. However, this only goes to those employed in the formal sector. It is estimated that over 50% of the workforce is in the informal sector, and these tend to be the poorest segment of society, especially those in rural areas. The legally required fringe benefits are significant, amounting to about 35% of nominal wage. There is also mandatory profit sharing, with workers receiving 15% of the profits. After a 90-day probationary period, unless the worker is terminated for "just cause," severance pay is legally required. It is substantial, equal to three months' pay for up to three years of service, and increases by one month's pay for each additional year. There are specified premiums for overtime work. In addition to cash benefits, there are noncash benefits such as pensions, medical services, subsidized meals, and, in the case of larger companies, stores to sell employees basic food items at cost. In 1992 the minimum wage was $28 per month. Payroll costs, including fringe benefits, are relatively small, representing 15% to 25% of production costs for the typical firm with mostly semiskilled labor (Price Waterhouse 1992).

In theory these strict labor laws apply to all salaried, minimum wage workers. In practice there are some major exceptions. *Maquiladora* operations are exempt from the severance rules. More important, over 50% of the labor force is in the informal sector, which is not covered by the labor laws. Even the large firms of the *gran industria* can achieve a more "flexible" workforce, evading these regulations for part of their workforce, by subcontracting with informal sector workers. It is estimated that about 20% of the workforce receives the minimum wage and is covered by these laws (Business International 1993).

Ecuador has never had a very strong labor union movement. Public-sector employees have been the most organized, with many more strikes in public than in private enterprises. Until 1970 less than 10% of the economically active population was organized. During the 1970s, under the reformist military government, headed by General Guillermo Rodríguez Lara, organized labor gained power, increasing its representation to 18% of the workforce (Corkill and Cubitt 1988, p. 68). In 1975 the three largest unions, representing almost half of organized labor, joined forces in the umbrella organization, the United Workers' Front (FUT), and held a successful nationwide one-day strike to protest the government's failure to deliver reformist promises. When the more conservative military junta deposed Rodríguez Lara in 1976, an aggressive line against organized labor was adopted. The legal process for approving new unions ceased, minimum wages were frozen for three years, causing a decline in real wages, and police were used to break up strikes (Schodt 1987, pp. 126–29). In 1979 the military stepped down. With the return to an elected government, minimum wages were increased, the antilabor laws were rescinded, and new laws that facilitated union organizing were passed. One-fifth of all unions organized since 1966 were approved in 1980 (Schodt 1987, pp. 149–53). At present, unions are common in the formal industrial sector, representing about

20% of the labor force. Most are local, with collective bargaining between the company and company union. Most organized labor is in Quito and Guayaquil. There are national unions in commercial banking, electricity, and transportation. Many of the unions are tied to the FUT for legal advice and support. The Ecuadorean Workers' Confederation (CTE), the other strong national confederation, dominates in textiles, public sector employees, and health. Union ties to political parties are weak.

It is estimated that the informal labor sector accounts for 55% of the urban economically active population. In the slums of Guayaquil it employs as much as 75% of the labor force (Corkill and Cubitt 1988, p. 32). This sector is characterized by lack of regulation, including wages, health, and safety, as well as lack of access to capital, both physical and human. The sector has the advantages of ease of entrance and the possibility of flexible hours, but the disadvantages of low wages, lack of security, and lack of government protection, resulting in marginalized living. In Ecuador, where labor legislation is complex and includes constraints on dismissing workers, the informal sector offers employers increased flexibility and decreased risks. It interacts with and subsidizes the formal sector by providing cheap goods and services, employing the formal sector's surplus labor, buying materials from it, and subcontracting with it. The shortage of work in the formal industrial sector and the rapid migration of population from poor rural communities have contributed to the rapid growth of this sector. The low wages and low consumer purchasing power of labor in this sector contrast sharply with the consumption of luxury goods by the middle and upper classes (expensive automobiles, condos, stereos, computers, etc.). The large proportion of labor working in the informal sector, most with very low productivity and very low wages, is a major contributor to the highly unequal distribution of income.

Macroeconomic Bases for Growth

Income, Investment, and Consumption Trends

Economic growth and development in Ecuador has not been a smooth, steady process; rather it has come in fits and spurts. Periods of rapid growth have followed the commodity booms, bananas during the early 1950s and oil in the early 1970s. The debt crisis that hit in 1982 led to a period of negative growth, resulting in a lower real per capita income in 1990 than in 1980. For this reason the 1980s are called the "lost decade."

Average per capita gross national product in U.S. dollars was $131 in 1950, rising to $181 in 1960, an average annual growth rate of 3.2% per year, much of that growth actually coming in the first half of the decade. From 1960 to 1970 it increased to $290, averaging 4.6% per year. The big jump in growth came with the oil boom. Per capita income growth averaged 12.5% during the 1970s. Its big spurt was between 1972 and 1975, with a 21.6% increase in 1973 alone. After 1975 it increased at a rate of about 3% per year until 1981, when it reached its peak of $1,350. With the debt crisis, the growth in per capita income fell to zero in 1982 and then declined. At an average rate of decline of 2.9% per year, per capita income reached a low of $940 in 1990, equaling that of 1978. (The per capita gross national income figures are calculated by the World Bank, using the Atlas method, which attempts to calculate a real exchange rate, adjusting for the relative inflation rates in the United States and Ecuador. Hence, these figures are basically in constant dollar terms.) With the 1990s positive growth returned. In real (1975 sucre) terms, per capita income grew at an average rate of 1.1% per year between 1990 and 1993, slow but positive.

The major components in Ecuador's national income accounts are consumption and investment. Government expenditures are divided between government consumption and investment expenditures and are treated as a part of total consumption and total investment, respectively. Between 1950 and 1980 total consumption expenditures grew at a reasonably steady rate of about 5.5% per year. With the economic crisis, falling real wages that resulted from high inflation, devaluations, and wage controls led to a drop in consumption. The average annual growth rate fell to 1.2% per year between 1980 and 1985 and remained at about 2% per year between 1986 and 1993. Given a population growth rate of over 2% per year, in per capita terms consumption declined.

In 1950 household consumption represented 75% of GDP. This proportion fell to 68% by 1980 and since then has increased slightly to 71% in 1993. Government consumption was 10% of GDP in 1950, rising to 15% during the oil boom years of the 1970s. Since 1980 there has been a concerted effort to decrease the role of government. Government consumption growth rates became negative and government consumption fell to 8% of GDP by 1993. Over the postwar period (with very small variation) close to 20% of consumption was of imported goods.

While consumption growth tends to be very steady, that of investment is very volatile. Between 1950 and 1985 gross domestic investment (private and public) grew at an average rate of 5.9%. However, the large fluctuations in that rate make the average mean very little. During the boom period of 1950–55, when the government was investing heavily in infrastructure, total investment grew an average of 16.6% per year and between 1970–75 at 12.9% per year. On the other hand, the rate of investment declined at an average annual rate of 6% between 1980 and 1985 and then declined more slowly, averaging -0.5% per year from 1986 to 1990. In the 1990s positive growth returned and investment grew at an annual rate of 6.3% between 1991 and 1993. Much of the fall in investment has been in the loss of public sector infrastructure investment. Its drop may constitute a deterrent to future growth. The increased investment of the 1990s is mainly private sector investment since the public sector's debt obligations still prevent much public sector investment. Table 7.3 shows investment as a proportion of GDP. This represented 8% in 1950, rising to 23% by 1975 and maintaining that level through the rest of the 1970s. With the capital shortage brought on by the debt crisis, it fell to 16% in 1985 and to 13% in 1990. Reversing this downward trend, it increased to 14% of GDP in 1993.

When income declines, savings and investment are expected to take up a disproportionate amount of the decline. People are loath to cut their standard of living and will decrease their rate of saving first. The figures given above clearly indicate that this is the case for Ecuador. Each decline in investment means that much less capital was created in that period, limiting the potential for production in the following period.

External Debt

Throughout the 1980s and to the present the large external debt and its drain on capital resources have been an overriding characteristic of Ecuador's economy. Ironically, the origins of the massive debt coincide with the oil boom. Development of the oil resources brought in large amounts of revenue, spurring spending and economic development. It also increased Ecuador's creditworthiness in the eyes of international bankers, at a time when the international banking system was highly liquid and looking for borrowers. The temptations of "easy" borrowing and the desire to spur development even faster led to rapid borrowing. In 1975 foreign debt amounted to only half a billion dollars. By 1980 it had mushroomed to $4.8 billion.

Some of this overborrowing was a miscalculation, and some was due to poor internal policy that made the borrowing artificially too profitable. In the mid-1970s international interest rates were low, around 7%. At the same time, oil prices were rising rapidly, so it appeared that revenues to meet debt servicing would be readily available. In addition Ecuador's military government had allowed the sucre to become overvalued and had controlled internal interest rates. As inflation climbed higher than the interest rate, making the real rate of interest negative, business firms became heavily indebted. Debt-to-equity ratios averaged

Table 7.3. Investment and Government Expenditures, 1950–93 (in millions of 1975 sucres)

	1950	1960	1970	1975	1980	1985	1990	1993
Total gross investment	3,474	8,985	13,576	24,907	34,975	24,618	23,961	28,742
Total investment as % of GDP	8	22	17	23	24	16	13	14
Net foreign investment in millions of U.S. dollars	4.7	8.0	88.6	95.3	70.0	62.0	82.0	115.0
Public sector investment	–	–	4,161	6,308	8,432	7,177	5,250	4,746
Public sector consumption	2,587	3,965	7,600	15,624	23,611	21,076	21,431	20,036
Total public sector expenditure	–	–	11,761	22,032	32,043	28,253	26,681	24,782
Central government expenditure as % total public sector (excluding debt source)	–	–	–	–	40.0	36.3	54.5	50.9
% central expenditure on defense[a]	–	–	15.7	–	12.5	11.3	12.9	–
% public sector expenditure on education[a]	–	–	27.5	–	34.7	27.7	18.2	19.8
% public sector expenditure on health[a]	–	–	11.0	–	7.8	8.3	11.0	5.4

Source: Banco Central del Ecuador.
[a] From World Development Report, World Bank.

six to one. The negative interest rates discouraged savings, diverting them into consumption, capital flight, and real assets. Bank savings deposits decreased from 55% of current account deposits at the beginning of the 1970s to 18% by 1980. The private banking system found a lucrative source of income to be borrowing abroad and lending at home. The number of banks increased from fifteen to thirty (Swett 1989, pp. 9–11). Overall private sector debt increased twelvefold between 1975 and 1980 and another 130% by 1982. These aggressive private loans were less favorable than loans secured by the government. The periods of the loans were shorter and the interest rates were mainly variable, tied to the U.S. prime rate or the LIBOR (London interbank offer rate), plus a spread for risk, which varied from loan to loan, but averaged about 2%.

Toward the end of the 1970s international interest rates began to rise. The U.S. prime rose to 9% in 1978. It rose again to 12.67 in 1979, to 15.27 in 1980, and to 18.87 in 1981. This almost tripling of interest rates increased debt service payments dramatically. From 1970 to 1974 total debt service was $55.6 million. It increased to $902.7 million between 1975 to 1980 and to $2,209.3 million between 1980 to 1984 (Benalcázar 1989, pp. 392–98). Initially, the rise in interest rates did not present a big problem, since oil prices rose even faster. The price of oil jumped from $12.50 per barrel to $40 per barrel between 1979 and 1980. This led to increased spending, both private and public, and increased domestic prices. In this two-year period public expenditures increased by 100%. Since official exchange rates were fixed, the sucre became even more overvalued.

Then oil prices started to fall. In 1981 they fell from $40 to $30 per barrel. The current account trade deficit rose to 10% of GDP and the government's budget deficit to 7% of GDP. In 1982 interest rates continued to rise and oil prices to fall. A weather condition called "el niño" created floods that caused production losses equal to 2.5% of GDP. In August Mexico declared that it could no longer meet its debt service payment, drying up credit from the international banking community to most of Latin America, and the debt crisis was officially on. While debt service during the 1960s and first half of the 1970s averaged around 12% of exports, it rose to an impossible 90% of exports in the early 1980s. Ecuador was unable to meet its payments and began postponing payment of some interest and capital, adding the unpaid amounts onto the debt and increasing future debt obligations.

Ecuador, as a small country, has very little bargaining power against the international banking consortium. In initial rescheduling agreements, the variable interest rate spread above the LIBOR was actually increased and the term of debts shortened. Though the terms of the debt were worse, Ecuador's inability to meet debt obligations forced the nation's Central Bank to accept the rescheduling. Also as a condition of rescheduling, the IMF placed conditions on the economy, forcing a decrease in public-sector spending, devaluation of the sucre, and the transformation of private debt into public debt. The Central Bank took over the dollar-denominated debt incurred by private businesses, leaving them with debt owed to the Central Bank, denominated in sucres. As the sucre devalued and inflation soared, private debt was lessened while the dollar-denominated debt's burden held by the government increased. This shift in the debt burden from private borrowers to the general public amounted to an enormous government subsidy to that part of the private sector that had borrowed heavily (mainly the wealthy business class), to be financed by taxation and a decrease in government services. It gave rise to the accusation that it was the wealthy who borrowed and the poor who paid. In 1985 the commercial debt was refinanced on more favorable terms and the spread over the LIBOR reduced to 1.75, which saved $250 million in debt service payments per year.

However, oil prices continued to fall and in 1987 a major earthquake ruptured the oil pipeline, costing $600 million in lost production along with $300 million in damage. An attempt at debt equity swaps, where debt instruments are purchased at a discounted rate and used for investment at face value, was soon discontinued due to corruption associated with the program. By 1990 the debt had risen to $11.8 billion, of which $1.6 billion was accumulated past debt service. By June 1994 the debt was $13.2 billion. In October 1994 Ecuador became one of the last Latin American nations to reach a debt agreement with commercial banks under the Brady Plan. Under this plan Ecuador's debt principal owed to 400 commercial banks is decreased by 45% and the remaining amount restructured over a 30-year period. Of the $7.6 billion owed to commercial banks, $4.5 billion is principal and subject to this reduction. Commercial banks can choose to take the reduction by decreasing the principal by 45% and charging the market rate of interest or by maintaining the principal and reducing the interest rate by 45% (58% of the banks chose to decrease the principal). The additional $3.1 billion is accumulated past interest, for which there is no reduction, but the agreement allows a ten-year grace period before repayment. Ecuador's hope is that this agreement will restore its status among the international banking community, opening the way for additional foreign capital. Between 1988 and 1993 debt interest and amortization payments exceeded new loans (including loans for refinancing old debt) by an average of $450 million per year. The net capital outflow that resulted from the debt burden accounts for the negative growth rates of the 1980s.

Inflation

Historically Ecuador has been a low inflation country. Before 1970 inflation was rarely above 5% and never above 10%. With the rapid influx of revenues during the oil boom it jumped up to an average of 17% per year between 1970 and 1975 and then settled back down to an average of 12% per year through the rest of the 1970s. Between 1979 and 1980 oil prices increased from $12.80 to $40 per barrel. The extra income was used to increase spending. Minimum wages were increased to $80 per month and the work week decreased from 44 to 40 hours. Government expenditures increased 100% between 1980 and 1982. Inflation rose to 14% in 1981 and to 16% in 1982. However, with the debt crisis inflation jumped to 48% in 1983, falling back to under 30% until 1988 when it jumped up to 58%, hitting its peak at 75% in 1989. Since then it has gradually decreased, falling to under 40% in 1994.

There are many theories that attempt to explain inflation and a variety of causes for inflation. In addition to the traditional demand pull, monetarist, cost-push, supply shock, and rational expectations theories of inflation there are the Latin American–initiated structural and inertial inflation theories. Each of these contains grains of truth that match reality at least sometimes in some places. The real world generally is best understood by applying some combination of these theories.

Ecuador's periods of high inflation coincide with periods of economic crisis and decline, suggesting that it is not an excess demand inflation, but rather is more likely coming from the cost and supply side. In perhaps overly simple terms, inflation can be thought of as the result of too much money chasing too few goods. This can happen either by expanding the money supply faster than the expansion of goods or with a constant money supply in the face of declining goods. In Ecuador's case both too rapid an expansion of the money supply and contraction from the supply side appear to have contributed to inflation. The net capital outflow due to the foreign debt and falling oil prices led to negative growth rates during the 1980s. The resulting inflation may have been due at least in part to the fact that the monetary base did not contract with the decrease in production (monetarist cause). It might also be explained by a struggle of various groups within the economy attempting to maintain their own standards of living in the face of a declining total (cost-push). Given the amount of monopoly power within the economy this struggle can create a strong inflationary spiral. As positive (though small) growth rates have returned in the 1990s, the inflation rate has been gradually declining.

The openness of Ecuador's economy adds to its vulnerability to inflationary pressures. Devaluations in the exchange rate increase inflation in two ways. To the extent that the economy is dollarized, meaning that though prices are quoted in sucres they are thought of in dollar terms, a devaluation will make those prices increase automatically. In addition, as a result of its long period of import substitution industrialization, Ecuador has a large amount of imported inputs in its production. When the currency devalues, the costs of these imported inputs increase, increasing costs and prices. Further, the openness limits government control of the money supply, since the inflow of foreign reserves adds to the monetary base. Empirically, the price of imports, growth in the money supply, and the growth rate of the economy have been shown to be among the most important influences on inflation in Ecuador. Inflationary expectations and inertia are also important so that inflation does not disappear immediately after the inflationary stimuli are gone (Anderson 1990, pp. 50–52).

Policy to control inflation is made within the Monetary Council, based in the Central Bank of Ecuador. It is charged with controlling money, credit, and exchange rate conditions in a manner "most favorable to development." While it is important to control the growth of the money supply, controlling it to the extent of limiting growth can be counterproductive, since slower growth appears to increase inflation in Ecuador. The Monetary Council must control money's growth enough to keep it in line with real growth, but not constrain it so much that it limits real growth. This is easier said than done. They have shifted from a planned devaluation of the currency to a more stable exchange rate in order to decrease the inflationary push from this source and especially to decrease inflationary expectations. Their current goal is to bring inflation down to about 20% per year.

Summary of Development Policy in Ecuador

Ecuador's economic development has been strongly influenced by the country's small size, its highly unequal income distribution, and its dependence on primary goods exports. Its development path during the postwar period has not been smooth; rather it has come in a couple of spurts, stimulated by banana and oil commodity booms. The nature of the banana boom tended to enrich the wealthy, landed classes faster than the general population, increasing the already unequal distribution of income and wealth. The industrialization that accompanied the oil boom decreased the inequality in income distribution, developing a middle class of industrial employees.

Through much of the postwar period, development policy followed the import substitution industrialization model, which entailed a large amount of government intervention in the economy in an attempt to spur economic development. To encourage the growth of the capital stock, below-market interest rates and overvalued exchange rates decreased the relative price of capital. Overprotection of the new industry and subsidized prices on imported inputs kept this industry from ever becoming efficient enough to be competitive internationally and from ever integrating vertically. There are two ironies in this policy. First, despite the preferential treatment of industry, Ecuador still relies on oil and agricultural products for its exports. Second, despite the majority of the population's living in rural areas, the development policy followed was directed almost exclusively toward urban industry and urban dwellers, often at the expense of the rural population.

With the economic decline brought on by the debt crisis in the 1980s development policy has taken on a new direction: decreasing the amount of government intervention by freeing interest rates and exchange rates to be set by the market; decreasing the amount of regulation of business; opening markets by lowering tariffs and nontariff barriers; encouraging rather than regulating foreign investment; and beginning to privatize state-owned enterprises. It remains to be seen whether this reverse in direction will be successful or whether it may go too far. Too much state intervention, especially in nonproductive directions, distorts development. On the other hand, in the case of a poor country like Ecuador with its unequal distribution, there is still a need for government to take an active role in economic development, especially in the areas of infrastructure and human capital development and in efforts to improve the distribution of income. It is unlikely that undirected market forces alone will spur development.

Over the postwar period the overall economic well-being of the country has improved. Per capita income has increased, and the industrial sector, though distorted, has become a major producer in the economy (see table 7.4). Increasing investment in education and health decreased illiteracy from 25% in 1974 to 12% in 1990 and increased life expectancy from fifty-eight to sixty-four years (see table 7.5). Those with access to safe water expanded from 12% to 59% of the population and the percentage of dwellings with electricity improved from 32% to 63% over the same period (World Bank 1987). The Gini ratio fell from .625 in 1970 to .445 in 1987.

Nonetheless, severe economic problems remain. The four decades of growth and "modernization" left the country with an overdeveloped bureaucracy and overprotected, monopolized industry, both working to maintain the wealth and power of the upper classes. The austerity measures adopted have placed the "adjustment" burden disproportionately on the poor. It is estimated that over half the population, approximately 5 million people, lives below the poverty threshold. Malnutrition is a problem for 57% of the population (Corkill and Cubitt 1988, p. 63). Real per capita income was lower in 1992 than it was in 1980. The sharp decline in government expenditures on infrastructure investment and education decreases Ecuador's potential for future development.

Table 7.4. Economic Indicators, 1950–90

	1950	1960	1970	1980	1990
1. GDP (in million 1975 sucres)	24,701	40,590	62,912	147,622	181,638
2. Per capita GDP	131	181	290	1,260	940
3. Average per capita growth Rate of change per decade		3.2 *(1950–60)*	4.6 *(1960–70)*	12.5 *(1970–80)*	-2.9 *(1980–90)*
4. Government expenditures (in million 1975 sucres)	3,629	6,660	11,761	32,043	26,681
5. Imports (in million US$)	41.2	115	274	2,253	1,862
6. Exports (in million US$)	74	145	190	2,481	2,714
7. Commercial trade balance (Exports-imports)	32.8	30	-84	228	852
8. Current account trade balance*			-133	-642	-166
9. Money supply (in million sucres)	1,038 *(1952)*	1,736	5,465	44,790	852,900
10. External debt (in million US$)	6.1 *(1952)*	24.6	256	5,997	12,105
11. Average annual rate of inflation (as a percentage)	1.4 *(1952)*	12	5	13.8 *(1970–80)*	38 *(1980–91)*
12. Free market exchange rate (in sucres per US$)	17.4 *(1952)*	17.6	23.18	27.8	880.43

Sources: 1. Banco Central del Ecuador; 2. World Bank Database; 3. Banco Central del Ecuador; 4–6. International Historical Statistics, The Americas 1750–1988; 7–8. World Debt Tables; 9–10. Banco Central del Ecuador; 11. International Financial Statistics and World Development Report; 12. Banco Central del Ecuador.
* Includes commercial balance, plus services plus debt services.

Table 7.5. Educational Levels, 1950–90

	1950	1962	1974	1982	1990
1. Infant mortality	139.5	12.0 (1960)	99.0 (1970)	6.0 (1980)	54.8
2. Life expectancy	48.4	53.1 (1960)	58.1 (1970)	64.3 (1980)	66.0
3. % illiterate rate total population 15+	43.7*	30.4*	26.1	16.4	11.7
4. % illiterate rate urban areas	–	–	10.0	6.2	5.4
5. % illiterate rate rural areas	–	–	35.5	27.7	20.5
6. No formal education % population 6+			26.2	17.3	
7. Basic literacy only % population 6+			.3	1.4	
8. 1–3 Yr. primary % population 6+			27.1	21.5	
9. 4–6 Yr. primary % population 6+			29.9	30.7	
10. 1–3 Yr. secondary % population 6+			7.8	10.7	
11. 4–6 Yr. secondary % population 6+			4.8	7.4	
12. 1–3 Yr. higher education % population 6+			1.2	2.5	
13. 4+ Yr. higher education % population 6+			.9	2.1	
14. Undeclared % population 6+			1.8	6.3	

Sources: 1–2. World Bank data; 3–14. Banco Central del Ecuador, *Boletín anuario.*
*10 and over.

Works Cited

Anderson, Joan B. 1988. *An Econometric Model of Real Growth, Inflation and Exchange Rate Changes for the Economy of Ecuador, 1950–1987.* Quito: Banco Central del Ecuador.

———. 1990. *Policy Alternatives for the Latin American Crisis.* New York: Taylor and Frances.

Banco Central del Ecuador. 1950a–92a. *Cuentas nacionales.* Quito: Banco Central del Ecuador.

———. 1950b–92b. *Memoria anual.* Quito.

———. Several years. *Boletín anuario.* Quito.

———. Several years. *Información estadística mensual.* Quito.

Benalcázar R., René. 1989. *Análisis del desarrollo económico del Ecuador.* Quito: Ediciones Banco Central del Ecuador.

Busey, James L. 1995. *Latin American Political Guide.* 20th ed. Manitou Springs, Colo.: Juniper Editions.

Business International. 1993. *Investing, Licencing and Trading Conditions Abroad: Ecuador.* Economist Intelligence Unit, December 1993. New York: Business International Corp.

Cardoso, Eliana, and Ann Helwege. 1992. *Latin America's Economy.* Cambridge, Mass.: MIT Press.

Comard, Wayne. 1990. Inflation, Interest Rates and Business Groups in Ecuador. Unpublished paper. Stanford University.

Corkill, David, and David Cubitt. 1988. *Ecuador: Fragile Democracy.* London: Latin American Bureau.

Dávalos, Xavier. 1993. La distribución del ingreso en el Ecuador. *Cuestiones económicas* 20 (May).

Denison, Edward F. 1962. *The Sources of Economic Growth in the United States and the Alternatives.* New York: National Bureau of Economic Research.

INEC. 1984. Industrial Census for Manufacturing and Minerals. Quito, Ecuador: INEC.

International Monetary Fund. Several issues. *International Financial Statistics.* Washington, D.C.: IMF.

Military Catering to Tourists. 1994. *Latinamerica Press* 26(37), October 13.

Price Waterhouse. 1992. *Doing Business in Ecuador.* N.p.: Price Waterhouse.

Psacharopoulos, George, et al. 1993. Poverty and Income Distribution in Latin America: The Story of the 1980s. *Latin American and the Caribbean Technical Department*, Report no. 27. Washington, D.C.: World Bank, April.

Schodt, David. 1987. *Ecuador.* Boulder, Colo.: Westview Press.

Swett, Francisco X. 1989. *Turnaround: The Political Economy of Development and Liberalization in Ecuador, 1984–88.* Occasional Papers no. 20. San Francisco: International Center for Economic Growth.

United Nations Development Programme. 1994. *Human Development Report.* Oxford: Oxford University Press.

U.S. Department of Commerce, Bureau of Economic Analysis. 1994. *Survey of Current Business* 74(8) (August).

Villalobos, Fabio. 1985. Ecuador: Industrialization, Employment and Distribution of Income: 1970–1978. In Louis Lefeber, ed., *Economía política del Ecuador*. Quito, Ecuador: Corporación Editorial Nacional.

Viteri, Galo. 1992. Diagnóstico de la inversión extranjera en el Ecuador. *Revista Economía* 89 (June).

Wilkie, James W., David E. Lorey, and Enrique Ochoa, eds. 1988, 1994. *Statistical Abstract of Latin America*. Los Angeles: UCLA Latin American Center Publications.

World Bank. 1987. *World Development Report*. New York: Oxford University Press.

——. 1992. *Social Indicators, 1992*. London: Oxford University Press.

——. Several issues. *World Debt Tables*. Washington, D.C.: World Bank.

——. Several issues. *World Development Report*. London: Oxford University Press.

8.
Cuba

Carmelo Mesa-Lago
University of Pittsburgh

Introduction

This chapter covers the period 1959–95, Cuba under the Revolution
(partial data on 1995 were added in a final revision of this chapter in
1996). This section provides a brief review of economic and social
policies and conditions on the island in the 1950s, prior to revolutionary
takeover and a summary of changes in overall economic policies under
the Revolution; specific polices are discussed in the remaining sections.

Overall Economic Policies in the 1950s

Several comparisons of Cuba with other Latin American countries in the
1950s ranked the island among the top two or three places in terms of
economic and social development. But the Cuban economy suffered
from serious problems that were corrected neither by the market nor by
the government (this section, unless otherwise specified, is based on
CERP 1965 and Mesa-Lago 1981).

Compared to other Latin American countries at similar levels of
development, in 1958 the Cuban state had a very low degree of ownership in production and services: none in industry and agriculture and a
very small proportion in banking, construction, transportation, and
trade. Public utilities, such as electricity and telephones, were owned by
U.S. corporations, which also controlled a significant share of banking.
The only extensive state ownership was found in education and public
health facilities.

Although Cuba had overwhelmingly a market economy, after the
Revolution of 1933 the state began to intervene in the regulation of labor
conditions as well as in economic affairs. In the late 1940s and 1950s
several important institutions, such as the National (Central) Bank of
Cuba, the Agricultural and Development Bank, and the Economic and
Social Development Bank were established. The last two banks provided

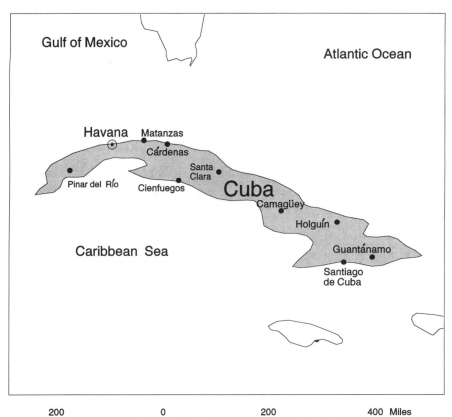

Gulf of Mexico

Atlantic Ocean

Havana   Matanzas
Cárdenas
Santa
Clara
Pinar del Río   Cienfuegos

Cuba

Camagüey

Holguín

Guantánamo

Santiago
de Cuba

Caribbean Sea

200   0   200   400 Miles

⊛ **Capital**
• **Major Cities**
   National Boundary
   Countries

credit for industrial promotion and agricultural diversification, while a Law of Industrial Stimulation introduced fiscal and tariff incentives for the creation of new industries. The state also expanded public construction and social services. In the 1950s the National Economic Council was created to program economic policies, but it lacked the real power to become an indicative planning agency.

Dependency on sugar was very high: in the 1950s the agricultural and industrial branches of sugar generated 28–29% of GNP, sugar exports accounted for about 80% of the total exports, and 20–25% of the labor force was employed in the sugarcane fields and mills (Pérez-López 1991). The price fluctuations of sugar in the world market, as well as the shifting U.S. sugar quota and prices, were exogenous factors that Cuba could not control. Because of the dominant role of sugar, these fluctuations provoked instability in growth. The sugar sector was basically stagnant and could not provide the needed dynamism to make the economy grow vigorously. However, there were some signs that sugar dependency was declining: in 1957–58 sugar originated only 25% of GNP in spite of high sugar output and exports during those years, and nonsugar industrial output grew 47% in 1947–58 (Pérez-López 1987). There were significant developments in the mining-industrial sector, including nickel extraction, petroleum refining, cement, glass, electricity, etc. In nonsugar agriculture, progress was reported in cattle, rice, and other crops (Baklanoff 1979).

Inflation in 1950–58 averaged 1% yearly. GNP per capita in constant prices increased at an annual rate of 1% in the same period. The investment ratio averaged 17% in 1955–58 and showed an upward trend, eliciting hope that the rate of growth would rise in the future (see table 8.1).

Cuban legislation on labor conditions and social security was among the most advanced in the region and the trade union movement, as well as collective bargaining, was strong although usually controlled by the government. However, in 1956–57, 16% of the labor force was openly unemployed and approximately 14% was underemployed (see table 8.2).

Furthermore, open unemployment increased more than twofold in the annual slack period of the sugar sector ("dead season") over the period of the harvest. The expansion of employment in construction, commerce, and industry was insufficient to absorb both the rapidly growing labor force and rural-to-urban migration. Scarce data from 1943–57 indicate that the rate of open unemployment was increasing.

There are no data on income distribution, but in 1949–58 the labor share of national income was 65%, the highest in the region: those employed enjoyed sufficient power to capture a significant share of national income, but their gains were largely obtained at the expense of

Table 8.1. Macroeconomic Indicators, 1956–93

Year	GSP[a] Million Pesos[b]	Gross Domestic Investment (GDI) Million Pesos[b]	GDI/GSP (%)	GDI/GSP (%)	Monetary Surplus/ Population Income %	Fiscal Deficit/ State Budget %	External Debt (billion dollars) Hard Currency	USSR + CMEA[c]	Exchange Rate (pesos per US$1) Official	Black Market
1956	2,471[d]	458[d]	–	17.1	–	–	–	0.0	1.00	–[g]
1962	5,169	572	11.1	–	90.8	–	–	–	1.00	–
1970	8,356	800	9.6	15.1[f]	83.1	–	–	–	1.00	–
1980	17,606	2,739	15.6	19.3	30.9	0.0	3.2	–	0.71	5.00[h]
1989–90	26,653	4,511	16.9[e]	–	40.0	13.7	7.3	30.0	1.00	8.00
1993	12,500	2,037	16.2	–	73.5	35.0	8.6	–	1.00	80.00[i]

Sources: ECLAC 1958–64; Mesa-Lago 1994a, 1994b; *Granma International*, January 4, 1995, pp. 4–5.
[a] Global Social Product based on old Soviet system of material product: not comparable with GDP.
[b] Current prices.
[c] At official exchange rate.
[d] GDP and gross fixed investment based on national accounts; the annual average GFI/GDP in 1955–58 was 17.2%.
[e] GDI declined by 43% in 1989–91.
[f] 1971.
[g] There was no black market.
[h] 1979.
[i] Annual average.

the unemployed and the peasants. In 1957–58 Cuba's national averages in education, health care, and social security were among the three highest in Latin America, but social service facilities were mainly concentrated in the capital city and urban areas, whereas their availability and quality declined sharply in rural areas. For instance, in 1953 the illiteracy rate in rural areas was 3.6 times higher than in urban areas and similar disparities were roughly estimated on income, infant mortality, and housing (see table 8.2). Most rural migrants to Havana lived in shantytowns and found low-paid work in the tertiary sector (domestic service, peddling) or became beggars. The high and growing percentage of the labor force engaged in tertiary activities was an indication of underemployment and a growing informal sector.

Cuba's economy was remarkably open: in 1957–58 the trade turnover (exports plus imports) equaled about half of GNP. Two-thirds of Cuban foreign trade was with the United States, and that commercial dependence invariably resulted in a deficit (U.S. investment in Cuba was possibly the second highest in Latin America). The Cuban peso was exchanged par with the U.S. dollar and was freely convertible in the world market (see table 8.1). According to one critical view, the Cuban economy was totally dependent on the United States, a situation that impeded a satisfactory degree of domestic integration on the island, perpetuated sugar dependency, obstructed industrialization, and induced significant inequalities. An opposing view contended that the small size of Cuba and its proximity to the most powerful world economy made integration inevitable and that the U.S. investment and transfer of technology were largely responsible for the relatively high development achieved on the island.

In summary, during the decade prior to the Revolution, the Cuban economy had a small rate of growth that largely benefited capital and employed labor. The dominant sugar sector was basically stagnant while the nonsugar sector, although expanding, was not dynamic enough to generate vigorous economic growth and absorb the labor transfer from agriculture. Open unemployment and underemployment were high and apparently increasing. The island ranked among the top countries in the region concerning social services, but national averages hid significant differences between urban and rural areas. Due to the openness of the Cuban economy, as well as its heavy dependence on sugar exports and U.S. quotas and preferential prices, fluctuations in the world sugar price and shifts in U.S. policies had significant repercussions on the island's economy, thus creating considerable instability. The Cuban economy was fully integrated with the U.S. economy and had very little independence, but there is no consensus on whether that situation was avoidable or on its overall consequences. Although successive Cuban govern-

Table 8.2. Indicators of Social Welfare, Late 1950s–93

Years	Labor Force, % of		Health Care				Education			Social Security Coverage[d], % of		Housing	
	Open Unemploy-ment	Female Partici-pation	Infant Mortality[a]	Physicians per 10,000 Inhab.	Hospital Beds per 10,000 Inhab.	Life Expect-ancy Years	Illiteracy Rate[b]	Enrollment, % Increase[c] Secondary	Higher	Total Population	Labor Force	Units Built per 1,000 Inhab.[e]	House Deficit
Late 1950s	16.4[f]	12.6[f]	33.4[h]	9.2[h]	4.2[h]	–	23.6[k]	–	–	4.2[h]	62.6	–	–
1960	11.8	–	41.5[i]	5.4[i]	–	64.0	3.9	14	3	–	–	2.4	655,000[l]
1970	1.3	18.3	38.7	7.1	5.0	68.5	12.9	25	5	100.0	88.7	0.6	755,000
1981	5.5	31.4	18.5	16.6	4.4	72.8	1.9	81	20	100.0	93.0	1.9	877,000
1988–89	6.0	35.0[g]	11.1	32.8	5.1	75.2	3.8	88	23	–	–	2.41	880,000[m]
1993	10–18	–	10.2[j]	39.0[j]	5.0	75.4	6.0	–	–	–	–	–	–

Sources: Mesa-Lago 1993a,1994a, 1994b, based on Cuban statistics.

[a] Per 1,000 born alive.

[b] 1950s and 1970, 10 years and older; 1980s excludes older than 49 years; 1993, 15 years and older.

[c] Percentage of the school-age cohort enrolled in public schools; in elementary education 100+.

[d] Total in health care; labor force in pensions.

[e] State civilian construction; 1960 is the annual average of 1959–63; in 1981 total construction was 2.8 per 1,000 and in 1985, 4 per 1,000 (private rates were 0.7 and 1.2, respectively).

[f] 1956–57.

[g] Author's estimate based on female participation in civilian labor force.

[h] 1958.

[i] 1962.

[j] 1992.

[k] 1953.

[l] 1964.

[m] 1985.

ments since 1933 gradually increased their intervention in the economy, particularly in the 1940s and 1950s, both state ownership and regulation were considerably lower in comparison with Latin American countries at the same level of development.

Overall Economic Policies under the Revolution: 1959–95

There is a fair consensus among foreign experts on the economic periodization under the Revolution (one exception is Zimbalist 1987). Cuban economists generally follow the same periodization but stress the continuity of the process (Rodríguez 1990). Here I identified seven stages in Cuban economic policy concerning the model of organization: (1) 1959–60, liquidation of capitalism and market erosion; (2) 1961–63, attempt to introduce an orthodox (Stalinist) central planning model; (3) 1964–66, debate over and test of alternative socialist models (Mao-Guevarist idealism versus pro-Soviet pragmatism); (4) 1966–70, adoption and radicalization of the Mao-Guevarist model (movement away from the market); (5) 1971–85, introduction of a timid Soviet (pre–Mikhail Gorbachev) model of economic (market-oriented) reform; (6) 1986–90, the Rectification Process and movement away from the market; and (7) from 1991 on, collapse of the Soviet bloc, economic crisis, and renewal of the move to the market. More than thirty-five years of revolutionary policies have been characterized by pendular shifts between the plan and the market, but with an overwhelming dominance of the former. Intertwined with the policy stages on economic organization were shifting policies concerning the chosen development strategy: (1) 1959–63, antisugar bias, industrialization, and agricultural diversification; (2) 1964–70, return to priority of the sugar sector with emphasis on huge crops; and (3) from 1971 on, a more balanced strategy with continuous predominance of sugar but with a better allocation of resources among various economic sectors (Mesa-Lago 1971, 1978, 1981, 1994a, 1994b).

Who Owns the Economy?

In 1959–90, before the collapse of the socialist camp, there was a steady move in Cuba toward full collectivization of the means of production, as well as egalitarianism (with a minor slowdown in 1971–85). The crisis of the 1990s forced the government to open up to foreign investment and joint-venture ownership; the domestic market reform, which began in mid-1993, has led to some expansion of the internal nonstate sector but without significant changes in ownership.

Producers

Government Ownership. In 1959–89 there was a steady increase in state ownership and operation in all economic branches: by 1961 it was 100% in wholesale and foreign trade, banking, and all social services (education, health, social security); by 1968 it was also 100% in industry, construction, and retail trade; and by 1989 it was 92% in agriculture (state farms and government-controlled cooperatives) and 99% in transportation (Mesa-Lago 1994b).

The proportion of state employment in the civilian sector (excluding the military sector) steadily increased from about 10% in 1958 to 86% in 1970, to 93.6% in 1979, and to 94.1% in 1989 (JUCEPLAN 1968 to 1976; CEE 1976 to 1991). There was a 0.5 percentage point decline in state employment in 1979–85, when self-employment was authorized, but the state sector resumed its expansion in 1986–89. Estimates for 1989 indicate that 95.2% of the labor force was employed by the state in both the civilian and military sectors; the remaining 4.8% was disaggregated as follows: 2.6% in "private farms," 1.4% in government-controlled cooperatives, 0.5% self-employed, and 0.3% in salaried employment in private farms (Mesa-Lago 1993b; CEE 1990).

Private Foreign Ownership. Until 1982 all foreign investment was banned in Cuba although there were partnerships with the USSR in certain ventures, but without ownership. That year a law regulating foreign investment was enacted, but it did not attract any significant external capital. At the end of the 1980s Cuba had the highest degree of state ownership within the whole socialist camp and obviously within Latin America (Mesa-Lago 1994b).

The economic reforms of the 1990s have reversed this ownership trend somewhat. In 1992 the constitution was amended to allow ownership by mixed enterprises and the transfer of state property to joint ventures with foreign capital. Rules for foreign investors were liberalized and incentives provided and a new law enacted in 1995. There are very few data on foreign investment, but it reached a cumulative $1.5 billion in 1991–94 and is mainly concentrated in tourism and, to less extent, in oil exploration and nickel. However, almost all sectors of industry are open to foreign investment now; most foreign partners are Spaniards, Canadians, Mexicans, and some Western Europeans. The amount of foreign investment has been acknowledged to be grossly insufficient by top Cuban officials; it is only a fraction of the $5 to $6 billion that Cuba annually received from the USSR and the Council of Mutual Economic Assistance (CMEA) in the 1980s (Mesa-Lago 1994a; Monreal and Rúa 1994).

Private Domestic Ownership. The size of private domestic legal ownership in 1994 was unknown, but it was probably considerably smaller than that of foreign investment and was concentrated in self-employment and agriculture, most of it illegal or underground. The private sector is expanding, however, and such a trend will be very difficult to reverse.

Individuals

Individuals' Distribution of Income. Cuba has not published data on income or wealth distribution under the Revolution in the 1970 and 1981 census or in the statistical yearbooks. The most important distributory measures took place in 1959–61, when most property was collectivized and the government increased minimum wages and pensions, cut down home rent and tariffs of public utilities, and nationalized and made social services free. The only information available on income distribution is very rough estimates by foreign scholars (Zimbalist and Brundenius 1989; Brundenius 1984; MacEwan 1981; see table 8.3) whose accuracy has been contested (Mesa-Lago 1981, 1994b). Distribution by family income in 1958–62 indicates a transfer from the wealthiest quintile to the poorest two quintiles. Distribution of personal income in 1953 and 1962 suggests that a higher income share of the wealthiest quintile shifted to the poorest two quintiles, but with a substantial transfer to the middle two quintiles. Subsequent data on personal income distribution in 1973, 1978, and 1986 show very minor additional transfers, mostly going to the two middle-income quintiles. The virtual universalization of free social services for the population (significantly increasing access to rural and marginal urban areas) and almost full

Table 8.3. Crude Estimates of Income Distribution, 1953–86

Quintile	Family Income		Personal Income					
	1958	1962	1953	1962	1973[a]	1978[b]		1986[c]
						Low	High	
0–20	5.7	9.5	2.1	6.2	7.8	7.8	11.0	11.3
21–40	8.9	12.2	4.4	11.0	12.5	12.4	13.8	14.7
41–60	12.5	13.5	11.1	16.3	19.2	19.7	16.5	17.0
61–80	18.3	18.3	24.5	25.1	26.0	26.7	22.7	23.2
81–100	54.6	46.5	57.9	41.4	34.5	33.4	36.0	33.8
TOTAL	100.0	100.0	100.0	100.0	100.0	100.0	100.0	100.0

Sources: Family income from MacEwan 1981; personal income from Brundenius 1984 and Zimbalist and Brundenius 1989. For criticism see Mesa-Lago 1994a.
[a] Excludes private sector.
[b] Includes private sector.
[c] The authors do not clarify whether the private sector is included or excluded.

employment played a major progressive role in distribution too. In 1989, 78% of the population income came from state employment, 16.7% from state pensions and other transfer payments, and 5.3% from the private sector (Pérez-López 1995). In spite of the statistical vacuum, there is a wide consensus that by the end of the 1980s Cuba had one of the most egalitarian economies in the world (Brundenius 1984; Mesa-Lago 1981, 1993b). Nevertheless, Cuban leaders have access to goods and services that usually are either unavailable or very scarce or of poor quality, such as housing, beach homes, cars and gasoline, stores with imported consumer goods, domestic servants, and travel abroad.

Market-oriented reforms introduced in the 1990s have reversed the previous trend, toward inequality. The small number of workers employed in joint enterprises (particularly tourism and oil) receive the bulk of their salaries in pesos, but part of them are paid a fraction in dollars. Contributing to expanding inequality are the 1993 legalization of hard-currency remittances by Cuban Americans and their possession by Cubans; the authorization of self-employment; the expansion of the black market and free agricultural markets; and the creation of state dollar shops. Professionals, university graduates, executives, and political cadres are banned from self-employment. Blacks and mulattos probably are now a majority in Cuba's population, but are only 3% to 5% of Cuban Americans in Florida; hence, those in Cuba receive a very small percentage of dollar remittances. Last but not least, rationing of food has ceased to be an equalizer because it barely provides for two weeks within the month; the lowest-income groups lack resources to buy in the agricultural and black markets as well as in state dollar shops because their prices are very high (Pérez-López 1995; Mesa-Lago 1994a).

Wealth and Land Distribution.   There are no data on wealth distribution. In 1989 distribution of total land was reported as follows: 82.2% in state farms, 15.6 in cooperatives, and 2% in "private" farms. In 1988, 78.8% of agricultural output was from state farms and 21.2% from private farms and co-ops (Pérez-López 1995).

Limits and Forms of Ownership and Control

Types of Ownership.   Until the end of the 1980s there were four types of ownership of means of production in Cuba: (1) state ownership of virtually all the economy; (2) pseudo-private ownership in agriculture; (3) state ownership but operation by agricultural production cooperatives; and (4) a tiny sector of cooperatives in fishing and some types of transportation. The economic reforms of the 1990s have created three new types of ownership: (5) joint ventures and mixed enterprises with foreign capital; (6) self-employed occupations; and (7) transformation of state farms into a new type of cooperatives, Unidades Básicas de Producción Agropecuaria (UBPCs; Basic Units of Agricultural Production).

1. State ownership of mining, industry, construction, transportation, commerce (domestic and foreign), banking, and social services was total, following the old Soviet model of the centrally planned economy. In construction, a 1980 law allowed individuals to build their own homes, but later a new law introduced tight controls for building, selling, buying, and exchanging dwelling units. Control in social services is still absolute; for instance, physicians are prohibited from having a private practice even in their free time. In 1968, 58,000 tiny businesses (food stands in the streets, family repair shops, tailors, etc.) were nationalized. Within agriculture, 78% of cultivated land was organized as huge state farms where workers received a salary; all their production went to the state. Family plots for the workers' own consumption in state farms were eliminated in 1967 and partly reestablished in the 1980s but as a collective parcel for all workers rather than a family plot.

2. Small plots of "private" land (about 200,000 with an average size of 33 acres) were distributed in 1959 and again by reforms in 1963. Although ownership of the land was granted to the farmers, there are significant limitations imposed on their rights: (a) the state has priority to buy the land when the farmer dies, retires, or wants to sell the farm (that option invariably has been exercised by the government); (b) inheritance is possible only when heirs have previously worked the land together with the owner; (c) a substantial part of the crop has to be sold to the state (procurement quota, or *acopio*) at prices set by the latter well below market prices; (d) the government provides credit, seeds, fertilizer, tools, and other inputs to the farmer, in exchange for commitments to cultivate specific crops and fulfill the *acopio*; (e) until 1980 the farm surplus produce (after the *acopio*) could be used only for self-consumption or bartered with other farmers; selling to outsiders or in the black market was prohibited and severely punished; (f) in 1980–86 the government authorized free farmers' markets where the surplus could be sold at prices set by supply and demand, but those markets were strongly criticized by Fidel Castro in 1982 and abolished in 1986 with the allegation that they charged very high prices and led to huge profits (the markets were reintroduced in 1994—see below); and (g) "private" farmers were under strong pressure to join an official association, Asociación Nacional de Agricultores Pequeños (ANAP; National Association of Small Private Farmers), which was controlled by the government and manipulated to support state goals even when the latter collided with the private farmers' own interests.

3. Agricultural production cooperatives (CPAs) were established in the early 1970s and pushed by the government since 1977. Private farmers who integrated their land into a CPA lost ownership of their land, became state employees (with a guaranteed salary and social security coverage), and had to sell all their crops to the state. The number of CPAs and their membership grew until 1983 and thereafter declined; many old farmers joined CPAs to receive state pensions, and the co-ops took out loans and began to suffer heavy losses. The CPAs were prohibited from selling any produce to the free farmers' markets; hence, this was a disincentive to join the co-ops vis-à-vis private farmers (who were allowed to sell in the free markets), and that was one of the reasons used by the government to shut down those markets in 1986.

4. Fishing cooperatives had a tiny share of ownership that gradually declined and became state owned (Mesa-Lago 1981, 1994b).

5. Joint ventures with foreign capital are given several incentives: (a) ownership of 49% of shares; in tourism and other strategic trades the foreign partner can have a majority of shares (in the 1995 law, 100% of foreign ownership is allowed, with some exceptions and restrictions); (b) rapid recuperation of investment (e.g., three years in tourism); (c) exemption on taxes on gross revenue, personal income, transfer of real estate and business, and custom duties for needed imports of equipment and inputs (taxes levied are 30% on profit and 25% on the payroll); (d) unrestricted repatriation of dividends, profits, and salaries; (e) state handling of unruly or unproductive workers, a ban on strikes, and very low wages (paid in pesos) for personnel; and (f) some insurance and state services. Disadvantages are the government bureaucracy, too many regulations and red tape, inability to hire, pay, and promote workers (this is done by a state agency), state inability to meet delivery deadlines, shortage of some inputs, and potential canceling of business. Currently, joint enterprises are only allowed in the hard-currency export sector or tourism; they cannot produce for the domestic market; therefore, such enterprises have no impact on domestic output and are not able to get inputs from the internal economy. Risks are very high: in 1992–95 three international business/economics publications (Business International, Euromoney, and the Heritage Foundation) ranked Cuba last or among the worst countries in terms of risks for foreign investors. The Helms-Burton bill, approved in 1996, penalizes foreign investors in expropriated United States business in Cuba (Pérez-López 1995; Mesa-Lago 1994a).

6. Self-employed persons were labeled vagrants by a 1971 law against loafing; they were authorized in 1978 and flourished until 1982, when they were criticized by Castro; in 1986–90 there was a government campaign against street vendors and sellers of services. In 1993, because

of the crisis, 117 self-employed occupations (mostly in services) were authorized but were subjected to strict regulations: (a) state employees can perform self-employed work only during weekends and vacations, while professionals, university graduates, and government leaders are banned from doing it; (b) registration and municipal approval are required, and the self-employed must buy a license and pay taxes; (c) the self-employed are prohibited from hiring wage earners and are subjected to state inspection ("excessive" prices and profits may result in government interference and increased taxation); and (d) state enterprises can neither buy products from the self-employed nor supply inputs to them (with certain exceptions). Some of these activities became very successful (restaurants, taxi drivers) and successfully competed with similar public services; hence, they were banned at the end of 1993, to be reintroduced in 1995. A decree enacted in mid-1994 created a new crime ("illegal enrichment"): defendants must prove their innocence; otherwise they are put in prison and their property is confiscated, and there is no appeal against the government decision. It is not surprising, therefore, that only 170,000 self-employed had registered in 1995, two years after their activities were permitted, but probably 500,000 to one million people are illegally performing that type of work (Pérez-López 1995; Mesa-Lago 1978, 1981, 1994a, 1994b).

7. In September 1993 the government approved the transformation of state farms into a new type of production cooperatives (UBPCs). There are similarities with the previous unsuccessful CPAs: their members do not get land ownership but an indefinite contract to rent it; the government largely decides what the UBPCs will cultivate; 60% to 80% of their crops must be sold to the state (acopio—a compulsory procurement quota imposed on private farmers by the state [a share of their crop must be sold to the government at prices set below the market prices]); and members can request loans to buy the agricultural equipment that belonged to the state farm, as well as needed inputs. The major differences from CPAs are that UBPC members are not paid a guaranteed salary but have a share of the cooperative profits (after deducting payment of rent, principal and interest of loans, and taxes) and they are authorized to sell any surplus at the free agricultural markets reintroduced in fall 1994, where prices are set freely, about ten times higher than the acopio prices. By the end of 1993 the government claimed that all state sugarcane farms had been converted into UBPCs, and by mid-1994 about half of the nonsugar state farms had been transformed into UBPCs. In addition to the UBPCs the government provided similar contracts to individuals for small isolated plots of land that could not be merged into co-ops (Mesa-Lago 1994a). As a result of these changes, at

the end of 1994, 51.8% of the agricultural land was operated by co-ops (40.6% by UBPCs and 11.2% by CPAs); 33.1% by state farms; and 15% by small private farmers and other co-ops (Deere 1995).

Labor Supply and the Role of Trade Unions. Until the crisis of the 1990s labor supply was tightly controlled by the government through the central planning apparatus: 95% of employment was in the state sector and shifts in jobs required government authorization; a mandatory labor booklet listed all the worker's merits (productivity, participation in government rallies, "voluntary" unpaid labor) and "demerits" (absenteeism, low productivity, etc.); and the scarcity of housing and the rationing system (which mandates purchasing the rations in a specifically located state store) also impeded free labor mobility.

Since 1993 labor mobility has increased and state employment declined (but we lack hard data on this). The growing private sector (and joint ventures) is providing strong incentives and attracting skilled workers from the state sector: professionals, such as physicians, are becoming restaurateurs, taxi drivers, and waiters. But legal restrictions are still impeding labor mobility. In 1995 the government announced (but did not implement) a plan to dismiss 500,000 to 800,000 workers in the state sector (mostly in paralyzed industry, mining, transportation, construction, and commerce). Unemployment compensation (60% of the monthly salary) will be paid until a "suitable" job is offered (mostly in agriculture); if the unemployed person refuses the offer, the compensation will be halted. It is expected that fired workers will find employment in the domestic private sector, but that requires the lifting of strict regulations and restrictions imposed on self-employment and agriculture and the authorization for Cubans to own small and medium-sized industrial enterprises; the number of jobs created in joint ventures is very small (Mesa-Lago 1993b, 1994a, 1994b).

Trade unions have been controlled by the government since the beginning of the 1960s; their function is not to defend workers' interests, but to be "transmission belts" for fulfilling planned output quotas, increasing labor productivity, and meeting other state goals. Wages are centrally determined for 95% of the labor force and are linked to fulfillment of planned output targets. Collective bargaining does not regulate working conditions but secures labor's commitment to the nation's economic goals. The traditional Marxist-Leninist explanation of these practices is that there is no conflict between the state and the worker's interest, since the former is the dictatorship of the proletariat; strikes are banned based on the same logic. As the economic reform advances, however, the trade unions may change their role (at least in the private sector) and become involved in the defense of the workers' interests (Mesa-Lago 1971, 1978, 1981, 1994b).

How Does the Economy Grow?

According to Marxist theory, after a successful socialist revolution there will be a transitional stage where the state (the dictatorship of the proletariat) will confiscate all means of production and exercise a monopoly; the "surplus value" (profit), previously "robbed" by the capitalists, will become "surplus product" and will be seized by the state. With a rational economic organization (planning) the state will manage an accumulation fund (investment to expand the means of production) and a consumption fund (which will finance production costs and social services), and full employment will be achieved. In the transitional stage (called socialism by V. I. Lenin) there will be remnants of capitalism such as "the law of value" (the market, supply and demand), scarcity, money, deductions from the labor product, state direction, distribution according to the workers' skill and effort, material incentives, and inequality. These "vices" will gradually disappear and, in the ultimate stage of communism, there will be economic abundance, distribution according to needs, a "new man" motivated by nonmaterial incentives, equality, and the withering away of the state. Karl Marx incorrectly assumed that the socialist revolution would take place in the most developed capitalist nations (Germany, England), but it actually occurred in unevenly, relatively poorly developed Russia. The Mensheviks argued that capitalist development should precede socialism, but Lenin and the Bolsheviks decided that the state would develop the economy and eventually reach communism. The civil war and the economic crisis forced Lenin to take a step back toward the market, and he launched the New Economic Policy (NEP) against Leon Trotsky's idea of communal communism. Joseph Stalin strengthened state power, collectivized agriculture (to control the labor surplus and generate revenue for industrialization), and created central planning combined with material incentives. After World War II the Stalinist model was initially applied in all new socialist states in Eastern Europe and China, but it was found inadequate by several countries that decided to take divergent paths to communism: workers' management and market tools in Yugoslavia, various combinations of the plan and the market in Hungary and Poland, communes and mobilization in China (which later shifted to market socialism). In the mid-1960s the USSR introduced a timid reform with a few market tools that proved to be a failure; two decades later Gorbachev launched perestroika (a further move to the market) and glasnost (political opening), which eventually led to the collapse of socialism in the USSR and Eastern Europe. Castro experimented in succession with several models, all of which failed: the Stalinist model of central planning and industrialization, the Mao-

Guevarist idealistic mobilization model, the 1960s Soviet timid economic reform, a third way between the Guevarist and Soviet approaches, and, currently, a slow, piecemeal market-oriented reform.

Microanalysis: The Public Sector and Growth

Planning. As shown in the previous section, regardless of the multiple changes in economic models, there was a steady trend in Cuba (in 1959–90) toward increasing state ownership and centralization in the operation of the means of production. The central planning apparatus was established in 1961 (Junta Central de Planificación, or JUCEPLAN) and the first medium-range plan (1962–64) was launched; its failure in 1963 (compounded by the lack of success in rapid industrialization) led to a debate on alternative models of economic organization (1964–66). Eventually Castro chose the Guevarist model (1966–70), but with his own interpretation: gigantic sugar harvests would be the engine of growth and the medium-range central plan was replaced by short-run sectorial plans (sugar, nickel, etc.) directly controlled by him. The double failure in 1970 of the model of organization and the development strategy forced Castro to accept the timid 1960s Soviet model of reform (the system of Direction and Planning of the Economy: SDPE); the central plan was reintroduced (1975–80, 1981–85, and 1986–90) with a few market tools. Gorbachev took power in the USSR at the same time that Cuba's trade deficit with and aid from the Soviets were at their peaks. Instead of moving further toward the market, Castro launched the antimarket Rectification Process (1986–90) and the central plan virtually vanished, although centralization of decision making increased. The failure of this experiment and the collapse of the socialist camp (ending all Soviet aid and subsidies) forced Castro, once again, to implement a market-oriented reform, but this time more radical than any one before: central planning has virtually disappeared, but there is an emergency program: the "Special Period" (Mesa-Lago 1978, 1994b).

Production by Government Enterprises and Financing. Until the 1990s production in Cuba was done by huge state monopolies organized as ministries or state committees (e.g., on sugar, agriculture, heavy industry, light industry, domestic and external trade). Except for the SDPE period (when profit was expected to become the major indicator of managerial performance), the central ministries and the planning apparatus set physical output targets that had to be fulfilled by state enterprises, farms, and agencies. Financing was done mainly through direct state budget allocations ("budgetary financing"): all profits and budget surpluses went back to the state, deficits were canceled, and there was no interest charged to the enterprises. There were attempts (namely under the SDPE) to introduce "self-financing": enterprises received bank loans that were expected to be paid back with interest, part of the profit could be kept by the enterprise, and, if there were losses, the enterprises might be shut down; this system, however, was never truly implemented (Mesa-Lago 1993a, 1994b).

Subsidies to State Enterprises. The government heavily subsidized production and prices of essential consumer goods. Obsolete technology, high labor costs, and managerial inefficiency led to losses in virtually all enterprises. Soviet aid and price subsidies helped to compensate for the deficit, but it reached 13.7% of the state budget in 1990 (see table 8.1). Prices of essential consumer goods, particularly food, provided by rationing were frozen in 1961–81 and only increased slightly later; thus, the gap between domestic and world prices expanded as did the deficit.

The Mixed and Private Sectors. The domestic economic reform of the 1990s has led to increasing autonomy of state enterprises and gradual decentralization. Foreign trade has ceased to be a central state monopoly as many public enterprises are now allowed to export and import. Joint ventures are expected to be self-sufficient and generate a profit (but no data are available). New pseudo-"private" corporations (*sociedades anónimas*) are being established, but their ownership remains public. The new co-ops (UBPCs) are supposed to be profitable, but in 1995 only 9% of them met that goal and increased output; of the remaining 91% unprofitable UBPCs, about half suffered from problems that were judged insoluble in the short run. I have already described the legal regulation of new mixed and "private" enterprises and self-employment.

There were four foreign banks operating in Cuba in 1995. The domestic banking system remains public and centralized: there are two public banks, the Central Bank (BNC) and the Popular Savings Bank (BPA); in addition there are two pseudo-private banks that operate for international trade (the International Financial Bank and the International Trade Bank). Joint ventures are financed by external capital and Cuba's government allocation. UBPCs can get loans from public banks with interest, and relatively autonomous enterprises are supposed to get credit in the same manner, but virtually no information is available on this (Pérez-López 1995; Mesa-Lago 1993b, 1994a, 1994b).

Macroanalysis

Cuba's Marxist economic model is gradually changing toward a mixed model that has not been defined yet. The continuum between a centrally planned economy and a comparative market economy is quite wide, and Cuban economic leaders do not seem to have reached a consensus yet on the point in such a continuum where the economy should stand. The old guard led by Castro wants to "perfect socialism" and preserve it as much as possible. The younger technocrat reformist group is very fragmented, although its members want to go much further to the market than the hard-liners and develop a "mixed economy." There is no model of economic analysis used so far in Cuba (Mesa-Lago 1994a).

The Population's Capacity to Save.   The capacity of the Cuban population to save is very small. In mid-1995 it was reported that 55% of the population saved (at the BPA), but 65% of the accounts had 200 pesos or less (equal to the monthly average wage and $8 in the black market); 22% of the accounts had from 201 to 2,000 pesos (the latter equal to $80 in the black market); 11% of the accounts had from 2,001 to 10,000 pesos; and only 2% had more than 10,000 pesos. Total deposits were equal to 59% of the population's income in 1995 but, once again, the purchasing power of such deposits was very low (BNC 1995).

Gross Investment.   Gross investment in Cuba is difficult to measure because the country does not follow the Western system of national accounts but follows the old Soviet system of the material product or global social product (GSP). As a percentage of GSP, gross investment increased from an annual average of 11.7% in 1962–65 to 12.6% in 1971–75 and 16.7% in 1976–80; the average declined to 15.9% in 1986–89 and decreased to 14.4% in 1993 (see table 8.1). Comparisons with Latin America are very difficult because Cuba has published the conversion of GSP into GDP for only a few years. Table 8.1 shows the comparison of investment/GDP in 1956 (17%), 1971 (15%), and 1980 (19%); the last was well below the Latin American average for that year (ECLAC 1982).

Interest Rate.   The interest rate has been fixed by the government from 1961 to the present. There are different rates for savings deposits, credits to agricultural co-ops and private farmers, loans to state enterprises, etc. Throughout the Revolution the interest rate has played a minor role in economic control as most of the economy has been financed by the state budget. As economic reform advances, the interest rate should have an increasing economic role, but so far it is still very minor.

Exchange Rate.   The foreign exchange rate is arbitrarily fixed by the government: in 1959–71 the peso was par with the U.S. dollar; in 1972–81 the peso appreciated to $1.40; in 1982–85 it declined to $1.20; and since 1986 it is par with the dollar again (see table 8.1 and Mesa-Lago 1994b). There are multiple exchange rates (e.g., for tourists, exports, etc.). The Cuban government has never explained how the exchange rate is set and the reasons for its changes. In the black market, the peso exchange for one dollar increased from 5 in 1979, to 8 in 1990, 15 in 1991, and 45 at the end of 1993; in August of that year—when the circulation of the dollar was legalized—the exchange rate jumped to 100 pesos and peaked in August 1994 at 120 pesos; it declined to 35 in November of that year and increased again to 50 at the end of 1994 and early 1995, to decline to 25 at the end of 1995. The causes of those fluctuations are not easy to explain for both domestic and foreign economists (see table 8.1 and Mesa-Lago 1994a, 1994b).

Foreign Debt and Investment. In 1960–90 Cuba received the equivalent of $65 billion in economic aid from the USSR, 60% in nonrepayable grants and price subsidies and 40% in loans under very generous conditions: long terms, very low interest, and postponements without interest (for diverse estimates of the value of Soviet aid to Cuba, see Pérez-López 1991; Zimbalist 1987, 1988; Mesa-Lago 1981, 1994b). In 1989 the USSR revealed that Cuba owed it 15.5 billion rubles, equivalent to $24.5 billion at the official exchange rate that year; the total debt with the USSR and CMEA was $30 billion at official exchange rates (see table 8.1). Because of the decline in the value of the ruble, the disappearance of the German Democratic Republic's mark, and the erosion of other Eastern European currencies, Cuba's debt with the former socialist camp has decreased significantly. The former CMEA countries have unsuccessfully requested that Cuba agree on an exchange rate in order to start paying the debt; except for Russia, the other countries have conditioned a resumption of trade on an agreement on debt payment. In per capita terms, Cuba's total debt in 1989 (combining the CMEA and hard-currency debt) was the highest in Latin America (Mesa-Lago 1993a).

Cuba's hard-currency debt (mostly with the Paris Club) increased from $3.2 billion in 1980 to $5 billion in 1986; that year Cuba suspended the debt service and requested new loans. The debtors refused to resume loans until Cuba starts servicing the debt. The result of the stalemate has been a growing hard-currency debt, which reached $8.6 billion in 1993 and $9.2 billion in 1995 (see table 8.1; BNC 1995). Toward the end of the 1980s the hard-currency debt equaled one-fourth of Cuba's GSP and by 1995 such debt must have been several times the value of Cuba's national product.

As already noted, cumulative foreign investment in Cuba was $1.5 billion in 1990–94, about 15% of the hard-currency debt. The annual average of foreign investment in 1990–94 was about 6% of the annual average Soviet aid Cuba received in the 1980s (Mesa-Lago 1993a, 1994a).

Foreign Trade. By the end of the 1980s Cuba was the CMEA country with the highest dependency on both foreign trade and intra-CMEA trade. Table 8.4 shows that (a) overall dependency on foreign trade increased from 23% to 51% in 1965–89; (b) the trade turnover rose from 1.3 to 13.5 billion pesos in 1959–89 but dropped to 3.2 billion in 1993; (c) the trade deficit increased 60 times in 1959–89, from 39 million pesos to 2.7 billion pesos (but the deficit declined to 900 million in 1993); (d) exports in 1993 were 21% of the 1989 level and imports were 25% of

Table 8.4. Foreign Trade and External Dependency, 1959–93 (in millions of pesos)

Year	Exports (f.o.b.)	% of Sugar in Total Exports[a]	Imports (c.i.f.)	Turnover	Balance	Turnover as a % of:				% of Deficit with USSR over Cuba's Total Deficit
						GSP	Soviet Trade	CMEA Trade		
1959	636	75	675	1,311	-39	–	1.0[b]	1.0		0
1965	691	86	866	1,557	-175	23.0	48.2	61.5		60.3
1970	1,050	77	1,311	2,361	-262	27.6	51.7	64.0		61.8
1980	3,967	88	4,627	8,594	-660	48.8	60.0	71.7		98.5
1989	5,392	76	8,124	13,516	-2,732	50.7	64.7	78.9		83.8
1993	1,530	63[b]	1,840	3,370	-310	–	19.2[c]	–		–

Sources: Mesa-Lago 1994a, 1994b.

[a] Excluding oil "reexports."

[b] In 1957–58 trade with the United States equaled 66% of Cuba's turnover.

[c] 1992.

that level; (e) Cuba's trade dependency on the CMEA increased from 1% to 79% in 1959–89 (dependency on Soviet trade alone grew from 1% to 65% in the same period but dropped to 19% in 1993); and (f) Cuba's trade deficit with the USSR, as a percentage of total deficit, rose from 60% to 98% in 1965–80 and decreased to 84% in 1989 (trade deficits with the USSR were automatically covered with Soviet credits) but was zero in 1993.

These data indicate the severe limitations Cuba confronts in shifting its trade toward the world market, as only about 10% of total trade was with market economies at the end of the 1980s. Furthermore, huge trade deficits were covered with Soviet soft loans,and such deficits would have been five times higher without Soviet price subsidies to both Cuban exports (sugar, nickel) and imports from the USSR (oil). The magnitude of Soviet aid, the generous terms of the Cuban debt with the USSR, and price subsidies protected the Cuban economy from the generalized crisis Latin America suffered in the 1980s, but also insulated the island from the world market and did not put pressure on Cuban leaders to diversify exports and increase their competitiveness. When trade with CMEA disappeared, Cuba's trade turnover declined by 75% (see table 8.4). Last but not least, thirty-five years of revolution, the enormous Soviet aid, and a radical transformation of the island economy, politics, and society were unable to change the major structural problem of Cuba's economy: excessive concentration on sugar exports. As table 8.4 shows, sugar exports as a percentage of total exports were about the same in 1959 and 1989; the decline in the 1990s has been due to both a drop in sugar output by one-half and the loss of Soviet price subsidies. Cuba simply lacks exportable goods to finance its needed imports and does not have access to hard-currency credit either.

Concepts of Growth

GSP, GDP, and PPP

From 1962 at least until 1989, Cuba used the old Soviet system of the material product, which significantly differs from the Western system of national accounts. Cuba's Global Social Product (GSP) excluded the value of "nonproductive services" (health, education, social security, defense, bureaucracy) and, because of such downward bias, GSP is smaller than GDP. But GSP does not use the value added method of national accounts and double counts the value of the same input, hence resulting in an upward bias that makes it bigger than GDP. Cuba has only published the full data and methodology for converting GSP into GDP for the year 1974, although a series of GDPs for 1970–80 was officially released (without providing the backup data); a new GDP series in constant prices for 1989–94 was released in 1995 but could not be evaluated in this chapter (BNC 1995). Changes in economic organization have compounded the problem: in the 1960s vertical integration of enterprises reduced double counting, while in the 1970s disaggregation of enterprises increased double counting. A comparison of GSP and GDP official series (for 1970–80) showed the former to be from 33% to 45% higher than the latter, indicating that the downward bias (exclusion of nonproductive services) was smaller than the upward bias (double counting).

To complicate things further, I am ignoring the valuation method Cuban used in 1962–69; a "complete circulation" valuation method was used in 1970–76 (with considerable double counting); and a shift to an "enterprise exit" valuation method occurred in 1975–89 (reducing double counting); Cuba stopped publishing data altogether after 1989. There are, therefore, at least three different GSP series, which cannot be connected. A series on constant prices (based on 1981) is available for 1975–89, but Cuba's statistical publications have never released data on the basket of goods and services used for the GSP deflator. Furthermore, the abnormal year of 1981 (because of very high inflation) was used as a base for fifteen years, causing considerable criticism. There are two Cuban series on inflation that cannot be connected: 1963–66 based on 1965 prices and 1976–89 based on 1981 prices. Finally, conversion of Cuban pesos to U.S. dollars has been done unilaterally by the Cuban government (the peso is not exchanged in the world market) without explaining shifts in the exchange rate. For all of these reasons, it is impossible to have a reliable series for Cuba's GDP or GNP, at constant prices and converted into dollars, for the entire revolutionary period, and Cuban economic growth has been the subject of bitter controversy (table 8.1 shows GSP in current pesos and estimated with divergent valuation methods). The use of purchasing parity power (PPP) exchange rates is equally impossible due to lack of data (Rodríguez 1990; Zimbalist and Brundenius 1989; Pérez-López 1987; Zimbalist 1987, 1988; Mesa-Lago and Pérez-López 1985a, 1985b, 1985c, 1992; Brundenius 1984).

Human Development Index

The United Nations Development Program (UNDP 1990 to 1994) began in 1990 to estimate a "Human Development Index" (HDI) that has included Cuba. Such an index is based on a series of social and economic indicators that are combined into an overall score. Cuba's score steadily declined and its rank gradually sank in 1990–94: 0.877 in 1990 (38th rank, from best to worst, among 130 countries); 0.732 in 1992 (61th rank among 160 countries); and 0.666 in 1994 (89th rank among 173 countries). The HDI, however, used real per capita GDP in U.S. dollars as one of its indicators, and we have seen in the previous section that such measurement is not feasible.

Economic Growth Trends

Although we lack an accurate complete series of Cuba's GDP growth, available data at least allow us to detect rough trends in economic growth and the factors (domestic and external) that explain significant oscillations (see Eckstein 1994; Pérez-Stable 1993; Rodríguez 1990; Roca 1988; Pérez-López 1987, 1991, 1994, 1995; Mesa-Lago 1978, 1981, 1993a, 1994a, 1994b; Ritter 1974).

The 1960s: Poor Performance.   Growth was probably fair in 1959–61 and 1964–65, but there was stagnation or economic decline in 1962–63 and, particularly, in 1966–70. Average growth in the decade was low due to the following reasons: (a) huge and rapid collectivization; (b) several changes in economic organization and development strategy; (c) idealistic errors of Mao-Guevarism (e.g., poor material incentives); (d) massive exodus of managerial personnel, professionals, and top skilled workers; (e) consumptionist policies in the early years that reduced investment, combined with poor capital efficiency and labor productivity; (f) low sugar output (in 1962–63) and chaos caused in 1970 by the failed effort to produce 10 million tons of sugar; (g) the cost of the U.S. economic embargo since 1961; and (h) the cost of military expenditures for domestic defense and subversion abroad.

The 1970s: Recovery and Slowdown.   There was a strong economic recovery in 1971–75 and a slowdown in 1976–80. Reasons for the former were (a) more rational economic organization and balanced development strategy; (b) halt of skilled labor exodus and payoff of previous investment in human and capital resources; (c) record sugar prices in the world market; (d) increased Soviet price subsidies and economic aid; and (e) lifting of the prohibition to trade with United States subsidiaries abroad in 1975 and increasing economic relations with Latin America and credit from market economies. The slowdown in 1976–80 was the outcome of (a) plagues that affected sugarcane, tobacco, coffee, and hog raising; (b) problems in the fishing and nickel industries; (c) obstacles to and complications in the implementation of the SDPE; (d) decline in sugar prices in the world market (although largely compensated by increases in Soviet price subsidies to sugar); (e) reduction in Western credit; and (f) costs of the Cuban military involvement in Africa.

The 1980s: Boom and Bust.   Growth rates in 1981–85 were probably the highest under the Revolution, but there was stagnation and decline in 1986–90. Factors responsible for the boom were (a) high sugar crops and a world sugar price increase (in 1980–81); (b) expansion of government expenditures (at the cost of growing budget deficits); (c) more economic incentives and timid use of some market tools under the SDPE (free farmers' markets, authorization of self-employment and private housing construction); (d) significant increase in Soviet price subsidies and soft loans with generous terms; and (e) growing credit supplied by market economies.

The antimarket reversal (officially called the "Rectification Process") in 1986–90 had a negative impact on the economy as a result of (a) a decline in economic incentives and elimination of some market tools (e.g., prohibitions or curtailment of free farmers' markets, self-employment, private housing construction); (b) concentration of economic decision making but lack of a coherent economic policy; (c) huge trade balance deficits and a cut in Soviet price subsidies; and (d) a halt in Western credit due to Cuba's cessation of its hard-currency debt service. *The 1990s: Worst Crisis under the Revolution.* The Cuban economy declined by about one-half in 1990–94 due to several factors: (a) a sharp decline in sugar output in 1993–94 and a shutdown of 60% to 80% of the industrial plant; (b) the end of Soviet and CMEA price subsidies and economic aid; (c) a decline in foreign trade turnover by 75% due to the disappearance of the Soviet camp and their price subsidies and trade credits (the sharp decline in imports of fuel, fertilizer, spare parts, etc., in turn, had devastating effects on domestic production); (d) tightening of the U.S. embargo in 1992 (the Torricelli law) and Bill Clinton's economic sanctions in 1994–95; and (e) a continuous halt of Western trade credit, although a moderate increase in foreign investment. The slow and timid introduction of market tools has, so far, not compensated for the negative factors summarized above and, therefore, has failed to stop the economic decline and generate a recovery.

Other Measurements of Social Welfare

Although the overall economic performance under the Revolution has been quite negative, Cuba was able (until the 1990s) to significantly cut open unemployment, expand the provision of free social services, and reduce income inequalities. The severe crisis of the 1990s, however, is dramatically reversing those accomplishments.

Employment. Cuba's open unemployment rate was 16.4% in 1956–57 and was gradually cut down to 1.3% according to the 1970 census (see table 8.2). Full employment was achieved through (a) creating jobs in the state sector (guaranteed year-round jobs in state farms, particularly in sugar plantations, thus eliminating seasonal unemployment, as well as jobs in the armed forces, social services, and the public bureaucracy); (b) rural to urban migration; (c) keeping the labor surplus on the payroll;

(d) extending the years of schooling; and (e) universalizing pension coverage and early retirement. But "full employment" was accomplished at the cost of overstaffing and declining labor productivity. As more rational employment policies were applied in the 1970s and timid market reforms were introduced in the first half of the 1980s (e.g., profit as a major indicator of managerial performance) unemployment pockets appeared and expanded. In the 1981 census, the unemployment rate reached 5.5%, and it rose to 6% toward the end of the 1980s. The attempt to keep unnecessary workers on the payroll in 1986–89 led to an annual decline in labor productivity of 2.6% (CEE 1989).

More market-oriented reforms in the 1990s, compounded by the shutdown of enterprises (due to lack of fuel or external demand), led to labor "dislocations" that, by 1993, affected from 10% to 18% of the labor force; but most of the surplus labor received unemployment compensation at a high cost. In 1995 the government set the proportion of "dislocated" plus unemployed workers at 22% and announced that from 500,000 to 800,000 workers would be dismissed, but they were not. The unemployed, however, would be paid 100% of their salaries in the first month and 60% thereafter, until a suitable job was offered (usually in agriculture; declining such an offer would terminate the compensation). The government hoped that those fired from public employment would find jobs in the private sector, but timid, slow reforms and excessive regulations made that prospect very difficult, which explains why the massive dismissal did not take place (Pérez-López 1995; Mesa-Lago 1978, 1981, 1994a, 1994b).

The percentage of females in the labor force gradually increased from 12.6% in 1956–57 to 18.3% in 1970, 31.4% in 1981, and probably 35% in 1988 (see table 8.2). In 1981 almost two-thirds of the females in the labor force were employed in the tertiary sector; in 1989, 90% of all administrative jobs and 64% of all service jobs, both in the civilian economy, were held by women, but only 33.7% of the executive jobs and 19.4% of blue-collar jobs were performed by females (CEE 1981, 1991; JUCEPLAN 1973).

Social Services: Education.   The national illiteracy rate in 1953 was 23.6% (one of the four lowest in the region), but the rate was 11.6% in urban areas and 41.7% in rural areas (see table 8.2). At the end of the literacy campaign, launched by the government in 1960, it was claimed that the illiteracy rate had been cut to 3.9%. By 1961 all private education was nationalized and a program was launched to reach universal compulsory elementary education, expanding schools and teachers, particularly in the countryside. According to the 1970 census, the national illiteracy rate among the population older than ten years was 12.9% (certainly not the 3.9% claimed in 1960, but about half the 1953 rate); the rate was 7% in urban areas and 22% in rural areas, which reduced the 1953 gap by one-half. The 1981 census excluded the population older than forty-nine years, still the most affected by illiteracy; hence the illiteracy rate was underestimated at 1.9%. More comparable data released in 1993 (population fifteen years and older) set the illiteracy rate at a more realistic rate of 6%. Enrollment in secondary education jumped from 14% to 25% in 1960–70, while enrollment in higher education increased for 3% to 5% in the same period; this was partly due to the nationalization of private schools and universities, but was also the result of an increase in facilities. By the end of the 1980s enrollment had risen to 88% at the secondary level and to 23% at the higher level. Mean years of school in 1992 were 8.1 for males and 7.9 for females. The crisis of the 1990s has afflicted education due to lack of pencils, paper, and books, cuts in school meals, and severe transportation difficulties (UNDP 1994; Mesa-Lago 1993b, 1994a, 1994b).

Health Care.   Prior to the Revolution, Cuba was at the top of Latin America in health standards (e.g., it had the lowest infant mortality rate), but facilities in the countryside were extremely poor. Cuba's birth rate increased from 26.1 to 35.1 per 1,000 in 1958–63 but thereafter steadily declined to 17.6 in 1989; the rate of population growth was 1.8% in 1958, 2.6% in 1963, and 1% in 1991.

The number of physicians per 10,000 inhabitants declined from 9.2 to 5.4 in 1958–62 due to the exodus of one-third of the total number of doctors. As a result of this problem, as well as scarcity of medicines and equipment and better statistical reporting, the infant mortality rate increased from 33.4 to 41.5 in the same period. Expansion of the population coverage and ratios of hospital beds and physicians, as well as supplies of medicines and equipment, led to a cut in the infant mortality rate to 36.4 in 1967. But a decline in the rates of physicians combined with increases in morbidity rates (in acute diarrhea, respiratory diseases, measles, typhoid, and tuberculosis) in the late 1960s resulted in a new increase of infant mortality to 46.7 in 1968, the highest in twelve years. Massive vaccination, increases in the ratio of physicians and other health personnel, more efficient use of a declining ratio of hospital beds, and elimination or sharp reduction of some diseases (polio, diphtheria, tuberculosis, tetanus, etc.) led to a steady decline of the infant mortality rate to 38.7 in 1970, 18.5 in 1981, 11.1 in 1989, and 10.2 in 1992. In the last year, the ratio of physicians was 43 per 10,000 inhabitants and the ratio of hospital beds was 5 per 1,000 inhabitants (see table 8.2). And yet morbidity rates of some contagious diseases (particularly those difficult to control through vaccination and venereal diseases) increased in the second half of the 1980s: acute diarrhea, acute respiratory problems, chicken pox, hepatitis, syphilis, and gonorrhea. The crisis of the 1990s has badly affected the health and nutrition status of the population due to absence of 300 medicines and severe shortage of soap, detergents, spare parts, insecticides, and food. Scabies and lice are common; 800 asthmatics lack medicines; and 50,000 people suffered from optic myeloneuropathy in 1994 due to vitamin deficiency. Rationing quotas provide barely enough food for one or two weeks of the month; the rest must be bought, at very high prices, in state dollar shops, free farmers' markets, or the black market; hence those suffering most are the lowest-income groups. In early 1995 the monthly average wage was worth $4 in the black market and could buy only four pounds of chicken or two pounds of pork or eight liters of milk (Mesa-Lago 1993b, 1994a, 1994b; Díaz-Briquets 1983).

Social Security. In 1958, 63% of the labor force was covered by pensions (old age, disability, survivors) through more than fifty social security funds, one of the highest coverage rates in Latin America. But there was no national health insurance (sickness-maternity program) and only 4.2% of the total population was insured. Together with Uruguay, however, Cuba had a widely expanded system of health-care cooperatives and clinics (combined with public hospitals) that covered most of the urban population; but rural protection by social security was minimal outside of plantations that grew sugarcane and other industrial crops. Laws enacted in 1959–79 unified all the pension funds into a state agency and expanded coverage to 93% of the labor force; a separate free national health care system legally protected all the population (see table 8.2). The number of pensioners increased from 154,000 to 1,370,000 in 1959–93, while social security expenditures jumped from 114 to 1,464 million pesos in the same period. In 1990 the costs of social security (both pensions and health care) took 9.3% of the GSP, one of the highest in the region. As the pension system matured and the population aged, the ratio of active workers to one pensioner declined from 14.7 to 4.2 in 1958–90. Financing of pensions and other monetary benefits is done through a 10% wage tax paid by enterprises (the worker does not contribute); health care is financed by the state budget; the deficit of the entire system, covered by the state, was 41% in 1990 and kept growing in 1991–95.

Pensioners have suffered the most under the crisis of the 1990s: their minimum pension equals less than $2 in the black market; they are afflicted by the lack of medicines and severe cuts in public transportation (many old people cannot ride bikes); and they are unable to stand in long queues for hours to buy the few available rationed goods. The mortality rate of those sixty and older (retirement ages are fifty-five for females and sixty for males) increased from 48 to 53 per 1,000 in 1989–93 (Mesa-Lago 1993b, 1994a, 1994b).

Housing. In contrast with the development of other social services, housing has been seriously neglected under the Revolution. Average annual housing units, built by the state civilian sector, per 1,000 inhabitants was 2.4 in 1959–63, decreased to 0.6 in 1970, increased to 1.9 in 1981 and to 2.4 in 1985, but steadily declined thereafter. Housing expenditures represented 6.5% of total government expenditures in 1984 and declined to 5.7% in 1987 and 2.1% in 1994. For those reasons, the housing deficit increased from 655,000 to 888,000 in 1959–85 and probably surpassed the one million mark in the early 1990s (see table 8.2). Not only has the number of dwelling units built been small, but a good part of the existing stock has disappeared because of lack of maintenance: in 1981 half of all housing had leaking roofs and 4.4% had to be propped up. The crisis of the 1990s has aggravated the already difficult situation. In 1995, 16% of all housing in the capital city had to be demolished, 24% was "repairable," 49% was mediocre to bad, and only 11% was considered to be in good shape (Mesa-Lago 1993b, 1994a, 1994b).

For information on income equality, see the section "Macroanalysis" above and table 8.3.

Who Contributes and Who Benefits from Growth?

This section reviews the contribution to and the benefits from growth of three sectors: the state, foreigners, and the people. Cuban statistics on these issues are either nonexistent or quite limited; hence, this section is the poorest in terms of hard data.

The State

I have analyzed how the Cuban state overwhelmingly owns all means of production, is almost the only source of investment, and employs virtually all the labor force. The crisis of the 1990s is changing the state hegemony as it is forced to allow increasing foreign investment and, to less extent, permit some individuals to perform certain occupations (but still without property rights).

Production Sectors. Within the state sector there are differences among the three major production branches: agriculture, industry (manufacturing, mining, and construction), and "productive services" (transportation, communication, and trade). A major problem is that "nonproductive services" are excluded for GSP and that has probably been the largest and most dynamic economic branch. Such exclusion also distorts the distribution by production share, as the proportions of the other three branches are inflated. To complicate things further, Cuban statistical yearbooks have published three series on the distribution of GSP by economic branches (all of them in current prices): (a) table 8.5 summarizes the longest series (1962–88), which is based on enterprise prices and

Table 8.5. Share of Production (GSP) and Labor Force by Economic Branches, 1962–88

Year	Distribution of GSP[a]			Distribution of the Labor Force[b]			
	Agriculture	Industry	Services	Agriculture	Industry	Services	Other
1962[c]	17.8	55.4	26.8	38.8	21.2	36.0	4.0
1970	14.7	53.1	32.2	30.0	36.3	41.3	2.4
1980[d]	11.6	44.5	43.9	22.3	27.8	46.3	3.6
1988	15.7	44.5	39.8	–	–	–	–

Source: Mesa-Lago 1994b.

[a] Longest series available out of three series (all in current price); excludes taxes. Industry includes manufacturing, mining, and construction. Services are only "productive" (transportation, communication, and trade) and exclude "nonproductive" services (personal, social services, defense, etc).

[b] Industry includes the same subbranches as in GSP. Services include "nonproductive." Other are "nonspecified."

[c] 1956–57 for labor force.

[d] 1981 for labor force.

excludes taxes; (b) a second, shorter series (1975–89) is based on producer prices and includes indirect taxes; and (c) a third series, equal in length to the second, theoretically distributes taxes among the three productive branches. The outcomes of the three series are substantially different.

Table 8.5 shows that the share of the agricultural branch in GSP declined from 17.8% in 1962 to 11.6% in 1980 but then grew to 15.7% by 1988. The industrial share declined from 55.4% in 1962 to 44.5% in 1980 and was stagnant by 1988 (within this branch, manufacturing generated 48.2%, 35.6%, and 35.9%, respectively). The productive service branch was the most dynamic, as its share of GSP grew from 26.8% in 1962 to 43.9% in 1980, but it decreased to 39.8% in 1988 (as the agricultural share expanded). Part of the growth of the productive service branch, however, was the result of inflation, which particularly affected foreign trade. The other branches were much less affected by inflation, as domestic prices were largely (although not totally) frozen in 1962–80; small price increases in wholesale and retail trade, particularly in food, resulted in an increase of the agricultural share in 1980–81 (from 11.6% to 16%), and small reductions in industry and productive services.

The second series, not shown in table 8.5, does not give data for 1962 and 1970; its principal difference from the first series (in 1975–88) is that about 10 percentage points of the productive service share are transferred to the manufacturing share. The major outcome is that the corresponding manufacturing share is bigger and its decline is very small, from

47.8% to 46.7% in 1975–88. The question is why the value of indirect taxes (taken from trade) was assigned only to manufacturing, instead of distributing it among all the nontrade branches.

The third series transfers an additional and growing portion of the trade share to manufacturing: about 10 percentage points in 1988 (or 20 percentage points compared with the first series). This series is expected to distribute taxes among each branch, but, as in the second one, they are all virtually assigned to manufacturing.

The resulting difference is that the manufacturing share dramatically declines in the first series (from 48.2% to 35.9%), decreases slightly in the second series (from 47.8% to 46.7%), and significantly increases in the third series (from 48.7 to 55.3%). Conversely, the trade branch in 1988 is 31.1%, 19.9%, and 11.8% in the three series. I have interpreted these differences as a manipulation to support the official view that industrialization progressed significantly under the Revolution.

The distribution of the labor force by economic branches in 1957–81 has the advantage (over the distribution of GSP) that it includes nonproductive services. The results, shown in table 8.5, confirm my points that the agricultural share declined (from 38.8% to 22.3%) and that the most dynamic sector of the economy was services (whose share increased from 36% to 46.3%). The industrial share increased (from 21.2% to 27.8%), but the manufacturing share was almost stagnant (17.4% in 1956–57, 20.3% in 1970, and 18.9% in 1981). The debate on these issues in the 1980s was passionate, to say the least, but it has become irrelevant in the 1990s because of the virtual collapse of industry (Rodríguez 1990; Zimbalist and Brundenius 1989; Zimbalist 1988; Mesa-Lago and Pérez-López 1985a, 1985b).

Sources of State Revenue and Budget Deficit. The major sources of government revenue until the 1990s were (a) profits of state enterprises and state farms; (b) the surplus extracted from the difference between prices of produce paid to both cooperatives and pseudo-private farmers (*acopio*) and market prices; (c) taxes paid by enterprises (circulation and social security taxes); and (d) differences in foreign trade taxes.

Because of the losses of most state enterprises and farms, the state had to subsidize them; hence in 1988 only 12.5% of state budget revenue was generated by profit. The circulation tax was the major source of state revenue in 1988 (44.7%), followed by "other" taxes (31%, from social security, etc.). Taxes paid by the population and the nonstate sector (mostly private farmers) only contributed 2% to the state budget. In 1988 the state allocated 37% of that year's revenue to finance production (subsidies, credit, etc.), a declining proportion from 44% in 1978. The biggest share of state expenditures (45%) went to social services, increasing from 33% in 1978. The remaining expenditures went to defense and security (10%), public administration (4%), and other activities (4%). Because state expenditures (mostly social services and subsidies) grew faster than revenue, the state budget suffered from increasing deficits (10% in 1989, 12.8% in 1990, 34.7% in 1993, as a percentage of budget expenditures), which were financed by foreign subsidies and monetary emission (see table 8.1). When the former ended in the 1990s, the printing machine became the only source to cover the deficit.

Excess Money in Circulation. Because the state fixed and froze virtually all prices (to protect low-income groups), inflation was "controlled." But the state had to ration consumer goods; the list of rationed goods steadily expanded until it virtually embraced all of them, while the ration quotas gradually declined. Because ration quotas are not guaranteed, queues became longer and demanded more time. People had very little on which to spend their surplus income, after buying the rationed goods: social services and sporting events were free; public utility rates were ridiculously low; and most of the population owned their homes or paid 6% of their salaries as rent (the lowest-income group was exempt from paying rent). Attempts to siphon off the surplus in the 1970s and early 1980s (through free farmers' markets, parallel markets, etc.) were abolished in 1986–90. The black market boomed, in spite of government efforts to control it (particularly in 1966–70).

The monetary surplus is the difference between the population's income and expenditures; as such difference grew, the cumulative surplus (monetary hangover) expanded and in 1970 reached 83% of the population income, or 388 pesos per capita. The severe scarcity of that year (at the end of the Guevarist period), and lack of alternatives to spend the surplus, provoked a dramatic jump in labor absenteeism: 20% of the labor force stayed home, and a virtual economic collapse ensued. With more material incentives and a few market tools, in the 1970s and 1981–85 the cumulative surplus proportionally declined to 30% of the population income and stagnated in the 1980s. But the crisis of the 1990s, the grave scarcity of goods, the expansion of the black market, the growing budget deficits (35% of the budget in 1993), and increasing monetary emission resulted in a sharp decline in the purchasing value of the peso. The monetary surplus rapidly grew and reached 74% of the population income in 1993, or 908 pesos per capita (more than twice the peak of 1970 and 4.5 times the monthly average wage of 1993). The surplus peaked in May 1994, when it probably surpassed the population income by 35%. The budget deficit also peaked at 35% in 1993 (see table 8.1). Top government officials stated, at the end of 1993, that excess money in circulation was a strong disincentive for work and production, being responsible for a 35% decline in the value of goods and services sold to the population in 1991–93. The budget deficit was a major cause of that phenomenon, and about half of it was generated by subsidies to state enterprises (Mesa-Lago 1994a).

Market-Oriented Reforms.   Several measures have been introduced since 1993 to reduce the monetary hangover, cut the budget deficit, strengthen the value of the peso, and create incentives to siphon off the surplus: (a) increases in prices of both consumer goods (but mostly nonessential, such as tobacco and alcohol) and public utilities (electricity, water, gas, mail, phone, but about half of the population is exempted and the increases are small); (b) taxes on the self-employed and new agricultural co-ops (UBPCs), but the revenue generated so far is small; (c) creation of the state dollar shops, reintroduction of free farmers' markets, and authorization for artisan markets (where prices are very high); (d) payment of a fraction of wages in dollars (actually in a new "convertible peso," exchanged on a par with the dollar and legal tender to buy in state dollar shops) to a small sector of the labor force employed in tourism, joint ventures, etc.; and (e) some cuts in subsidies to state enterprises.

These steps are in the right direction and the government claims that, at the end of 1994, the monetary hangover had been cut by 15% and the budget deficit from 35% to either 19% or 10% (according to different estimates). There is no way to check the accuracy of these figures, however, and the most important reforms still have to be implemented: (a) complete elimination of subsidies to state enterprises; (b) establishment of an income/wage tax as well as a social security tax payable by workers; (c) dismissal of as many as 800,000 unneeded workers in the state sector; (d) true privatization of agriculture as well as small and medium-sized industrial enterprises (authorizing Cuban citizens to own these means of production); (e) a price reform that should allow prices of consumer goods to be largely set by the market; and (f) emission of a truly convertible peso. Until these reforms are implemented, the fundamental flaws of the Cuban economy will not be corrected (Mesa-Lago 1994a).

Foreigners

Cuba is not a member of international/regional financial organizations (International Monetary Fund, International Bank for Reconstruction and Development, Inter-American Development Bank) and hence they do not contribute to its growth.

I have already discussed the size of foreign investment ($1.5 billion cumulative by the end of 1994) and the incentives/benefits provided to it by the state, as well as its disadvantages. But the figure on foreign capital is misleading, because part of it is in debt-equity swaps and not all the capital has been disbursed (as it might be spread over various years). There is virtually no information on what the contribution of foreign investment to Cuba's economic growth is. In order to provide a rough assessment, I will briefly review the experience of three areas where foreign investment is crucial: tourism, oil, and nickel.

Tourism. Tourism concentrates most foreign investment (the total is unknown; estimates range from $300 to $600 million): two-thirds of new tourist rooms are financed by external capital (mainly coming from Spain), and the investment can reportedly be recovered in three years. And yet the overall contribution of tourism (including both domestic and foreign investment) to Cuba's economy is small. In 1994 the government reported 617,300 foreign tourists and 24,000 tourist rooms, which generated a "gross revenue" of $850 million; but Cuba's "net revenue" (profit) was estimated to be only one-third of "gross revenue," or $280 million. The explanation of that gap is that virtually all inputs to cater to tourists must be imported with hard currency. The proportion of profit actually declined from 60% in 1985 to 33% in 1994, indicating the increasing cost of required imports. In 1992 there were 62,000 jobs in the foreign-tourist sector, only 1% of total civilian employment. The multiplier effect of tourism on the domestic economy is minimal as it has very little link with foreign enclaves. Cuba did not meet the initial tourism goals for 1995 of 2 million tourists (successively cut down to 1.5 million, 1 million, and 850,000); 50,000 rooms (later reduced to 30,000); and $1.2 billion (later decreased to $1 billion and $900 million). It came close to meeting the goal of 1 million tourists (BNC 1995; Pérez-López 1994; Mesa-Lago 1993a, 1994a, 1994b; La Sociedad Económica 1993).

Oil and Energy. Oil exploration and extraction is vital for Cuba: the country produces only 15% of its needs; at least one-third of its import value is fuel; the Soviet supply of crude declined by 72% in 1987–94 and all price subsidies were terminated; and the fuel shortage has had severe negative effects on domestic production and exports. Since 1991 several foreign corporations have been awarded exploration contracts by the government. The pioneer—French Total—discovered oil offshore in Cárdenas Bay in 1992, but the crude was of very low quality and brought less than one-third the world price; after another try in a different location on the island, Total withdrew all operations at the end of 1994. A Mexican consortium (including state-owned PEMEX) in 1994 signed a contract with Cuba to invest $100 million (in addition to a debt-equity swap) to complete and modernize the Soviet-made refinery in Cienfuegos; but the Mexican crisis of 1995 provoked the suspension of that contract. The Soviet-made, but incomplete, nuclear power plant of Juraguá was expected to save 2 million tons of oil annually and to supply 12% of

Cuba's electricity needs, but the construction was halted in 1992 because the Russians left. In 1993–94 Moscow gave Havana $30 million to preserve the nuclear plant and began the search for a third-party capitalist to invest the $250 to $500 million needed to finish the plant. In 1995 a consortium of five countries was formed, but the required investment was raised to $800 million, more than half of the total foreign investment in Cuba (Mesa-Lago 1994a, 1994b; and additional information from Cuba's media).

Nickel.   Nickel is Cuba's major export after sugar and the island has one-fourth of the world's reserves of that mineral. Agreements signed in 1973–90 with the USSR and CMEA called for the construction of two new plants and modernization of two existing U.S.-made plants: production was planned to increase from 39,000 to 106,500 tons in 1981–86; by 1986 output was only 46,000; in 1991 the Soviets pulled out, demand for the product dropped, costs became very high, and output declined to 33,000 tons. Corporations from Canada and Holland reportedly have invested $150 million to modernize the two old U.S. plants and complete/modernize the Soviet plant, almost finished in 1989. Production, nevertheless, decreased to 30,200 in 1993 and 26,900 in 1994 (BNC 1995; Mesa-Lago 1993a, 1994a, 1994b).

The People

We have seen that Cubans "own" a tiny segment of their country's economy, mainly in agriculture and some services, and they are subjected to strict regulations and state controls. The economic reform of the 1990s has not changed that situation (at least by mid-1995). As employees of the state, Cuban workers have obviously contributed to economic growth, but their productivity has been very low and has dramatically declined in the 1990s. As the "private" sector expands, the potential for an increase in output and productivity could be significant in the long run. The operation of the small pseudo-private farms has been an example of that potential: in 1986 that sector operated only 6.5% of Cuba's agricultural land, but its share in total output of key crops was as follows: 74% of tobacco, 64% of vegetables, 61% of cacao, 55% of corn, 53% of plantains and fruits (except citrus), 48% of coffee, 28% of tubers and bananas, 25% of beans, 15% of rice, and 13% of citrus (calculations based on CEE 1986). As the state and cooperative sectors reduced the size of the "private" farms (from 6.5% to 2% in 1986–89), agricultural production declined. The private farms' productivity was considerably higher than that of state farms and co-ops; the transformation of state farms into UBPCs has not solved the problem as only 9% of them were profitable in 1995. The enormous success of private restaurants and taxi drivers, which began in August 1993 as forms of self-employment and favorably competed (in price and quality of goods and services) with their state counterparts, moved Castro to prohibit them at the end of 1993; such a ban, however, has been impossible to enforce.

The 95% of the labor force employed by the state at the end of the 1980s typically minimized their work effort as they enjoyed job safety, a guaranteed salary, equality, and basic social needs. But they lacked economic incentives and disincentives and their lives were frugal, with poor chance for improvement. Workers enjoyed those benefits through the end of the 1980s, but their productivity was very low and plummeted in the 1990s; the severe crisis virtually destroyed the easy benefits they had before. The challenge of the future is whether former state workers will be willing to trade their safety net (rapidly disappearing anyway) for economic incentives that would stimulate labor productivity and raise their real purchasing power and living standards. The example of "private" farmers, the self-employed, and even black market speculators suggests that such a challenge will be met. But the remarkable revolutionary accomplishments in social services (education, health care, social security) should be maintained, although obviously reformed to make them more efficient and financially viable in the long run.

Works Cited

Baklanoff, Eric. 1979. Economic Development after World War II. In Robert Freeman Smith, ed., *Background to Revolution: The Development of Modern Cuba*, pp. 219–26. Huntington, N.Y.: R. A. Krieger.

Banco Nacional de Cuba (BNC). 1982 to 1989, 1995. Informe económico (IE) 1982 to 1989 and 1994. Havana: BNC.

Brundenius, Claes. 1984. *Revolutionary Cuba: The Challenge of Economic Growth with Equity*. Boulder: Westview.

Comité Estatal de Estadística (CEE). 1976 to 1991. *Anuario estadístico de Cuba (AEC), 1975 to 1989*. Havana: CEE.

———. 1981. *Principales características laborales de la población de Cuba: Encuesta demográfica*. Havana: CEE.

———. 1986 to 1990. *Boletín estadístico de Cuba (BEC), 1985 to 1989*. Havana: CEE.

Cuban Economic Research Project (CERP). 1965. *A Study on Cuba*. Coral Gables: University of Miami Press.

Deere, Carmen Diana. 1995. The New Agricultural Reforms. In *Cuba: Adapting to a New Post-Soviet World*. NACLA Report on the Americas 29:2 (September–October): 13–17.

Díaz-Briquets, Sergio. 1983. *The Health Revolution in Cuba*. Austin: University of Texas Press.

Eckstein, Susan. 1994. *Back from the Future: Cuba under Castro*. Princeton: Princeton University Press.

Economic Commission for Latin America and the Caribbean (ECLAC). 1958 to 1994. *Economic Survey for Latin America 1957 to 1992*. Santiago: ECLAC.

JUCEPLAN. N.d.*Compendio estadístico de Cuba (CEC) 1966–1968*. Havana.

——. 1968–1973. *Boletín estadístico (BE) 1966–1971*. Havana.

——. 1974–1976. *Anuario estadístico de Cuba (AEC). 1972–1974*. Havana.

——. 1973. *Censo de población y viviendas 1970: Datos fundamentales de la población*. Havana: Instituto del Libro.

——. N.d. *Compendio estadístico de Cuba (CEC), 1966 to 1968*. Havana: Instituto del Libro.

MacEwan, Arthur. 1981. *Revolution and Economic Development in Cuba*. New York: St. Martin's Press.

Mesa-Lago, Carmelo, ed. 1971. *Revolutionary Change in Cuba*. Pittsburgh: Pittsburgh University Press.

——. 1978. *Cuba in the 1970s: Pragmatism and Institutionalization*. Albuquerque: University of New Mexico Press.

——. 1981. *The Economy of Socialist Cuba: A Two-Decade Appraisal*. Albuquerque: University of New Mexico Press.

——. 1993a. *Cuba after the Cold War*. Pittsburgh: University of Pittsburgh Press.

——. 1993b. The Social Safety Net in the Two Cuban Transitions. In Cuban Research Institute, *Transition in Cuba*. Gainesville: CRI, Caribbean Center of Florida International University.

——. 1994a. *Are Economic Reforms Propelling Cuba to the Market?* Coral Gables: University of Miami, North-South Center.

——. 1994b. *Breve historia económica de Cuba socialista: Políticas, resultados y perspectivas*. Madrid: Alianza Editorial.

Mesa-Lago, Carmelo, and Jorge Pérez-López. 1985a. The Endless Cuban Economic Saga: A Terminal Rebuttal. *Comparative Economic Studies* 27(4) (Winter): 67–82.

——. 1985b. Imbroglios on the Cuban Economy: A Reply to Brundenius and Zimbalist. *Comparative Economic Studies* 27(1) (Spring): 47–83.

——. 1985c. A Study of Cuba's National Product System, Its Conversion to the System of *National Accounts and Estimation of GDP Per Capita and Growth Rates*. Washington, D.C.: World Bank.

——. 1992. Cuban Economic Growth in Current and Constant Prices, 1975–1988: A Puzzle on the Foreign Trade Component of the Material Product System. *Statistical Abstract for Latin America* 29, part 1, pp. 598–615. Los Angeles: UCLA Latin American Center Publication.

Monreal, Pedro, and Manuel Rúa. 1994. Apertura y reforma de la economía cubana: Las transformaciones institucionales (1990–1993). *Cuadernos de nuestra América* 21 (January–June).

Pérez-López, Jorge. 1987. *Measuring Cuban Economic Performance*. Austin: University of Texas Press.

——. 1991. *The Economics of Cuban Sugar*. Pittsburgh: University of Pittsburgh Press.

——, ed. 1994. *Cuba at a Crossroads*. Gainesville: University Press of Florida.

——. 1995. *Cuba's Second Economy*. New Brunswick: Transaction.

Pérez-Stable, Marifeli. 1993. *The Cuban Revolution: Origins, Course and Legacy.* New York: Oxford University Press.

Ritter, Archibald R. M. 1974. *The Economic Development of Revolutionary Cuba.* New York: Praeger.

Roca, Sergio, ed. 1988. *Socialist Cuba: Past Interpretation and Future Challenges.* Boulder, Colo.: Westview Press.

Rodríguez, José Luis. 1990. *Estrategia del desarrollo económico de Cuba.* Havana: Editorial Ciencias Sociales.

La Sociedad Económica. 1993. *Bridging the Gap: Cuban Tourism in the 1990s.* Bulletin 29 (April 19).

United Nations Development Program (UNDP). 1990 to 1994. *Human Development Report, 1990 to 1994.* New York: Oxford University Press.

Zimbalist, Andrew, ed. 1987. *Cuba's Socialist Economy toward the 1900s.* Boulder: Lynne Rienner.

——, ed. 1988. *Cuban Political Economy: Controversies in Cubanology.* Boulder: Westview.

Zimbalist, Andrew, and Claes Brundenius. 1989. *The Cuban Economy: Measurement of Analysis of Socialist Performance.* Baltimore: Johns Hopkins University Press.

Index